Praise for *Ellen White Under Fire*

"Good stuff! Perceptive! A book long overdue! Straightforward and clear in dealing with irresponsible Ellen White bashing. Whether you love Ellen White or hate her, this is a book that you need to read."—George Knight, professor emeritus of church history, Andrews University

"Dr. Jud Lake traces the history of Ellen White's critics from the earliest days of her ministry until the present. He demonstrates how an accurate understanding of inspiration prevents one from falling into the false expectations raised by her critics. . . . This invaluable book provides a real service to all who have read charges made against Mrs. White and have wanted clear, factual answers to refute those false claims."—James R. Nix, director, Ellen G. White Estate, Silver Spring, Maryland

"Jud Lake takes you on a historical journey of Ellen White apologetics that is a *tour de force*. This brilliant book, written in a lucid style, lays bare the charges of the critics. Lake tackles difficult topics and then offers compelling reasons why Ellen G. White remains both relevant and authoritative as the prophetic voice for the Seventh-day Adventist Church."—Michael Campbell, pastor, Montrose, Colorado

"Jud Lake has produced a book that is a model of SDA apologetics. His defense of Ellen White is marked by thorough research . . . and a balanced theological perspective grounded in responsible biblical exegesis. The entire effort comes wrapped in a graciousness and respect for those who have mounted the attacks on Ellen White. . . . This book is simply a must read for any honest-hearted person who has issues with the prophetic ministry of Ellen G. White."—Woodrow W. Whidden, professor of historical and systematic theology, Adventist International Institute of Advanced Studies, Cavite, Silang, Philippines

"*Ellen White Under Fire* is specifically designed to answer questions raised by current Web sites critical of Ellen White. Every Adventist who has friends that use the Internet needs the concepts in this book. It clearly exposes the deceptive methods and arguments used by current critics. . . . I highly recommend it to all students of Ellen White."—Jerry Moon, associate professor of church history and chair of the church history department, Seventh-day Adventist Theological Seminary, Andrews University

"Jud Lake is to be commended for addressing the deeper issues behind all the attacks on Ellen White. *Ellen White Under Fire* provides a careful analysis of the major issues in the writings of Ellen White—inspiration, authority, and interpretation. His chapter summaries are useful for students and teachers in reviewing the material, and the extensive endnotes provide an excellent resource for further studies. The book will be a real help for those confronted by the multitude of Web sites and books attacking Ellen White."—Gerhard Pfandl, associate director, Biblical Research Institute

"Jud Lake joins previous apologists with a contemporary defense of Ellen G. White and her writings. His defense is the result of years of study and is accurate and compelling. This book is a must read for every Seventh-day Adventist and all who want to know the truth about Ellen G. White."—Norman R. Gulley, research professor in systematic theology, Southern Adventist University

"*Ellen White Under Fire* is one of the best books to come out in recent years dealing with the prophetic ministry of Ellen White. It doesn't dodge the hard questions but treats them in a thoughtful, reflective, and engaging way. While respectful of opposing views, it makes a persuasive case for the viewpoint that Ellen White was called to be the Lord's special messenger and that her writings continue to have value and relevance today. Make sure that you obtain this book. Then make sure that you read it!"—Greg A. King, dean, School of Religion, Southern Adventist University

ELLEN WHITE
UNDER FIRE

ELLEN WHITE UNDER FIRE

JUD LAKE

Identifying
the Mistakes
of Her Critics

Pacific Press® Publishing Association
Nampa, Idaho
Oshawa, Ontario, Canada
www.pacificpress.com

Cover design by Gerald Lee Monks
Cover design resources from iStockphoto.com
Inside design by Steve Lanto

Copyright © 2010 by Pacific Press® Publishing Association
Printed in the United States of America
All rights reserved

The author assumes full responsibility for the accuracy of all facts, quotations, and references as cited in this book.

Scriptures quoted from KJV are from The King James Version.

Scripture quoted from NASB are from *The New American Standard Bible*®, copyright © 1960, 1962, 1963, 1968, 1971, 1972, 1973, 1975, 1977, 1995 by The Lockman Foundation. Used by permission.

Scripture quotations marked NIV are from the HOLY BIBLE, NEW INTERNATIONAL VERSION®. Copyright © 1973, 1978, 1984 by International Bible Society. Used by permission of Zondervan Publishing House. All rights reserved.

Scriptures quoted from NKJV are from The New King James Version, copyright © 1979, 1980, 1982, Thomas Nelson, Inc., Publishers.

Scriptures quoted from RSV are from the Revised Standard Version of the Bible, copyright © 1946, 1952, 1971 by the Division of Christian Education of the National Council of the Churches of Christ in the U.S.A. Used by permission.

You can obtain additional copies of this book by calling toll-free 1-800-765-6955 or by visiting http://www.adventistbookcenter.com.

Library of Congress Cataloging-in-Publication Data:

Lake, Judson Shepherd.
 Ellen White under fire : identifying the mistakes of her critics / Jud Lake.
       p. cm.
 Includes bibliographical references.
 ISBN 13: 978-0-8163-2408-8 (hard cover)
 ISBN 10: 0-8163-2408-5 (hard cover)
 1. White, Ellen Gould Harmon, 1827-1915. 2. Seventh-day Adventists—Doctrines. 3. Seventh-day Adventists—Apologetic works. I. Title.
   BX6193.W5L35 2010
   230'.6732—dc22
                                          2010013872

10 11 12 13 14 • 5 4 3 2

Dedication

To Ellen G. White, who remained
true to her prophetic calling
in spite of the scorn of her critics
and left a legacy of writings
faithful to the Lord Jesus Christ
and His Word, the Bible.

Acknowledgments

I am sincerely grateful to several groups of people. First, the following specialists and skilled scholars who read the manuscript in its early stage and offered their critiques and suggestions to make it better and more accurate: Jack Blanco, Michael Campbell, Kwabena Donkor, Herbert Douglass, Norman Gulley, Greg King, George Knight, Jerry Moon, Craig Newborn, Gerhard Pfandl, and Woodrow Whidden. At the Ellen G. White Estate, Jim Nix and Tim Poirier read the manuscript and offered invaluable counsel. Their expertise in the Ellen White materials proved most helpful. Clifford Goldstein also read the manuscript and wrote the foreword, for which I am grateful. Additionally, the editors at Pacific Press were not only patient and supportive, but skilled at bringing this book to publication. Any remaining errors and omissions are certainly my responsibility.

Second, Merlin Burt, director of the Center for Adventist Research in the James White Library at Andrews University, was a most helpful guide while I camped out there doing research. The administration at Southern Adventist University—namely, Gordon Bietz, president, and Bob Young, senior vice president for academic administration—showed interest in this book and offered encouragement along the way. Star Stevens, secretary in the School of Religion, helped with editing during the early stages of writing and saved me hours of time. The theology students who sit through my class, "Prophetic Ministry of Ellen G. White," have, through their probing questions year after year, stimulated my thinking about the issues in this book. And my colleagues in the School of Religion are not only great companions in academia but also great encouragers to one of their own trying to write a book on top of carrying a full teaching load.

Finally, special appreciation goes to a wonderful life companion, Bonnie, who not only endured my countless hours in the study, but also encouraged me in my efforts to vindicate the truth about Ellen White.

Ultimately, it was God's faithfulness that brought this work to completion. "Commit your works to the LORD and your plans will be established" (Proverbs 16:3, NASB).

Soli Deo Gloria.

TABLE OF CONTENTS

Introduction 13
Foreword 17

PART I: THE CRITICS AND THEIR CRITICISMS
Chapter 1   Ellen White Under Fire.. 21
Chapter 2   Nothing New Under the Sun 29
Chapter 3   Dudley M. Canright: Father of Ellen White Criticisms 45
Chapter 4   Canright's Legacy and the Church's Response 65

PART II: ISSUES AT THE HEART OF THE DEBATE
Chapter 5   Revelation-Inspiration: The Foundation of God's Communication With Us ... 90
Chapter 6   Ellen White and Models of Inspiration 106
Chapter 7   Authority, Part 1: The Position of the Pioneers 132
Chapter 8   Authority, Part 2: Dual Authorities 149
Chapter 9   Interpretation, Part 1: Correct Principles 179
Chapter 10   Interpretation, Part 2: Applying Correct Principles 190
Chapter 11   The Big Picture, Part 1: Understanding Ellen White's Message 206
Chapter 12   The Big Picture, Part 2: Vindicating Ellen White's Message 221

PART III: RESPONDING IN THE AFFIRMATIVE
Chapter 13   An Evangelical at Heart 248
Chapter 14   The Best Defense Is a Good Offense 264
Conclusion   Why I Believe in Ellen White's Prophetic Ministry 280

APPENDIXES
Appendix A   Seven Contemporary Views of Ellen White: A Taxonomy 286
Appendix B   Uriah Smith's Defense of Ellen White's Prophetic Ministry ... 289
Appendix C   "Our Use of the Visions of Sr. White," by John Nevins Andrews 292
Appendix D   Resources for Answering the Critics of Ellen White 296

Endnotes 298

Introduction

About six years ago, a student in my Adventist Heritage class asked my opinion on several books he had ordered from a Web site. As I read through the books, it became obvious that the authors were determined to discredit Seventh-day Adventism and Ellen White's prophetic gift. Interested in what other critics were saying, I searched the Internet and found several anti-Adventist and anti-Ellen White Web sites. Having never before encountered criticisms through this medium and on such an intensive level, I was very concerned. Ellen White had always been a great blessing in my life, and what I read about her on the Web sites didn't fit my experience with her writings. So, I began a detailed investigation of these criticisms and the church's response. This investigation became a passion, and now much of my academic interest is focused on this issue.

Over the last several years, as I have engaged with students, pastors, and concerned Adventists, I have sensed a need for more information regarding the deeper issues behind all these criticisms of Ellen White. This book addresses that need. And it offers more than just answers to specific charges. (Other books—for example, Francis D. Nichol's classic *Ellen G. White and Her Critics*—have provided that kind of response). This book will take the reader behind the Ellen White criticisms and address the larger issues. It will give a sense of history regarding these criticisms and provide strategies for dealing with them. Ultimately, it will impart confidence that Ellen White's prophetic ministry can withstand the greatest scrutiny.

This book will show readers outside of the Adventist community that Ellen White wasn't the fanatic her critics make her out to be, that her prophetic gift doesn't threaten the final authority of the Bible, and that she was a Christian woman with a deep evangelical piety whose voice deserves to be heard in its original historical and literary contexts, regardless of whether one agrees or disagrees with her theology.

This book approaches the topic of Ellen White criticisms under three headings. Part I shows the need for this book by setting forth the intensity of the war on Ellen White via the Internet and explains the nature of Ellen White apologetics. Additionally, it covers the history of Ellen White criticisms and how the church has responded over the years. This first section is very important as a foundation, because the past illuminates the present. It will provide a new perspective on the criticisms circulating on the Internet today.

Part II digs beneath the surface and deals with the larger issues underlying the criticisms of Ellen White. For example, many critics advancing the plagiarism charge espouse a view of inspiration not found in the Bible. The nature of Ellen White's authority is another issue that affects how detractors, as well as supporters, approach her writings. Four chapters in this section are devoted to these two vital topics. Another issue behind every criticism of Ellen White is interpretation. Do critics follow valid principles of interpretation, or do they ignore these principles? The only way to arrive at a correct understanding of Ellen White's meaning is through correct principles of interpretation—an issue to which four chapters in this section are devoted.

Part III looks into Ellen White's understanding of the basic principles of biblical Christianity and affirms the evangelical, biblical framework for her prophetic ministry. It also deals with practical issues relating to the defense and advocacy of Ellen White's prophetic gift. The last chapter provides strategies for responding to her critics, proposing that in this matter too, "the best defense is a good offense." Finally, the book ends with my own testimony as to why I believe in Ellen White's prophetic ministry.

The appendixes contain material that supplements the body of the book. The first appendix contains seven contemporary views of Ellen White, something most useful to any person interested in current issues regarding her and her work. One will also find two historic statements that represent how Seventh-day Adventist pioneers viewed Ellen White's prophetic gift. The last appendix provides a list of resources online and in book form that give specific answers to the charges against Ellen White.

Finally, one additional component of this book should be helpful to many readers. At the end of each chapter is a concise summary of its main arguments. This will benefit those who want a chapter review before moving on to the next chapter, such as students reading this book for a class. These summaries will also be ideal for those who like to read through a book in one short sitting and then get into details later.

Roy Graham, in his doctoral dissertation *Ellen G. White: Co-Founder of the Seventh-day Adventist Church,* noted that "it seems inevitable that anyone who made the kind of claims [Ellen White did] with reference to her work and ministry would be subject to critical examination."* He was right. Indeed, Ellen White will continue to be a controversial figure as long as Adventism continues to thrive. This book invites critical examination of her prophetic ministry, but it also asks that those who would examine her work do so fairly and, as far as possible, objectively. As one who claimed to possess the prophetic gift, Ellen White deserves to be heard through her own voice rather than through the voice of her critics.

Jud Lake
Southern Adventist University
Collegedale, Tennessee

---

*Roy Graham, *Ellen White: Co-Founder of the Seventh-day Adventist Church* (New York: Peter Lang, 1985), 355.

Foreword

Not long into Jud Lake's *Ellen White Under Fire*, I thought, *This should have been done long, long ago.* Though other books have dealt with this difficult and sometimes painful issue—difficult because we can't explain everything perfectly; painful because people have been hurt badly—I can't think of anything else that deals with this crucial topic so thoroughly and in such detail.

For me, the issue of Ellen White and her prophetic gift was resolved a long time ago. Certainly, questions remain. They do regarding just about everything in life. But looking at all the logical options to explain her and her life, I concluded—based on her writings, based on her life, and based on the fruit of her ministry—that the most logical explanation for her life and her work is that she had the prophetic gift. Nothing in the years since, not even the new "revelations," has done anything to change my mind. If anything, the years of reading her have only served to strengthen my belief in the divine sanction of her ministry.

Of course, questions remain, particularly as to her role, her authority, and how we are to interpret and use her writings. I imagine questions will continue until the Second Coming; to say that Ellen White manifested the prophetic gift doesn't automatically mean we understand everything about that gift—how it operates and how it should be used by those who believe in it.

Jud Lake's book does two things, and it does them well. First, it describes the history of the attacks on Ellen White and her ministry going back to the earliest days in the 1850s, to the Messenger party, through the sad case of Dudley Canright, and on into our time with the attacks of a former Adventist minister named Dale Ratzlaff. (Those who have read my *Graffiti in the Holy of Holies* know that I am very familiar with him.) Jud shows what many of us who have been familiar with the issues have known all along, which is that over the years the attacks really haven't changed much. They get a bit more sophisticated, a bit more detailed, but all are based on the same distortions, the same false premises, the same misrepresentations.

Second, and more important, not only is Jud's book descriptive, it's also prescriptive. That is, Jud helps the reader understand how the prophetic gift works, how it should be read, and how we can best interpret it. He doesn't focus only on the problem; he also helps us understand what's going on and how to protect ourselves from the kind of misinformation that has led—and most likely will lead—others astray.

Jud put a lot of time into researching and writing this book. The reader probably will have to put some time into reading it too. But there's no doubt in my mind that the time spent reading it will be time well spent.

We've been given a wonderful gift in the ministry of Ellen White. Many know that. Jud's work, Lord willing, could in the end help many more understand that as well. Increasing people's appreciation for her ministry is, I believe, his heart's desire. That, I believe, is what impelled him to write this book. The church, and all other honest seekers for truth, should be glad he did.

Clifford Goldstein
Silver Spring, Maryland
March 2010

Part I

THE CRITICS AND THEIR CRITICISMS

CHAPTER 1

Ellen White Under Fire

Never before have criticisms of the Seventh-day Adventist Church been more accessible to the average church member and the general public. Scores of Web sites and blogs denouncing the church and its doctrines are available at the simple click of a mouse.[1] From bizarre personal attacks to more sophisticated criticisms, opponents of the Seventh-day Adventist Church relentlessly pound its teachings on the World Wide Web.[2] It's no exaggeration to say that the war on Adventism is a global war.[3]

The major target of all this criticism is Ellen White.[4] Because of her claim to the prophetic office and her foundational role in the development of the Seventh-day Adventist Church and its teachings, she has become a lightning rod, her credibility as a prophet the target of most strikes on Adventist theology.[5]

Presently, http://www.ellenwhiteexposed.com,[6] is the most extensive Web site devoted exclusively to discrediting Ellen White. On the main page one will find a list of "Article Collections," with such links as "Plagiarism," "Visions Examined," "Myths," "Shocking Quotes," "Ellen White versus the Bible," "Health," "Confusion," "The Shut Door," "1844 Movement," and "Contradictions." Each of these sections, in turn, contains numerous links to many pages of text criticizing Ellen White's prophetic ministry.[7]

Books targeting Ellen White are also easily available on the Internet. Salient examples are *White Out: An Investigation of Ellen G. White; More Than a Profit, Less Than a Prophet; Prophet or Pretender; The Fake Controversy;* and *White Washed: Uncovering the Myths of Ellen G. White.*[8] Several older books are still available, such as *The White Lie* and *The Life of Mrs. E. G. White, Seventh-day Adventist Prophet: Her False Claims Refuted.*[9] Unquestionably, this negative campaign against Ellen White is hurting her credibility.[10]

Overview of Ellen White criticisms

I have organized the contemporary criticisms of Ellen White into twelve basic categories that summarize the main charges against her prophetic ministry.[11] At the end of each category, the reader will find an Internet source that provides an Adventist response to the specific charges.

1. *Ellen White plagiarized most of her writings.* This is the most pervasive charge against Ellen White. She allegedly copied up to 90 percent of her writings from others[12] and claimed she received the information in visions from God. Popularized in Walter Rae's *The White Lie,* this criticism receives significant coverage on the anti-Ellen White Web sites.[13]

   Answer: http://ellenwhiteanswers.org/answers/plagarism.

2. *In her early ministry, Ellen White taught the shut door theory.* This criticism receives a great amount of attention on the various Web sites and in books. The "shut door" is a term used to describe the belief that the door of human probation was closed to the world following the October 22, 1844, disappointment.[14] The critics claim that the young Ellen taught this theory during the years 1844–1851 based on her early visions. Along with plagiarism, the shut-door charge is a major emphasis for Ellen White's critics.[15]

   Answer: http://ellenwhiteanswers.org/answers/shutdoor.

3. *Ellen White contradicted the Bible.* One Web site claims she contradicted the Bible more than fifty times.[16] From small issues such as whether or not Adam was with Eve when she was tempted to larger issues such as the investigative judgment and the great controversy theme, the critics say Ellen White got it wrong. If she contradicted Scripture so frequently, they argue, how can she be a true prophet of God? Furthermore, they say, Ellen White and her followers claim her writings are equal with the Bible's inspiration and authority, which violates the *sola scriptura* principle.

   Answer: http://www.ellen-white.com/Contradictions.html.

4. *Ellen White contradicted herself in both what she taught and what she did.* It is claimed that she condemned eating meat while still eating meat; she condemned unclean

meats while still eating them; she condemned vinegar but was addicted to it, etc. Furthermore, her later writings supposedly contradict the earlier writings.[17]

Answer: http://ellenwhiteanswers.org/answers/healthinconsistencies.

5. *Ellen White misunderstood the gospel.* According to this charge, the fact that Ellen White said that Christians should never say "I am saved," shows she believed that Christians can't have assurance of salvation. She allegedly taught a "faith in Christ plus good works equals salvation" theology that is contrary to the gospel.[18]

Answer: http://ellenwhiteanswers.org/answers/answershardsayings.

6. *Ellen White's prophecies failed.* Critics claim that especially in her early ministry she made a host of predictions that never came true.[19] For example, it is claimed she predicted that Christ would come 1845, that the final pestilence would begin in 1849, and that Christ would come in 1856. Since these events didn't happen, she is a false prophet.[20]

Answer: http://ellenwhiteanswers.org/answers/answershardsayings.

7. *Ellen White derived all of her health insights from contemporary health reformers.* Critics claim she derived all her health teaching from human sources rather than from God.[21] Ronald L. Numbers's book, *Prophetess of Health: A Study of Ellen G. White,* is a major source for this charge.[22]

Answer: http://www.whiteestate.org/issues/prophetess-of-health.pdf.

8. *Ellen White's visions were the result of temporal-lobe epilepsy.* Her visions, is it alleged, weren't visions but rather "a unique form of epilepsy known as complex partial seizure."[23] The supernatural element is thus discounted.[24]

Answer: http://www.whiteestate.org/issues/visions.html.

9. *Ellen White suppressed theological mistakes in her writings.* Critics claim that by comparing her early writings with later writings, one can find numerous deletions of theological mistakes and that Ellen White herself is chiefly responsible for this alleged deception.[25]

Answer: http://www.whiteestate.org/books/egwhc/EGWHCc17.html#c17.

10. *Ellen White endorsed the mistakes of the Millerites.* According to this view, William Miller used fifteen faulty proofs that Christ would

come in 1843. Ellen White endorsed these proofs and therefore is a false prophet.[26]

Answer: http://ellenwhiteanswers.org/answers/mischarges/millerproofs.

11. *Ellen White made some "strange" statements.* For example, she allegedly said that tall people live on Jupiter, Satan has better success with women than with men, wigs cause insanity, and God doesn't love children who misbehave.[27]

Answer: http://ellenwhiteanswers.org/answers/answershardsayings.

12. *Church leaders have covered up Ellen White's mistakes and failures.* This suppression, according to some critics, is one of the greatest cover-ups in the history of the Christian church. Some critics call for the church to be forthright and tell the real truth about Ellen White.[28]

Answer: http://ellenwhiteanswers.org/gen_dyn.php?file=media/pdf/Coonplagiarism.pdf.

As noted in the introduction, it is beyond the purview of this book to give specific answers to all the charges against Ellen White. For those interested in more Seventh-day Adventist answers to these charges, appendix D contains a list of Web URLs and books.

How shall we respond to these criticisms?

Some time ago, I received an email from a Seventh-day Adventist who had encountered some of the anti-Ellen White material on the Internet. Although this person had been raised in the Adventist Church, she was shocked at the intensity of the criticisms and deeply concerned that she had no immediate answer to them. Like this person, more and more Adventists feel overwhelmed with the sheer volume of material criticizing Ellen White. They're bewildered and unsettled, wondering if they've been deceived.

How shall those who highly value the prophetic ministry of Ellen White respond to this aggressive and negative campaign? My personal response has been mixed. At times I feel frustrated when reading the anti-Ellen White books and Web sites. The rhetoric can be quite negative, and the view of Ellen White presented on these sites is a far cry from the real Ellen White revealed in her writings and in Adventist history. Other times, though, I find myself glad for these criticisms. They've led me to study the issues about Ellen White—and that has blessed me and strengthened my understanding of the prophetic gift. Exploring the background of the many charges and finding satisfactory answers has increased my faith in her prophetic ministry significantly from what it was before.

Many Adventists who read this negative material shake their heads and discard it, while some end up rejecting Ellen White's prophetic ministry and leave Adventism.[29] Others, however, feel angry at these criticisms and take some kind of action, such as condemning the critics via email or engaging them in debate. This is not the best idea. Debates can easily turn into hostile engagements, and some of the anti-Adventist publications tend to exploit angry Adventist letters by publishing them and giving a rejoinder. We have the option of a better response—a calm and rational response provided through Christian apologetics.

Apologetics

The term *apologetics* comes from the Greek word *apologia,* which in the New Testament[30] means to give "a reasoned defense" of the Christian faith "in light of objections raised against it and of offering positive evidence on its behalf."[31] Activities such as providing a reasoned defense of Christ's resurrection in the face of objections,[32] advancing arguments for the existence of God,[33] or answering skeptics of the Bible's reliability[34] are all a part of the apologetic enterprise. A defense of Ellen White's prophetic ministry would fall under this larger umbrella of defending the Christian faith in the sense that Seventh-day Adventists believe she was a postcanonical prophet who upheld biblical Christianity and, in particular, pointed her readers to Scripture and exalted Jesus Christ as Lord and Savior. Additionally, Adventists believe that the Bible itself teaches that the prophetic gift would continue after the closing of the scriptural canon. As such, in the Adventist context, defending her prophetic ministry against critics is a part of defending the Christian faith.

Christian apologists frequently base their reason for, and approach to, apologetics on 1 Peter 3:15, which says, "sanctify Christ as Lord in your hearts, always *being* ready to make a defense to everyone who asks you to give an account for the hope that is in you, yet with gentleness and reverence" (NASB; emphasis added). The "hope" Christians defend in this context is the resurrection of Christ from the dead and the salvation found in Him (see 1 Peter 1:3).

In 1 Peter 3:15, the apostle gives important counsel regarding the enterprise of apologetics. The Greek word he used here is *apologia.* In other words, he was calling for a carefully reasoned, well organized, and intellectually satisfying response to the questions of outsiders and the challenges of opponents regarding the Christian faith. So, the Christian defense of the gospel is to be credible. Furthermore, Christians should continually be "ready" to answer and defend the hope of salvation in Christ and make their defense with a spirit of "gentleness and respect." Ultimately, Christians should maintain "Christ as Lord in their hearts" and seek to honor Him in the way they deal with challenges to the faith.

This passage contains lessons that can be applied to defending the prophetic ministry of Ellen White, as well as Adventist teaching in general. First, our "defense" of her prophetic gift must be credible—carefully reasoned, well organized, and intellectually satisfying. The critics speak as if we have no defense for Ellen White, and they arrange their criticisms in such a way as to overwhelm the reader with the apparent problems. Like the person who sent me the e-mail, many Adventists are not equipped to answer the maze of criticisms and don't know how to respond. But there *are* answers to the many charges, and we must present them in a responsible and credible way.

Second, it behooves every believer in Ellen White's prophetic gift to be "ready" with a reasoned defense. Simplistic answers won't do. Issues such as Ellen White's relationship to the Bible, the nature of her inspiration, the integrity of her claims, the ethics of her personal life, the nature of her literary borrowing, her stance on the divinity of Jesus Christ, and many others must be fully understood by those who support her prophetic ministry. Not all of us will be asked to make a formal defense, but all of us will need to resolve the issues in our own minds. In the age of the Internet, the criticisms are only a mouse-click away. Readiness is essential for all, not just pastors and theologians.

The third lesson from 1 Peter 3:15 is that our defense of Ellen White's prophetic ministry must be made with "gentleness and respect." The construction in the Greek indicates this defense must be made "in company with" gentleness toward people and humility before God.[35] One commentator suggests that Peter may have in mind "a profound acknowledgment of the power of God and of one's own poverty and dependence on Him."[36] This kind of God-centered attitude will certainly find expression in how we treat those opposed to our faith. While we can be confident in light of research findings that favor Ellen White's prophetic status, we should discard defensiveness and contentiousness. Arguing in highly adversarial ways about Ellen White—or any other theological subject, for that matter—tends to alienate people. If we honor "Christ as Lord in our hearts" and depend on Him for help, we can defend our faith in a way that glorifies God and respects our fellow human beings, even when they oppose us. Thus, we can "[keep] a clear conscience, so that those who speak maliciously against your good behavior in Christ may be ashamed of their slander" (1 Pet. 3:16, NIV).

However, when our opponents bear false witness against us, we must firmly protest. Jude called it contending for the faith (Jude 3). Jesus and Paul, for example, held nothing back when their opponents confronted them and truth was at stake. Consequently, there will be times when we'll need to meet aggressive tactics with vigorous argument. Nevertheless, in our apologetic activity we should never lose sight of "gentleness and respect."

Conclusion

Ellen White understood and accepted the fact that her life and work would always be under attack. "I expect that the raid will be made against me till Christ comes," she wrote. "Every opposer to our faith makes Mrs. White his text. They begin to oppose the truth and then make a raid against me."[37]

In the midst of the assault on her prophetic credibility, her philosophy regarding the criticisms emerged: "Every charge should be carefully investigated; it should not be left in any uncertain way, the people should not be left to think that it may be or it may not be." They "must be undeceived," she declared, and "must not be left to believe a lie."[38]

This statement and others like it are the basis for the apologetic approach advocated in this book.[39] When every charge is carefully investigated in light of the literary and historical contexts of Ellen White's life and writings, a different picture emerges from the one found in the critical Web sites and books. The truth awaits our investigation.

One area extremely helpful in addressing Ellen White criticisms is the history of those criticisms and the church's response. Understanding this aspect of Adventist history, to which the next three chapters are devoted, is vital to understanding the contemporary situation.

Chapter Summary

1. The Internet has made criticisms of Seventh-day Adventism more accessible today than ever before.
2. Many Web sites, blogs, and books are dedicated exclusively to discrediting the Seventh-day Adventist Church and its teaching.
3. Ellen White is at the center of the target for most of the criticism of Seventh-day Adventism.
4. Presently, http://www.ellenwhiteexposed.com is the most extensive and popular Web site devoted exclusively to discrediting Ellen White.

Chapter Summary

5. The criticisms of Ellen White can be divided into twelve categories:
   a. She plagiarized most of her writings.
   b. She taught the shut-door theory in her early ministry.
   c. She claimed inspiration equal to the Bible and contradicted the Bible.
   d. She contradicted herself.
   e. She misunderstood the gospel.
   f. Her prophecies failed.
   g. She derived all her health insights from contemporary health reformers.
   h. She experienced temporal-lobe epilepsy rather than authentic visions.
   i. She suppressed theological mistakes in her writings.
   j. She endorsed the mistakes of the Millerites.
   k. She made some strange statements.
   l. Church leaders have covered up her mistakes and failures.
6. The response of church members to the Ellen White criticisms is varied: most reject the criticisms; some become angry and attack the critics; others reject Ellen White and leave the church.
7. The best type of response is one modeled on the enterprise of Christian apologetics—a reasoned defense of the Christian faith in light of objections raised against it; one that offers positive evidence on its behalf.
8. First Peter 3:15, 16, the key text Christian apologists use as their reason for, and approach to, apologetics, can be applied to the defense of Ellen White. Based on those verses,
   a. Our "defense" of her prophetic gift must be credible—carefully reasoned, well-organized, and intellectually satisfying.
   b. Every believer in Ellen White's prophetic gift, not just pastors and theologians, must be "ready" to answer the charges with a reasoned defense.
   c. The defense of Ellen White's prophetic ministry must be made with "gentleness and respect" toward our detractors.
9. Ellen White believed that every charge against her should be carefully investigated and answered.

CHAPTER 2

Nothing New Under the Sun

"From the beginning of my work," Ellen White wrote in 1883, "I have been pursued by hatred, reproach, and falsehood. Base imputations and slanderous reports have been greedily gathered up and widely circulated by the rebellious, the formalist, and the fanatic." This "warfare," she recounted, "has been kept up for nearly forty years."[1] This chapter is about that "warfare" and the church's response during the first forty years of Ellen White's seventy-year prophetic ministry. Solomon's memorable saying, "There is nothing new under the sun" (Eccles. 1:9, NIV), certainly applies to criticisms of Ellen White. While our nineteenth-century pioneers never could have imagined the Internet with its marvelous technology, criticisms of Ellen White were as familiar to them as the whinnying of the horses that provided much of their transportation.

The criticisms and the church's responses[2] during Ellen White's first four decades of prophetic ministry can be organized under three headings: the Messenger party, the Marion party, and Miles Grant.[3] In the next chapter I'll discuss Dudley M. Canright, who was the most influential critic of Ellen White during the last three decades of her life.

The Messenger party

The first organized opposition[4] to Ellen White's prophetic ministry arose in 1853 from two early Sabbatarian Adventist ministers, H. S. Case and C. P. Russell, who, after wrongly accusing a woman of saying a vile word, received a rebuke from Ellen White.[5] The two men were offended by the rebuke and began railing publicly against James and Ellen White. By mid-1854, they had attracted a following, and James White wrote in the *Review and Herald* that this group talked "of starting a paper in which to vindicate their own course, and expose us, especially Mrs.

W[hite]'s views. From what we know of these men, and their present excited state of feeling, we may expect from them the most gross misrepresentations, and shameful abuse."[6] In the fall of that year, Case, Russell, and their followers did begin to publish a paper, which they titled *Messenger of Truth*. They hoped their paper would replace the *Review and Herald*. Because of the name of their paper, they were dubbed the "Messenger party."

The early issues of the *Messenger of Truth* justified the actions of Case and Russell, opposed James White's leadership, and challenged the visions of Ellen White.[7] Subsequent issues advanced personal attacks on the character of James White and continued criticism of Ellen White's visions.[8] In November 1854, the publishing committee of the *Review and Herald* issued a response to the *Messenger of Truth* and its "unfavorable statements" about Seventh-day Adventists. "The contemptible course which these persons have pursued," stated the committee, "evinces that there is nothing to which they will not stoop; and that they are never likely to be out of scandal with which to assail those who have incurred their displeasure."[9]

J. N. Loughborough, pioneer evangelist, administrator, and church historian, recalled the attacks in the *Messenger of Truth*: "Many falsehoods were inserted in its pages, which annoyed us in our work in the message; and as it was our first experience with such an open attack, we thought it our duty to refute their slanderous statements." But these "efforts at answering their falsehoods had only resulted in their manufacturing more," he added.[10]

By mid-1855, the opposition from the Messenger party became so intense that five leaders of the sabbatarian Adventists, including James White and J. N. Loughborough, planned an aggressive campaign to refute the charges.[11] During the evening of June 20, however, Ellen White received a vision about the Messenger party and how to deal with them.

"The *Messenger* party has arisen," she penned, "and we shall suffer some from their lying tongues and misrepresentations, yet we should bear it all patiently; for they will not injure the cause of God, now they have left us, as much as they would have injured it by their influence had they remained with us."[12]

In the vision, Mrs. White was shown the course of action the sabbatarian Adventists should take. "I saw that the people of God must arouse and put on the armor. Christ is coming, and the great work of the last message of mercy is of too much importance for us to leave it and come down to answer such falsehoods, misrepresentations, and slanders as the *Messenger* party have fed upon and have scattered abroad. Truth, present truth, we must dwell upon it. We are doing a great work, and cannot come down. Satan is in all this, to divert our minds from the present truth and the coming of Christ."[13] As a result, the Adventist leaders decided to abandon their plans to refute the Messenger party and made no further allusion in the *Review and Herald* to the negative propaganda published in the *Messenger of Truth*.[14]

On November 16, 1855, at a major conference in Battle Creek, the sabbatarian Adventist leaders voted a resolution that would guide them in the years ahead as to how to react to their enemies. This resolution was published in the December 4, 1855, *Review and Herald:* "Whereas, Inquiries have been made as to what course we designed to pursue in the future, in reference to the misstatements of the enemies of present truth, therefore, for the information and satisfaction of the brethren abroad, *Resolved,* That we henceforth devote ourselves exclusively to the advocacy and defense of the present truth, committing ourselves in all things to Him who judgeth righteously, after the example of our Pattern, in affliction and in patience."[15]

The significance of this resolution should not be missed. It was influenced by Ellen White's June vision of not "coming down" and answering the falsehoods and slander in the *Messenger of Truth*. The lesson was unmistakable: Don't allow Satan to "divert our minds from the present truth and the coming of Christ."[16] This meant that the leaders shouldn't spend all of their time on the "misstatements of the enemies" but rather "devote" themselves to both the "advocacy" and "defense" of the truth. In other words, "defense" of the truth—the act of defending it against attacks—should never be separated from "advocacy" of truth—the act of arguing in favor of truth and presenting positive evidence for it. This policy resulted in many *Review* articles advocating and defending "present truth."[17] In addition, it resulted in major apologetic activity regarding the biblical doctrine of spiritual gifts as manifested in Ellen White's prophetic ministry.

The Marion party

The "Marion party"[18] had a much longer and more extensive influence than the Messenger party. Elements of this group challenged Ellen White's prophetic ministry up through the 1880s.

B. F. Snook and W. H. Brinkerhoff. The "Marion party" grew out of resistance to the establishment of the church's General Conference in 1863. B. F. Snook, president of the newly organized Iowa Conference, and W. H. Brinkerhoff, its first secretary, opposed formal church organization and the name "Seventh-day Adventist." They felt Sabbatarian Adventists should instead take the name "Church of God." In addition, they criticized Ellen White's visions and James White's leadership, stirring up turmoil in the new conference.

In June 1865, James and Ellen White attended a special session of the Iowa Conference to address the situation. They carefully and patiently answered the questions and criticisms of the two leading conference officers, Snook and Brinkerhoff. Following the meeting, both men apologized and later wrote detailed letters with confessions of their wrongs, which were published in the *Review and Herald* of July 25, 1865. In these letters, both men expressed themselves in apparently sincere terms and affirmed their confidence in the Seventh-day Adventist Church and Ellen White's prophetic guidance.[19]

Snook's and Brinkerhoff's change of heart, however, was short lived. Their objections to Ellen White's visions and their pursuit of independence for their conference revived within weeks, and they engaged in a rebellion that was much more intense than the first one. They spent weeks framing objections to the visions and went from church to church in the state of Iowa, endeavoring to destroy confidence in the denomination and in Ellen White.[20] They established their headquarters in Marion, Iowa (hence the name "Marion party"), and by the spring of 1866, they "had succeeded in drawing off with them forty-five of the sixty members of the Marion church."[21]

Their most significant move in 1866, however, was the publication of a polemical book titled *The Visions of E. G. White, Not of God*.[22] This book drew together things they had already been saying in their preaching and publications.[23] The two men challenged Ellen White's claim to inspiration, accused her of teaching the shut-door theory, attempted to prove inconsistencies and contradictions in her writings, asserted that she ignored the right to exercise private judgment apart from her visions, and insisted that she and the church considered her writings another Bible.[24] Accordingly, they refused to accept Ellen White's visions as "divine revelation."[25]

There is a striking resemblance between the series of objections in *The Visions of E. G. White, Not of God* and the material on the anti-Ellen White Web sites today. A simple comparison between the two reveals that contemporary critics are recycling many of the very same objections Snook and Brinkerhoff used almost a century and a half ago.[26]

The church's response to Snook and Brinkerhoff. The charges made by Snook and Brinkerhoff were widely disseminated, so in response, Uriah Smith prepared a manuscript answering their objections. The manuscript wasn't published, however, until a group of ministers and church leaders examined it "to decide upon its merits, and the disposition that should be made of it."[27] Upon examination, the manuscript received their approval, and they chose to publish it. Most of the manuscript was also read before a joint session of the General and Michigan conferences of Seventh-day Adventists, and the following action was taken and published in the *Review and Herald* of June 12, 1866: "*Resolved,* That we, the members of the General and Mich. State Conference, having heard a portion of the manuscript read, which has been prepared by Bro. U. Smith, in answer to certain objections recently brought against the visions of Sister White, do hereby express our hearty approval of the same. *Resolved,* That we tender our thanks to Bro. Smith for his able defense of the visions against the attacks of their opponents."[28]

In this same issue of the *Review and Herald,* Smith published the first installment of his manuscript as the beginning of a five-part series titled "The Visions—Objections Answered" that ran until July 31. Throughout the series he listed thirty-nine objections and provided accompanying answers. Objection 1, for example, was titled "The Bible and the Bible Alone," and objection 39 was "Suppression."[29] Other objections included in the series were "The Shut Door" (objection 4, which included Smith's comments on the alleged Camden vision),[30] and "The Negro Race Is Not Human" (objection 37),[31] based on the controversial amalgamation statement.[32]

In the first installment of the series, Smith set forth several important principles before he engaged the specific objections. First, he explained the Seventh-day Adventist understanding of the spiritual gifts spoken of in the New Testament and how Ellen White's visions were a manifestation of one of these gifts. He specified that the visions were "published in the works entitled, *Experience and Views, Testimonies to the Church, and Spiritual Gifts,* Vols. I–IV."[33]

Second, he explained that the visions have been proven "genuine" by "every test which can be brought to bear upon" them. "The evidence which supports them, internal and external," he declared, "is conclusive." These visions "agree with the Word of God and with themselves." They are "calm, dignified, impressive," and "commend themselves to every beholder, as the very opposite of that which is false or fanatical."[34]

Third, Smith discussed the "fruit" of the visions in five points: (1) "They tend to the purest morality," (2) "They lead us to Christ," (3) "They lead us to the Bible," (4) "They have brought comfort and consolation to many hearts," and (5) "Negatively, they have never been known to counsel evil or devise wickedness."

After discussing these positive fruits of the visions, he argued: "Yet with all this array of good fruit which they are able to present, with all this innocency of any charge of evil that can be brought against them, they everywhere encounter the bitterest opposition."

Then as a lead-in to his response to the first objection, Smith wrote directly of

Snook and Brinkerhoff's publication: "Some of those who so strenuously oppose the visions, have a series of objections which they offer in justification of their course. In these objections, they everywhere betray a consciousness of a painful scarcity of material; and hence there is throughout a labored effort to make the most of every little point that can be seized upon, and present it in a greatly magnified or perverted light."[35] This is a pointed statement, but the correctness of Smith's assessment unfolded as he answered each objection.

Following the publication of the series, several articles in the *Review and Herald* highly commended Smith's work. Author and church leader J. N. Andrews,[36] for example, wrote, "The series of articles on this subject by Bro. Smith, are well worthy of the attentive perusal of the readers of the *Review*. I ask those who have not read them, to take time and read them with care, and those who have read them hastily, to give them further attention."

Andrews then expressed his hope that "we may have these articles in pamphlet form."[37] A month later, Pastor C. O. Taylor[38] wrote, "Many of those same objections have perhaps troubled you. Read the answers. Read twice, yea thrice, and even more, till you can see the point, and light and peace will be the reward of your labor."[39]

Two years later, in 1868, Smith expanded his original manuscript into a 144-page book titled *The Visions of Mrs. E. G. White, a Manifestation of Spiritual Gifts According to the Scriptures*[40]—obviously, a play on the title of Snook and Brinkerhoff's book *The Visions of E. G. White, Not of God*. The expansions in Smith's widely distributed book included thirteen more objections with accompanying answers and two appendixes.[41] The first appendix included several recent confessions of people expressing sorrow about their warfare against Ellen White's prophetic ministry. The second appendix contained the original confessions of Snook and Brinkerhoff, first published in the *Review and Herald* of July 25, 1865.[42]

Uriah Smith's article series in the *Review and Herald* and its later expansion in book form can be considered the denomination's first apologetic work regarding Ellen White's prophetic ministry. As an application of the 1855 policy of "advocacy and defense of present truth," both forms of this apologetic work balanced the answering specific charges and falsehoods with argument for and affirmation of the validity of Ellen White's prophetic gift.

Smith's work remains relevant in several ways. First, it gives us a glimpse of how our pioneers viewed Ellen White's writings in relationship to Scripture. Second, Smith's work answered many charges that are still circulating today. And third, it shows today's church that our pioneers had nothing to hide regarding Ellen White's claim to the prophetic gift.

Other critics from the Marion movement. After Snook and Brinkerhoff left the Marion movement,[43] various other individuals continued their dispute against the Seventh-day Adventist Church and Ellen White. The Marion party ultimately became known as the Church of God (Adventist) and established their headquarters at Stanberry, Missouri.[44] Later, H. E. Carver took over the movement. Like Snook and Brinkerhoff, Carver embraced the Sabbath and three angels' messages but struggled with Ellen White's visions and eventually rejected them. He published the anti-Seventh-day Adventist paper *Advent and Sabbath Advocate* and authored the book *Mrs. E. G. White's Claims to Divine Inspiration Examined,* first published in 1870 and revised in 1877.[45] In this book he provided his version of what happened to Snook and Brinkerhoff and attempted to refute Uriah Smith's 1868 defense of Ellen White.

James White responded to the first edition of Carver's book in the *Review and Herald* of June 13, 1871. Although he didn't mention Carver or Carver's book by name, White addressed the issues Carver raised.

> When men can show that the manifestation of the spirit of prophecy among us is unscriptural, and that Mrs. W.'s writings and her oral appeals to the people are calculated to lead the people from God, from the Bible, from Christ, from the Holy Spirit, from the keeping of the commandments of God, from the duties set forth in the teachings of Christ and the apostles, and from the simplicity and purity of the Christian life; then, and not till then, will they have a reasonable excuse for their persistent opposition of the work, and their persecution of the person through whom God speaks to his people.[46]

White's obvious implication was that neither Carver nor any other critic had actually proved Ellen White to be a false prophet who led people away from the teaching of the Scriptures.

Toward the end of his book, Carver attempted to refute Uriah Smith's claims about the "fruits" of the visions.[47] At one point he argued that the "Camden vision," already considered spurious at this time, provided evidence that Ellen White's visions don't lead to the "purest morality" or "to Christ."[48] James White responded to this argument and the others with this challenge: "When the opposition can find in all her writings one unchaste word, one sentence that lowers the character of God, of Christ, the work of the Holy Spirit, or the standard of Christian holiness, or that leads from the sacred Scriptures as a rule of faith and duty, then it will be time to warn the people against them. Until they can meet the subject fairly, their sneers are hardly worth noticing, as it is both difficult and unpleasing to review and answer a sneer."[49]

In further response to Carver's attack on Smith's "fruits," White closed the article with a lengthy quotation from the very section in Smith's *The Visions of Mrs. E. G. White, A Manifestation of Spiritual Gifts According to the Scriptures* that Carver attempted to refute. It is obvious that James White believed Carver's attempt to refute Smith's defense of Ellen White had failed.

Another minister who left the Adventist ranks was H. C. Blanchard, who authored the critical work titled *The Testimonies of Mrs. E. G. White Compared With the Bible*,[50] published in 1877. Exercised on the issue of health reform, Blanchard endeavored to show that Ellen White's teaching on that topic contradicted the Bible. In 1884, both Carver's and Blanchard's books were being sold at the office of the *Advent and Sabbath Advocate* in Marion, Iowa.

Criticisms by A. C. Long and company. Perhaps the most controversial book published by the Marion group against Ellen White was A. C. Long's *Comparison of the Early Writings of Mrs. White with Later Publications,* published in Marion, Iowa, in 1883.[51] Although this book didn't provide any new arguments against Ellen White, it was widely circulated and caused Adventists and non-Adventists alike to question Ellen White's visions. The basic argument in the book was that many of Ellen White's early statements were suppressed and hidden from the general public because of their heretical nature. Long concluded that "fifty-nine lines of her first three visions are omitted from her late published works."[52] This same kind of suppression argument is made today by online critics and in such works as Dirk Anderson's *White Out: An Investigation of Ellen G. White.*[53]

The publication of Long's book was triggered by the republication in 1882 of the earliest visions of Ellen White in book form: *Christian Experience and Views of Mrs. E. G. White* (1851); *Supplement to Experience and Views* (1854); and *Spiritual Gifts,* volume 1 (1858).[54] These three out-of-print works were combined and published as *Early Writings,*[55] which remains in print. In the *Review and Herald,* of December 26, 1882, the president of the General Conference, G. I. Butler, penned an article announcing the new book: "A Book Long Desired." In this article he made a mistake that A. C. Long exploited: Butler declared that the contents of *Early Writings* were "the very first of the published writings of Sister White." In addition, he chastised the critics for their "lying insinuations" of "suppression," saying that they now "have the opportunity" to examine her early visions "to show up their supposed errors."[56]

Arthur White explained the mistake: "When Butler explained the publication of *Early Writings,* he was doing so in terms of the republication of Ellen White's early books, notably the first, *Experience and Views.* He made no reference to the fact that her first vision had been published in several forms in 1846 and 1847—an article, a broadside, a pamphlet by James White. When the account of her first vision appeared in her first book, there were some deletions of which he was either unaware or had overlooked. Copies of these very early items were extremely scarce."[57]

A. C. Long possessed one of these rare copies, and he seized the opportunity to exploit Butler's mistake. After finding that "fifty-nine lines of her first three visions" were omitted in *Early Writings,* Long shot back at Butler. "Upon whose character falls these 'lying insinuations' now?" he wrote. "Who now 'appears in their real character by the publication' of these suppressions?"[58]

At that point, the church faced two unbearable circumstances. First, Long, joined by two other dissidents—J. S. Green, an attorney who had left the Seventh-day Adventist Church, and Alexander McLearn, ex-president of Battle Creek College—published an "Extra" of the *Advent and Sabbath Advocate,* which contained numerous other criticisms of Ellen White. Second, the publication of Long's critical book was creating quite a stir in Adventist circles. The "wide distribution" of these criticisms, therefore, "gave rise to questions demanding answers."[59]

The church responds to A. C. Long and company. The church published a meticulous reply to Long's charges in a sixteen-page *Review and Herald Supplement* bearing the date of August 14, 1883. This was the most significant apologetic effort regarding Ellen White's prophetic gift to appear in the *Review* since Uriah Smith's series of articles in 1866. The *Supplement* contained seventeen articles that addressed issues raised by Long and other critics over the years. The three lead articles dealt specifically with the suppression charge. In the first article, "Suppression and the Shut Door," J. H. Waggoner argued that just because "a publication, or any part of it, is not *republished,* is no evidence of intention to suppress it, as long as no effort is made to recover or to check the circulation and use of the copies made." After addressing issues related to the shut door, he continued to argue that "intention" is the real issue and that no one can prove any evil intention as to why certain statements were omitted from Ellen White's earlier writings.[60]

In the second article, "Early Writings and Suppression," Butler himself responded to Long and acknowledged his mistake published eight months before in the *Review and Herald.* He wrote, "There is but one inaccuracy in that article, and that is found in this clause: 'These were the very first of the published writings of Sister White.' This statement is not strictly true, though we supposed it was at the time we wrote it. We had never seen any earlier published writings of hers, and others of long experience the same as we did. But since writing to Bro. Andrews, and talking with others longer in the truth, we have found that we were mistaken."

After correcting another statement by Long, Butler gave a concise history of the "manner of publishing some of the earlier visions of Mrs. White." He traced the publication of her first vision from its original form in the *Day-Star* (1846) to its slightly edited form in James White's *A Word to the Little Flock* (1847) to its final edited version in the 1851 *Experience and Views*. He explained that a "few years after these works were published, they went out of print." He said that at the time he was writing, in 1883, *Experience and Views,* its *Supplement,* and other documents are made available in *Early Writings* for "those who have embraced the truth at a comparatively recent date."

Then Butler spoke pointedly about the history of the "suppression" charge. In his choice of words, one gets a feel for the robust spirit of apologetics in those days. "The first we ever heard of this howl of 'suppression' was back in 1866, when Snook and Brinkerhoff got out a little pamphlet against the visions, full of gall and bitterness. This was followed in 1870 by another slippery document from the pen of H. E. Carver. Our people and the visions have survived both of these attacks, and still prosper. And now comes Mr. Long's poor imitation of both of these men; and after examining the three together, we cannot see that he has a single new idea which they did not have."

One won't find this kind of spirited language in any of today's issues of the *Review*. In the formative years of the church paper, the rough-and-tumble of debate was a regular occurrence, and the language sometimes took on an aggressive character.

In perhaps the most compelling argument in the article, Butler countered Long's charge that "fifty-nine lines" were suppressed in *Early Writings*.

Perhaps there never was a more unjust charge made than this, that we have "suppressed" the visions, because there were some portions of them of which we were ashamed. Mr. Long thinks he has found "fifty-nine lines" which we have "suppressed." From a rough estimate, we judge there are at least 150,000 lines extant of her different published works. Surely, according to his own statement, it is but a very small proportion of her writings we were ashamed of,—fifty-nine lines out of 150,000. But now all of these fifty-nine lines are published, and accessible, and all who want them are invited to obtain them.[61]

The reference to the publication of the "fifty-nine lines" refers to the third article in the *Supplement*, "A Venerable Document," also by Butler. In this article he introduced the republication of James White's original 1847 *Word to the Little Flock,* which contained two of Ellen White's visions later included in *Early Writings,* but without any lines omitted. Butler explained:

> Within the last few years there has been a strong desire among our people to procure the earlier writings of Sr. White. "Early Writings" was published last year to meet this want, and a large number of copies have been sold. These visions, with the exception of a few sentences, are contained in that volume. A few of our people have desired to obtain them exactly as they were originally published in "Word to the Little Flock." To gratify this desire, the Publishing Association has printed them entire in a little tract, and all who wish them can obtain them.[62]

Thus, Long's charge of "fifty-nine lines" suppressed in *Early Writings* was answered by republishing those lines in their original context in the pamphlet *A Word to the Little Flock.* It is noteworthy that while today's critics circulate the suppression charge concerning the book *Early Writings,*[63] *A Word to the Little Flock* is in print for all to read.[64]

Ellen White responds to A. C. Long. Ellen White usually didn't respond to her critics. However, due to the significant influence of Long's book, she made a rare departure from this practice. Initially, she published an article in the *Review and Herald* of August 28, 1883, titled "Our Present Position." In this article she encouraged fellow believers in the midst of the current attacks on her prophetic ministry. "Brethren and sisters," she penned, "let not your souls be disturbed by the efforts of those who so earnestly seek to arouse distrust and suspicion of Sister White." Attacks like these "have been repeated hundreds of times during the past forty years; but my labors have not ceased; the voice of warning, reproof, and encouragement has not been silenced."[65]

Then two months later, again in the *Review and Herald,* she spoke about the influence of Long's book and applied her experience to fellow believers: "The same enemy that is ever on my track, will be on yours also. He will suggest, conjecture, fabricate all sorts of reports, and those who wish them true will believe them."[66]

Her final and most direct response to A. C. Long was a sixteen-page explanation of the omissions in her earlier writings, titled "An Explanation of Early Statements." The complete document was published in *Selected Messages,* volume 1, and addresses each omission, explaining the background and rationale. "So far from desiring to withholding anything that I have ever published," she wrote, "I would feel great satisfaction in giving to the public every line of my writings that has ever been printed."[67] This explanation also addressed the shut-door charge and provides an important response to the issue. Every Seventh-day Adventist and any other Christian interested in this issue should read this material in its entirety.[68] It provides Ellen White's side of the story.

Miles Grant

One of the most influential and outspoken non-Sabbatarian critics of Ellen White was Miles Grant, Advent Christian leader and editor of the periodical *The World's Crisis*.[69] He gave wide exposure to arguments against Ellen White in his 1874 publication *The True Sabbath: Which Day Shall We Keep? An Examination of Mrs. Ellen White's Visions*.[70] Grant focused mostly on the shut-door issue and claimed that "not a single prophecy or vision of hers can be produced that may not have been given by a demon."[71] He included a number of testimonies by those who had associated with Ellen White during the early years and claimed that she engaged in fanaticism and time setting.

The church published a response to Grant's attacks on the Sabbath and Ellen White in the *Review and Herald* of April 14, 1874.[72] Ellen White also addressed Grant's criticisms in a private letter to J. N. Loughborough on August 24, 1874: "I hereby testify in the fear of God that the charges of Miles Grant, of Mrs. Burdick, and others published in the *Crisis* are not true." She then refuted each statement point by point.[73]

Over the years Grant pursued Mrs. White, apparently even following her to Torre Pellice, Italy, in 1885 and setting up meetings in a hall directly above the one where she was speaking.[74] Reflecting on this, she wrote:

> During all these years one of the principal burdens of his work seems to have been to follow on my track, and spread these statements which have been manufactured by false witnesses, some of whom had become disaffected because they had been reproved for their wicked course. It has been shown again and again, both by pen and voice and by the testimony of many witnesses, that these reports have no foundation in truth; but what cares he for this? He loves his falsehoods too well to give them up. And now we are charitable enough to venture the opinion that having repeated them so many times he really believes many of them to be true, and feels as zealous as ever Saul did, believing that in trying to tear down my influence he is doing God service.[75]

Over the years, Ellen White refused to enter into controversy with Grant. She explained why:

It has ever been against my principle to enter into controversy with any one, or to spend my time in vindicating myself against the attacks of those who do not hesitate to adopt any means to pervert the truth, or to cast stigma upon those who stand in defense of the law of God. Nothing would please Satan and his followers better than to have me engage in this work; for then they would give me enough to keep me busy all the time, and thus my real work would be left undone. But this is not the work that God has given me.[76]

Although Ellen White responded to critics like A. C. Long a few times, as a general rule she followed the principle proclaimed above during the many years of her prophetic ministry.

Conclusion

History is replete with lessons for the present. This is certainly the case with the history of Ellen White criticisms and the church's response. I suggest that the following lessons will be helpful as we contemplate this part of our church history.

1. The first and most obvious lesson is that intense warfare against Ellen White's prophetic credibility has been around from the beginning and shouldn't shock us. Critics of the past aggressively used every tool of the press within their means to silence her voice. Things have not changed, except for the added avenue of publication that Internet technology has provided, of course.

2. For the most part, the content of today's Ellen White criticisms is recycled from nineteenth-century criticisms. G. I. Butler was right when he said that A. C. Long's book contained nothing new. Long simply recycled what H. E. Carver had said, and H. E. Carver recycled what B. F. Snook and W. H. Brinkerhoff had said, and B. F. Snook and W. H. Brinkerhoff recycled what the Messenger party had said. Granted, each generation presented criticisms in a new form, but the substance was the same. Today, these same old criticisms are sprinkled across the anti-Ellen White Web pages and masked with a fresh new face. Again, there is "nothing new under the sun."

3. The early apologetic work of the church has already answered many of today's criticisms of Ellen White. For example, Uriah Smith's 1868 *The Visions of E. G. White, a Manifestation of Spiritual Gifts According to the Scriptures* and the August 13, 1883, *Review and Herald Supplement* have addressed many issues raised today, such as the suppression and shut-door charges. Not surprisingly, most contemporary critics ignore these answers of yesteryear.

4. Responding to Ellen White's critics is important, but it shouldn't keep us from focusing on the positive message of Adventism—a soon-coming Savior. The 1855 resolution at the conference in Battle

Creek emphasized both "the *advocacy* and [the] *defense* of present truth" (emphasis added), thus presenting a balance in dealing with criticisms of Adventism. Advocacy of truth should go hand in hand with defense of the truth. The two shouldn't be separated in the work of the church. The same is true of our individual lives. Each of us should be able to defend the truth of Ellen White's prophetic ministry, as well as argue the benefits of it.

5. Just as past criticisms failed to silence the prophetic voice of Ellen White, so will the present criticisms fail to silence it. As long as we continue the policy of our pioneers, "the advocacy and defense of present truth," the prophetic voice will continue to speak and invigorate the hearts of people. But for this to happen, all supporters of Ellen White's prophetic ministry should consider what it means to advocate and defend these writings. Thus, parts I and II of this book address the defense of the prophetic gift, and part III deals with its advocacy.

Such are the key lessons from the first forty years of Ellen White criticisms and the church's response.

As the decade of the 1880s came to a close and the Marion party faded into the background, Ellen White would experience another wave of attack more intense than all those before it. Dudley M. Canright, longtime minister and defender of Seventh-day Adventism, left the church and launched a thirty-year campaign against it, with Ellen White as his primary target. His experience and the church's response to him are the subjects of the next chapter.

Chapter Summary

1. The first organized opposition to Ellen White's prophetic ministry came from a group called the Messenger party (1854–55), who launched a periodical titled *Messenger of Truth*, which they hoped would replace the *Review and Herald*.
2. Their tactics were personal and aggressive toward the developing group of Sabbatarians, especially James and Ellen White.
3. During 1855, the opposition from the Messenger party became so intense that church leaders planned on an aggressive campaign to refute the charges.
4. Ellen White received a vision guiding church leaders away from this aggressive campaign of refutation, and they complied with her guidance.

Chapter Summary

5. The church's positive response to the vision eventually resulted in an important resolution voted at a major conference in Battle Creek during November 1855. The resolution stated that the church would "devote [itself] exclusively to the advocacy and defense of the present truth."
6. This resolution, which kept the church from spending all its energy answering criticisms, translated into many *Review and Herald* articles advocating and defending the truth of Seventh-day Adventism. As such, it was a guide on how to address attacks on the church and its teaching.
7. The Marion party (based in Marion, Iowa), had a much longer and more extensive influence than the Messenger party and produced a number of former Seventh-day Adventist critics who published the following books against Ellen White:
   a. *The Visions of E. G. White, Not of God* (1866), by B. F. Snook and W. H. Brinkerhoff.
   b. *Mrs. E. G. White's Claims to Divine Inspiration Examined* (1870), by H. E. Carver.
   c. *The Testimonies of Mrs. E. G. White Compared With the Bible* (1877), by H. C. Blanchard.
   d. *Comparison of the Early Writings of Mrs. White With Later Publications* (1883), by A. C. Long.
8. The church responded to the Marion party with four apologetic works:
   a. Uriah Smith's church-approved response to Snook and Brinkerhoff's book in a five-part article series, "The Visions—Objections Answered," published in the *Review and Herald,* June 12 through July 31, 1866.
   b. Smith's article series expanded into a book, *The Visions of Mrs. E. G. White, a Manifestation of Spiritual Gifts, According to the Scriptures* (1868).
   c. The church's *Review and Herald Supplement,* August 14, 1883—composed of seventeen articles mostly defending Ellen White's prophetic ministry in response to A. C. Long's influential book.
   d. Ellen White response to Long's book, comprised of a sixteen-page explanation of the omissions in her writings: "An Explanation of Early Statements." This response is significant because Ellen

Chapter Summary

White rarely responded to critics herself.

9. Miles Grant, the most influential and outspoken non-Sabbatarian critic of Ellen White, published the periodical *The World's Crisis* and the book *The True Sabbath: Which Day Shall We Keep? An Examination of Mrs. Ellen White's Visions* (1874).
10. In reflecting on Grant's intense criticism of her, Ellen White felt that he repeated his criticisms so many times that he came to believe them to be true and to believe that he was doing God's service in criticizing her. She never entered into controversy with Grant.
11. Five lessons emerge from this chapter:
    a. Criticisms of Ellen White have been around from the beginning of her prophetic ministry, so the fact that people criticize her today shouldn't shock us.
    b. For the most part, the content of today's Ellen White criticisms is recycled from nineteenth-century criticisms.
    c. The early apologetic work of the church has already answered many of today's Ellen White criticisms.
    d. Answering Ellen White's critics is important, but it shouldn't keep us from focusing on the positive message of Adventism—a soon-coming Savior.
    e. Just as past criticisms failed to silence the writings of Ellen White, so will the present criticisms fail to silence her prophetic voice.

CHAPTER 3

Dudley M. Canright: Father of Ellen White Criticisms

Dudley Marvin Canright was born September 22, 1840, in Kinderhook, Michigan, the third child of seven born to Hiram and Loretta Canright.[1] He was baptized into the Methodist Church at age sixteen; and in 1859, at age nineteen, was converted to Seventh-day Adventism through the preaching of James White. He listened to the preaching, devoured Adventist books, and studied his Bible day and night. He longed to convert others to his newfound faith. His mother was his first convert.[2]

Canright felt called to the ministry and at age twenty-one traveled to Battle Creek to talk with James White, who encouraged him to try it out. Canright experienced success from the beginning. The *Review and Herald* reported the fruitfulness of his ministry during these early years.[3] After holding meetings in Vassar, Michigan, with Elder Isaac Van Horn in July 1864, Canright wrote in the *Review and Herald:* "Present truth looks clearer and more beautiful to us the more we study it. Praise the Lord for a religion that agrees with the Bible, common sense, and the wants of men."[4] He was ordained to the gospel ministry on May 29, 1865. J. N. Loughborough and James White conducted the service. On April 11, 1867, he married Lucretia Cranson, a nineteen-year-old orphan raised in part by James and Ellen White. Within a short time Canright became one of the most forceful and successful preachers of the Seventh-day Adventist message.

Canright worked in the Seventh-day Adventist Church as an ordained minister for twenty-two years. In the early years he was known as a gifted communicator and debater who successfully refuted opponents of Seventh-day Adventism. From his prolific pen came hundreds of articles published in the *Review and Herald* and *Signs of the Times®* advocating and defending present truth.[5] He wrote some of the most affirming statements ever written about the Seventh-day Adventist message and Ellen White's prophetic ministry.

Canright's on-and-off relationship with Ellen White

During the decade between 1873 and 1883, Canright left the Adventist ministry three times due to ill feelings toward Ellen White and her testimonies.[6] His relationship to her during this time can best be described as on and off.[7] According to his own words,[8] the first time he took a leave of absence from the ministry (1874), it was because he and his wife received a strong letter of correction (testimony) from Ellen White.[9] "I felt that it was too severe," he recalled, "and that some of it was not true." He "quit preaching for a short time," but "soon got mostly over this" and went back into the work of ministry, although he still "did not feel exactly right toward Sr. White, nor fully accept the testimony."[10]

Interestingly, a few short years later, he penned one of his strongest affirmations of Ellen White's prophetic ministry in a ten-part series of articles titled "A Plain Talk to the Murmurers: Some Facts for Those Who Are Not in Harmony With the Body," published in the *Review and Herald*, March 15–June 14, 1877.[11] In article 4 of this series, he described Ellen White as an "unassuming, modest, kind-hearted, noble woman" who is "not self-conceited, self-righteous, and self-important, as fanatics always are." He went on to say, "I have heard Sr. White speak hundreds of times, have read all her testimonies through and through, most of them many times, and I have never been able to find one immoral sentence in the whole of them, or anything that is not strictly pure and Christian; nothing that leads away from the Bible, or from Christ; but there I find the most earnest appeals to obey God, to love Jesus, to believe the Scriptures, and to search them constantly." Reflecting upon his personal experience, he said, "I have received great spiritual benefit times without number, from the testimonies."[12]

Canright's second leave of absence from the Adventist ministry occurred in 1880, when he received another strong testimony of rebuke from Ellen White.[13] "This I did not receive at all well," he explained, "but felt hard toward Sr. White, and soon quit the work entirely."[14] For four months, according to his recollection, he questioned Adventist doctrine. "I looked in every direction to see if there was not some mistake in our doctrine, or if I could not go some other way." He even "talked with ministers of other churches to see what they would say." But he found "in every case" that "they were wholly ignorant on the subject, and that their arguments were not better than those I had heard and refuted a hundred times."[15] Eventually he traveled to Battle Creek to counsel with George Butler and both James and Ellen White about his doubts and trials.

After several months of this kind of searching, Canright went back to preaching the Adventist message again. He wrote out his experience and published it in the September 13, 1881, *Review and Herald* under the title "Danger of Giving Way to Discouragement and Doubts."[16] In this article he affirmed the Adventist message: "If the Bible does not plainly and abundantly teach the doctrines of the third angel's message, then I despair of ever knowing what it does teach." He was determined to learn from this experience: "Of course I regret now that I gave way to discouragements and doubts; but I think I have learned a lesson by it which I shall not need to learn again as long as I live."[17]

Within a year Canright left the Adventist ministry for the third time (in the autumn of 1882), due to continuing doubt regarding Adventist doctrine and Ellen White's prophetic ministry. He had tried preaching "practical truths largely," but this didn't work. "Still I was not heartily in sympathy with all parts of the work," he recalled in 1884, "especially the testimonies." Thus, he "went to farming" and "resolved to live a devoted life."[18] From 1882 to 1884, he tilled the soil.

In December of 1883, Canright wrote in a personal letter[19] to A. C. Long that farming was keeping him "very busy and hard at work." Tilling the soil, he told Long, "is what I naturally love to do the best of anything and so I feel well contented." As to preaching for the Adventists, he confessed, "I have entirely given up preaching and have no intention of ever engaging in it again." Concerning Ellen White, he said he disliked her "very much indeed." As far as he was concerned, she was "self deceived," and her "visions" were "not from God" but "wholly the fruit of her own imagination." He had "often seen her show a bitter, vindictive spirit toward those who cross her path."

The next statement in the letter is significant: "But you cannot separate her visions and work from the third [angel's] message as held by our people. If her visions are not of God, then that entire work is not, for they have grown up together. Hence, as you can see, my faith in the whole thing is shaken. As far as I can see at present, much of it may be true or it may not be. I do not feel positive about any of these speculative points as I used to."

Ellen White obviously played a central role in Canright's feelings about the Seventh-day Adventist Church. While he expressed doubts about Adventist teaching, his relationship to her seemed to be the deciding factor in how he related to Adventism as a whole. As to the leading men in the church, especially Elder Butler, Canright expressed great appreciation for them. "I am a member of the church still and I do all I can to help it," he said.

"But if I were situated differently, I would just as soon join some other church."[20]

Reflecting on this two-year absence from the Adventist ministry, he wrote, "I soon found my doubts and fears increasing, and my devotion decreasing, till, at length, I found myself largely swallowed up in my work with little time, taste, or interest for religious work. I felt sure that the testimonies were not reliable, and that other things held by our people were not correct. So it always is when a person lets go of one point of the truth—he begins to drift he knows not whither."[21]

In September 1884, at the pleading of friends, Canright attended the "Northern Michigan camp meeting with Eld. Butler." Here they both spent a long time in "consultation, prayer, and careful examination" of his difficulties. "I began to see," he wrote, "that, at least, some of my objections were not tenable, and that I myself was not right and in the light." As a result of this time with his old friend Butler, he saw Ellen White and the church in a new light. "I saw that I had put a wrong meaning on some things, and that other things were certainly true. If those were true, then I had certainly been wrong all the way through. Light came into my mind, and for the first time in years I could truly say that I believed the testimonies. *All my hard feelings toward Sr. White vanished in a moment, and I felt a tender love towards her*" [emphasis added].[22]

His most significant statements of resolve to stay loyal to Seventh-day Adventism were penned when he returned from this third leave of absence. When one reads these statements without letting the knowledge of Canright's later defection influence the reading, one sees a freshness and sincerity in these statements that is quite moving. In describing his reconversion experience on Friday, September 26, 1884, at the northern Michigan camp meeting, he wrote in the *Review and Herald*:

I felt in my heart the most remarkable change that I ever experienced in all my life. It was a complete reversion of all my feelings. Light and faith came into my soul, and I felt that God had given me another heart. I never felt such a change before, not even when first converted, or when I embraced the message, nor at any other time. I believe it was directly from heaven,—the work of the Spirit of God. I now believe the message as firmly and more understandingly than ever before; and I want to say to all my friends everywhere, that now I not only accept, but believe the testimonies to be from God. Knowing the opposition I have felt to them, this change in my feelings is more amazing to myself than it can be to others.[23]

Referring to this reconversion experience, he said, "Such nearness to God, such earnest devotion, such solemn appeals to live a holy life can only be promoted by the Spirit of God. Where that is, there I want to be. I am fully satisfied that my own salvation and my usefulness in saving others depends upon my being connected with this people in this work. And here I take my stand to risk all I am, or have, or hope for, in this life and the life to come, with this people and this work."[24]

Speaking to ministers, he said:

> Brethren, I will say this: So far as I am concerned, I will start right here; and all that I have, all that I am, I will put into this work, and take my risk of everything. I will never do this backing up any more; and I believe that if I ever go back from this I am lost. All I have I will give to this cause. I believe there is in this truth that which will save men. I have seen drunkards saved by it, and the wickedest of men saved by it; and may God help us to triumph with it when Jesus comes.[25]

For the next two years Canright labored successfully in the Adventist Church, preaching, teaching, and writing.[26] Nearly every issue of the *Review and Herald* contained an article from his productive pen. His best-remembered article of this period, "To Those in Doubting Castle," appeared in the February 10, 1885, *Review and Herald*. Again he affirmed Ellen White's prophetic ministry in no uncertain terms: "Again, the tendency and influence of the testimonies is not, like the teachings of Spiritualist mediums, to lead away from the Bible, away from God, and away from faith in Christ; nor, like Mormonism, to lead to sensuality, dishonesty, and crime; but they lead to faith in the Holy Scriptures, devotion to God, and a life of humility and holiness. Can a corrupt tree bear good fruit? Jesus said not. What is a tree known by?—Its fruit. Here is a tree which has been standing among us for forty years, and bearing fruit."[27]

Things went fine for him until the General Conference session of 1886. This meeting changed his relationship to Seventh-day Adventism forever.

The General Conference session of 1886

Over the years, several reasons for Canright's defection from Seventh-day Adventism have been suggested: disappointed ambitions, an unstable character, preparation for a debate over the Sabbath with D. R. Dungan, and a conflict over the nature of the law during the 1886 General Conference session. Of these several reasons, the last one is the most compelling. Canright himself refers to this General Conference debate as the turning point in his thinking about Seventh-day Adventism.

Legalism during the 1870s and 1880s. To fully appreciate the impact of the 1886 General Conference Session on Canright, we must examine Adventism's understanding of the law and salvation during the 1870s and 1880s. The first generation of Seventh-day Adventists believed in salvation by grace through faith,[28] but over the years they began to lose sight of the Christ-centered nature of their distinctive doctrines, such as the perpetuity of the law and the nearness of the Second Coming. Their concern for the breach in God's law regarding the seventh-day Sabbath began to eclipse their appreciation for righteousness by faith, and it was assumed as a "basic truth rather than emphasized as the dominant truth."[29] Consequently, "in early Seventh-day Adventist sermons, books, and periodicals there is but scant mention of justification by faith and salvation by grace."[30] The central feature of their unique end-time message—a personal, saving relationship with Jesus Christ—had gradually and imperceptibly slipped from their consciousness.

Denominational historians Richard Schwarz and Floyd Greenleaf summarized the situation accurately: "By the 1870s and [18]80s a new generation of Seventh-day Adventists had arisen. Ridiculed as legalists and Judaizers by fellow Christians, persecuted in some areas, these Seventh-day Adventists searched the Bible to sustain their Sabbath beliefs. They found it a veritable arsenal of proof texts, which could be marshaled with crushing logic to demonstrate the perpetuity of the Sabbath. They courted debate and, imperceptibly to themselves, tended to become just what they were charged with being: legalists looking to their own actions for salvation rather than to Jesus Christ."[31] Consequently, *obedience,* rather than *faith,* became the keyword for most Adventists during this period.[32]

Canright himself, a champion of traditional Adventism, reflected the thinking of the day in an 1874 *Signs of the Times®* article when he declared that the mission of Seventh-day Adventists was *not* to emphasize "the subjects of faith, repentance, conversion, free salvation, and the other cardinal doctrines of Christianity." There is "no necessity for much time and labor to be spent upon these subjects" because the "battle has been fought and these doctrines are not disputed." They only had "to be assented to." Rather, the mission of the church was to emphasize the prophecies, the law, the "coming day of wrath," and the preparation necessary "to stand in the day of trouble."[33] In effect, Canright and many others were convicted that Adventism's prophetic warnings should take the front seat, and basic Christian teaching the back seat.

That Ellen White didn't share this understanding of the Adventist message held by Canright and other church leaders is obvious from her writings during this period. She believed that these salvation themes should be much more than just "assented to." For years she had been emphasizing the prophecies, the law, and the nearness of the end *in the context of faith, repentance, conversion, free salvation, and the other cardinal doctrines of Christianity.* In 1864, for example, she wrote about the "merits" of Christ being the only ground of our favor with God,[34] and in 1869, she wrote a pamphlet on correctly understanding His atonement titled "The Sufferings of Christ."[35] Here she exalted the theme of salvation through Christ alone. "The death of Christ proclaimed the justice of His Father's law in punishing the transgressor," she explained, "in that He consented to suffer the penalty of the law Himself in order to save fallen man from its curse."[36] She insisted, "We should take broader and deeper views of the life, sufferings, and death of God's dear Son."[37] Canright and others had missed this theme in her writings. But her emphasis was unmistakable: "It is impossible for us to exalt the law of Jehovah unless we take hold of the righteousness of Jesus Christ."[38] In reflecting on her teaching over the years, she stated in 1889 that for forty-five years she had been presenting the "matchless charms of Christ."[39]

The legalistic trend in the teaching and preaching of the church during the 1870s and 1880s had caused Ellen White great concern, and she addressed it repeatedly. In 1879, she complained, "Too often this truth is presented in cold theory," and "sermon after sermon upon doctrinal points is delivered to people who come and go, some of whom will never have another as favorable opportunity of being convicted and converted to Christ."[40] In 1880, she exclaimed, "I long to see our ministers dwell more upon the cross of Christ, their own hearts, meanwhile, softened and subdued by the Saviour's matchless love which prompted that infinite sacrifice."[41] Her most memorable statement, although penned in 1890, referred to this legalistic period in the church: "As a people, we have preached the law until we are as dry as the hills of Gilboa that had neither dew nor rain." Instead, she proclaimed, we "must preach Christ in the Law" and "not trust in our own merits at all, but in the merits of Jesus of Nazareth."[42] Thus, Ellen White was determined to neutralize the "Pharisaism" of the day, the "feeling that we are righteous, and all our acts are meritorious."[43]

She also expressed concern over the debating spirit among Seventh-day Adventist ministers. "There are many speakers," she wrote in 1882, who "can say sharp, crank things, going out of their way to whip other churches and ridicule their faith." But only a few possessed true "humility of soul." (It's possible that Canright may have been one of the debaters on her mind, as he was considered a champion debater of traditional Adventism.) "These sharp, self-important speakers profess to have truth in advance of every other people, but their manner of labor and their religious zeal in no way correspond with their profession of faith." Only when "the love of God is burning on the altar of their hearts," she declared, will these ministers "present Christ who taketh away the sins of the world" and "not preach to exhibit their own smartness."[44]

Controversy over the law. With this general background in mind, we will now examine the controversy over the law that brought things to a head for Canright.[45] Since the mid-1850s, Adventist preachers had interpreted the "added law" in Galatians 3:19–25 as the ceremonial law rather than the moral law. The foremost champion of this interpretation was D. M. Canright himself, who in 1876, in his *Two Laws*[46]—a "major contribution to Adventist thinking on the law"[47]—argued that the Bible made a general distinction between the ceremonial and moral laws.

In the early 1880s, Canright revised this book by expanding the section on the law in Galatians from six to twenty-four pages.[48] In this enlarged discussion of Galatians 3, Canright argued that the moral law "convicts a man of sin" but does "not lead him to Christ for pardon." Rather, he stated, the "typical law" (ceremonial law) and "the gospel" in the New Testament "point" the sinner to Christ.[49] In contrast, in the *Signs of the Times*® published between 1884 and 1886, Ellet J. Waggoner made a different emphasis. He said that "the law literally *drives* the sinner to Christ."[50] Waggoner and his coeditor of *Signs of the Times*®, Alonzo T. Jones, argued that Galatians had the Ten Commandments in mind, rather than the ceremonial law. Thus, by 1886, the law issue of Galatians 3 had become a major controversial issue.

At the heart of this controversy were the General Conference president, George I. Butler, and the editor of the *Review and Herald,* Uriah Smith. Both Butler and Smith, the traditional old guard, were concerned about the theology of the young progressives A. T. Jones and E. J. Waggoner. In the context of late nineteenth-century evangelicalism's protest against the perpetuity of the law and the apparent imminent Sunday law, Butler and Smith felt that this was no time to compromise the church's traditional teaching on the distinction between the two laws. In fact, as far as they were concerned, this issue had already been settled, and they were resolute in their position. Jones and Waggoner were also just as resolute as to what they were teaching, and they felt they were more in harmony with the context of Galatians. History would acknowledge their position as more correct. But for the time being, the traditional old guard and the young progressives were locked in combat, and neither side was about to compromise. Such was the immediate context for the 1886 General Conference Session, the twenty-fifth annual session of the General Conference.

As the session approached, Butler endeavored to resolve the struggles over the law to his advantage, and his three-part strategy involved Dudley Canright. First, he corresponded with Ellen White over the summer to enlist her aid against Jones and Waggoner, "men who had been bold enough to advocate in print theological and prophetic viewpoints contrary to long-established Adventist positions." Butler appealed to her authority to "settle the interpretative problem by providing a testimony on the correct interpretation of the law in Galatians."[51] Ellen White, however, would have nothing to do with any of her testimonies providing the final word on interpreting Scripture and never gave Butler any encouragement to this end.[52]

Second, by the end of August, Butler composed his own "brief comment on Epistle to the Galatians" regarding the issue of the law—an eighty-five-page book titled *The Law in the Book of Galatians* that was a direct attack on Waggoner's position.[53] In addition, Butler and his forces brought out a new edition of Canright's *Two Laws,* with its expanded discussion on the law in Galatians. As I have noted, Canright was considered a good debater and able defender of traditional Adventism, particularly its view of the two-law theory. So his work on the law was an asset to Butler's cause.

Butler's final strategic move was to use the 1886 General Conference Session itself to put Jones and Waggoner in their proper place and jettison their "false teachings" on the law and salvation. Thus, when the session convened in November, Butler provided every attendee with a copy of his *Law in the Book of Galatians* and organized a nine-member committee to settle the prophetic issues and the nature of the law in Galatians "once and for all." He arranged for someone other than himself to appoint the committee members. S. N. Haskell was chosen for this task, and the nine appointees on the committee were G. I. Butler, S. N. Haskell, U. Smith, E. J. Waggoner, J. H. Morrison, M. C. Wilcox, B. L. Whitney, W. Covert, and, of course, D. M. Canright.

Butler had hoped the committee would compose a creedal statement, but this was not to be. According to his account, the committee "had an argument of several hours" over the law issue, "but neither side was convinced."[54] The nine-member committee was split, five to four: Canright, Smith, Covert, and Morrison sided with Butler; Haskell, Whitney, and Wilcox sided with Waggoner.[55] Realizing he couldn't get the creedal statement he wanted, Butler settled for a resolution that disallowed "doctrinal views not held by a majority of our people" to be taught in Adventist schools or published in denominational papers until they had been "examined and approved by the leading Brethren of experience."[56]

Turning point for Canright. The debate over the law in Galatians in this committee was the turning point in Canright's relationship with Adventism.⁵⁷ In *Seventh-day Adventism Renounced,* he recalled,

> In our General Conference that fall, a sharp division occurred between our leading men over the law in Galatians. One party held it was the ceremonial law, the other the moral law—a square contradiction. After a long and warm discussion the conference closed, each party more confident than before. There was so much disagreement over other points of doctrine, and a good deal of warm party feeling. This, with other things, brought up my old feelings of doubt, and decided me that it was time for me now to examine and think for myself, and not be led or intimidated by men who could not agree among themselves.⁵⁸

Canright mentioned this division several times in his book. "Elder Waggoner leads one party and Elder Butler the other."⁵⁹ Thus, in the weeks following the 1886 General Conference session, Canright "used every minute" he could in "carefully and prayerfully examining all the evidence on the Sabbath, the law, the sanctuary, the visions, etc., till," he said, "I had not a doubt left that the Seventh-day Advent faith was a delusion."⁶⁰

According to George Knight, in the heat of the debate over the law, Canright "must have grasped the fact that Waggoner had a valid point"—that contextually, the law in Galatians was the moral law. This interpretation flattened Canright's argument about Galatians in the second edition of his *Two Laws.* "But instead of adopting Waggoner's view of the Ten Commandments as leading individuals to Christ, Canright dropped both the perpetuity of the law and Adventism." In Canright's thinking there was no middle ground. His law-oriented theology couldn't account for "the truth of the gospel of salvation by grace through faith." Although "he had grasped the fact that the Adventist leadership was confused on the question of the covenants and had placed the law above the gospel," in the end, he never found the proper relationship of law and gospel and chose to "reject the law and join the gospel-oriented Baptists."⁶¹

Ellen White told Butler that she was shown the 1886 General Conference Session in vision (she was in Switzerland at the time and couldn't attend it), and she felt it was a "terrible conference." "The Lord was not pleased with that meeting," because "your spirit, my brother, was not right," she said. "The manner in which you treated the case of Dr. Waggoner was perhaps after your own order, but not after God's order." She quickly got to the heart of the matter: "We must not crowd and push one another because others do not see just as we see. We must treat others with Christ-like courtesy, even if they differ with us."⁶² It's noteworthy that the inability of the brethren to "agree among themselves" was an influential factor in Canright's decision to leave Adventism.

Ellen White had foreseen "a time of trial" facing the church in connection with the 1886 General Conference Session. She warned that "great evils would be the result of the Phariseeism which has in a large degree taken possession of those who occupy important positions in the work of God."[63] It appears that Canright's departure and future war on Adventism were in view, for he was not only a culprit of this "Phariseeism," but a casualty, of it as well.

Canright's final departure from Adventism

According to his own words, Canright "laid the matter before the leading men at Battle Creek," "resigned all the positions" he held, and "asked to be dismissed from the church." His request was "granted February 17, 1887,"[64] at a special meeting called at Otsego, his home church. During the meeting, Canright was invited to "make any statement he chose to the church."[65] Butler, who was present, described Canright's words as "very kind and conciliatory."[66]

Canright spoke for about an hour, explaining the reasons for his departure. "He said in substance," according to Butler's account, "that he could go no longer with Seventh-day Adventists" and had "ceased to believe that the law was binding, and did not expect to keep another Sabbath." In short, "he had no faith in the message, the sanctuary, the two-horned beast, the testimonies, health reform, etc." He also "spoke in regard to the shut door movement in 44, how he knew that the testimonies taught" this doctrine for many years. Canright also told the church that "he had been passing through a constant struggle for twenty years to believe these things but now it was over and he could not do it any more."[67]

While Canright disagreed with Adventist doctrine, however, he had only positive things to say about Adventists as a people. He was "perfectly satisfied with the treatment he had received among Seventh-day Adventists" and said "he should never pursue the course of some others had who have left us, becoming bitter assailants of our people," but instead "his only desire was to labor for the salvation of souls."[68] Butler summarized the interview by saying that "there was no unpleasant language used, no unkind expressions; and though, of course, there was great sadness of heart to think that one so long associated with us should depart from the faith we hold so dear, yet everything passed off pleasantly."[69]

Thus, Canright's departure from Seventh-day Adventism in February 1887 was marked by peace. Within a short time, however, this peaceful atmosphere disappeared. The word *apostasy* was used several times in the *Review and Herald* in reference to Canright's departure (unwisely so, in my view), and he took offense at it.[70] In addition, in the March 22 *Review and*

Herald, Butler rebuked those Adventists who were sending Canright letters "calculated to create an acrimonious spirit, imputing unworthy motives, and saying things of a personal nature which better by far be left unsaid."[71] Whatever the case, a few short months after Canright's peaceful departure from Seventh-day Adventism, he began to wage war on the church. While there has been discussion as to who broke the truce first, it appears that both sides were at fault.[72]

On April 5, 1887, Ellen White wrote to denominational leaders Butler and Smith that she believed Canright's course was "contemptible." In her thinking, though, Butler and Smith didn't fully grasp what had happened to Canright. "I can see farther in this matter from that which the Lord has shown me, than you can," she told them. "But his course, his sudden change, speaks for itself." Evidently she saw Canright's future war on Adventism and appropriately remarked to Butler and Smith, "I believe we will have to have far more of the Spirit of God in order to escape the perils of these last days."[73] She was on the mark, because Canright's war against Adventism defined the last thirty-two years of his life.

Canright's campaign against Ellen White and Adventism

In the late spring and summer of 1887, several months after his departure from Adventism, Canright began traveling from place to place speaking on the "exposure of Adventism." He charged "two dollars per night" to reveal Adventism's "fanaticism." He also penned articles against Adventist teaching in the religious papers of the various churches. In September, during a large Adventist camp meeting in Grand Rapids, Michigan, Canright obtained permission from the city newspaper offices to insert articles in their papers against Adventism. The articles came out as the camp meeting convened and were circulated throughout the city. In addition, Canright circulated another handbill "with a bitter personal attack upon Mrs. White." Thousands of copies were scattered on the campground of the Adventist camp meeting.[74]

These initial articles and camp-meeting handbills led to a lengthy response by church leaders in a *Review and Herald Extra* issued on November 22, 1887. This twenty-page *Extra,* together with a second four-page *Extra* on February 21, 1888, were reprinted in 1888 and 1895 as a booklet entitled *Replies to Elder Canright's Attacks on Seventh-day Adventists.*[75] Four pages of the first *Extra* were devoted to answering Canright's charges against Ellen White.[76] This *Extra* also began the practice of having the "Adventist" Canright refute the attacks of the "Baptist" Canright by printing in column format his arguments defending the law to respond to his later arguments dismissing the law.[77]

In 1888, Canright published the first edition of *Seventh-day Adventism Renounced*. This book had gone through fourteen editions by 1914, and it became his most important book against his former church.[78] It contained extensive criticism of the history and teaching of Seventh-day Adventism. Although Canright devoted only one chapter to criticizing Ellen White's prophetic gift, critical remarks about her were interwoven throughout the book.[79]

In 1889, Canright traveled all the way from Michigan to Healdsburg, California, to present a series of lectures based on *Seventh-day Adventism Renounced*. After the lectures in February, he engaged in an eight-night-long debate with William Healey, a Seventh-day Adventist evangelist. During these debates, in addition to criticizing the distinctive Adventist beliefs, Canright set forth the charge that Ellen White plagiarized most of her writings. Consequently, these meetings have appropriately been called "The Genesis of the Plagiarism Charge."[80] J. N. Loughborough responded to this charge by publishing Mrs. White's writings and those of the other writer in question in parallel columns, thus demonstrating the "falsity of Canright's claims." Loughborough was the first to use this approach.[81]

Over the years Canright went on to publish other works against Adventist teachings, such as a ten-tract series, *Adventism Refuted in a Nutshell* (1889), and two books: *The Lord's Day From Neither Catholics Nor Pagans* (1915) and *The Complete Testimony of the Early Fathers* (1916).[82] The culmination of his thirty-two-year-long campaign against Ellen White was his 291-page book *Life of Mrs. E. G. White, Seventh-day Adventist Prophet: Her False Claims Refuted*, published in 1919.[83] It was the forerunner of all future criticisms of Ellen White and occupied the attention of Adventist apologists for decades, as the next chapter will show.

Interestingly, Canright died on May 12, 1919, and *Life of Mrs. E. G. White* was published two months later, in July of 1919. The two books, *Seventh-day Adventism Renounced* and *Life of Mrs. E. G. White* became his legacy.[84]

Observations from Canright's experience

When Canright left the Seventh-day Adventist Church in early 1887, the church was on the threshold of a major theological change. The law-centered theology of the General Conference leadership, headed by G. I. Butler and Uriah Smith, was about to clash with the Christ-centered theology of E. J. Waggoner and A. T. Jones at the 1888 Minneapolis General Conference session. This historic conference, filled with drama and controversy, changed the theological focus of the church from being law-centered to being Christ-centered. At the forefront of this change was Ellen White, who led the way in promoting the vital, life-giving message of righteousness by faith. In the years following 1888, she, Jones, and Waggoner were determined to get this vital message to the church through pen and pulpit.

But D. M. Canright wasn't around to hear the message of 1888 or to experience the ensuing revival. He was outside of the church, engaged in a campaign against it. During his thirty-two-year-long campaign against Adventism, he either failed to recognize or refused to acknowledge the positive impact of the 1888 message on the church.

The irony of Canright's experience is that Ellen White rejected the same law-centered Adventism that he rejected. In a definitive statement, she described the 1888 message as a "most precious message" that presented "the righteousness of Christ" and directed all "to His divine person, His merits, and His changeless love for the human family." Nothing can ever "diminish the efficacy" of Christ's "atoning sacrifice," she said. "The message of the gospel of His grace was to be given to the church in clear and distinct lines, that the world should no longer say that Seventh-day Adventists talk the law, the law, but do not teach or believe Christ." This is the foundation, she explained, that "is made manifest in obedience to all the commandments of God." Because the Seventh-day Adventist Church had been "looking to man and expecting much from man" in the years prior to 1888 and "not looking to Jesus, in whom our hopes of eternal life are centered, God gave to His servants [E. J. Waggoner and A. T. Jones] a testimony that presented the truth as it is in Jesus, which is the third angel's message, in clear, distinct lines."[85] This message was quite different from the law-centered Adventism that Canright had experienced and even championed, during the 1870s and 1880s.

What Canright missed during the years following 1888 was a revival in Adventism unrivaled by anything before it. In March of 1889, for example, Ellen White wrote, "I have never seen a revival work go forward with such thoroughness, and yet remain so free from all undue excitement."[86] And in July of the same year, she stated, "The tidings that Christ is our righteousness has brought relief to many, many souls."[87] Although some of the old law-centered traditionalists resisted, the message of righteousness by faith forged ahead in the 1890s through ministerial institutes and General Conference sessions.

One area in which this revival was especially noticed was education. In 1891, W. W. Prescott, leader of the Adventist educational program, called a meeting in Harbor Springs, Michigan, on the subject of educational reform. Jones preached a series of sermons from the book of Romans, and Ellen White spoke on "such topics as the necessity of a personal relationship with Christ, the need for spiritual revival among Adventist educators, and the centrality of the Christian message to education." Participants described the meetings as a "spiritual feast." As a result, this historic convention changed the course of Adventist education. Study of the Bible became central to the curriculum, Adventist doctrine was taught in the context of "a proper knowledge of the gospel" and "a belief in Jesus Christ as a living personal Savior," and the Christ-centered teachings of Jones and Waggoner became a part of all college studies.[88] Thus, as a result of the 1888 experience, Seventh-day Adventists "could preach a full message that taught the distinctively Adventist doctrines within the context of the saving work of Christ."[89]

In his years of fighting Ellen White and Adventism, Canright never mentioned this theological change and resulting revival in Adventism. He had thrown out the entire package and viewed it as hopelessly legalistic and erroneous. As late as 1914, in the last edition of his *Adventism Renounced,* he continued to assert that the "constant theme" of Adventism "is the law, law, law." In spite of contrary evidence, he insisted that Adventists preach the law "ten times as much as they preach Christ."[90] It is noteworthy that in the last edition of *Adventism Renounced,* published in 1914, Canright mainly cites Adventist literature published prior to 1888.[91] He certainly was right when he said that the moment he took his "stand decidedly" to leave Adventism in 1887, the "matter was settled forever."[92] He never looked back—even to check the correctness of his arguments!

Because of this decided stance, Canright apparently never studied Ellen White's post-1888 literary production. He never mentioned or cited any of her many articles in the *Review and Herald* that affirmed justification by faith and free salvation. Neither did he reference her Christ-centered books uplifting the theme of righteousness by faith:

- 1890 *Patriarchs and Prophets*
- 1892 *Gospel Workers* (first edition)
- 1892 *Steps to Christ*
- 1896 *Thoughts From the Mount of Blessing*
- 1898 *The Desire of Ages*
- 1900 *Christ's Object Lessons*
- 1903 *Education*
- 1905 *The Ministry of Healing*
- 1911 *The Acts of the Apostles*
- 1915 *Gospel Workers* (second edition)
- 1917 *Prophets and Kings*[93]

As noted by denominational historians, the continuing influence of these books "has prevented Seventh-day Adventists from ever again falling into quite the same danger from legalism that existed in the 1870s and 1880s."[94]

Canright's failure to acknowledge this wealth of Christ-centered writing and the church's promotion of it was indicative of a stratagem.[95] Once he rejected the idea that God was a supernatural source of Ellen White's messages, he looked only "for natural and psychological ways to explain both the content of her messages and the phenomena she experienced while in vision."[96] He thus narrowed his focus to perceived problems in her writings and dismissed all contrary evidence.[97] This trend continues today in those who follow in Canright's path.

Another point of interest is that Canright's criticisms of Ellen White didn't reflect how she viewed the relationship of her writings to the Bible. In both *Adventism Renounced* and *Life of Mrs. E. G. White,* for example, Canright claimed that Adventists view Ellen White's writings as "another Bible." Just before Canright left the Adventist Church, he heard Butler and Smith appeal to Ellen White for an authoritative word on the law in Galatians 3. But he wasn't at the 1888 General Conference session when she turned the attention of the delegates back to the Bible and away from her writings as the final word on any biblical subject. Furthermore, she spelled out the final authority of the Bible in 1889.[98] "The *Testimonies* are not to belittle the word of God," she explained, "but to exalt it and attract minds to it, that the beautiful simplicity of truth may impress all."[99] Canright failed to notice these words.

Thus, in his campaign against Seventh-day Adventism, Canright was fighting the pre-1888 Adventism, not the Adventism that had moved on to greater understanding of God's plan for humankind. His criticisms were focused on the Adventism he remembered. His charges may have been true of pockets of Adventism, but the denomination as a whole had outgrown them.[100]

Conclusion

Dudley M. Canright's departure from Seventh-day Adventism and his subsequent lengthy campaign to discredit its prophetic messenger can be considered a critical turning point in the history of Ellen White criticisms for four reasons. First, in the culmination of his work in *The Life of Mrs. E. G. White,* he recycled the criticisms of Ellen White's prophetic ministry from 1845 to the late 1880s, covered in the previous chapter.

Second, he conceived new criticisms against her, such as the plagiarism and epilepsy charges. He was also the first one to systematically associate Ellen White with cult leaders[101] of the eighteenth and nineteenth centuries, such as Emanuel Swedenborg, Ann Lee Stanley, Joseph Smith, Mary Baker Eddy, and Charles T. Russell.

Third, Canright raised almost all the issues that would be directed against Ellen White in the future.[102] Most of the criticisms circulating on the Internet today are recycled from Canright's complaints. Even when an occasional new criticism is posted, it still stands in the framework of his stratagem.

Fourth, Canright provided a model that almost all future critics of Ellen White would copy. From the non-Adventist evangelical critics of the early twentieth century to the former Adventist critics of today, most of them have followed the pattern he laid out in *Life of Mrs. E. G. White* and have considered this volume to be influential in their thinking. In this sense, therefore, Canright can be called the "father" of Ellen White criticisms.

In the next chapter we will survey the church's response to Canright over the years and observe his influence on two well-known contemporary critics of Ellen White.

Chapter Summary

1. Converted to Seventh-day Adventism at age nineteen by the preaching of James White, Dudley Marvin Canright became an avid follower of the Seventh-day Adventist message and was ordained to the gospel ministry on May 29, 1865.
2. He worked in the church as an ordained minister for twenty-two years and was well known as a gifted communicator and debater who could successfully refute opponents of the Seventh-day Adventist message.
3. Canright penned some of the strongest and most affirming statements ever written about the Seventh-day Adventist message and Ellen White's prophetic ministry.
4. During the decade 1873–1883, Canright left the Adventist ministry three times due to ill feelings toward Ellen White and her testimonies. His relationship with her during this period was on and off.
    a. Each time he left the ministry, his leaving was related to his receiving a testimony of rebuke from Ellen White.
    b. Each time he returned to the ministry, he published an article in the *Review and Herald* affirming Ellen White's prophetic gift.
    c. His strongest affirmation of Seventh-day Adventism and Ellen White's prophetic gift was published in the *Review and Herald* after this third leave of absence.
5. From 1884 to 1886, Canright labored successfully in the Adventist Church, preaching, teaching, and writing.

ELLEN WHITE UNDER FIRE

Chapter Summary

6. The General Conference Session of 1886 was the turning point in Canright's relationship to Seventh-day Adventism.
7. During the 1870s and 1880s, the Adventist Church had become steeped in legalism and Canright was a part of this trend.
    a. Canright himself, a champion of traditional Adventism, reflected the thinking of the day in an 1874 *Signs of the Times*® article in which he declared that the mission of Seventh-day Adventists was *not* to emphasize the subjects of faith, repentance, conversion, free salvation, or other cardinal doctrines of Christianity. Instead, he felt the church's mission was to emphasize the unique view of end-time events related to the prophecies and the law.
    b. Ellen White didn't hold this understanding that was held by Canright and many other church leaders. She believed that the law and end-time events should always be proclaimed in the context of the saving work of Christ and spoke out against the legalistic trend in the teaching and preaching of the church. She believed Adventist ministers must preach Christ in the law and not trust in their own merits.
8. The controversy over the law in the 1886 General Conference Session brought things to a head for Canright.
    a. The General Conference leadership, particularly G. I. Butler and Uriah Smith argued that the law Paul wrote about in Galatians 3:19–25 was the ceremonial law rather than the moral law. Canright had been the foremost champion of this position in his book *Two Laws*, originally published in 1876, and enlarged in the early 1880s. In this book he also argued that the moral law only convicts sinners but does not lead them to Christ.
    b. During the years 1884–1886, Ellet J. Waggoner argued the opposite in the *Signs of the Times*®, saying that the law in Galatians 3:19–25 is the moral law and that law *does* lead sinners to Christ.
    c. Thus, by 1886, the law issue of Galatians 3 had become a major controversial issue in the church.
9. At the 1886 session, General Conference President Butler strategically orchestrated events so that his view of the law would prevail, and Canright was a big part of his strategy.

Chapter Summary

    a. When the General Conference convened in November, Butler provided every attendee with a copy of his book, *Law in the Book of Galatians*.

    b. He also promoted Canright's new edition of *Two Laws,* with its expanded discussion on the law in Galatians.

    c. He arranged for a nine-member committee, which included Canright, and he intended this committee to secure his position on the law with a voted creedal statement.

10. During the committee meetings, of which Canright was an intimate part, a major debate took place about the law in Galatians.

11. In the heat of this debate over the law, Canright evidently grasped the fact that Waggoner had a valid point, that contextually, the law in Galatians was the moral law. This interpretation flattened Canright's argument about Galatians in the second edition of his *Two Laws.* However, instead of adopting Waggoner's view of the Ten Commandments as leading individuals to Christ, Canright gave up both the perpetuity of the law and Adventism.

12. After thinking through the issues for several months, Canright resigned all his positions in the church, and at a special meeting called at his home church in Otsego, Michigan, on February 17, 1887, he asked to be dismissed from the church. His request was granted in an atmosphere of peace and kindness.

13. This peaceful exit from Adventism was shortlived. The word *apostasy* was used several times in the *Review and Herald* in reference to Canright's departure, and some Adventists wrote condemning letters to him. Consequently, a few months after his peaceful departure from Adventism, Canright began to wage war on the church.

14. Through public meetings and the publishing of books and pamphlets, Canright waged war on the Adventist Church and Ellen White for the next thirty-two years of his life. His two most significant books were *Seventh-day Adventism Renounced* and *Life of Mrs. E. G. White, Seventh-day Adventist Prophet: Her False Claims Refuted.*

15. Observations from Canright's experience:

    a. When Canright left the Seventh-day Adventist Church in early 1887, the church was on the threshold of a major theological change. Although controversial, the 1888 General Conference Session was a

Chapter Summary

major turning point in Adventism's theology. At that session, a Christ-centered theology confronted the traditional law-centered theology.

  b. In the years following 1888, Ellen White, A. T. Jones, and E. J. Waggoner proclaimed this Christ-centered message of righteousness by faith to the membership of the church. Canright was engaged in fighting the church and either refused to acknowledge this message or never heard it.
  c. Neither did Canright acknowledge Ellen White's post-1888 literary production, which included such Christ-centered books as *Steps to Christ* and *The Desire of Ages*.
  d. Throughout his thirty-two-year-long campaign against Adventism and Ellen White, Canright continued to argue against the pre-1888 Adventism. He never acknowledged the change in Adventist theology that took place after 1888.
16. Canright's departure from Seventh-day Adventism and his subsequent campaign to discredit Ellen White was a critical turning point in the history of Ellen White criticism.
  a. He recycled all Ellen White criticisms from 1845 to the late 1880s.
  b. He conceived of new criticisms against her, such as the plagiarism charge.
  c. He raised almost all issues that would be thrown against Ellen White in the future.
  d. He provided a model of criticism that almost all future critics of Ellen White would copy.
17. As such, D. M. Canright can be called the "father" of Ellen White criticism.

CHAPTER 4

Canright's Legacy and the Church's Response

D. M. Canright's influence on the critics of Seventh-day Adventism and Ellen White during the twentieth and twenty-first centuries has been enormous. Canright's books were kept in circulation during the decades following his death, and non-Adventist evangelicals used them to assail Adventist teachings. Clearly, anti-cult evangelical writers such as William Irvine and Jan Karel Van Baalen were informed by D. M. Canright and categorized Adventism as a cult.[1] Ellen White was a focal point of the criticisms, with Canright's *Life of Mrs. E. G. White, Seventh-day Adventist Prophet: Her False Claims Refuted* as the major source. By 1960, Walter Martin, cult expert and major player in the *Questions on Doctrine* story,[2] could write in his book *The Truth About Seventh-day Adventism* that "D. M. Canright laid the foundation for all future destructive criticism of Seventh-day Adventism, and careful research has confirmed the impression that nearly all subsequent similar publications are little more than repetitions of the destructive areas of Canright's writings."[3]

In the 1970s, Canright's influence in several academic corners of the Seventh-day Adventist Church became evident.[4] In 1976, for example, Ron Numbers published his *Prophetess of Health: A Study of Ellen G. White*—the most significant critical publication on Ellen White since Canright's *Life of Mrs. E. G. White*. Although Numbers didn't reflect the same attitude seen in Canright's writings, he reached similar conclusions.[5] In the early 1980s Walter Rea published his noted *The White Lie,* trumpeting the charge of plagiarism in Ellen White's writings.[6] Many in the church were caught off guard by Rea's book, but it was a recycling of a charge already advanced by Canright in the late 1880s, as noted in the previous chapter.

Then, in late 1990s, Ellen White criticisms went global on the Internet. By 1998, Dirk Anderson's Web site, http://www.ellenwhite.org,[7] was circulating anti-Ellen White material, and eventually the Web site included Canright's *Life of Mrs. E. G. White*. More recently, not only can Canright's books *Adventism Renounced* and *Life of Mrs. E. G. White* be downloaded free on the Internet, but reprinted hard copies are available at online bookstores. Thus, in the early twenty-first century, Canright's writings are more accessible than ever before.[8] Indeed, part of the epitaph on his tombstone carries much greater significance today than it did in 1919: "An author of world renown."

The main arguments of Canright's *The Life of Mrs. Ellen G. White*

Before we examine the church's response to Canright, a concise summary of his book against Ellen White will be helpful. The main arguments of the book are presented below in summary form. The numbers in parentheses are the page numbers as found in the Shurtliff edition of Canright's *Life of Mrs. Ellen G. White*.[9]

1. Ellen White claimed that every line she wrote, "whether in articles, letters, testimonies or books," was "dictated to her by the Holy Ghost, and hence must be infallible" (1).
2. Like the followers of Mary Baker Eddy and Charles T. Russell, Seventh-day Adventists "accept their leader as the only infallible oracle of God" (14).
3. "Over and over Mrs. White claimed her writings to be inspired of God, and placed them on a level with the Bible" (16). Therefore, Adventists have another Bible and should be honest and state in their creed that they believe the writings of Mrs. White to be the word of God (17–23).
4. Throughout her life Mrs. White was sickly, self-centered, boastful on occasion, and taught her people to look to her for guidance and instruction in every move and every detail of life. But her mistakes in her alleged inspired writings disprove her claim to divine inspiration (25–51).
5. Her view of the sanctuary was erroneous (55–57).
6. Until 1851, she taught the shut-door theory, that probation for sinners ended on October 22, 1844, and "revelation after revelation" during this time period confirmed this theory (59–81).
7. She and other church leaders suppressed damaging statements in her writings (83–97).
8. Ellen White suffered from hysteria, epilepsy, catalepsy, and ecstasy, which produced her visions (99–109).

9. Ellen White was a great plagiarist (111–123).
10. She used her prophetic gift to get money (125–128).
11. She contradicted herself, thus disproving her high claim to inspiration (129–133).
12. Her early visions contained childish, extravagant, and crude expressions and some historical blunders (135–137).
13. Uriah Smith, longtime editor of the *Review and Herald,* rejected her testimonies (139–142).
14. She made many predictions that failed, especially regarding the Civil War (143–149).
15. She claimed to know the secret sins of others when she really didn't (151–155).
16. She was influenced to write her testimonies to individuals by what others told her (157–164).
17. She broke the Sabbath for nine years (165–167).
18. She was wrong in her teaching about the "reform dress" (169–173).
19. Her vision about the planets was false (175–178).
20. She contradicted herself in her teaching about Sunday laws (179–181).
21. "Mrs. White's claims to being an inspired prophet of God have been maintained very largely by deception, both on her part and on the part of her defenders and supporters" (185).

As noted in the previous chapter, Canright recycled most of the above charges from earlier critics, he originated some of them, and all continue to circulate in today's anti-Ellen White books and Web sites.

1919 to 1936: A. G. Daniells's response to Canright's charges

The first full response to Canright's *Life of Mrs. E. G. White* came in the form of correspondence between Arthur G. Daniells, General Conference president at the time, and F. G. Dufty, a Canadian Adventist who had been a conference treasurer for several years.[10] Dufty had read Canright's book shortly after it came off the press and resonated with its contents. On October 15, 1919, he wrote to Daniells, asking for his response to the book. Daniells fired a hasty letter back to Dufty on November 4, 1919, characterizing Canright's book as being among other things, "absolutely untrustworthy" and "scurrilous." Evidently, Daniells had read Canright's book cursorily; in his letter, he provided no evidence for his claims.

In a five-page letter written on December 27, 1919, Dufty challenged Daniells to support his "serious charges" against *Life of Mrs. E. G. White* with "clear, definite proof."[11] It would be almost two years before Daniells would answer Dufty's challenge. His answer has no specific date attached to it, but was written sometime in mid to late 1921. After apologizing to Dufty for the long delay, Daniells explained to him: "Since making these statements in my letter to you on December 4, 1919, I have taken time to examine Mr. Canright's book, *Life of Mrs. E. G. White,* with much greater care than I had given it before writing you." Then he reinforced his previous charges: "In all candor and sincerity I declare that this book is such a 'mixture of truth and error,' such a weaving together of 'unfair interpretations and absolutely false representations' that it must be pronounced most unfair, misleading, and 'untrustworthy.'"[12] Interestingly, Daniells apologized for using the word *scurrilous* in the letter "without due consideration to its real meaning." He then added, "I am sorry for having done so. It is my purpose to be fair and honest in all things."[13]

This forty-four-page letter contained Daniells's answers to the fifteen questions put to him by Dufty regarding Canright's book. Throughout the document, Daniells addressed various statements by Ellen White and church leaders that he felt were "garbled" or taken out of context.[14] The charges receiving the most attention were the shut door, suppression, and plagiarism charges that comprised chapters 7, 8, and 10 in Canright's book.

Daniells was especially interested in Canright's chapter devoted to the shut-door charge, which began with the words: "*The Shut Door, or Probation for Sinners Ended Oct. 22, 1844.* The above title indicated the theory held and dogmatically taught by all Seventh-day Adventists until the autumn of 1851. . . . Mrs. White had revelation after revelation in her visions during this time confirming this theory."[15]

After citing this passage from Canright's book, Daniells said to Dufty,

> I have been testing the accuracy of this statement and I shall give you the results of my findings. It may be well for me to state that during the last fifteen years the officers of the General Conference Committee have made earnest efforts to secure a copy of every document that was printed by our pioneers in the early days of our cause. We have called for these through the columns of our papers, and have carried on correspondence with elderly people who have been identified with us the longest period of time. We have also corresponded with the descendants and acquaintances of the oldest believers who have passed away. In this endeavor we have been able to secure a copy of nearly every document of which we have ever heard.[16]

The next sentence was at the heart of Daniells's defense of Ellen White: "*In these printed documents we have all the published utterances of Mrs. White from 1844 to the autumn of 1851, the period to which Mr. Canright refers in the excerpt given above.*" Daniells then proceeded to give Dufty "every one of Mrs. White's statements regarding the 'shut door' and the close of probation"[17] in the order in which they occurred and in the "exact language in which they were first printed."[18] Daniells also listed all of Ellen White's articles and letters that dealt with the shut door up to the time of 1851. After devoting fourteen pages of the letter to the shut-door charge, Daniells wrote, "I am compelled, by the documents we have in our possession, to state that there is not a single statement in the writings of Mrs. White from 1844 to 1851 that declares that she was shown in vision that salvation for sinners ended in 1844."[19]

Unimpressed with Daniells's answers, Dufty replied on January 11, 1922, chiding the president for taking so long to reply to his previous letter. Dufty said, "The long delay has convinced me that either you were not familiar with the subject notwithstanding its intimate connection with the origin and history of the denomination, or that it must indeed be a difficult one to handle, and Mr. Canright's book is a very hard book to answer."[20]

Although Dufty took issue with a number of the matters Daniells had written about, he gave special attention to the shut door and the charge of suppression. At one point he articulated the complaint of most anti-Adventist critics over the years. The shut-door doctrine, he said, is "an awful doctrine" that "misrepresented God." It "had its conception in a misunderstanding and misinterpretation of a passage of Scripture, based on the unscriptural doctrine of time-setting, and led to very bad and far-reaching evil results." It "misrepresented Christ" and "taught that He had rejected 'all the wicked world,' which he had not done."

The shut door, Dufty said, led "Mrs. White to have false 'visions,' teaching and upholding this false doctrine as from God, which led her and her husband later to leave out and suppress portions of these 'visions,' and this to others [sic] publishing and circulating the false statement and representation that Mrs. White never believed or taught the 'shut door' doctrine." This "misrepresentation," he declared, "has been persisted in now for seventy years, and is upheld in so late a document as your recent answer." He concluded by saying that this teaching "ought to be acknowledged and repented of, rather than suppressed and denied."[21]

At the core of Dufty's criticisms about the shut door was the belief that nothing of prophetic significance really happened on October 22, 1844. Once this belief is jettisoned, everything else generally follows in its trail, and the shut door becomes permanently attached to Ellen White's visions.

Not surprisingly, after his correspondence with Daniells, Dufty, with his family and a number of other Adventists, left the Montreal Seventh-day Adventist Church.[22] Daniells, however, was unmoved by Dufty's negative actions because Dufty had failed to respond to several of Daniells's strongest arguments against the charge that Ellen White believed and taught the shut door based on her visions.[23]

Several years later, Daniells expanded his material on the shut-door charge and published it in the *Review and Herald* of November 25, 1926, under the title "The Shut Door and the Close of Probation: The Position of the Spirit of Prophecy Between 1844 and 1851, as Revealed in Original Sources of Our Early Documents and Periodicals."[24] In doing so, he placed before all readers of the *Review* the very statements that Canright claimed the church had suppressed. Three years later, Francis M. Wilcox, editor of the *Review and Herald*, published a seven-part series on the shut-door charge titled "The Shut Door and the Close of Probation: Faith of the Early Believers Regarding These Questions," which ran in the church's paper from December 19, 1929, to January 30, 1930.[25]

At the end of the seventh article, Wilcox announced that his series would be followed by another series on the shut door by A. G. Daniells. Preparing the way for Elder Daniells's series, the editor wrote, "We believe that our readers will study with interest his discussion of this question which is of interest to every Seventh-day Adventist."[26] Thus, Daniells's original article published in the *Review and Herald*, November 25, 1926, was reissued in a four-part series from February 6 to February 27, 1930.[27] Additionally, Daniells's article series was reprinted in a pamphlet, "The Shut Door and the Close of Probation,"[28] and later, both Wilcox's and Daniells's article series were reprinted in another pamphlet entitled "The Faith of the Pioneers: Relating to the Shut Door and the Close of Probation."[29] Both pamphlets were distributed by the Review and Herald® Publishing Association during the early 1930s.

It should also be noted that Daniells published a follow-up article on the shut-door charge in the *Review and Herald* of January 14, 1932, titled "The Shut Door and the Close of Probation: An Important Statement from Mrs. E. G. White."[30] During this time, while the Ellen G. White Estate was still organizing and filing Ellen White's letters, a letter from Ellen White to J. N. Loughborough regarding the shut door was brought to Daniells's attention. This letter corroborated all of the Ellen White statements he had published previously. In the letter, Mrs. White said: "I never have stated or written that the world was doomed or dammed. I never have under any circumstances used this language to any one, however sinful. I have ever had messages of reproof for those who used these harsh expressions."[31]

Following the letter, Daniells stated,

> This clear statement, made by herself, is precisely the conclusion I reached after a very careful study of all her published statements from 1844 to 1852. I accept this statement at one hundred per cent for all that it is intended to convey. I must conclude that she knew better than any one else what was revealed to her. Furthermore, I must in all fairness allow her to testify for herself. Her letter, written in 1874, agrees with the views, teaching, and experiences of the pioneers of this movement from 1844 to 1852 as recorded in the publications that have been preserved.[32]

Daniells would reach the peak of his apologia for Ellen White's prophetic ministry in his classic *The Abiding Gift of Prophecy*,[33] completed shortly before his death in 1935 and published the following year. In a memorable remark toward the end of the manuscript, he reflected on his personal knowledge of Ellen White's life and writings:

> In this present year of our Lord 1935, Mrs. White has been at rest twenty years, while I have been toiling on. I had had twenty-three years of direct observation of her lifework. Since her death I have now had twenty additional years for thoughtful reflection and study of that life and its fruits. Now, at an advanced age, with the constraint of expressing only sober, honest truth, I can say that it is my deep conviction that Mrs. White's life far transcends the life of anyone I have ever known or with whom I have been associated. She was uniformly pleasant, cheerful, and courageous. She was never careless, flippant, or in any way cheap in conversation or manner of life. She was the personification of serious earnestness regarding the things of the kingdom. I never once heard her boast of the gracious gift God had bestowed upon her, or of the marvelous results of her endeavors. She did rejoice in the fruitage, but gave all the glory to Him who wrought through her. I realize that these are grave statements, but they come from the deepest conviction and soundest judgment that I am capable of rendering. They are uttered in the sobering atmosphere of my last illness, as I face the Judge of all the earth, before whose presence I realize that I soon shall stand.[34]

One can detect in this statement the background of Canright's statement in the *Life of Mrs. E. G. White*, where he wrote that "no writer is perhaps better qualified to give the facts" regarding Mrs. White's faults and failures than he was because of his "intimate association" with her in the early days.[35] Such was Arthur G. Daniells's defense and advocacy of Ellen White in response to D. M. Canright's charges.

It is important to note that during the summer of 1919, about the time when Canright's book was published, Daniells was engaged in the significant 1919 Bible Conference, in which several frank discussions took place regarding Ellen White's inspiration, authority, and the use of historical sources in her writings.[36] The discussions that occurred indicate that Daniells and other church leaders were articulating an understanding of Ellen White's inspiration quite different from what Canright was arguing in his book.[37] Canright claimed that Ellen White and her followers believed that "every line" she wrote was "directly inspired by God."[38] In contrast, Daniells and other key thought leaders at this conference rejected a rigid view of verbal inspiration regarding Ellen White's inspiration. This subject will be discussed in more detail in chapter 6.

1930 to 1960: Responses to Canright's charges

Meeting at the Elmshaven office. Another response to Canright's book came in the form of a meeting held at the Elmshaven office of the Ellen G. White Estate, August 15 to 17, 1930.[39] Although *The Life of Mrs. E. G. White* had been published in 1919, ten years later it remained the source Protestants turned to for information about Ellen White. The purpose of the meeting was to "Answer D. M. Canright's Misrepresentations." With between seven to ten participants present at every meeting, the council addressed specific criticisms one after the other. The discussion focused on "giving information which either meets the attack or a background which makes the point of no effect."[40] W. C. White, Ellen White's son and most knowledgeable participant of her life and work, was present at every meeting.

Brief statements. The next response to Canright was a twenty-seven-page pamphlet by W. C. White and D. A. Robinson titled *Brief Statements Regarding the Writings of Ellen G. White* (1933). The pamphlet was directed mainly at the issue of plagiarism.[41] It focused on the supernatural origin of Ellen White's writings in the midst of her literary borrowing and addressed important questions related to her literary work. Some fifty years later, the trustees of the Ellen G. White Estate reprinted this document and inserted it in the *Adventist Review* of June 4, 1981,[42] in response to the plagiarism charges raised by Walter Rea.[43]

William H. Branson. The most significant and direct response to Canright in the 1930s was the belated and full-scale one William H. Branson supplied in his *Reply to Canright: The Truth About Seventh-day Adventists,* published in 1933 and later titled *In Defense of the Faith, The Truth About Seventh-day Adventists: A Reply to Canright.*[44] The focus of Branson's response was on answering Canright's *Adventism Renounced* rather than his *Life of Mrs. E. G. White,* although he did devote one chapter to Canright's criticisms of Ellen White. Branson's work was a welcome tool to Adventist ministers who were encountering Protestant pastors prejudiced by Canright's arguments, such as found in William C. Irvine's *Timely Warnings.*[45] Branson popularized the method of pitting Canright's arguments as an Adventist against his later arguments as a Baptist. A notable example is found in the chapter on Ellen White.

Let us note a few of his most flagrant contradictions on this point. From his volume under review we quote the following statements published in 1889.

Mr. Canright the Baptist speaking: "She has a harsh, uncharitable spirit. . . . Her severity and harshness have driven many to despair." Ibid., p. 160.

In 1877 Mr. Canright the Adventist said: "I know Sister White to be an unassuming, modest, kind-hearted, noble woman. These traits in her character are not simply put on and cultivated, but they spring gracefully and easily from her natural disposition."

In 1889 he said she "is simply a religious enthusiast, and a fanatic," and "is always telling what great things she has done." "Hear her laud herself."

In 1877 he testified of her: "She is not self-conceited, self-righteous, and self-important, as fanatics always are. . . . I have ever found Sister White the reverse of all this."

Of her writings he said, in 1889: "These inspired Testimonies now embrace ten bound volumes. Thus they have another Bible, just the same as the Mormons have. *Seventh-day Adventism Renounced,* p. 136.

In 1877 he said of these same writings that there is "nothing that leads away from the Bible, or from Christ"; and in 1885, just four years before he wrote his renunciation of Adventism, he added: "The tendency and influence of her Testimonies is not, like the teachings of Spiritualist mediums, to lead a way from the Bible, away from God, and away from faith in Christ; nor like Mormonism."

Now we submit to our readers that Mr. Canright could not have been sincere in both instances when these conflicting statements were made about the character and work of the same person. If he was sincere in his published utterances regarding Mrs. White in 1877, when he claims to have had eighteen years' acquaintance with her, and in 1885, at which time his acquaintance had lengthened to twenty-six years, then he could not have been sincere in 1889 when he clearly contradicted all that he had previously written of her. On the other hand, if he was sincere in his later statements, it surely proves insincerity on his part in what he had formerly said.[46]

Branson's book continues to be a valued response to Canright's arguments in *Adventism Renounced*.[47]

Francis D. Nichol. Two decades after Branson's defense of Seventh-day Adventism, Francis D. Nichol published (in 1951) what has been the most significant and comprehensive response to the arguments of D. M. Canright: *Ellen White and Her Critics: An Answer to the Major Charges That Critics Have Brought Against Mrs. Ellen G. White.*[48] In the introduction to his book, Nichol tells the reader he has provided a "composite of the critics' arguments," that "Canright is often cited" because "he first and most fully set forth in print the major accusations against Mrs. White," and that "others have largely copied from him."[49]

As editor of the *Review and Herald* since 1945 and general editor of the soon-to-be published *Seventh-day Adventist Bible Commentary*,[50] Nichol was one of the most influential writers of the period. His previous apologetic works, *Answers to Objections: An Examination of the Major Objections Raised Against the Teachings of Seventh-day Adventists* and *The Midnight Cry: A Defense of William Miller and the Millerites*,[51] had shown his considerable ability as a church apologist.

Nichol's 703-page apologia for Ellen White was the definitive answer of Seventh-day Adventists to Canright's *Life of Mrs. E. G. White*. Although somewhat dated in some places, it "remains the most complete answer to a wide spectrum of challenges against Ellen White's prophetic gift."[52] *Ellen White and Her Critics* has been online for several years now at the official Ellen G. White Estate Web site, http://whiteestate.org. It is noteworthy that most contemporary critics of Ellen White rarely, if ever, engage the comprehensive answers Nichol provided more than half a century ago.

1960 to 2000: Responses to Canright and other critics

Two significant publications rolled off the press during this period that were apologetic in tone but more biographical in form: Norman F. Douty's *The Case of D. M. Canright,* published in 1964, and Carrie Johnson's *I Was Canright's Secretary,* published in 1971.[53] Douty wrote as a Baptist pastor sympathetic to Canright, whereas Johnson wrote as a Seventh-day Adventist who was critical of Canright.

In 1962, prior to publishing *The Case of D. M. Canright,* Norman Douty published a critique of Adventist doctrine titled *Another Look at Seventh-day Adventism.* In this book he argued that Adventism is "characterized by heresy" and thus "cannot be esteemed a Scriptural church."[54] With these presuppositions in mind, it is natural that he would be supportive of D. M. Canright's campaign against Adventist teaching. In *The Case of D. M. Canright,* Douty wrote of both Canright's experience while an Adventist and his experience after leaving Adventism. This book is carefully researched and contains helpful insights. As noted earlier, the way some Adventists handled Canright's exit from Adventism was unfortunate, and reading Douty reminds us to see the fault on both sides.

Having said this, however, it seems clear to me that Douty wrote this book with the presupposition that Adventists were wrong and Canright was right. In his conclusion, after presenting in the preceding chapters his "numerous facts," he states that Canright was "a sincere, upright, good man," and because of this, "his testimony against Adventism cannot be brushed aside." Then he reiterates the basic thesis he presented at the beginning of the book: that the Seventh-day Adventist Church is "responsible for the false witness against Canright." As such, "in bearing this false witness against Canright, Adventism has expressly violated the ninth commandment." He then chides Adventism for breaking the law it so earnestly contends to uphold.[55]

Whether or not the Adventist Church has borne a false witness against Canright is certainly debatable.[56] Douty is parochial in his presentation of the evidence and tends to be one-sided. Nevertheless, his perspective deserves to be heard.

The favorite treatment of Canright within Adventism is Carrie Johnson's *I Was Canright's Secretary,* published in 1971. Mrs. Johnson claims she was secretary to Canright for several months in 1913, which Douty disputes.[57] Much of the book serves as a narration of Canright's experience as a Seventh-day Adventist minister and can be corroborated with documented evidence. The parts of the book that deal with Johnson's personal experience with Canright, however, are supported only by her word.[58] She recounts some very interesting experiences in her encounters with Canright but, like Douty, is parochial in her concerns. A fair and impartial biography of Canright is yet to be written.

Too often in our defense of the faith we resort to criticizing the character of D. M. Canright. No doubt he had his ups and downs in his relationship with the Adventist Church. But whether he was an "upright, good man," an embittered antagonist, or both is not the main issue. The focus should be on his arguments, not his character. Canright was a fascinating person, and his story should be told.[59]

During the 1960s and 1970s, Arthur White, son of W. C. White and secretary of the White Estate at the time, provided responses to Canright's charges against Ellen White in his class for pastors in training, "Prophetic Guidance," and he published them in *Notes and Papers Concerning Ellen G. White and the Spirit of Prophecy*.[60] In the 1980s and through the early 1990s, Roger Coon, then associate secretary of the White Estate, also taught the class "The Writings of Ellen G. White" at the Seventh-day Adventist Theological Seminary at Andrews University. In his class lectures he provided responses to contemporary criticisms of Ellen White. By his carefully researched and logical answers to critics, he laid the foundation for modern Ellen White apologetics.[61] Other professors of Ellen White studies build on this foundation at the seminary and at other Adventist universities.[62]

Although Canright's influence is still felt, other critics have emerged who have demanded the attention of Ellen White apologists. In 1981, Robert W. Olson published his *One Hundred and One Questions on the Sanctuary and Ellen White*, which dealt with various charges against Ellen White such as plagiarism, historical errors, and the shut door.[63] This book was written as a response to issues raised by Desmond Ford.[64] During the years 1981–1986, Arthur White published his six-volume biography of Ellen White, which contains 2,917 pages.[65] While the major purpose of the series was to provide detailed biographical coverage of Ellen White's life, the author did periodically respond to her critics. One other important development in the 1980s was the church's response to Walter Rea and his plagiarism charge. The studies by Vincent L. Ramik and Fred Veltman helped disseminate a better understanding of Ellen White's literary borrowing.[66]

The last apologetic work on Ellen White in the twentieth century was Herbert Douglass's *Messenger of the Lord: The Prophetic Ministry of Ellen G. White*, published in 1998.[67] This major work was intended as a textbook for undergraduate and graduate classes on Ellen White in the tradition of T. Housel Jemison's college textbook *A Prophet Among You*, published in 1955.[68] Douglass covered every major issue relating to Ellen White's life and prophetic gift and devoted an entire section to criticisms of Ellen White.[69] This comprehensive textbook is still used in classes today and can be read online at the Ellen G. White Estate Web site: http://whiteestate.org.

2000 to the present: Responses to the critics

The first five years of the twenty-first century saw the release of several apologetic volumes. First was Clifford Goldstein's *Graffiti in the Holy of Holies*, released in 2003. Goldstein was responding to Dale Ratzlaff's *The Cultic Doctrine of*

Seventh-day Adventists, and he devoted a chapter to Ratzlaff's criticisms of Ellen White.[70] In 2005, Don McMahon's *Acquired or Inspired: Exploring the Origins of the Adventist Lifestyle* was published and demonstrated that Ellen White was remarkably accurate and more advanced than others of her day in the counsel she gave on health issues.[71] In addition, a CD-ROM containing the writings of health reformers of Ellen White's day comes with the book so the reader can compare them with Ellen White's writings on health. In that same year, McMahon partnered with Leonard Brand in *The Prophet and Her Critics.*[72] This volume, based on McMahon's previous book, examined the research designs used by Ronald Numbers and Walter Rea. Based on the evidence presented in their book, the authors concluded that the health principles contained in the writings of Ellen G. White originated from a divine source—God.[73]

Additionally, in 2005, Alden Thompson published his *Escape From the Flames: How Ellen White Grew From Fear to Joy—and Helped Me to Do It Too,* in which he applied the concepts from his earlier book, *Inspiration: Hard Questions, Honest Answers,* to the writings of Ellen White.[74] His driving thesis was that the Spirit led the young Ellen White "from an early emphasis on God's power (fear), to a deeper appreciation of His goodness (joy)."[75] While not all students of Ellen White agree with Thompson's conclusions in this book, his purpose was to help readers avoid extreme positions such as, on the one hand, elevating Ellen White too high or, on the other, completely rejecting her because of the critics' charges.

The year 2006 saw the release of Graeme Bradford's *More Than a Prophet: How We Lost and Found Again the Real Ellen White.* This book is an expansion of the author's two previous volumes, *Prophets Are Human* and *People Are Human.*[76] Bradford's purpose was to defend Ellen White's prophetic ministry, but his approach to New Testament prophets in relationship to Ellen White has caused concern to some in the church.[77]

In 2011, the Review and Herald will release a major publication edited by two professors at the Adventist seminary, Denis Fortin and Jerry Moon: *The Ellen G. White Encyclopedia.*[78] Containing contributions by Adventist scholars from all over the world, this work is the most comprehensive study of Ellen White's life and prophetic ministry ever published. While not specifically apologetic in tone, various articles address issues related to Ellen White apologetics. This is a must-have study for every Adventist home and for anyone interested in information about Ellen G. White. Released in 2010 was William Fagal's *101 Questions About Ellen White and Her Writings.*[79] This easy-to-read book provides concise answers to many issues relating to Ellen White, including ones raised by her critics.

Finally, a word should be said about Web sites defending Ellen White. On the official Web site of the Ellen G. White Estate, http://whiteestate.org/, one will find many pages of response to Ellen White criticisms. Other Web sites I have found helpful are

- http://www.ellenwhite.info/
- http://ellen-white.com/
- http://dedication.www3.50megs.com/egw.html
- http://adventist-defense-league.blogspot.com
- http://sdaforme.com

Of course there is my own Web site, http://ellenwhiteanswers.org/, where I have provided research-based answers to Ellen White criticisms. More discussion on these Web sites can be found in appendix D.

Today, many critics of Ellen White are sprinkled across the landscape. Nevertheless, whether recognized or not, the influence of D. M. Canright, the father of Ellen White criticisms, lies behind each personal campaign against her ministry. Two of these critics exert notable influence, and a brief case study of their experience will be helpful in understanding the Adventist background of Ellen White's critics.

Canright and two contemporary critics of Ellen White

The two well-known contemporary critics of Ellen White who follow in the tradition of D. M. Canright are Dirk Anderson and Dale Ratzlaff. Both of them recycle Canright's old charges and point to his writings as a factor in their decision to leave Adventism. Because of their influence in circulating criticisms of Ellen White at the present time, brief biographical sketches and analyses of their experience are in order.

Dirk Anderson.[80] This man, the author of several books against Ellen White and editor of two anti-Ellen White Web sites, grew up in the Seventh-day Adventist Church and attended its school system up to the collegiate level. He describes his childhood experience as living in a "state of constant fear mingled with expectancy." He was "afraid of the coming persecution and time of trouble" but "looked forward to Christ's coming." The idea of having to "stand perfect without an intercessor" before God at the end of time was a "heavy burden to bear" for a child. "I tried to be perfect and I tried to keep the Sabbath perfectly," he recalls, "but I always seemed to come up short." Seeing the lack of "perfect people" in the Adventist Church and its schools also caused him great concern.

"At the age of 21 I was converted," says Anderson. Through a "sense" of his "own sinfulness" and the reading of a book by Morris Venden, he discovered that "salvation is by faith." Prior to this he had believed that his salvation depended on keeping the Ten Commandments. "I began to see things in a whole new light" and "surrendered myself to God and dedicated myself to him." Excited by his new experience, he began reading Ellen White's writings daily, a practice that continued for more than ten years.

Here's how Anderson describes the influence Ellen White had on his life:

> Ellen White's writings had a dramatic impact on my life. In my reading I began to discover many rules that I and most of the SDA's I knew were not following. I began making a list in order to obey them. My wife resisted this process, but I pushed forward. We were already vegetarians. Now we largely eliminated dairy products, vinegar, eggs, and sugar from our diet. You are probably thinking, what did we eat? Not much! My weight dropped below normal levels and I lost energy. The insufficient diet combined with the stress of trying to live a perfect life took a toll on my health from which I have never recovered. In addition to dietary changes, I made other changes. I refused to even wear a wedding ring and insisted my wife do likewise. I avoided associating with non-SDA's except for the purpose of converting them to Adventism. I avoided going to doctors and avoided using drugs of any type, including aspirin. We took down all the photographs of children and family from our walls because Mrs. White said that was idolatry. I cancelled our life insurance because Mrs. White said SDA's do not need life insurance. I neglected buying stocks for retirement because Mrs. White said to avoid such investments. I even went so far as to ask my wife to find a female gynecologist because Mrs. White said it was improper for a woman to have a male gynecologist.

After involving himself with an independent ministry for some time and finding the experience frustrating, Anderson discovered material on the Internet "attacking Mrs. White as a prophet." Enraged and indignant, he felt a need to take action. "I had become adept at identifying which of Ellen White's rules a person was not following and I was eager to criticize them for being lax in not following her standards." But, he says, "now I took on the new mission of defending her on the Internet." However, Anderson was troubled by this experience because he discovered that one of the Adventist pioneers he was quoting was mistaken. This led him to question what was true and what wasn't true in the Adventist portrayal of Ellen White.

The event that led Mr. Anderson out of Seventh-day Adventism and into a campaign against Ellen White was his reading of D. M. Canright. His own words best describe this experience:

About a month later a former SDA pastor, Dale Ratzlaff, challenged me to read Canright's book about Ellen White. I decided to read the book with the intent of refuting it. I read it and found it very disturbing, but I was determined to prove it wrong. So I went over to the local SDA university library and began digging out all the old documents I could find on Ellen White and the pioneers. I spent many hours sifting through material. To my amazement, I could not find anything to refute Canright. In fact, everything I found seemed to support what Canright wrote. I was perplexed. I began digging into the shut door teaching and discovered that Ellen White had indeed seen the door of salvation shut to sinners in 1844 in at least one of her visions. I read the vision over and over again struggling to make sense of it. I wrestled with the vision, using my best mental gymnastics to try and change it so that I could make sense of it, but I failed. I could not get around it. Mrs. White had seen a falsehood in vision. I was confused and upset. I decided to study further before making a decision.

This experience eventually resulted in Anderson's leaving the Adventist Church: "I was finally forced to admit, by the overwhelming weight of evidence that Mrs. White was not a prophet of God." So he left the Seventh-day Adventist Church and since the late 1990s has launched and maintained several Web sites, such as http://www.ellenwhiteexposed.com and http://www.nonsda.org and has authored several books: *White Out: An Investigation of Ellen G. White*; *More Than a Profit, Less Than a Prophet*; *Prophet or Pretender*; and *The Fake Controversy*.[81]

Dirk Anderson's testimony is worthy of a brief analysis. First, his experience of seeking to live a perfect life and never quite reaching the mark was caused by an unfortunate misunderstanding of biblical perfection. The latter is a subject that has been the subject of many a debate in Adventist circles, and one can only wish that while Anderson was still an Adventist he would have read George Knight's *I Used to Be Perfect*. In this book, Knight explains that reaching a "fixed" and "static" standard of sinless moralistic behavior—which appears to be what Mr. Anderson was trying to do—isn't the biblical idea of perfection. "Being perfect," Knight says, "is a dynamic state in which dedicated Christians continue to advance in Christian living."[82] A careful reading of Ellen White on this subject confirms that Knight's understanding harmonizes with hers.[83]

Second, Anderson never seemed to have grasped the assurance of righteousness by faith the writings of Ellen White contain despite all his intense reading of her writings during the years he was an Adventist.

Third, Mr. Anderson's account of his rigid application of Ellen White's counsels represents an extreme approach to these writings, which are so full of balance and common sense. I don't blame him for abandoning the legalistic and destructive lifestyle he had thought he must live. Ellen White herself wrote that "health reform becomes health deform, a health destroyer, when it is carried to extremes."[84] Dirk Anderson is certainly not alone in this experience. I have encountered extreme approaches to Ellen White's writings over the years and found them to be a type of bondage. Anderson correctly described this kind of experience as producing a "judgmental, critical, harsh spirit" and the "loss of spiritual life."

The main problem with Mr. Anderson's testimony, however, is that he leaves the impression that any serious reading of Ellen White will inevitably lead to a negative, critical spirit and rejection of her prophetic ministry. I haven't found this to be true in my experience or in the experience of many others who read Ellen White with the correct principles of interpretation. A well-written corrective to misinterpreting Ellen White's writings is George Knight's *Reading Ellen White*, published around the time Anderson was beginning to question her.[85] Applying the principles in this book would have helped Anderson avoid extreme interpretations while he was an Adventist. Unfortunately, the same pattern of misinterpretation that characterized his approach to Ellen White's writings as an Adventist also characterizes his approach to her writings as a former Adventist who has become a critic. I will discuss the issue of interpretation in chapters 9 and 10.

Fourth, and most important, Mr. Anderson was significantly influenced by D. M. Canright's book *Life of Mrs. Ellen G. White, Seventh-day Adventist Prophet, Her False Claims Refuted*. As noted above, after reading this book, he tried to refute it and went to the library of the local Adventist university to look for material. After researching for hours, he "could find nothing to refute Canright." I can only wonder what he did when he came across F. D. Nichol's *Ellen White and Her Critics*. Did he read through this book carefully, or did he put it aside, thinking it couldn't refute Canright? I don't know. But it is interesting that on his Web site and in his books, he rarely mentions Nichol's massive apologetic and never seriously engages with its contents. In fact, most contemporary critics of Ellen White rarely engage with Nichol's answers to Canright's charges. Why? Because Nichol's work, although dated in some places, provides a thorough refutation of Canright.

Nevertheless, Canright's criticisms of Ellen White permeate Anderson's works. Furthermore, he follows Canright's stratagem of ignoring the literary and historical context of Mrs. White's writings and distorting the meaning of her statements. We will assess an example of Anderson's criticisms in chapter 10. Ultimately, Anderson's approach to criticizing Ellen White continues the work of D. M. Canright, the father of Ellen White criticisms.[86]

Dale Ratzlaff. This critic is a former "conservative, fourth generation Seventh-day Adventist." He "received all his formal education in SDA schools, graduated from the Seventh-day Adventist Theological Seminary, pastored two Seventh-day Adventist churches, and taught Bible in a Seventh-day Adventist school for seven years."[87] Mr. Ratzlaff and his wife were strong supporters of Ellen White but eventually concluded that the 1844 judgment was not biblical. During this time, he read D. M. Canright's books and other authors who influenced his thinking.[88] His conclusions about the sanctuary judgment eventually brought him into conflict with his conference administration. He was given the option to "teach all of the Fundamental Beliefs of the SDA church or resign."[89] Choosing to resign, he raised up another church outside of Adventism and pastored there for some years. During this time he jettisoned Ellen White's prophetic gift and the Sabbath.

In 2000, Mr. Ratzlaff established Life Assurance Ministries (LAM) and published the magazine *Proclamation!* which continues to the present time.[90] The staff and writers of *Proclamation!* focus on former Adventists and other evangelicals by criticizing Adventism's teachings. Recently, Ratzlaff wrote that he feels "God calling us to expand our ministry to questioning, transitioning and former Seventh-day Adventists and to help evangelical pastors and lay members learn how to better minister to the approximately 300,000 Adventists who leave that church each year."[91]

The *Historical Dictionary of the Seventh-day Adventist Church* contains an article on Mr. Ratzlaff and makes several references to his works.[92] His books *The Cultic Doctrine of Seventh-day Adventists, Sabbath in Christ,* and *Truth About Seventh-day Adventist Truth*[93] are promoted and sold on his Web site.[94] Recently, he completed his autobiography, *Truth Led Me Out: A Seventh-day Adventist Pastor Courageously Studies His Way to Biblical Truth,* and he plans to continue speaking and writing about the Adventist Church.[95] Ratzlaff's activities and publications have made him a major influence in the world of Adventist criticism.

Regarding the gift of prophecy, Ratzlaff believes the Adventist Church will no longer be able "to keep people from finding out the truth regarding Ellen White and her many: (1) self-contradictions; (2) contradictions with Scripture; (3) anti-gospel statements; (4) historical errors; (5) massive plagiarism; (6) statements contrary to scientific findings; and (7) foolish statements."[96]

While I was reading *Truth Led Me Out*, I noticed that when Ratzlaff finally discovered the real gospel—that sinners are saved by grace and not works—he thought it incompatible with Adventism.[97] Several times in the book he pits assurance of salvation against Ellen White's statement that Christians should never say "I am saved."[98] In his thinking, Ellen White was opposed to people's finding assurance of salvation—as was Adventist theology in general. "Historic Adventism," he writes, had "made sanctification part of the *foundation of acceptance with God*, and that clouded the gospel."[99] In Mr. Ratzlaff's thinking, this works-oriented theology was most fully expressed in the Adventist investigative judgment, which, according to him, could not be substantiated from Scripture and which undermined assurance of salvation in Christ.[100] Thus, his view of Adventism didn't fit with the biblical view of righteousness by faith in which one's acceptance with God is based on the imputed righteousness of Christ alone and not the works of man. Because he couldn't reconcile his view of traditional Adventism and its investigative judgment with righteousness by faith, Ratzlaff resigned from the Adventist ministry and left the church.[101]

There is an interesting parallel between Ratzlaff and Canright. As demonstrated in the previous chapter, Canright, like many of his fellow Adventist ministers, never really grasped the fact that Ellen White taught salvation by faith alone in Christ and resisted an overemphasis on the law. He was a product of the pre-1888 legalistic Adventism, and when confronted with the facts regarding the true nature of the law in relationship to the gospel, he found it incompatible with his understanding of Adventism. Rather than embrace the concept of law and gospel working together, he threw out the law altogether, resigned from the Adventist ministry, and left the church. Consequently, he missed the intensity and clarity of expression with which Ellen White wrote of the relationship of justification by faith to the law during the years following 1888.

In a similar way, Dale Ratzlaff never seemed to fully understand Ellen White's teaching on salvation. He did mention his positive experience in reading *Selected Messages,* volume 1, which contains some of Ellen White's key messages surrounding the 1888 meetings.[102] But, evidently, these strong gospel statements didn't affect his general understanding of Ellen White's teaching on salvation. Later, he apparently dismissed these kinds of statements because he believed that her writings contained numerous "self-contradictions."[103]

Furthermore, since leaving the Adventist Church in the early 1980s, Mr. Ratzlaff has never interacted with the studies related to the centennial of 1888, which set forth the profound impact this message had on the church and Ellen White. Such studies as George Knight's *A User-Friendly Guide to* the 1888 Message, Woodrow Whidden's *Ellen White on Salvation,* and *The Ellen G. White 1888 Materials,* volumes 1–4, have helped Adventists understand the vital role Ellen White played in setting the church on the right theological track regarding salvation.[104] Like Canright, Ratzlaff is either unaware of these studies or refuses to acknowledge them. As a self-proclaimed specialist on Adventism, one would expect him to be aware of these studies and to interact with them.

The theme of salvation through Christ's merits is clearly evident in Ellen White's writings. (See chapter 12 for specific examples of Ellen White's teaching on assurance of salvation.) It balances her statements that discourage people's saying, "I am saved." This statement, by the way, must be interpreted in light of its immediate context,[105] something that Mr. Ratzlaff never understood as an Adventist and continues to ignore in his treatment of Ellen White.

Conclusion

As one can see, the most determined critics of Ellen White today are former Seventh-day Adventists who once believed earnestly in her prophetic gift. Both Dirk Anderson and Dale Ratzlaff continue the Adventist tradition of seeking truth. Like D. M. Canright, though, they believe the truth is not in the Seventh-day Adventist Church and its teachings. Dale Ratzlaff's quest for truth led him to reject first the Adventist teaching on the sanctuary and 1844 judgment, next Ellen White's prophetic ministry and the Sabbath, and then all Adventist doctrine. Today he considers himself a "Christian" with no denominational affiliation who teaches the simple gospel of Christ and actively opposes Seventh-day Adventism.[106] Dirk Anderson's search for truth led him to reject Ellen White and then Adventism, which he now refers to as a "restrictive Christian organization." He considers himself a Christian who is on a life journey. Truth is not found "in a book, or a religion," but in the "journey that we call life."[107]

My conviction is that the Bible contains objective truth, or reality, and we discern it only through applying the correct principles of interpretation with the aid of the Holy Spirit. Have Canright, Anderson, and Ratzlaff applied correct principles for interpreting the Bible in their campaign against Adventism? Have they applied correct principles of interpretation to Ellen White's writings? Later chapters will address these questions.

This brings to an end the first section of our study—the history of Ellen White criticisms. The next section, the heart of this book, will go behind the scenes of the criticisms and study the underlying issues of revelation-inspiration, authority, interpretation, and the big picture in Ellen White's message. These are the big methodological issues that will reveal the shakiness of the platform upon which the critics of Ellen White stand.

Chapter Summary

1. Canright's influence on the critics of Seventh-day Adventism and Ellen White in the twentieth and twenty-first centuries has been enormous. By 1960, Walter Martin could write that nearly all publications against Adventism and Ellen White were little more than repetitions of Canright's criticisms. In the 1970s, Canright's influence was felt in several academic areas of the Seventh-day Adventist Church. In the early 1980s, his influence was felt in the charge of plagiarism. In the late 1990s, Ellen White criticisms went global on the Internet. Through the Internet, Canright's writings have become more accessible and widespread today than they ever were before.
2. Canright's major book against Ellen White, *The Life of Mrs. E. G. White: Her False Claims Refuted,* published in 1919, can be summarized in twenty-one basic assertions.
3. Responses to Canright's charges—1919–1936:
   a. A. G. Daniells's responses came in answer to letters repeating Canright's charges written by F. G. Dufty, a Canadian who had worked in the Adventist Church for years.
   b. Daniells answered fifteen questions put to him by Dufty about Canright's book.
   c. In answering, Daniels focused mostly on the shut-door issue.
   d. Daniells's initial research and answer to Canright's shut-door charge was expanded and published several times up to the early 1930s.
   e. Daniells's last book, *The Abiding Gift of Prophecy,* was a major defense and advocacy of Ellen White's prophetic gift.
4. Responses to Canright's charges—1930–1960:
   a. During August 15–17, 1930, a series of meetings took place at the Elmshaven office of the Ellen G. White Estate on how to answer the charges in Canright's *Life of Mrs. White.*
   b. A twenty-seven-page pamphlet by W. C. White and D. A. Robinson, *Brief Statements Regarding the Writings of Ellen G. White,* was published in 1933. It dealt mainly with the issue of plagiarism. It was republished and inserted in the *Adventist Review* of June 4, 1981.

Chapter Summary

   c. William H. Branson published his *In Defense of the Faith, The Truth About Seventh-day Adventists: A Reply to Canright* in 1933. It contained one chapter addressing Canright's charges against Ellen White.

   d. The most significant and comprehensive response to Canright's arguments against Ellen White was Francis D. Nichol's *Ellen White and Her Critics: An Answer to the Major Charges That Critics Have Brought Against Ellen G. White*—a volume that contemporary critics of Ellen White rarely engage.

5. Responses to Canright and other critics—1960–2000:

   a. In 1964, Norman F. Douty, a Baptist critic of Seventh-day Adventism, published his defense of D. M. Canright, *The Case of D. M. Canright*. He argued that Adventists were bearing a false witness in their criticism of Canright. Douty was parochial in his presentation but nevertheless needs to be heard.

   b. In 1971, Carrie Johnson published her *I Was Canright's Secretary*, a critique of Canright's life and teachings. While much of the book can be corroborated with documented evidence, parts of it are based solely on Johnson's testimony. Like Douty, Johnson is parochial in her presentation. A fair and impartial biography of Canright is yet to be written.

   c. During the 1960s and 1970s, Arthur White provided responses to Canright in his seminary class "Prophetic Guidance," taught to ministerial students.

   d. In the 1980s and 1990s, Roger Coon also provided responses to criticisms of Ellen White in his seminary class "Writings of Ellen G. White."

   e. Others continue this tradition at the Adventist seminary and at Adventist universities today.

   f. In 1980, Robert W. Olson published his *One Hundred and One Questions on the Sanctuary and Ellen White*, which dealt with issues raised by Desmond Ford.

   g. The last apologetic work on Ellen White in the twentieth century was Herbert Douglass's *Messenger of the Lord: The Prophetic Ministry of Ellen G. White*, published in 1998 and used in many university and college classes on Ellen White.

Canright's Legacy and the Church's Response

6. Responses to critics—2000 to the present

   Chapter Summary

   a. The first five years of the twenty-first century saw the release of several apologetic volumes: Clifford Goldstein's *Graffiti in the Holy of Holies* (2003), Don McMahon's *Acquired or Inspired? Exploring the Origins of the Adventist Lifestyle* (2005), and Leonard Brand and Don McMahon's *The Prophet and Her Critics* (2005).
   b. Alden Thompson's *Escape From the Flames* (2005) and Graeme Bradford's *More Than a Prophet: How We Lost and Found Again the Real Ellen White* (2006) affirm Ellen White but give a different perspective from the other apologetic works.
   c. *The Ellen G. White Encyclopedia,* edited by Denis Fortin and Jerry Moon, will be published in 2011. While not directly apologetic, this work addresses issues related to apologetics.
   d. Presently, several Web sites provide a defense of Ellen White's prophetic ministry:

      http://whiteestate.org/
      http://www.ellenwhite.info/
      http://ellen-white.com/
      http://dedication.www3.50megs.com/egw.html
      http://adventist-defense-league.blogspot.com
      http://sdaforme.com
      http://ellenwhiteanswers.org/

7. Canright's influence on two contemporary critics of Ellen White
   a. Dirk Anderson, author of several books against Ellen White and editor of two anti-Ellen White Web sites, is a former Seventh-day Adventist with a legalistic background. Influenced by reading the works of D. M. Canright, he left the Adventist Church and began opposing its teachings and especially Ellen White. His story is instructive regarding the style of many who turn against Ellen White.
   b. Dale Ratzlaff is a former Seventh-day Adventist who pastored for thirteen years and then left Adventism because he disagreed with its doctrine of the investigative judgment. After rejecting the Sabbath and Ellen White's prophetic ministry, he launched a ministry to former Seventh-day Adventists and is the founding editor of the

Chapter Summary

anti-Adventist periodical *Proclamation!* He is the most well-known critic of Adventism and Ellen White today.

   c. Ratzlaff's experience parallels Canright's in their refusal to acknowledge the Christ-centered teaching in mainstream Adventism and Ellen White's writings.
   d. Neither of these critics ever really understood Ellen White's teaching on salvation while they were Seventh-day Adventists. This misunderstanding has been carried over into their campaigns against her.

Part II

ISSUES AT THE HEART OF THE DEBATE

CHAPTER 5

Revelation-Inspiration: The Foundation of God's Communication With Us

"In the past God spoke to our forefathers through the prophets at many times and in various ways, but in these last days he has spoken to us by his Son" (Heb. 1:1, 2, NIV). This well-known biblical declaration tells us that God is a personal Being who spoke through prophets and ultimately communicated with the human race through His Son Jesus Christ. The "many times" and "various ways" provide a glimpse into the manner in which the divine Author spoke through the human prophets. This manner of communication is known as the divine-human mystery of revelation-inspiration, the foundation of God's communication with us.

The nature of inspiration is a major underlying issue in the debate on Ellen White. All detractors and supporters of her prophetic ministry either knowingly or unknowingly presuppose a view of inspiration. If that view is too rigid or too loose, then chances are strong that those who hold that view will misunderstand, undermine, or even discard Ellen White's writings. The same is true of the Bible. An incorrect view of how inspiration worked in the prophets can befog the biblical message. So, in this chapter we'll explore the phenomenon of inspiration and its sibling, revelation, in the experience of the biblical writers.

Scripture testifies to both revelation and inspiration in the biblical writers, and it is the starting place for understanding this divine-human process. Once we've established the manner of God's communication with the biblical prophets, then we'll compare Ellen White's claim to the prophetic experience with this normative experience. Throughout this discussion, we will use the works of evangelical and mainstream Adventist theologians to explain and define the concepts of revelation, inspiration, and illumination.

In order to address the nature of Ellen White's prophetic experience, we'll also

Revelation-Inspiration: The Foundation of God's Communication With Us

need to examine the theory of "degrees of inspiration." Ultimately, Ellen White either possessed the authentic prophetic gift, or what she communicated was the product of an excited imagination, or, even worse, it was a fraud. I believe that when the revelation-inspiration experience of the biblical writers is correctly understood and Mrs. White's prophetic experience is found to parallel theirs, her claim to revelation-inspiration is indeed credible.

Revelation

Theologians generally say there are two kinds of revelation: general revelation and special revelation. General revelation refers to the manifestation of God through nature, history, and human experience; it is accessible to all people at all times and in all places (see, e.g., Dan. 2:21; Rom. 2:11–16; Acts 14:16, 17). Psalm 19:1, 2, for example, tells us that the created order speaks about God: "The heavens declare the glory of God; the skies proclaim the work of his hands. Day after day they pour forth speech; night after night they display knowledge" (NIV). The message of this particular manifestation of God, however, is general and inexact rather than specific and detailed.[1]

Special revelation is "God's manifestation of Himself to particular persons at definite times and places, enabling those persons to enter into a redemptive relationship with him."[2] Because human beings lost the direct communication they had with God before the fall into sin (Gen. 2:17; 3:24), they needed more than general revelation because of their spiritual and moral limitations (1 Cor. 2:14). Through special revelation, God addressed human beings in their sinful state and disclosed specific truths about Himself, His character, and His purposes (Deut. 29:29; Heb. 1:1, 2). The Bible provides the record of this special revelation to the human race.

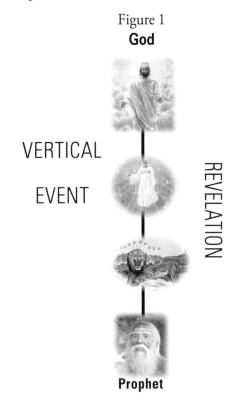

Figure 1

The words translated as *reveal* in the Bible, *galah* in the Hebrew Old Testament (e.g., Amos 3:7) and *apokaluptō* in the Greek New Testament (e.g., Rom. 1:7) both express the idea of uncovering something that is hidden or concealed. Special revelation is thus a disclosure of specific knowledge about God that human beings can't obtain on their own. Adventist theologian Raoul Dederen, who specialized in the study and teaching of revelation-inspiration at the Seventh-day Adventist Theological Seminary, provided a helpful definition of *revelation*. He said it is "a divine act in which God discloses Himself to a specially chosen instrument and conveys to him a knowledge of Himself and of His will which man could not have attained on his own."[3]

The content of the Bible has come through special revelation. As recorded in Genesis 3:15, immediately after Adam and Eve's fall into sin, God announced the goal of all future divine revelations: the person and mission of Jesus Christ. He would be the divine content of this special revelation, and God availed Himself of every means to communicate this to human beings.[4]

In attempting to explain the way God communicated His message in ancient times, theologians have used the term *modalities* to describe the different forms or manners in which God manifested Himself and His will to the world.[5] These modalities have been classified into the following categories:

1. *Theophanies* (visible manifestations or appearances of God): to Abraham (Gen. 17:1, 22; 18:1); to Isaac (Gen. 26:2); to Jacob (Gen. 32:30); to Moses (Exodus 33:11); and to Gideon (Judges 6:12, 14–18).
2. *Dreams and visions* (Num. 12:6; Dan. 2:19, 28; 7:1; 10:7, 8; Matt. 1:20; 2:13).
3. *Angels* (Gen. 32:1; Dan. 10:11, 12; Luke 2:8–14; Acts 8:26; Heb. 1:14).
4. *Casting of lots* (Num. 26:55, 56; 1 Sam. 14:41; Acts 1:21–26). This modality was used only in a spiritual context, however; never as magic (Prov. 16:33).
5. *Urim and Thummim* (stones on the high priest's breastplate): (Exod. 28:30; Num. 27:21; 1 Sam. 28:6).
6. *Divine speech:* God's warning about the Flood (Gen. 6:13); promises to Abraham (Gen. 12:1–4); giving of the Ten Commandments (Exod. 20:3–17); instructions on the tabernacle (Exod. 25–27). The introductory formula "Thus says the Lord" appears literally hundreds of times in the Old Testament.
7. *Miracles and signs:* the Flood (Gen. 6–9); the plagues on Egypt (Exod. 7–10); Israel's passage through the sea (Exod. 14:13–31).
8. *The ultimate and definitive modality of God's special revelation: the life, teachings, miracles, death, resurrection, and ascension of Jesus Christ* (Matthew, Mark, Luke, John, and the rest of the New Testament as the inspired apostolic interpretation of Jesus Christ).

All of these modalities were divine acts or *vertical events* in which God revealed information about Himself and His will to specially chosen human beings, the prophets.

Inspiration

While revelation was a vertical event in which God communicated truth to human recipient(s), inspiration was the "relaying of that truth from the first recipient(s) of it to other persons, whether then or later."[6] Inspiration was thus a horizontal process that preserved and continued the original revelation. This process involved both oral proclamation and the writing of Scripture. The prophetic oracles in the Bible, for example, were essentially delivered orally before being put into writing (e.g., Isa. 7:3, 4; 39:5–8; Jer. 7:2; 33:6). The same is true of Jesus' teaching (e.g., Matt. 5–7).[7] The Scriptures, however, were the "culmination of revelation and its primary product," the "deposit of divine truth for the doctrinal, moral and spiritual welfare of God's people."[8] In this sense, Scripture is itself revelation and the final modality of special revelation.[9]

The Bible attests to its own inspiration.[10] In the foundational text 2 Timothy 3:15–17, Paul declared, "All Scripture is given by inspiration of God, and is profitable for doctrine, for reproof, for correction, for instruction in righteousness, that the man of God may be complete, thoroughly equipped for every good work" (NKJV). The immediate context tells us that Paul wasn't really addressing the nature of inspiration; rather, he was explaining to Timothy the use of Scripture in the church. Nevertheless, his terminology is instructive. First, he used the term *theopneustos*, translated as "inspired." Literally, the word means "God-breathed," which describes the process of how the biblical writers were enabled to write what God wanted. The word doesn't give any details as to whether or not it was the person or the words that were inspired, only that God was the Author, rather than the writer, of Scripture.

Second, Paul states that "all Scripture" (*pasa graphē*) was "God-breathed." This phrase indicates that not part but *all* of the Scriptures were inspired. Hence, no part of the writings of Scripture is without inspiration. Paul's language indicates he had in mind the Old Testament writings; but in the larger framework of his epistles, "all Scripture" included both the Old and New Testaments (1 Thess. 2:13; 1 Cor. 2:13; 7:25, 40; 11:2, 23). The rest of the text addresses the usefulness of Scripture for the church and for Christian life, indicating that all of the Scriptures are trustworthy and reliable for "doctrine," "reproof," "correction," and "instruction in righteousness."

Peter emphasized that human beings were the writers of Scripture: "For prophecy never came by the will of man, but holy men of God spoke as they were moved by the Holy Spirit" (2 Pet. 1:21, NKJV). Yet, these humans were "moved by the Holy Spirit." The word Peter uses here for "moved" is *pheromenoi,* which suggests the idea of being carried along by the Holy Spirit. Hence, he underscores the fact that human beings wrote Scripture under the guidance of the Holy Spirit.[11] None of it was the product of the "will of man."[12]

In light of this scriptural teaching, Professor Dederen[13] proposed the following definition of inspiration: "another divine act or divine initiative in which God enables a prophet to receive and to communicate the content of revelation in a trustworthy and authoritative way."[14] This "divine initiative" involved the communication and conservation of divine truth through *inscripturation,* the process of casting that truth in written form. Thus, Moses was told to put in writing for future generations what the Lord told him (Exod. 17:14; Deut. 31:9). Years later, shortly before his death, Joshua instructed Israel to "be very courageous to keep and to do all that is written in the Book of the Law of Moses" (Josh. 23:6, NKJV).

The vertical-horizontal nature of revelation-inspiration

Revelation and inspiration worked together in God's plan of communicating His will to humankind. Revelation was the vertical work of God in disclosing divine truth (through dreams, visions, information) to the prophet. The movement was vertical—from God to humans. Inspiration was the horizontal work of God in which the prophets were enabled to communicate the content of revelation in a trustworthy and reliable way (through oral proclamation and "inscripturation"—the writing of what became Scripture) to the intended audience. The movement was horizontal—from inspired human to other humans. The prophet was the human agent who connected revelation-inspiration.

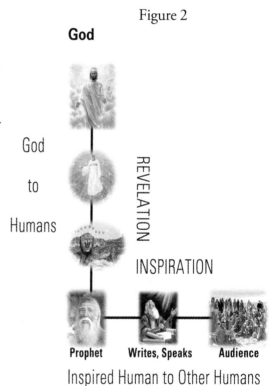

Figure 2

For the purpose of clarity and discussion, one can maintain "some kind of distinction between the two categories, especially since they sometimes function separately." But, according to Dederen, "since both are elements of a single process of divine self-revelation, revelation and inspiration are not easily separated," nor are they "successive steps in a series." Hence, the hyphen indicates the unity and oneness between the two: revelation-inspiration.[15]

Ultimately, this process is how we got our Bible—how the Word of God came to humankind. Ellen White herself understood the Bible to be revelation: "The more we search the Bible, the deeper is our conviction that it is the word of the living God, and human reason bows before the majesty of divine revelation."[16] Furthermore, the Bible is "a complete revelation of the attributes and will of God, in the person of Jesus Christ; and in it are set forth the obligation of the human agent to render wholehearted service to God and to inquire at every step, 'Is this the way of the Lord?' "[17]

Illumination

One other divine act distinct from revelation-inspiration completes the process of God's communication with humankind. It is the process of "illumination," defined by Dederen as "a divine act by which God enables any person in a right relationship with Him to come to a correct understanding of that which has been revealed."[18] Illumination takes place when Christians sincerely ask for the guidance of the Holy Spirit to understand Scripture.

Illumination should never be equated with revelation-inspiration. Sometimes Christians confuse the two. For instance, when a believer gains a life-changing insight into spiritual truth, he or she may claim it came through divine inspiration. And sometimes a person may be especially blessed by a sermon and then suggest that the preacher was divinely inspired like the prophets while preparing it. However, these are experiences of illumination and shouldn't be confused with the authoritative revelation-inspiration experience of the prophets. Through the centuries, confusion regarding these processes has caused serious problems in Christian communities.

Figure 3

Another way to explain the difference between revelation-inspiration and illumination is that the latter is a form of authority available to all Christians (sometimes referred to in Adventist circles as "pastoral authority"). However, revelation-inspiration is prophetic authority, which is limited to canonical, noncanonical, and postcanonical prophets. Chapter 8 discusses the different kinds of authority.

In sum, illumination is a gift from God to aid us in understanding the biblical record of His original revelation to the human race. The Holy Spirit completes the process of God's communication with human beings by making the original revelation personal to each reader of Scripture (John 14–16; Eph. 3:14–19; 1 Thess. 1:5).[19] The Bible is the product of revelation-inspiration and the focal point of illumination, which are God's methods of communicating His will to human beings. As a material shaped into a triangle is a very strong structural component, so a tightly connected combination of revelation, inspiration, and illumination makes a strong framework for the communication of God's will.

Mrs. White captured this dynamic of God's communication with us when she wrote: "In the Bible we have the unerring counsel of God. Its teachings, practically carried out, will fit men for any position of duty. It is the voice of God speaking every day to the soul."[20] Regarding the work of the Holy Spirit in illumination, she wrote, "The Holy Spirit is beside every true searcher of God's Word, enabling him to discover the hidden gems of truth. Divine illumination comes to his mind, stamping the truth upon him with a new, fresh importance."[21]

Degrees of inspiration

Are there degrees of inspiration in the Bible? Are all true prophets inspired in the same manner and to the same degree? The answer to these questions is important and will bring clarity to Ellen White's understanding of her prophetic gift.

According to 2 Timothy 3:16, "all Scripture" (*pasa graphē*) is "God-breathed." Therefore, no part of the Bible is less inspired than another part. Ecclesiastes, for example, is no less inspired than Isaiah; James no less inspired than Romans. The same is true of the individuals who are inspired (2 Pet. 1:21). When Balaam delivered his oracles (Num. 23, 24), he was speaking with as much inspiration as David, who exclaimed, "The Spirit of the Lord spoke by me, His word was on my tongue" (2 Sam. 23:2, NKJV). Furthermore, the noncanonical prophetess Huldah was just as inspired as the canonical prophet Jeremiah, her contemporary. As René Pache said, "In essence, divine inspiration knows no degrees."[22] The inspiration in all of Scripture and in every inspired person is full and complete, regardless of the prophet's canonical or noncanonical status.

A helpful analogy is a pregnant woman. There are no degrees of being pregnant—ask any woman who has ever been pregnant. Either you're pregnant or you're not! The same thing is true of the prophetic gift of inspiration: either the person is inspired or he or she isn't inspired; according to Scripture, there is no partial inspiration or degrees of inspiration.

Surprisingly, in 1884, the General Conference president at the time, George I. Butler, introduced the theory of "degrees of inspiration" to the Seventh-day Adventist Church through a series of ten articles in the *Review and Herald*.[23] "God has not always inspired men in the same manner or degrees," he argued. In the Bible there are lesser degrees of inspiration analogous to the "soft light of the moon," and there are the greater degrees of inspiration analogous to the "effulgence of the sun." Although "the nature of the light of both is the same," he reasoned, "they vary in degree."[24]

With this understanding of inspiration in mind,[25] Butler proposed a hierarchy within the biblical canon comprising four levels. The first and highest level was "the books of Moses and the words of Christ," in which God spoke directly. The second level involved the "the writings of the prophets and apostles and a portion, at least, of the psalms." This level of inspiration came through "dreams and visions."[26] The third level consisted in "the historical books," whose writers experienced nothing more than "a spiritual invigoration of the memory."[27] The fourth and lowest level was "the Proverbs, Ecclesiastes, the Song of Songs, and the book of Job."[28] Butler concluded that, for example, in parts of the book of Job "there is a very much modified form of inspiration, if there is any at all."[29]

Butler's articles were put in pamphlet form, and by the late 1880s were exerting an influence in some Adventist communities.[30] In 1889, Ellen White responded to the situation in no uncertain terms:

> Both in the Battle Creek tabernacle and in the college the subject of inspiration has been taught, and finite men have taken it upon themselves to say that some things in the Scriptures were inspired and some were not. I was shown that the Lord did not inspire the articles on inspiration published in the *Review,* neither did He approve their endorsement before our youth in the college. When men venture to criticize the Word of God, they venture on sacred, holy ground and had better fear and tremble and hide their wisdom as foolishness. God sets no man to pronounce judgment on His Word, selecting some things as inspired and discrediting others as uninspired. The testimonies have been treated in the same way; but God is not in this.[31]

In the years 1886 and after, Mrs. White wrote several essays on the complex issue of revelation-inspiration—essays that set forth what she believed to be the biblical view of the subject. The references to these essays are listed below in chronological order:

- 1886: "Objections to the Bible," *Selected Messages,* book 1, 19–21
- 1888: "Introduction," *The Great Controversy,* v–xii
- 1888: "The Inspiration to the Word of God," *Selected Messages,* book 1, 15–18
- 1889: "The Mysteries of the Bible," *Testimonies,* volume 5, 698–711[32]

In these essays Ellen White rejected the "degrees of inspiration" theory proposed by Butler in 1884 and articulated a comprehensive view that affirmed the entire Bible as the revealed and inspired Word of God. (As the next chapter will show, mainstream Seventh-day Adventism follows Ellen White in this view of inspiration.) Reflecting on Butler's degrees theory, she penned the following words, which summarized her conviction on the inspiration of Scripture:

> The Bible presents beautiful truths that all may understand, and at the same time it deals in deep mysteries and doctrines, which will require deep thought to understand. But nothing is to be misinterpreted, misapplied, or weakened as lightly inspired, if inspired at all. *God does nothing by halves. His Word is inspired.* And God designs that men shall take the Scriptures as His inspired Word, and any man that shall venture to distinguish between the portions of God's Word, exalting one and belittling another, and taking away from another, places himself in a dangerous position[33] (emphasis added).

Since God "does nothing by halves," Mrs. White understood her own writings to be no less inspired than those of the biblical writers. "The Holy Ghost is the author of the Scriptures and the author of the Spirit of Prophecy [a reference to her writings]."[34] This statement is consistent with her view that inspiration has no degrees and is full and complete in all true prophets.

Ellen White's experience of revelation-inspiration

Now that we have established the vertical and horizontal aspects of God's method of communicating His will to human beings and concluded that inspiration knows no degrees, we are ready to look at Ellen White's experience of revelation-inspiration. If she did possess the authentic prophetic gift, then we would expect her experience of revelation-inspiration to be the same as that of the biblical writers.

Significantly, this is precisely what we find in Mrs. White's explanation of her prophetic experience. "I am just as dependent upon the Spirit of the Lord in relating or writing a vision, as in having the vision," she said.³⁵ This statement is instructive for understanding her experience of revelation-inspiration, for in it we find the same divine vertical and horizontal activity as that found in the biblical writers. Observe first of all that revelation and inspiration were connected in the person of Ellen White. These two divine acts worked together in her prophetic experience just as they did in the biblical writers.

Second, notice that her experience of "having the vision" corresponds to the vertical event of revelation. Ellen White specialists estimate that over the course of her seventy-year ministry, Mrs. White received approximately two thousand dreams and visions. These visions dealt with a broad array of subjects. "Men and women received admonition, encouragement, and reproof regarding their personal lives and their Christian influence. Individuals and groups received insights, caution, and direction in general ideas, including education, health, administrative policy, evangelistic and publishing principles and church finance."³⁶ In addition, the visions provided theological insights into world history and its grand finale through the concept of the great controversy between Christ and Satan. Emphasis of various Bible truths was also at the heart of many visions.³⁷

In 1860 Mrs. White provided a glimpse into some of her visionary experiences:

As inquiries are frequently made as to my state in vision, and after I come out, I would say that when the Lord sees fit to give a vision, I am taken into the presence of Jesus and angels, and am entirely lost to earthly things. I can see no farther than the angel directs me. My attention is often directed to scenes transpiring upon earth. At times I am carried far ahead into the future and shown what is to take place. Then again I am shown things as they have occurred in the past.³⁸

Such was the vertical event of "having the vision" in Ellen White's experience.

Third, the horizontal process of inspiration involved "relating or writing a vision."³⁹ About a week after her first vision in December 1844, seventeen-year-old Ellen Harmon was commissioned in another vision to "make known to others what I have revealed to you."⁴⁰ Thus began the task of delivering to others the messages she received in vision, a large and often distressing task that occupied most of her time for the next seventy years (1845–1915).

According to her own description and those who worked with her, the visions lasted anywhere from a few minutes to an hour or more but would often take weeks and months to put in writing.⁴¹ Here's how Mrs. White described her experience of relating the visions to others:

After I come out of vision I do not at once remember all that I have seen, and the matter is not so clear before me until I write, then the scene rises before me as was presented in vision, and I can write with freedom. Sometimes the things which I have seen are hid from me after I come out of vision, and I cannot call them to mind until I am brought before a company where that vision applies, then the things which I have seen come to my mind with force. I am just as dependent upon the Spirit of the Lord in relating or writing a vision, as in having the vision. It is impossible for me to call up things which have been shown me unless the Lord brings them before me at the time that he is pleased to have me relate or write them.[42]

This horizontal process of communicating the messages involved three different modes. First was the oral presentation. At times, especially in the early days, Mrs. White met face-to-face with the individuals for whom the message was intended and transmitted it by word of mouth. Most of what was given her, however, focused on groups, and she communicated it by speaking in public services in churches, camp meetings, and General Conference assemblies.[43] She once wrote, "When I am speaking to the people I say much that I have not premeditated. The Spirit of the Lord frequently comes upon me. I seem to be carried out of, and away from, myself; the life and character of different persons are clearly presented before my mind. I see their errors and dangers, and feel compelled to speak of what is thus brought before me. I dare not resist the Spirit of God."[44]

Mrs. White also communicated her messages through manuscripts and personal letters. As her grandson Arthur White explained, "Painstakingly she wrote, page after page, presenting the views given her and conveying the instruction, cautions, encouragement, and warnings imparted to her for others."[45] Copies of the letters were usually made by a secretary; today the Ellen G. White Estate houses approximately eight thousand of these letters and manuscripts (including various testimonies and diary material).[46]

Ellen White's visions were communicated in printed articles and books as well. At the time of her death in 1915, she had published more than five thousand articles in Seventh-day Adventist periodicals and more than twenty books. The number of her books has quadrupled since that time, the posthumous volumes being topical compilations from her manuscripts, letters, and published writings. Adventist historian George Knight said it well: "The amount of Ellen White's literary output is staggering."[47]

It is important to note that not "everything that Ellen White wrote was directly linked to a vision." She used memory and crosschecking for dates and events in her earlier letters and historical research in the development of her book *The Great Controversy*. Moreover, "as a wide reader, she selected and adapted ideas and phraseology from other writers when she felt that they had said it as well as it could be said to get her message across."[48] (I will discuss literary borrowing, a common occurrence in Ellen White's writing experience, in more detail later.)

Another important insight into Ellen White's work, according to Knight, "comes from the realization that not all of her counsel to individuals and the church originated in the form of specific visions for the unique situation at hand."

She compared her experience to that of Paul, whose mind had been informed regarding Christian principles and dangers to the church in a general and broad manner through the previous visions he had received. As a result, the apostle was able to judge developments in the church with divine insight even though he may not have had a specific vision for a particular situation. Thus, Mrs. White wrote, "the Lord does not give a vision to meet each emergency which may arise." Rather, it is often God's method "to impress the minds of His chosen servants with the needs and dangers of His cause and of individuals, and to lay upon them the burden of counsel warning" (5T 684, 685). A great deal of her counsel seems to fall into this last category—a category in which the divine principles originally given in vision found their way, through the impress of the Holy Spirit, into a wide variety of specific situations to which those principles could apply.[49]

Such was the horizontal work of the Holy Spirit in Ellen White's experience of inspiration based on her own words.

In light of the above understanding of the vertical and horizontal work of the Holy Spirit, Seventh-day Adventists believe that Ellen White experienced revelation-inspiration in the same manner and to the identical degree as the biblical writers. Holding such an understanding of her work, Mrs. White wrote in 1876, "In ancient times God spoke to men by the mouth of prophets and apostles. In these days He speaks to them by the testimonies of His Spirit. There was never a time when God instructed His people more earnestly than He instructs them now concerning His will, and the course that He would have them pursue."[50]

Conclusion

This chapter has argued that revelation-inspiration as found in the Bible is the very foundation of God's communication with humans and that Ellen White's seventy-year prophetic ministry was a manifestation of that divine communication in recent times. Now a caveat is in order. This discussion could be *misconstrued* to mean that Seventh-day Adventists believe Ellen White's visions and writings are *equal to the Bible in every way* and thus an *addition* to the canon of Scripture. Please carefully note, however, that the part of this discussion pertaining to Ellen White has focused *only* on the phenomenon of revelation-inspiration in her experience, *not* on her authority in relationship to the Bible. We have not yet addressed the following question: *If Ellen White was inspired in the same way and to the identical degree as the biblical writers, then doesn't she have the same authority as the Bible?* This is not only a valid question but an extremely important one, and chapters 7 and 8 will explore this matter in considerable detail. For now, it will be helpful to remember that while there are *no* degrees of inspiration, there *are* degrees of authority.

In the end, either Ellen White possessed the authentic gift of revelation-inspiration at a time when many claimed to have divine communications,[51] or she was the victim of an excited imagination and thus nothing more than a self-appointed visionary. *The side upon which one stands in this matter will most likely be influenced by the model of inspiration she or he espouses.* Accordingly, the next chapter will explore different models of inspiration and their relationship to how people understand—or misunderstand—Ellen White's inspiration.

Chapter Summary

1. Revelation-inspiration is the foundation of God's communication with us and a major underlying issue in the debate on Ellen White.
2. Without a correct understanding of biblical revelation-inspiration, one stands on unstable ground, vulnerable to misinterpreting divine truth.
3. Theologians generally classify revelation in two ways: general revelation and special revelation. General revelation refers to the manifestation of God through nature, history, and human experience and is general rather than specific. Special revelation is the specific manifestation of God's redemptive plan to particular persons at definite times and places.
4. Revelation is therefore defined as a divine event in which God discloses Himself to a specially chosen instrument and conveys to him a knowledge of Himself and His will, that human beings couldn't have attained

Chapter Summary

on their own. It is a vertical work—God to human beings.

5. God revealed Himself to the prophets in forms or manners known as modalities: theophanies, dreams and visions, angels, casting of lots, Urim and Thummim, divine speech, and miracles and signs. The ultimate modality of God's revelation was Jesus Christ.

6. *Inspiration* is defined as another divine act or divine initiative in which God enables a prophet to receive and to communicate the content of revelation in a trustworthy and authoritative way. It's a horizontal work—from an inspired human to other humans.

5. Revelation and inspiration aren't easily separated. Their connection is in the human agent—the prophet who receives the vision and communicates it to others.

6. Illumination is a divine act by which God enables any person in a right relationship with Him to come to a correct understanding of that which has been revealed. It is a gift from God to aid us in understanding the biblical record of His original revelation to the human race. It should never be equated with the authoritative revelation-inspiration experience of the prophets. Throughout history, the confusing of illumination with the processes of revelation-inspiration has caused serious problems in Christian communities.

7. Illumination (sometimes called "pastoral authority" in Adventist circles), is an authority available to all Christians, whereas the authority conveyed through revelation-inspiration—prophetic authority—is limited to canonical, non-canonical, and post-canonical prophets.

8. God's method of communicating with human beings through the Bible can be visualized as a sturdy right triangle comprised of revelation and inspiration as the vertical and horizontal sides, with illumination forming the third side.

9. Scripture knows no degrees in the inspiration of its text or of its writers. Either a person is inspired or he or she isn't inspired.

10. General Conference President George I. Butler proposed the theory of degrees of inspiration in a ten-part articles series in the *Review and Herald* during 1884. Ellen White objected, saying, "God does nothing by halves." She said all of Scripture is equally inspired.

Chapter Summary

11. During the years 1886–1889, Ellen White wrote several essays to counteract Butler's view of inspiration, articulating in those essays what she believed to be the biblical view of inspiration. These writings advocate a comprehensive view of inspiration that affirms the entire Bible as the revealed and inspired Word of God.

12. If there are no degrees of inspiration, then Adventists are logically consistent in claiming that Ellen White had the same kind of revelation-inspiration experience as did the biblical writers. If so, then, both the vertical (revelation) and horizontal (inspiration) processes were at work in her experience.

13. Ellen White's experience of "having the vision," as mentioned in volume 1, page 293, of her *Spiritual Gifts* series, corresponded to the vertical element of revelation.
    a. Mrs. White received approximately two thousand dreams and visions.
    b. These visions dealt with a broad array of subjects. They provided men and women admonition, encouragement, and reproof regarding their personal lives and their Christian influence. Through them individuals and groups received insights, caution, and direction in general ideas, including education, health, administrative policy, evangelistic and publishing principles, and church finance.
    c. In addition, the visions provided theological insights into world history and its grand finale through the concept of the great controversy between Christ and Satan. Many of the visions also served to emphasize of various Bible truths.

14. Ellen White's experience of "relating or writing a vision" as spoken of in that same *Spiritual Gifts* statement, corresponded to the horizontal element of inspiration.
    a. About a week after her first vision in December of 1844, seventeen-year-old Ellen Harmon was commissioned in another vision to "make known to others what I have revealed to you." Thus began the task of delivering to others the messages she received in vision, a large and often distressing task that occupied most of her time for the next seventy years (1845–1915).
    b. This horizontal process of communicating the messages involved

three different modalities: oral presentation, manuscripts and personal letters, and printed articles and books.

Chapter Summary

   c. At the time of her death in 1915, she had published more than five thousand articles in Seventh-day Adventist periodicals and more than twenty books. The number of books has quadrupled since that time, the posthumous volumes comprising topical compilations from her manuscripts, letters, and published writings.

   d. It is important to note that not everything that Ellen White wrote was directly linked to a vision. She used memory and cross-checking when writing of dates and events in her earlier letters, and historical research played a role in the development of her book *The Great Controversy*. Moreover, she had read widely, and in order to get her message across, she selected and adapted ideas and phraseology from other writers when she felt they had said well what she wanted to communicate.

   e. Not all of Ellen White's counsels to individuals and the church originated from visions specifically given for the situation at hand. Through the impress of the Holy Spirit, she applied divine principles originally given in vision to a wide variety of situations that those principles fit.

15. In light of the above understanding of the vertical and horizontal work of the Holy Spirit, Seventh-day Adventists believe that Ellen White experienced revelation-inspiration in the same manner and to the same degree as did the biblical writers.

16. This discussion could be *misconstrued* to mean that Seventh-day Adventists believe Ellen White's visions and writings are *equal to the Bible in every way* and thus an *addition* to the canon of Scripture. But this discussion focused *only* on the phenomenon of revelation-inspiration in her experience, *not* on her authority in relationship to the Bible.

CHAPTER 6

Ellen White and Models of Inspiration

In his book *Seventh-day Adventism Renounced*, D. M. Canright claimed that Ellen White believed "the very words in which her visions are recorded are of divine inspiration." He described a time when he saw her "scratch out a whole page or a line or a sentence and write it over differently." But "if God gave her the words," he argued, "why did she scratch them out and alter them?" He also accused her of copying "subject matter" from "other authors" and then passing it off as "all revealed to her directly from heaven."[1] Based on this rigid view of inspiration, Canright rejected Ellen White as an inspired prophet.

Does inspiration mean that every word a prophet writes is inspired? Or does it affect only the thoughts, allowing freedom and creativity of expression? Can an inspired author edit his or her writings or use words from uninspired sources? These questions are at the heart of the debate on whether or not Ellen White was truly inspired.

This chapter will address these questions and the issues related to Ellen White's literary borrowing by discussing six models of inspiration. These six models result from the theorizing of theologians regarding what inspiration is and how it worked in the writers of the Bible.[2] By comparing these positions, we can identify the model of inspiration that best represents the one found in Scripture. This process will also help identify unbiblical positions that have been used to discredit Ellen White's prophetic gift. Models one through three are found mostly outside of the Seventh-day Adventist Church, and models four through six are found within the church.[3] Approaching inspiration this way will help clarify misunderstandings and accurately set forth the official position of Seventh-day Adventism.

The models of inspiration

1. The community model of inspiration. This model places inspiration in the community of believers rather than in the text of Scripture. Protestant theologian Paul J. Achtemeier advocates this view when he writes that inspiration is "located and occurs as much in the community of faith" as it does "in the process of giving final shape to the biblical books."[4] Thus, it "is the experience of the community of faith with the Bible that gives the basis for the confession of the authority of that Bible."[5] In this model, inspiration comes from the community rather than from a few prophets like Moses, Jeremiah, Daniel, Matthew, Paul, and John. It extends over a large number of anonymous individuals who changed and edited the various texts of Scripture.[6] It is similar to what evangelical theologian Millard Erickson calls the "intuition theory," which takes away the supernatural element and emphasizes human ability.[7] Evangelicals and most Adventist theologians reject this theory.

2. The encounter model of inspiration. This model focuses on the personal, subjective encounter between God and the prophet in the revelatory experience and rejects any objective communication of propositional truth.[8] One of the founders of this theory, German theologian Emil Brunner, stated, "The Biblical revelation in the Old and New Testaments deals with the relation of God to men and men to God." According to Brunner, this revelation "contains no doctrine of God as He is in Himself."[9] Thus, in this view of revelation, God reveals Himself to the prophet void of any cognitive content about Himself, and the prophet writes about this encounter in his or her own words without any divine guidance. Consequently, the Scriptures are not the Word of God but rather a word about the Word—a subjective account or personal testimony of what the biblical writers remember from the relational encounter experience. As such, Scripture contains errors and mistakes both in historical details and in theological statements.

It is important to note that Brunner understood revelation as an ongoing process involving not only the prophets but also the readers of the Bible. He saw it as a wordless encounter between God and humans that happens to all believers in all generations.[10] When believers come to the Bible, they may experience an encounter with God, but this encounter is void of biblical truth. Doctrinal belief is therefore subjective and at the discretion of the believer.

The encounter theory has had some influence on the thinking of some Adventist theologians during the latter part of the twentieth century.[11] Strong critical responses penned by Raoul Dederen in the 1970s,[12] however, diminished the influence of the encounter theory of inspiration, and today, Adventist theologians generally reject it,[13] emphasizing instead a holistic view of inspiration as both personal and propositional.

Scripture is clear that more than just a personal encounter took place between the prophet and God. First Samuel 3:21, for example, states, "Then the Lord appeared again in Shiloh. For the Lord revealed Himself to Samuel in Shiloh by the word of the Lord" (NKJV). Notice that what the Lord revealed was both "Himself" and content about Himself—"the word of the Lord."[14] Thus, when believers come to the Bible, they encounter not only the person of God but also truth about God and they are summoned to obey that truth.

3. The verbal-plenary model of inspiration. The best-known model of inspiration within evangelical Christianity is the verbal-plenary model, championed by the Presbyterian theologian Benjamin B. Warfield, who maintained that verbal inspiration best safeguards the plenary inspiration of the biblical books.[15] The term *verbal* places the focus of inspiration on the text of Scripture with all its verbal relationships, and the word *plenary* (from the Latin word *plenarius*, which means "full") emphasizes that every part of Scripture is inspired.[16] The idea is that the "work of the Holy Spirit is so intense that each word is the exact word God wants used at that point to express the message."[17]

Advocates of this model of inspiration take great care to distance this viewpoint from a mechanical, word-for-word dictation, and it's unfair to impose that view on them.[18] They don't believe that God violated the human personality in the process of inspiration. Rather, they believe God worked in such a way that the biblical writers' "thinking and writing was both free and spontaneous," yet "divinely elicited and controlled."[19] Nevertheless, this model places the emphasis on the divine side of inspiration and minimizes the human contribution.

Adventist theologian Fernando Canale sought to demonstrate that this model of inspiration replaces the "biblical notion of God with the Greek idea of a timeless God."[20] Greek philosophy, with its roots in Plato and Aristotle,[21] interprets ultimate reality as a timeless realm, whereas "the Bible considers reality to be temporal and historical." According to Canale, "timelessness is the conception that reality in general and God in particular are essentially and necessarily void of, and incompatible with, time and space." Because those influenced by Greek philosophy thought of God as dwelling in timeless perfection, they believed His "actions cannot be conceived as His personal, historical involvement and operation within history, but rather as historical manifestations of His one eternal act outside of history."[22] The early church fathers incorporated this understanding of God into their theology and passed it on to the Catholic fathers, who, in turn, transmitted it to Protestants.

"Consequently," Canale explains, "the biblical affirmation that the Holy Spirit led the prophet's writing was understood on the assumption that God operated as an irresistible sovereign influence, overruling any initiative originating in human freedom."[23] While this view maximizes the divine influence, it minimizes human freedom as the "Holy Spirit overshadows the human agency and overrides all human limitations, errors, and sins." Scripture, then, is viewed "as having divine objectivity, perfection, accuracy, and inerrancy."[24] This is the source of the evangelical doctrine of inerrancy.

While this model values the Bible as the Word of God, it doesn't match the data in the Bible that shows God operating from within human history, not outside of it, and cooperating with human agents in their sphere of understanding. Several Seventh-day Adventist teachers and authors, both early and late in the twentieth century, advocated this verbal-plenary view of inspiration.[25] In general, however, Adventists have not espoused it.

4. The dictation model of inspiration. Sometimes called mechanical dictation, this model takes the verbal-plenary model one step further by teaching that God actually dictated the words to the biblical writers. Called the "typewriter theory" in the mid-twentieth century, the dictation model views the mental activity of the biblical writers as suspended while "the mechanical transcription of words [was] supernaturally introduced into their consciousness."[26] Like the verbal-plenary model, this model also suffers from adopting the timeless view of God, and it, too, fails to engage the biblical data on inspiration. It pictures God as dictating the words from His timeless realm of perfection and depositing them into the mind of the human agent while never meeting the prophets at their level of existence within the temporal realm.

Although Protestant theology in general has rejected this model, it has exerted a considerable influence within some segments of Seventh-day Adventism. One of the best-known examples of the verbal dictation model at work in Adventist history is the reaction roused in 1883 by the proposed revision of the *Testimonies*.

Since 1881, Ellen White had been working with her staff to "revise wording, correct imperfect grammar, and improve clarity of expression" in the first twenty-eight pamphlet-sized *Testimonies*.[27] The project had received some resistance from the church leadership in Battle Creek, so when W. C. White traveled with his mother to the November 1883 session of the General Conference, he took with him a report of the revision project and "called for a resolution of explanation and General Conference support."[28] The proposed resolution, possibly written by W. C. White, passed and was published in the *Review and Herald* of November 27, 1883.

Whereas, Many of the testimonies were written under the most unfavorable circumstances, the writer being too heavily pressed with anxiety and labor to devote critical thought to the grammatical perfection of the writings, and they were printed in such haste as to allow these imperfections to pass uncorrected.

Whereas, We believe the light given by God to his servants is by the enlightenment of the mind, thus imparting the thoughts, and not (except in rare cases) the words in which the ideas should be expressed; therefore—

Resolved, That in the re-publication of these volumes such verbal changes be made as to remove the above-mentioned imperfections, as far as possible, without in any measure changing the thought [emphasis original].[29]

The most notable feature in this action by the 1883 General Conference Session is the "disavowal of belief in verbal inspiration and the consequent expression of support for Ellen White's making 'verbal changes' to remove 'imperfections.' "[30] For those who believed in verbal dictation, however, the idea of changing the words in Ellen White's writings was outrageous. An ensuing "hailstorm of opposition" erupted from the believers in Battle Creek. Alden Thompson vividly describes the reaction among those in whom the verbal-inspiration view was already entrenched: "Nobody was going to touch their *Testimonies*!"[31]

Uriah Smith was under pressure to implement this action, but he dragged his feet due to opposition from believers and the possibility that critics would exploit the changes in wording.[32] Ellen White expressed her concern to Smith when she wrote in February of 1884 that the language used in the first edition "is not the best." It should be "made correct and grammatical." The fact that the "work is delayed," she penned, "does not please me." Fear of the critics should not stop this production: "I think that anything that shall go forth will be criticized, twisted, turned, and boggled, but we are to go forward with a clear conscience, doing what we can and leaving the result with God." Then she pressed Smith and his colleagues: "I do not want this work dragging any longer. I want something done, and done now."[33]

Finally, in 1885, the revisions in wording were made. There were fewer of them than Ellen White had originally hoped for, but the first four volumes of *Testimonies for the Church* rolled off the press anyway. Although these four volumes have been reprinted numerous times over the years since then, they have remained unchanged.[34] The word-oriented understanding of inspiration also remained unchanged in the minds of some Adventist believers in spite of the official General Conference action against it.[35]

D. M. Canright evidenced the most notable manifestation of this more rigid view of inspiration. Shortly after he left the Adventist Church, he published the first edition of his *Seventh-day Adventism Renounced*. As noted at the beginning of this chapter, he used the more mechanical, word-for-word view of inspiration to discredit Ellen White's prophetic gift. He cited her statement in *Spiritual Gifts*, volume 2: "I am just as dependant upon the Spirit of the Lord in relating or writing a vision, as in having a vision." Then he wrote, "Here she claims the very *words* in which her visions are recorded are of divine inspiration" (emphasis original)—despite the fact that she said nothing at all here about the words she used.

Canright then gave six reasons why he "positively" knows "that the words in her written 'testimonies' are not inspired": 1. She rewrote sentences and pages. 2. She incorporated in her writings changes her husband suggested. 3. She employed editorial help. 4. She used the writings of others in her books. 5. In republications of her early works, she suppressed some passages.

The sixth reason came as no surprise to Ellen White and others, who, as noted above, expected critics to exploit the editorial changes in volumes 1–4 of *Testimonies for the Church*. Canright wasted no time making this charge: "In 1885 all of her 'testimonies' were republished in four volumes" with an "average" of "*twenty-four changes of the words on each page*" (emphasis original). He put great stress on these word changes: "Her words were thrown out and other words put in and other changes made, in some cases so many that it was difficult to read the two together." Canright's use of the mechanical, word-for-word view of inspiration here is unmistakable. He concluded: "Taking, then, the words which were put in by her husband, by her copyist, by her son, by her editors, and those copied from other authors, probably they comprise from one-tenth to one-quarter of all her books. Fine inspiration that is!"[36]

Canright exaggerated the number of changes made in the 1885 edition of the *Testimonies*. Nevertheless, his mechanical view of inspiration didn't tolerate *any* change in the wording. In later editions of *Seventh-day Adventism Renounced*, he repeated these six charges.[37]

Canright's charges of editorial changes in the prophet's writings had little impact on those who remembered the 1883 General Conference action that rejected the mechanical view of inspiration. Moreover, Ellen White never claimed, as Canright charged repeatedly, that her "very words" were inspired. Her June 14, 1906, letter to Dr. David Paulson, the founding president of Hinsdale Sanitarium, provides the clearest evidence against Canright's charge. Paulson, a classic example of someone who held the dictation model of inspiration that some Adventists held at the time stated in his initial query, "I was led to conclude and most firmly believe that *every* word that you ever spoke in public or private, that every letter you wrote under *any* and *all* circumstances, was as inspired as the Ten Commandments" (emphasis original). Ellen White's response was direct: "My brother," she penned, " you have studied my writings diligently, and you have never found that I have made any such claims, neither will you find that the pioneers in our cause ever made such claims." In the rest of the letter she reinforced this statement with citations from her earlier writings on the topic.[38]

Further evidence that Ellen White rejected the mechanical view of inspiration is found in her approval of the revisions in the 1911 edition of *The Great Controversy*. In a statement about the new edition made to those attending the current General Conference session, W. C. White, speaking on behalf of his mother, explained, "Mother has never laid claim to verbal inspiration, and I do not find that my father, or Elder Bates, Andrews, Smith, or Waggoner, put forth this claim. If there were verbal inspiration in writing her manuscripts, why should there be on her part the work of addition or adaptation? It is a fact that Mother often takes one of her manuscripts, and goes over it thoughtfully, making additions that develop the thought still further."[39]

In spite of Ellen White's rejection of verbal dictation and the 1883 General Conference action also rejecting this approach, members of the Adventist denomination continued to hold a rigid view of inspiration into the first half of twentieth-century Adventism, and it still persists in some quarters today.[40] The historic 1919 Bible Conference and the "dark cloud of verbal inspiration"[41] caused all kinds of trouble and is well documented in books on Adventist history.[42] The two most visible leaders at that meeting, A. G. Daniells and W. W. Prescott, argued for thought inspiration, but those who believed Ellen White's works were the product of verbal inspiration opposed them strongly.[43] To avoid open controversy in the church after the conference, discussions of how inspiration works—which the church needed—were put aside, and pastoral concerns and evangelism took center stage.

Over the years, the mechanical view of inspiration that persisted in the church was a ticking time bomb. Herbert Douglass described the situation: "When it is not made clear for generations that prophets do change with personal growth, that prophets do use other sources for bringing precision and force into their messages, rigid minds experience a terrifying awakening when the truth is brought forth. Assurance built on words and not the central message, begins to collapse."[44]

At the 1982 International Prophetic Guidance Workshop, Roger Coon, then associate secretary of the White Estate, stated that "most Seventh-day Adventists probably have a seriously impaired view of inspiration/revelation." Because they have a "bias toward" a "strictly verbal (mechanical dictation) position," these Adventists cannot handle "factual data contrary to their view." Instead of "adjusting their theory to fit demonstrated facts," they tend to lose confidence in Ellen White's prophetic ministry and "throw out the baby with the bath water."[45]

Coon was right, for in the years since 1982, the time bomb has exploded. Many church members have lost confidence in Ellen White's prophetic gift because of the charge that she copied from other authors. Those with a mechanical view of verbal inspiration have a hard time handling the idea of inspired authors using the writings of others to express their inspired thoughts. But for those with a broader, more holistic view of inspiration, the issue of plagiarism "is considered from other standpoints, such as intent, fair use, quality of selectivity, and ultimate originality of the author's contribution."[46]

Besides the plagiarism issue, other problems are associated with a mechanical view of Ellen White's inspiration, such as a rigid approach to interpretation and a critical spirit. George Knight has addressed the issue of interpretation and verbal inspiration effectively in his book *Reading Ellen White: How to Understand and Apply Her Writings,* and it deserves repeated reading by students of Ellen White. As to the critical spirit, Herbert Douglass said it well when he declared that nothing seems to be more unnerving to the verbal inspirationist than to be told that Ellen White's words (and certain biblical words or details) need to be understood in terms of "time, place, and circumstances." To speak in this way, he noted, awakens insecurity and the cry of "liberalism."[47]

C. S. Longacre, a longtime Seventh-day Adventist church leader early in the twentieth century, has a lesson for those who set up an unrealistic standard for Ellen White's inspiration and then reject her:

> You and some others who have made shipwreck of your faith in Mrs. White's testimonies set up your standards of infallibility for her writings and what she said from time to time, which she never set up for herself or her writings, and because she did not measure up to those standards which you set up for her, you naturally throw her overboard and try to make her out as a false prophet. The trouble with A. T. Jones, the Ballengers [and others] who lost faith in Mrs. White's testimonies was that they took very extreme positions, and made a veritable deity and superwoman out of Mrs. White and all she ever said and

wrote in any form and shape, and when she did not measure up to the "straw man" or false standards they had set up for her in her private and personal correspondence and in off-hand counsel she gave, then they lost faith and branded her as a false prophet. That is where most of the extremists on the Testimonies do end.[48]

5. The thought model of inspiration. In contrast to the community and encounter models, which place inspiration in either a community or a noncognitive relational encounter, the thought model places inspiration in the biblical writer's thoughts. "The spirit of God works by directing the writer to the thoughts or concepts, and allowing the writer's own distinctive personality to come into play in the choice of words and expressions."[49] In thus emphasizing the biblical writer's freedom to express the divine thoughts in human words, this model departs from the verbal-plenary and dictation models.

Since the time when Ellen White's 1886 manuscript on inspiration was published in the *Selected Messages,* book 1 (1958), the thought model of inspiration has become more influential in the Adventist Church.[50] In that manuscript she stated that it "is not the words of the Bible that are inspired, but the men that were inspired." She explained that inspiration "acts not on the man's words or his expression but on the man himself, who, under the influence of the Holy Spirit, is imbued with thoughts." The following sentence found in this context is often cited: "The writers of the Bible were God's penmen, not His pen."[51]

The previous section on the dictation model provides the context for understanding the development of the thought model in Adventist history. The 1883 General Conference Session voted a significant action that reflected Ellen White's view, which affirmed thought inspiration and disavowed verbal inspiration: "We believe the light given by God to his servants is by the enlightenment of the mind, thus imparting the thoughts, and not (except in rare cases) the very words in which the ideas are expressed."[52] This statement marked a clear departure from verbal inspiration, but it "was a sign along the way, not a theory."[53]

In his important essay "Revelation and Inspiration," published in *Understanding Scripture: An Adventist Approach,* Fernando Canale acknowledged several advantages of the thought model of inspiration: (1) it "provides a middle way between modernistic non-cognitive encounter revelation and absolutely inerrant classical verbal inspiration"; (2) it "has the positive effect of directing the interpreter's attention to the weightier matters discussed in Scripture and away from minutiae"; and (3) it "has the obvious advantage of accounting for biblical phenomena that do not fit within the verbal inspiration theory."⁵⁴

Unfortunately, though, these advantages have been diminished in recent years by those who have taken the idea of thought inspiration too far and problematically concluded that it "works on the thinking process of biblical writers but stops short of reaching their words." As such, those who hold to this model have assumed "a dichotomy between thought and words." Since thoughts "are independent from words," Scripture therefore contains "a limited verbal errancy in matters of detail at the level of words."⁵⁵

Even though this model pictures God as accommodating Himself to the human personality more adequately than does the verbal-plenary theory, it doesn't view inspiration as reaching the words—and thus not reaching the whole person. Consequently, in this thought-word dichotomy, God isn't acting fully within human history and remains partially in the timeless zone, thus creating an unbiblical disjunction between the human writer and the divine action.

Critics of Ellen White focus on this approach to inspiration and accuse Adventists of tearing down Scripture to build up Ellen White. Dale Ratzlaff, for example, stated that since he left the Adventist Church, his "concept of inspiration has become more conservative while Adventism's has become more liberal to allow for the obvious errors in EGW and still claim divine inspiration for them."⁵⁶ And Norman Douty, in his *Another Look at Seventh-day Adventism,* accused Adventists of being inconsistent in arguing, as he understood it, that inspiration is wordless. Because thought is expressed in words, he said, "there is no such thing as an inspiration of thoughts without words."⁵⁷ This problem of making a dichotomy between thoughts and words continues to challenge some Adventist theologians today.⁵⁸

6. The "whole-person" model of inspiration. Because of the problems associated with the thought model of inspiration, after carefully studying Scripture and Ellen White's writings, several Adventist theologians have discovered a broader view of inspiration. Several terms have been used to describe it: "entire inspiration," "comprehensive inspiration," "total inspiration," "historical-cognitive inspiration," the "Biblical Model,"⁵⁹ and "whole-person inspiration"—the term proposed here.

This model of inspiration goes a step further than the thought model, recognizing that while the words of Scripture weren't the primary focus of the process of inspiration, it did reach the words of the biblical writers—however, not in the same sense as taught in the verbal-plenary or dictation models. In those two models—and especially in the dictation model—God deposits the words into the biblical writers' minds from a timeless realm outside of human experience. But in the whole-person model, God met the biblical writer in his or her experience of daily life—the temporal realm—and the whole person was affected by the experience: thoughts, emotions, temperament, educational background, and powers of expression. God thus "acted in human space-time-history and spoke divine truths in the human cognitive sphere of the prophets, and then guided those prophets to express the divine truths in human ways of logic, thought, and expression."[60]

Adventist theologian Norman Gulley described this model of inspiration with precision:

> The prophets' freedom to write was the same as their freedom to speak the messages. God was guiding them in the writing process as He guided them in the speaking process. The prophets were filled with the God-breathing power of the Holy Spirit and wrote or spoke faithfully all that God communicated to them. But the prophets were not in a trance, operating like a fax or dictation machine. They were not speaking in tongues and uttering incomprehensible gibberish. They were participating in the process of inspiration. The mind of each prophet was fully in operation as the Holy Spirit gave them freedom to write or to speak. The cognitive, linguistic, logical powers of the prophets were under inspiration from the Spirit as God worked through their free use of these powers. The Spirit guided the prophets to express truths in the best language, logic, aesthetics, and words the prophets could muster. This accounts for the many types of writing in Scripture. For inspiration has the mark of the divine and the human in it.[61]

Gully concluded that "in this necessary accommodation, the Holy Spirit imparts divine truths through human expression and thereby gives an indissoluble Word of God as Scripture, with all the authority, authenticity, and trustworthiness of a divine gift."[62]

This is the best way to understand Peter's statement that the human instrument was "moved" (NASB) or "carried along" (NIV) by the Holy Spirit (2 Pet. 1:21) and Paul's emphasis that "*all* Scripture (*pasa graphē*) is inspired" (2 Tim. 3:16, NASB). Hence, the "primary locus of inspiration is in people," yet "what they spoke or wrote was the inspired word of God."[63] This model, according to many Adventist theologians,[64] represents the Seventh-day Adventist view of inspiration.

Correctly understood, Ellen White teaches that inspiration affects not only the thoughts of the biblical writers but also their words—the whole person:

> The Bible is written by inspired men, but it is not God's mode of

thought and expression. It is that of humanity. God, as a writer, is not represented. Men will often say such an expression is not like God. But God has not put Himself in words, in logic, in rhetoric, on trial in the Bible. The writers of the Bible were God's penmen, not His pen. Look at the different writers.

It is not the words of the Bible that are inspired, but the men that were inspired. Inspiration acts not on the man's words or his expressions but on the man himself, who, under the influence of the Holy Ghost, is imbued with thoughts. But the words receive the impress of the individual mind. The divine mind is diffused. The divine mind and will is combined with the human mind and will; thus the utterances of the man are the word of God.[65]

Ángel Rodríguez, Adventist theologian and director of the Biblical Research Institute at the General Conference, wrote the following commentary:

> According to her [Ellen White], God addresses the *total personality* of the person and not only one aspect of the personality of prophets, e.g., the verbal skills of the prophets. Second, what she is describing is the mysterious process through which the divine message is "incarnated" into the human condition. The divine mind, she says, is diffused. And by that she means that the divine mind and will are combined with the human mind and will in such a way that what is expressed by the human instrument—"the utterances of the man"—"are the word of God"[66] (emphasis added).

Ellen White, therefore, "does not separate in a drastic way the reception of the message from its delivery." While she "emphasizes that the words used were not given to the prophet from the divine language or vocabulary," she "insists that in recording the message the Spirit was directly involved."[67]

In her own experience of inspiration, Ellen White described how the Spirit sometimes helped her with words: "He lays out my work before me, and when I am puzzled for a fit word to express my thoughts, He brings it clearly and distinctly to my mind."[68] On another occasion she described her freedom of expression in the context of divine guidance: "Although I am as dependent upon the Spirit of the Lord in writing my views as I am in receiving them, yet the words I employ in describing what I have seen are my own, unless they be those spoken to me by an angel, which I always enclose in marks of quotation."[69] Nevertheless, words were important in her thinking: "I tremble for fear lest I shall belittle the great plan of salvation by cheap words."⁷⁰

So, the "process of revelation/inspiration reaches the words even though the words themselves are not inspired, that is to say they do not represent the divine language *per se* and neither were they dictated by the Spirit." Nevertheless, "the Spirit guided in the writing process in the sense that the Spirit made sure that the prophets used to the best of their abilities their own vocabulary to express the message they received in a trustworthy and reliable form."⁷¹

Raoul Dederen explained with precision the thought-word issue in revelation-inspiration:

> Since the thoughts rather than the words are inspired, shall we conclude that we are at liberty to treat the text of Scripture as being of little importance? Some, in fact do maintain that God suggested the thoughts and the general trend of His revelation, leaving the prophet free to express them in his own language, as he liked. Quite apart from the fact that ideas are not most usually transferred by means other than words, this scheme ignores the fact that if the thought communicated to a prophet is of the essence of a revelation, then the form in which it is expressed is of prime significance. The exegetical study of the Scriptures in their original languages would lose much of its meaning if God has not guided the prophet in the writing of his message. It is patent to any student of Scripture that more than infrequently the meaning of a whole biblical passage may rest on a word (as in Mt. 22:45—Ps. 110:1), a singular or a plural number (Gal. 3:16—Gen. 12:17), the tense of a verb (Jn. 8:58—Ex. 3:14), the details of a prophecy (Dan. 7, 8, 9), the precision of a promise (Heb. 2:11, 12—Ps. 22:2), or the silence of a text on a certain point (Heb. 7:3—Gen. 14:18–20).

Thus, while inspiration was flexible enough to allow for "personal matters" and freedom of expression, according to Dederen, "everything points to the fact that God who imbued the prophets' minds with thoughts and inspired them in the fulfillment of their task also watched over them in their attempts to express 'infinite ideas' and embody them in 'finite vehicles' of human language."⁷²

On a practical level, how did this happen in the inspiration of the biblical writers and Ellen White's experience? Canale provided a helpful answer:

> The goal of inspiration is not to upgrade the human mode of thinking or of writing but to ensure that writers do not replace God's truth with their own interpretations. The Holy Spirit's guidance did not over-

rule the thinking and the writing process of Biblical writers but supervised the process of writing in order to maximize clarity of ideas and to prevent, if necessary, the distortion of revelation, or changing divine truth into a lie. In other words, we should not conceive of the continuous guidance of the Holy Spirit in the process of writing as continuous divine intervention, causing the choice of every thought and word in Scripture. Instead, we should consider a less intrusive pattern of inspiration, one more consistent with the freedom of human writers.[73]

This understanding best reflects the view of "whole-person inspiration," or the "Biblical Model," as Canale called it.[74] Human effort and divine guidance are combined in such a way that "the utterances of the man are the word of God."[75]

Canale explained the results of such a view of inspiration: "On the foregoing basis we can affirm the total reliability of Scripture within the parameters of the normal human limitations of the thought and the linguistic process. Since the whole Bible is revealed and inspired within the level of human thought and language, it does not represent divine perfection; yet, its words reliably disclose God's thoughts and will to us. This view of inspiration explains why certain discrepancies and the lack of absolute precision in matters of detail that we find in the phenomena of Scripture do not affect the trustworthy communication of revealed contents."[76]

Ellen White herself reflected on the discrepancies in the Bible when she remarked, "All the mistakes will not cause trouble to one soul, or cause any feet to stumble, that would not manufacture difficulties from the plainest revealed truth." To those who criticize the Bible, her counsel was, "Brethren, cling to your Bible, as it reads, and stop your criticisms in regard to its validity, and obey the Word, and not one of you will be lost." Her own testimony was, "I take the Bible as it is, as the Inspired Word. I believe its utterances in an entire Bible."[77]

So, Seventh-day Adventists embrace a broad, comprehensive view of inspiration that is found in the Bible itself. The Bible shows inspiration to be a multifaceted process involving various modes, such as the theophanic mode (Exod. 3:1–5), the prophetic mode (Rev. 1:1–3), the verbal mode (Exod. 31:18), the historical/research mode (Luke 1:1–3), the wisdom mode (Eccl. 1:1, 12–14; 12:9–11), and the poetic mode (Psalms).[78] Others have suggested also the witness mode, the counselor mode, the epistolary mode, and the literary mode.[79] Hence, biblical inspiration is comprehensive, entire, and complete, allowing human freedom and creativity, yet influencing the text in such a way that the entire Bible is the Word of God.

In light of the whole-person model of inspiration embraced by mainstream Seventh-day Adventism, when detractors say Adventists tear down the Bible to build up Ellen White, they reflect a mistaken understanding of the church's official position on inspiration. While Seventh-day Adventists don't espouse the traditional, classical model of verbal inspiration, they still have a high view of the Bible and consider it to be the revealed and inspired Word of God.[80] To state their understanding as anything less is to misstate the facts.

Inspiration and literary borrowing: a case study

Many Christians who adhere to the verbal-plenary or dictation models of inspiration believe that the prophetic mode (supernatural dreams and visions) was the only vehicle of God's communication in the Bible. As noted above, the whole-person model of inspiration recognizes numerous modes through which the Spirit of God worked with human beings to produce Scripture. One of these modes relevant to the issue of literary borrowing is that of historical research. In this mode, the biblical author produced inspired writings independent of dreams and visions. He received information through research—reading, studying, compiling, and editing material from various documents (literary borrowing) generated by both inspired and uninspired authors. Nevertheless, God was providentially present, and He was supervising the entire process.

The biblical writers borrowed from each other and even from some uninspired writings. Examples abound throughout the Bible. Moses borrowed from the ancient Near Eastern world in the structure of Deuteronomy, and Micah (4:1–3) borrowed from Isaiah (2:2–4). The scribe who compiled 2 Kings (18–20) also drew from Isaiah (36–39). In Ecclesiastes 12:9, 10, Solomon states that he borrowed proverbs from wise sages and incorporated them into his book of Proverbs. Matthew and Luke based their Gospels on the structure of Mark, and John drew from Greek philosophical terminology in his use of the word *logos,* translated as "word" in John 1:1–3. John, however, gave a new meaning to the term when he stated, in verse 14, that the *logos* became flesh.

Paul cited the Greek poets Aratus (Acts 17:28), Epimenides (Titus 1:12), and Meander (1 Cor. 15:33), though he never mentioned their names. And John borrowed lines from the book of Enoch that he used in Revelation—the biblical book Christians might think would be one of the least likely to contain literary borrowing because of the prophetic visions that form its basis. Notice the following examples:

- "After that I saw . . . a multitude beyond number and reckoning, who

stood before the Lord of Spirits"—Enoch 40:1 (cf. Revelation 7:9).
- "And I saw and behold a star fell from heaven"—Enoch 86:1 (cf. Revelation 9:11).
- "They were all judged and found guilty and cast into this fiery abyss"—Enoch 90:26 (cf. Revelation 20:15).
- "And the first heaven shall depart and pass away, and a new heaven shall appear"—Enoch 91:16 (cf. Revelation 21:1).
- "The horse shall walk up to the breast in the blood of sinners"—Enoch 100:3 (cf. Revelation 14:20).
- "Their names shall be blotted out of the book of life"—Enoch 108:3 (cf. Revelation 3:5).[81]

The classic example in the Bible of the research mode of inspiration is the Gospel of Luke.[82] In the prologue, Luke states, "Many have undertaken to draw up an account of the things that have been fulfilled among us, just as they were handed down to us by those who from the first were eyewitnesses and servants of the word. Therefore, since I myself have carefully *investigated everything* from the beginning, it seemed good also to me *to write an orderly account* for you, most excellent Theophilus, so that you may know the certainty of the things you have been taught" (Luke 1:1–4, NIV; emphasis added).

How did Luke pull together the particular miracles, parables, and teachings for his Gospel from all the written accounts he investigated? How did biblical writers in general select from literary sources without a vision from God? Canale, writing in the framework of the whole person model of inspiration, suggested that God was "supervising the process of their free production in the mind of the writer."

Canale specifically addresses the issue of literary borrowing: "Although God could have led them to occasionally select literary sources through miraculous intervention, generally prophets did their homework and chose content and literary sources themselves without miraculous interventions. Yet, this does not mean that they chose their sources independent of divine direction. It only means that divine activity worked in them, stealthily shaping the hermeneutical and theological perspective from which biblical authors thought, wrote, and chose their sources."[83]

This explanation best captures how Luke put his unique Gospel together. The particular events he chose for his narrative of Christ's life were the result of both his own choosing and the Spirit's choosing. He did his "homework" and chose "literary sources" without "miraculous interventions," yet the Holy Spirit was working in him, "stealthily shaping" his research and choice of sources. The research mode, therefore, doesn't negate the quality of the biblical writers' inspiration.

The same is true in Ellen White's experience of inspiration. The well-known fact that she used other authors in her writings doesn't negate the quality of her prophetic inspiration any more than it does that of the authors of the books of the Bible. Juan Carlos Viera, a former director of the White Estate, provides a helpful explanation of how inspiration and literary borrowing worked together in Ellen White's experience:

> The messenger of the Lord was fully aware that God did not give her the exact words to use. In most cases, she was presented with graphic scenes—like those we would see today as movie films—without comprehensive statements or comments. On occasion she heard words and expressions, but even these had to be integrated within a more comprehensive description. Ellen White was aware of her limitations as a writer, but she was also aware of the limitless possibilities of enriching her language, her vocabulary, and her literary culture through reading. As is the case with any self-educated person, what she read immediately became an integral part of her fund of knowledge and her culture. That was her language, enriched by hundreds of pages read. Ellen White was a great reader. Her library—about fourteen hundred volumes at the time of her death—would give pause to more than one scholar of her time, and even today.
>
> When the messenger arose at two or three in the morning to write—she regularly used these first hours of the day to do so—certain expressions, literary figures, and well-formed sentences, came to mind from her reading. In fact, it seems that she did not go back to her library to check a statement word for word, but rather quoted it as she remembered it, or because it was already integrated into her language. Studies carried out in recent years show that the quotations cited word for word constitute only a small percentage.
>
> Why did she do it? Simply because prophets are allowed to use their own language. That language includes all that they may have memorized throughout a lifetime, including passages from their reading. Just as the apostle Paul mentioned a Cretan poet without mentioning his name (Titus 1:12) and other biblical authors referred to well-known writings in their times, modern prophets are allowed to use the expressions, literary figures, or phrases they have learned or read, in order to communicate the divine message that they have received.[84]

W. C. White, Ellen White's son and most important interpreter, provides in a letter to L. E. Froom another insight into how inspiration worked with his mother in her use of other authors:

> Many times in the reading of Hanna, Farrar, or Fleetwood, she would run on to a description of a scene which had been vividly presented to her, but forgotten, and which she was able to describe more in detail than that which she had read. Notwithstanding all the power that God had given her to present scenes in the lives of Christ and his apostles and his prophets and his reformers in a stronger and more telling way than other historians, yet she always felt most keenly the results of her lack of school education. She admired the language in which other writers had presented to their readers the scenes which God had presented to her in vision, and she found it both a pleasure, and a convenience and an economy of time to use their language fully or in part in presenting those things which she knew through revelation, and which she wished to pass on to her readers.[85]

For those like Canright who espouse a more rigid view of inspiration, Ellen White's literary borrowing poses a special problem. If God gave her the exact words, they argue, why would she need to use the words of noninspired writers to express the divine revelation? Inspired writers get all their information directly from God, so they don't need to borrow expressions from the writings of other human beings.

This understanding of inspiration doesn't take into account the literary borrowing done by the writers of the Bible. As noted above, the Bible is replete with literary borrowing as well as many other modes of divine-human communication.

The model that best explains the variety of the modes of inspiration we find in the Bible is the whole-person model. It accounts for the inspired writers using the best words they could muster to express the divine concepts—even when these words came from sources that were not divinely inspired.[86] Of the six models discussed in this chapter, therefore, the whole-person model best sets forth the phenomenon of inspiration as found in the Bible.

Conclusion

This taxonomy of the six models of inspiration provides several important insights with regard to the debate on Ellen White's inspiration

1. Although Adventists have struggled throughout their history to understand the doctrine of inspiration, contemporary Adventist theologians have, after carefully studying Scripture, concluded that Ellen White's understanding and explanation of inspiration effectively captures the whole person dynamic of inspiration found in the Bible.

2. The biblical doctrine of inspiration rejects the Greek idea of the timelessness of God. The Bible clearly shows God as acting from within human space-time-history, speaking divine truths in the human cognitive sphere of the prophets and guiding them in articulating these divine truths in their own unique manner of expression.

3. Many critics of Seventh-day Adventism and Ellen White who left the church and migrated into evangelical Christianity appear to espouse the verbal model, sometimes in its more rigid forms, and, like D. M. Canright, critique Ellen White according to this unbiblical standard.[87] Others adapt views similar to the community and encounter models of inspiration and find her writings to be full of error.

4. An unbiblical view of inspiration renders one incapable of correctly interpreting Ellen White's writings. Inspiration and interpretation go together like hand and glove. For example, supporters who espouse a more rigid view of inspiration tend to place too much emphasis on her words and sentences void of their literary context and consequently develop legalistic interpretations and applications. Detractors with a more rigid view of inspiration also tend to emphasize words and sentences over context, but instead use this view as a weapon to discredit Ellen White's teaching. Neither of these approaches to inspiration and interpretation is biblical or correct.

5. In contrast, whole-person inspiration as found in the Bible leads the interpreter to focus on the big picture of Ellen White's writings and to examine carefully the literary and historical contexts of a particular passage before reaching a conclusion on its final meaning.[88]

6. Ellen White's use of literary borrowing to express the content of her visions was no different from the practice of the biblical writers. They often used literary borrowing to express the divine truths given them through revelation, and this biblical practice is best explained with the whole-person model of inspiration that takes into account both divine guidance and human participation.

The issue of the final status of the Bible's authority is not to be confused with Ellen White's authority. The next two chapters are devoted to this vital issue. As is true of inspiration, if one is wrong on Ellen White's authority in relationship to the Bible, essentially everything else will be wrong, as well.

Chapter Summary

1. A study of the different theories of inspiration will shed light on the debate regarding Ellen White's inspiration. Thus, for the purpose of clarifying the nature of inspiration as it has been understood in Adventist

Ellen White and Models of Inspiration

Chapter Summary

history and as to how it functions in Scripture and Ellen White's experience, six basic models of inspiration are examined in this chapter.

2. The first three models are found mostly outside of Adventism, and the last three models are found within Adventism.
3. *The community model of inspiration* places the inspiration in the community of believers rather than in the text of Scripture. Because this model places the authority in the community that reads the Bible rather than in the Bible itself, most evangelicals and Adventist theologians have rejected it.
4. *The encounter model of inspiration* focuses on the personal, subjective encounter between God and humans in the revelatory experience and rejects any objective communication of propositional truth. Consequently, the Scriptures are merely a subjective account or personal testimony of what the biblical writers remember from the relational encounters they have experienced. This theory influenced the thinking of some Adventist theologians during the latter part of the twentieth century. Raoul Dederen penned strong critical responses in the 1970s, and today, most Adventist theologians reject the encounter theory of inspiration.
5. *The verbal-plenary model of inspiration* is the most well-known model of inspiration in evangelical Christianity today. The term *verbal* places the focus of inspiration on the text of Scripture with all its verbal relationships, and the word *plenary* (from the Latin word plenarius, meaning "full") emphasizes that every part of Scripture is inspired. Thus, the words of Scripture receive great attention in this model of inspiration. Advocates of this model often take great care to distance themselves from a mechanical, word-for-word dictation, and it is unfair to characterize them as holding this view.
    a. The verbal-plenary model of inspiration espouses a nonbiblical, Greek idea of God's timelessness. Consequently, it is believed that the Holy Spirit acted from outside of history and overshadowed the human agency, overriding all human limitations, errors, and sins. Such is the origin of the evangelical doctrine of inerrancy. This model doesn't match the data in Scripture that shows God operating from within human history—not outside of it—and cooperating

Chapter Summary

with the human agent in the revelation-inspiration experience.

    b. In general, Seventh-day Adventists haven't espoused the verbal-plenary view of inspiration.

6. *The dictation model of inspiration* takes the verbal-plenary model one step further by teaching that God actually dictated the words He wanted the biblical writers to write. It is the most rigid model of inspiration. Like the verbal-plenary model, this model also suffers from adapting the timeless view of God, and it fails to engage the biblical data on inspiration.

    a. Although most Protestant theologians have rejected this model, it has exerted considerable influence within some segments of Seventh-day Adventism.

    b. One of the best-known examples of the verbal-dictation model at work in Adventist history is the reaction in 1883 to the proposed revision of the *Testimonies*. Ellen White wanted grammatical errors corrected, but many resisted because they opposed changing any words in her writings. Church leadership hesitated to make the changes due to this resistance from members at Battle Creek.

    c. After a voted action at the 1883 General Conference Session disavowing of belief in verbal inspiration and recommending the proposed changes, the opposition grew stronger.

    d. When the changes in wording were finally implemented in 1885, Ellen White conceded to fewer revisions than she had originally hoped for, and the first four volumes of *Testimonies for the Church* rolled off the press. Although these four volumes have been reprinted numerous times over the years, they have remained unchanged since that time.

    e. The most notable proponent of the more rigid view of inspiration was D. M. Canright. Shortly after he left the Adventist Church, he published the first edition of his *Seventh-day Adventism Renounced* (in 1888). He used the more mechanical, word-for-word view of inspiration to discredit Ellen White's prophetic gift.

    f. Canright charged that Mrs. White claimed that "the very *words* in which her visions are recorded are of divine inspiration." He

Ellen White and Models of Inspiration

counted the number of changes on each page of the revised *Testimonies* and exclaimed, "Fine inspiration that is!"

Chapter Summary

g. Canright's charges of editorial changes in the prophet's writings had little effect upon those who remembered the 1883 General Conference action that rejected the mechanical view of inspiration.

h. Ellen White never claimed, as Canright charged repeatedly, that her "very words" were inspired. Her June 14, 1906, letter to Dr. David Paulson provides the clearest evidence against Canright's charge.

i. Paulson, a classic example of the dictation model of inspiration operating in Adventism at the time, stated in his initial query, "I was led to conclude and most firmly believe that *every* word that you ever spoke in public or private, that every letter you wrote under *any* and *all* circumstances, was as inspired as the Ten Commandments" (emphasis original). Ellen White's response was direct. "My brother," she penned, " you have studied my writings diligently, and you have never found that I have made any such claims, neither will you find that the pioneers in our cause ever made such claims."

j. In spite of Ellen White's rejection of verbal dictation and the 1883 General Conference action against it, a rather rigid view of inspiration continued into the first half of twentieth-century Adventism and still persists in some Adventists today.

k. At the 1982 International Prophetic Guidance Workshop, Roger Coon, then associate secretary of the White Estate, stated that "most Seventh-day Adventists probably have a seriously impaired view of inspiration/revelation." Because they have a "bias toward" a "strictly verbal (mechanical dictation) position," these Adventists cannot handle "factual data contrary to their view." Instead of "adjusting their theory to fit demonstrated facts," they tend to lose confidence in Ellen White's prophetic ministry and "throw out the baby with the bath water."

7. *The thought model of inspiration* places inspiration in the writer's thoughts rather than in the words he or she writes. Thus it departs from the verbal-plenary and dictation models. In this understanding of

Chapter Summary

inspiration, the spirit of God directs the writer to the thoughts or concepts, and allows the writer's own distinctive personality to come into play in the choice of words and expressions.

   a. Since 1958, when Ellen White's 1886 manuscript on inspiration was published in *Selected Messages,* book 1, the thought model of inspiration has become more influential in the Adventist Church.

   b. In that statement, Ellen White said that it "is not the words of the Bible that are inspired, but the men that were inspired." She explained that inspiration "acts not on the man's words or his expression but on the man himself, who, under the influence of the Holy Spirit, is imbued with thoughts." The following sentence found in this context is often cited: "The writers of the Bible were God's penmen, not His pen."

   c. This model has several advantages: 1. It provides a middle way between modernistic noncognitive encounter revelation and classical absolutely inerrant verbal inspiration. 2. It has the positive effect of directing the interpreter's attention to the weightier matters discussed in Scripture and away from minutiae. 3. And it has the obvious advantage of accounting for biblical phenomena that don't fit within the verbal-inspiration theory.

   d. Unfortunately, though, some have taken the idea too far and problematically concluded that thought inspiration works on the thinking process of biblical writers but stops short of reaching their words.

   e. Consequently, they have assumed a dichotomy between thought and words and concluded that since thoughts are independent from words, Scripture therefore has a limited verbal errancy in matters of detail at the level of words.

   f. Because of the problems associated with the thought theory of inspiration, several Adventist theologians have carefully studied Scripture and Ellen White's writings on inspiration and discovered a broader view of inspiration.

8. *The whole-person model of inspiration* goes a step further than the thought model. It recognizes that while the words of Scripture were not the primary focus of inspiration, the process of inspiration did influ-

Ellen White and Models of Inspiration

Chapter Summary

ence the words of the biblical writers, though not in the same sense as taught in the verbal-plenary or dictation models. Those two models, and especially in the dictation model, say that God "deposited" the words into the biblical writers' mind from a timeless realm outside of human experience.

9. The whole-person model says that God met the biblical writers in their experience of daily life—the temporal realm—and the whole person was affected by the experience—thoughts, emotions, temperament, and powers of expression. God thus acted in human space-time-history, spoke divine truths in the cognitive sphere of the human prophets, and then guided those prophets to express the divine truths in human ways of logic, thought, and expression. In this necessary accommodation, the Holy Spirit imparted divine truths through human expression and thereby gave an indissoluble Word of God as Scripture, with all the authority, authenticity, and trustworthiness of a divine gift.

10. This is the best way to understand Peter's statement that the human instrument was "moved" (NASB) or "carried along" (NIV) by the Holy Spirit (2 Pet. 1:21), and Paul's emphatic statement that "*all* Scripture (*pasa graphē*) is inspired" (2 Tim. 3:16, NKJV). Hence, the primary locus of inspiration is in people, yet what they spoke or wrote was the inspired word of God. This model, according to many Adventist theologians, best represents the Seventh-day Adventist view of inspiration.

11. Correctly understood, Ellen White teaches that inspiration affects not only the thoughts of the biblical writers but also their words—the whole person. She understood that human effort and divine guidance were combined during inspiration in such a way that, as she put it in volume 1 of *Selected Messages,* page 21, "the utterances of the man are the word of God."

12. So, Seventh-day Adventists embrace a broad, comprehensive view of inspiration that is found in the Bible itself. The Bible shows that inspiration is a multifaceted process, involving various modes of communication, such as the theophanic mode (Exod. 3:1–5), the prophetic mode (Rev. 1:1–3), the verbal mode (Exod. 31:18), the historical/research mode (Luke 1:1–3), the wisdom mode (Eccles. 1:1, 12–14; 12:9–11), and the poetic mode (Psalms). Hence, biblical inspiration is comprehensive, entire, and complete, allowing human freedom and creativity yet

Chapter Summary

influencing the text in such a way that the entire Bible is the Word of God.

13. In light of the whole-person model of inspiration embraced by mainline Seventh-day Adventism, when detractors say Adventists tear down the Bible to build up Ellen White, they reflect a mistaken understanding of the church's official position on inspiration. While Seventh-day Adventists don't espouse the classical model of verbal inspiration, they still have a high view of the Bible and consider it to be the revealed and inspired Word of God. To state their understanding as anything less is to misstate the facts.

14. Many Christians who adhere to the verbal-plenary or dictation models of inspiration believe that the prophetic mode (supernatural dreams and visions) was the only vehicle of God's communication in the Bible. But clearly, the historical or research mode figured in the composition of the Bible. In this mode of inspiration, biblical authors produced inspired writings independent of dreams and visions. They received information through research—reading, studying, compiling, and editing material from various existing documents generated by both inspired and uninspired authors. In other words, literary borrowing played a role in the writing of the Bible. Nevertheless, God was providentially present, supervising the entire process.

    a. The Bible is replete with examples of literary borrowing in which the research mode of inspiration is at work.

    b. The same is true in Ellen White's experience of inspiration. The well-known fact that she used other authors in her writings doesn't diminish the quality of her prophetic inspiration.

    c. For those like Canright who espouse a more rigid view of inspiration, Ellen White's literary borrowing poses a problem. If God gave her the exact words, they argue, why would she need to use the words of noninspired writers to express the divine revelation? This understanding of inspiration doesn't take into account the literary borrowing found in the biblical writers.

15. The whole-person model provides the best explanation of the variety of modes of inspiration in the Bible. It accounts for the inspired writers using the best words they could muster to express the divine concepts, even when those words came from noninspired sources.

Ellen White and Models of Inspiration

Chapter Summary

16. This taxonomy of the six models of inspiration provide several important insights with regard to the debate on Ellen White's inspiration:

    a. Although Adventists have struggled throughout their history to understand the doctrine of inspiration, contemporary Adventist theologians have, after carefully studying Scripture, concluded that Ellen White's understanding and explanation of inspiration effectively captured the whole-person dynamic of inspiration found in the Bible.

    b. The Bible clearly shows God as acting from within human space-time-history, speaking divine truths in the cognitive sphere of human prophets, and guiding them as they articulated these divine truths in their own unique manner of expression.

    c. Many critics of Seventh-day Adventism and Ellen White who have left the church and migrated into evangelical Christianity appear to have espoused the verbal model, sometimes in its more rigid forms—and like D. M. Canright, they critique Ellen White for not measuring up to this unbiblical standard.

    d. An unbiblical view of inspiration renders one incapable of correctly interpreting Ellen White's writings.

    e. The whole-person model of inspiration as found in the Bible leads the interpreter to focus on the big picture of Ellen White's writings and to examine carefully the literary and historical contexts of a particular passage before reaching a conclusion as to its meaning.

    f. Ellen White's use of literary borrowing to express the content of her visions was no different from the practice of the biblical writers.

CHAPTER 7

Authority, Part 1: The Position of the Pioneers

"The Bible and the Bible, *only*, is not the creed of Seventh-day Adventists," contended Dudley M. Canright. "It is the Bible *and something else;* it is the Bible *and the writings of Mrs. White*" (emphasis original).[1] Church leaders "urge the 'testimonies' of Mrs. White upon their people constantly, in their sermons and church papers." She is quoted more than the Bible, "and with the same authority." Her word is final: "Any interpretation she puts on a text, or any statement she makes on any subject, settles it beyond dispute. It is what God says, and that ends it."[2] So went Canright's argument against Adventism and its "prophetess" in 1919. The same argument persists in many anti-Adventist publications and Web sites.

The issue of Ellen White's authority in relationship to the Bible's authority probably has raised and continues to raise more controversy than does any other matter related to her prophetic ministry. Chapter 5 concluded that Ellen White's inspiration was the same as the Bible writers' and then raised the following question: If Ellen White was inspired in the same manner and to the identical degree as the Bible writers, then don't her writings have the same authority as the Bible? Such an important question deserves a thoughtful response. This chapter provides the first part of that response by examining what the Adventist pioneers and Ellen White herself said on the subject.

A sampling of statements by the pioneers

James White was a leader and cofounder of the Seventh-day Adventist Church and the husband of Ellen G. White.[3] He acknowledged the leading of the Holy Spirit in his wife's visions but made it clear they were never to be viewed as an addition to the Bible. The following statement comes from his first major publication, *A Word to the Little Flock* (1847),[4] in which he wrote an untitled piece to introduce his wife's first vision. White recognized that the belief that God still communicated with human beings through visions was a "very unpopular position to hold on this subject," but he believed it was a biblical one. After giving biblical justification for the modern gift of prophecy, he spelled out the relationship of his wife's visions to the Bible: "The Bible is a perfect, and complete revelation. It is our only rule of faith and practice. But this is no reason, why God may not show the past, present, and future fulfillment of his word, in these last days, by dreams and visions; according to Peter's testimony [Acts 2:17–20]. True visions are given to lead us to God, and his written word; but those that are given for a new rule of faith and practice, separate from the Bible, cannot be from God, and should be rejected."[5]

The next statement comes from an article White published in the *Review and Herald,* April 21, 1851, and is important because he wrote it several months before Ellen's first book was published (in August 1851)—*A Sketch of the Christian Experience and Views of Ellen G. White.*[6] While James worked with his wife to prepare this written account of her early visions, he articulated with clarity in "The Gifts of the Gospel Church" where the visions stood in relation to the Bible:

> Every Christian is therefore in duty bound to take the Bible as a perfect rule of faith and duty. He should pray fervently to be aided by the Holy Spirit in searching the Scriptures for the whole truth, and for his whole duty. He is not at liberty to turn from them to learn his duty through any of the gifts. We say that the very moment he does, he places the gifts in a wrong place, and takes an extremely dangerous position. The Word should be in front, and the eye of the church should be placed upon it, as the rule to walk by, and the fountain of wisdom, from which to learn duty in "all good works."[7]

Another statement by James White is also significant, particularly when seen in the context of the time. For years Adventists had differed with each other on when the Sabbath began and ended. By 1855, after careful Bible study, a consensus emerged that the Sabbath should be kept from sunset to sunset. Joseph Bates, however, persisted in the 6:00 P.M. to 6:00 P.M. position that some had held. At that point, Ellen White received a vision that confirmed the sunset-to-sunset position, and Bates, along with several others, accepted the consensus of the group. "The question then arose as to why God didn't just settle issues by providing visions in the first place." James White made the following reply in the article "Time to Commence the Sabbath," *Review and Herald,* February 25, 1868, providing "a crucial understanding of the role of his wife's gift" in relationship to the Bible:[8]

> It does not appear to be the desire of the Lord to teach his people by the gifts of the Spirit on the Bible questions until his servants have diligently searched his word. . . . Let the gifts have their proper place in the church. God has never set them in the very front, and commanded us to look to them to lead us in the path of truth, and the way to Heaven. His word he has magnified. The Scriptures of the Old and New Testament are man's lamp to light up his path to the kingdom. Follow that. But if you err from Bible truth, and are in danger of being lost, it may be that God will in the time of his choice correct you, and bring you back to the Bible, and save you.[9]

Uriah Smith, a longtime editor of the *Review and Herald* and apologist for the church,[10] provided a memorable analogy on the role of the prophetic gift in the last days in "Do We Discard the Bible by Endorsing the Visions?" *Review and Herald,* January 13, 1863. His article rebutted the argument that to believe Ellen White's "visions is to leave the Bible, and to cling to the Bible, is to discard the visions."

> Suppose we are about to start upon a voyage. The owner of the vessel gives us a book of directions, telling us that it contains instructions sufficient for our whole journey, and that if we will heed them, we shall reach in safety our port of destination. Setting sail we open our book to learn its contents. We find that its author lays down general principles to govern us in our voyage, and instructs us as far as practicable, touching the various contingencies that may arise, till the end; but he also tells us that the latter part of our journey will be especially perilous; that the features of the coast are ever changing by reason of quicksands and tempests; "but for this part of the journey," says he, "I have provided you a pilot, who will meet you, and give you such directions as the surrounding circumstances and dangers may require; and to him you must give heed." With these directions we reach the perilous time specified, and the pilot, according to promise, appears. But some of the crew, as he offers his services, rise up against him. "We have the original book of directions," say they, "and that is enough for us. We stand upon that, and that alone; we want nothing of you." Who now heed that original book of directions? those who reject the pilot, or those who receive him, as that book instructs them? Judge ye.
>
> But some, through lack of perception, or lack of principle, or the ebul-

litions of an unconquerable prejudice, one, or all combined, may meet us at this point like this: "Then you would have us take Sister White as our pilot, would you?" It is to forestall any efforts in this direction, that this sentence is penned. We say no such thing. What we do say is distinctly this: that the gifts of the Spirit are given for our pilot through these perilous times, and wherever and in whomsoever we find genuine manifestations of these, we are bound to respect them, nor can we do otherwise without in so far rejecting the word of God, which directs us to receive them. Who now stand upon the Bible, and the Bible alone?

Let no one then be frightened at this false alarm. A moment's consideration will show who receive the Bible, and who do not. Whoever receives it fully, will receive the pilot according to its directions. We do not, then, discard, but obey, the Bible by endorsing the visions; while we should just so far reject and disobey it, as we should refuse to receive the provisions it has made for our comfort, edification, and perfection.[11]

Smith based this conclusion on his analysis of the scriptural passage Joel 2:28–32 and the general biblical framework for the continuation of spiritual gifts to the end of time. (See chapter 8 for discussion of the biblical evidence on this point.)

George I. Butler, General Conference president and church leader in various capacities during the latter part of the nineteenth century,[12] responded to criticisms of Ellen White's visions in "The Visions: How They Are Held Among Seventh-day Adventists," *Review and Herald Supplement,* Aug. 14, 1883. Although Butler made his share of theological mistakes (see chapters 3 and 5), this was one of his better moments:

> The majority of our people believe these visions to be a genuine manifestation of spiritual gifts, and as such to be entitled to respect. We do not hold them to be superior to the Bible, or in one sense equal to it. The Scriptures are our rule to test everything by, the visions as well as all other things. That rule, therefore, is of the highest authority; the standard is higher than the thing tested by it. If the Bible should show the visions were not in harmony with it, the Bible would stand, and the visions would be given up. This shows plainly that we hold the Bible the highest, our enemies to the contrary, notwithstanding.[13]

Mrs. Sarepta Myrenda Irish Henry was a prominent figure in the national leadership of the Women's Christian Temperance Union (WCTU) during the late 1800s. She became a Seventh-day Adventist in 1896 while a patient at the Battle Creek Sanitarium.[14] As a new convert to Adventism with an evangelical background, she was perplexed by Ellen White's "testimonies." Reflecting on this experience two years later, she wrote: "The manner in which her work [Mrs. White's writings] was first brought to my notice was such as to give me an entirely false conception of it. . . . I supposed these Testimonies were considered as an appendix to the Bible, and of equal authority with it, that there were those among our people who even judged the Bible by these writings."[15]

After wrestling with this issue, Mrs. Henry sought an interview with W. C. White that proved to be most helpful. (Ellen White was in Australia at the time, so the two couldn't meet.[16]) "The conversation with Elder White," she recalled, "was one in which I will never forget, because of the peculiar circumstances, as well as the tender spirit manifested by him, and yet it brought me no permanent relief from the burden of my question." Her question was this: "Suppose I should find some point in these writings with which I could not agree," what then, she wondered, "would I do with it?" The Bible, she affirmed, "had my unquestioning obedience; but while the Testimonies might be good, sound, helpful, they were not, I had been compelled to notice, of sufficient authority to command obedience and silence controversy in those who had professed to have been always led by them."

So, in addition to her struggles with the authority of Ellen White's work in relation to the Bible, she was bothered by the fact that many Adventists she knew weren't shaping their lives by the *Testimonies*. Her discussions with Adventists around Battle Creek led her to observe, "I found coupled with a professed belief in their authority, a practical disbelief in the *Testimonies*." As a member of the WCTU who valued temperance, she found it perplexing that many Adventists didn't follow Mrs. White's teaching on healthful living.[17]

This conflict in Mrs. Henry's soul became so great that she sought a special season of prayer with her Adventist brethren. If the *Testimonies* were God's message for this time, Mrs. Henry "wanted to know it," and in her own words, "only God could make me know it." This special season of prayer brought a breakthrough in her understanding. It also resulted in a most helpful analogy for understanding the relationship between Ellen White's writings and the Bible. She said,

We all bowed in prayer, and I stated the case to God, with as deep a sense of need as I had ever known in my life. All the great and marvelous blessings of my life were for the time forgotten in this present need, and as must always be true, I was heard. The manifestation of the power of the Spirit of God was as clear as sunlight; and in that light I saw the Testimony as simply a lens through which to look at the Truth. It at once grew from a lens to a telescope, a perfect, beautiful telescope, directed toward the field of the heavens:—(that field the Bible); subject to all telescopic conditions and limitations. Clouds may intervene between it and a heaven full of stars,—clouds of unbelief, of contention; Satan may blow tempests all about it; it may be blurred by the breath of our own selfishness; the dust of superstition may gather upon it; we may meddle with, and turn it aside from the field; it may be pointed away toward empty space; it may be turned end for end, so that everything is so diminished that we can recognize nothing. We may change the focus so that everything is distorted out of all harmonious proportions, and made hideous. It may be so shortened that nothing but a great piece of opaque glass shall appear to our gaze. If the lens is mistaken for the field we can receive but a very narrow conception of the most magnificent spectacle with which the heavens ever invited our gaze, but in its proper office as a medium of enlarged and clearer vision, as a telescope, the Testimony has a wonderfully beautiful and holy office. Everything depends upon our relation to it and the use which we make of it. In itself it is only a glass through which to look, but in the hand of the Divine Director, properly mounted, set at the right angle and adjusted to the eye of the observer, with a field, clear of clouds, it will reveal truth such as will quicken the blood, gladden the heart, and open a wide door of expectation.

"The failure," Mrs. Henry concluded, "has been in understanding what the Testimonies are and how to use them. They are not the heavens, palpitating with countless orbs of truth, but they do lead the eye and give it power to penetrate into the glories of the mysterious living word of God."[18]

Denton E. Rebok, church administrator and educator,[19] reported that Ellen White "herself said that Mrs. S. M. I. Henry had caught the relationship between the writings of the Spirit of prophecy and the Bible as clearly and as accurately as anyone could ever put it into words."[20]

William A. Spicer, church administrator and missionary, told about hearing Ellen White's last sermon at the General Conference Session of 1909 in his book

The Spirit of Prophecy in the Advent Movement.[21] This story is often repeated by Adventist teachers and ministers.

> Well I remember the last words this faithful servant ever spoke in the general assembly of the movement. At a world's General Conference in Washington, D.C., she came to the platform, on the last day of the session, to speak a farewell word to the delegates who had come in from the four quarters of the earth. She felt impressed that she would never attend another General Conference; and she never did. What would be the last message by personal presence, in such an assembly, by one who had been so many years the agent through whom the writings of the Spirit of prophecy had come? Mrs. White spoke a few words of good cheer and farewell, and then turned to the pulpit, where lay a Bible. She opened the book, and held it out with hands that trembled with age. And she said: "Brethren and sisters, I commend unto you this Book."
>
> Without another word, she closed the book, and walked from the platform. It was her last spoken word in the world assembly of the remnant church. Well was it symbolic of the lifelong ministry through this gift, ever exalting high, supreme above all, the Holy Scriptures as the foundation of the faith of the people of the advent movement.[22]

This story beautifully captures Ellen White's lifelong passion to exalt the Bible and point souls to it. She could have held up *The Desire of Ages* or *The Great Controversy* or any of her other books before that audience, but instead she held up the Holy Scriptures. This was, indeed, her last official address at the General Conference in session before her death. In that circumstance, this physical uplifting of the Bible was more than just a respectful gesture; it was an act symbolic of her lifelong conviction that the Bible was the supreme source of authority for the Seventh-day Adventist Church and the individual Christian.

Ellen White's teaching on the relationship of her writings to the Bible

It is noteworthy that a search for Ellen White's usage of the words *Bible, Scripture,* and *Word of God* produces more than thirteen thousand hits on the *Ellen G. White Writings Comprehensive Research Edition* CD-ROM.[23] References, quotations, and allusions to the Bible literally permeate her writings.

Ellen White concluded her first book of visions, *A Sketch of the Christian Experience and Views of Ellen G. White* (1851), with a significant nod to the Bible as the supreme source of authority, thus setting a tone that would resonate throughout her writings: "I recommend to you, dear reader, the Word of God as the rule of your faith and practice. By that Word we are to be judged. God has, in that Word, promised to give visions in the 'last days'; not for a new rule of faith, but for the comfort of His people, and to correct those who err from Bible truth."[24]

Sixty years later, in the introduction to the 1911 edition of *The Great Controversy,* she affirmed the final authority of Scripture in relationship to the work of the Spirit in her ministry: "In His word, God has committed to men the knowledge necessary for salvation. The Holy Scriptures are to be accepted as an authoritative, infallible revelation of His will. They are the standard of character, the revealer of doctrines, and the test of experience.... The Spirit was not given—nor can it ever be bestowed—to supersede the Bible; for the Scriptures explicitly state that the Word of God is the standard by which all teaching and experience must be tested."[25]

Throughout her prophetic ministry, Mrs. White repeatedly affirmed the Protestant principle of *sola scriptura:*

- "The Bible, and the Bible alone, is to be our creed, the sole bond of union; all who bow to this Holy Word will be in harmony."[26]
- "The Bible, and the Bible alone, is to be the rule of our faith. It is a leaf from the tree of life, and by eating it, by receiving it into our minds, we shall grow strong to do the will of God. By our Christlike characters we shall show that we believe the word, that we cleave to the Bible as the only guide to heaven."[27]
- "The words of the Bible, and the Bible alone, should be heard from the pulpit."[28]
- "In our time there is a wide departure from their [the Reformers'] doctrines and precepts, and there is need of a return to the great Protestant principle,—the Bible, and the Bible only, as the rule of faith and duty."[29]
- "God will have a people upon the earth to maintain the Bible, and the Bible only, as the standard of all doctrines, and the basis of all reforms."[30]

Reflecting on her early experience and that of her colleagues in founding the Seventh-day Adventist Church, she wrote, "We then took the position that the Bible, and the Bible only, was to be our guide; and we are never to depart from this position."[31]

She repeatedly set forth her writings as subject to the Bible, rather than an addition to it: "The Lord desires you to study your Bibles. He has not given any additional light to take the place of His Word. This light is to bring confused minds to His Word, which, if eaten and digested, is as the lifeblood of the soul."[32] "Brother J would confuse the mind by seeking to make it appear that the light God has given through the *Testimonies* is an addition to the Word of God, but in this he presents the matter in a false light. God has seen fit in this manner to bring the minds of His people to His Word, to give them a clearer understanding of it."[33]

Ellen White's most memorable analogy of the relationship of her writings to the Bible is found in the often-quoted statement: "Little heed is given to the Bible, and the Lord has given a lesser light to lead men and women to the greater light."[34] The "greater light–lesser light" comparison suggested that "just as the moon derives its light from the sun and reflects only what that source emits, so her messages are seen as deriving their authority from Scripture, serving only to mirror the principles presented therein."[35]

On April 30, 1871, Ellen White had a dream, which led to perhaps her most significant discussion on the relationship of her writings to the Bible. In this dream she saw herself addressing a "large company" at an important church meeting. After surrounding the "precious Bible" with several of her *Testimonies for the Church*, she explained to the group:

> If you had made God's word your study, with a desire to reach the Bible standard and attain to Christian perfection, you would not have needed the *Testimonies*. It is because you have neglected to acquaint yourselves with God's inspired Book that He has sought to reach you by simple, direct testimonies, calling your attention to the words of inspiration which you had neglected to obey, and urging you to fashion your lives in accordance with its pure and elevated teachings.
>
> The Lord designs to warn you, to reprove, to counsel, through the testimonies given, and to impress your minds with the importance of the truth of His word. The written testimonies are not to give new light, but to impress vividly upon the heart the truths of inspiration already revealed. Man's duty to God and to his fellow man has been distinctly specified in God's word; yet but few of you are obedient to the light given. Additional truth is not brought out; but God has through the *Testimonies* simplified the great truths already given and in His own chosen way brought them before the people to awaken and impress the mind with them, that all may be left without excuse.
>
> Pride, self-love, selfishness, hatred, envy, and jealousy have beclouded the perceptive powers, and the truth, which would make you wise unto

salvation, has lost its power to charm and control the mind. The very essential principles of godliness are not understood because there is not a hungering and thirsting for Bible knowledge, purity of heart, and holiness of life. The *Testimonies* are not to belittle the word of God, but to exalt it and attract minds to it, that the beautiful simplicity of truth may impress all.[36]

In speaking to the General Conference leaders on the eve of the 1901 General Conference Session, Ellen White stated unequivocally how she felt about the relationship of her writings to the Bible. In this important address to the leaders of the denomination, she urged them to hold as their primary authority Bible principles rather than her words. "Lay Sister White to one side. Do not quote my words again as long as you live until you can obey the Bible. When you make the Bible your food, your meat, and your drink, when you make its principles the elements of your character, you will know better how to receive counsel from God. I exalt the precious Word before you today. Do not repeat what I have said, saying, 'Sister White said this,' and 'Sister White said that.' Find out what the Lord God of Israel says, and then do what He commands."[37]

One of the distinguishing characteristics in Ellen White's published books is the scriptural indexes. They show evidence of an author who knew her Bible well and saturated her books with passages from all over the Bible. Merlin Burt, director of the Center for Adventist Research at Andrews University, conducted a random examination of chapters from some of Ellen White's books to determine the amount of scriptural quotations, references, and allusions they contain. Here's what he found:

- *Patriarchs and Prophets,* chapter 37 ("The Smitten Rock") has eight pages of text. The chapter is based on Numbers 20:1–13. Besides this topical connection to the Bible, there are thirty direct scriptural quotations and many linguistic inferences.

- *Prophets and Kings,* chapter 5 ("Solomon's Repentance") has twelve pages of text with twenty-two direct quotations from the Bible. It also contains lengthy quotes from Ecclesiastes. Roughly five of the twelve pages are direct scriptural quotations.

- *The Desire of Ages,* chapter 17 ("Nicodemus") is based on John 3:1–17 and contains almost continuous textual reference through the commentary. Additionally there are thirteen other direct references to Scripture.

- *The Acts of the Apostles,* chapter 51 ("A Faithful Undershepherd") is based on the first epistle of Peter. Apart from repeated reference to verses in that epistle, there are thirteen other direct references to Scripture.

- *The Great Controversy,* chapter 27 ("Modern Revivals") begins with the words, "Wherever the word of God has been faithfully preached results have followed that attested to its divine origin." The eighteen pages of this chapter contain sixty-five direct quotations from Scripture. These quotes come from twenty-four different books of the Bible—seven books of the Old Testament and seventeen New Testament books. There are dozens of other brief quotes and allusions to Bible texts. This chapter is truly saturated with Scripture.

- *Testimonies for the Church,* volume 2, pages 261–268 ("A Birthday Letter") contains a letter that was written July 27, 1868, to her second-born son, James Edson White. It is a testimony encouraging him to give his life entirely to Jesus. In her conclusion she said, "Educate your mind to love the Bible." There are fewer direct scriptural quotes (only three), but she has used another thirteen scriptural allusions. While not as saturated with Scripture as many other parts of her writings, she has nevertheless seamlessly interwoven the Bible in her letter, and it is a part of her final appeal.

- *Education,* pages 135–145 ("Business Principles and Methods") contains sixty-one direct quotes from Scripture, many from Proverbs. Altogether she quotes from twenty different books of the Bible—thirteen from the Old Testament and seven from the New Testament. She begins the chapter with the following words: "There is no branch of legitimate business for which the Bible does not afford an essential preparation."

- *The Ministry of Healing,* pages 241–259 ("Mind-Cure") contains twenty-three direct quotes from the Bible.

- *Steps to Christ,* pages 9–15 ("God's Love to Man") contains thirty-one direct and indirect references to the Bible. This chapter, like some others listed above, is permeated with Scripture.[38]

Without question, any person who carefully reads what Ellen White has written can't miss the centrality of the Bible to all her writings. She did more to exalt the Bible and draw minds to it than any other modern claimant to the prophetic gift.[39] Her view of the Bible is best captured in the following statement: "The Bible is God's voice speaking to us, just as surely as though we could hear it with our ears. If we realized this, with what awe would we open God's word, and with what earnestness would we search its precepts! The reading and contemplation of the Scriptures would be regarded as an audience with the Infinite One."[40]

Conclusion

Based on the evidence presented in this chapter, it is clear that the pioneers of Seventh-day Adventism all spoke with one voice regarding Ellen White's writings and the Bible. They viewed her prophetic gift as subordinate to the Bible and in no way an addition to it. Notwithstanding this fact, D. M. Canright persisted with his charge that Seventh-day Adventists officially placed Ellen White's writings on the same level with the Bible. In one of his arguments, shortly after he left Adventism early in 1887, he stated that, in her claim to speak for God, Ellen White vaulted herself "right into the place of God himself."

In part of an extended response to Canright's claim, Uriah Smith penned the following late in the fall of that same year:

> When a person under such circumstances [experiencing visions] receives a message from the Lord to be imparted to men, could he, or she, say anything less than that it was a message from the Lord, and whatever treatment they accorded to it, it was to the Lord and not to her? In so saying she does not "vault herself right into the place of God himself," as is "slanderously reported" Rom. 3:8; *Advocate,* Oct. 8, 1887. If, to illustrate, the President of the United States should send a message by a courier to the collector of customs at New York, and the courier should tell the collector that it was a message from the President, and that as he treated it, so he would be treating the President, would he thereby "vault himself right into" the presidential chair? Nonsense![41]

As significant as the statements in this chapter are, we must not end here in responding to the issues raised by Canright. Contemporary critics continue to press the issue that Seventh-day Adventists have "dual authorities," which, they argue, is a violation of the Reformation teaching of *sola scriptura*. It is to this issue that we now turn.

Chapter Summary

1. The matter of Ellen White's authority in relationship to the Bible's authority is perhaps the most controversial issue regarding Ellen White's prophetic ministry, both in the past and currently.
2. If Ellen White was inspired in the same way and to the identical degree as the Bible writers, then don't her writings have the same authority as does the Bible? This important question deserves a thoughtful response.
3. This chapter provides the first part of that response by examining what the Adventist pioneers and Ellen White herself said on the subject.
4. James White, leader and cofounder of the Seventh-day Adventist Church and husband of Ellen G. White, acknowledged the leading of the Holy Spirit in his wife's visions, but he made it clear they were never to be viewed as an addition to the Bible.
   a. In his first major publishing venture, *A Word to the Little Flock* (1847), James White made it clear that "the Bible is a perfect, and complete revelation" and "our only rule of faith and practice."
   b. "True visions," he declared, "are given to lead us to God, and his written word; but those that are given for a new rule of faith and practice, separate from the Bible, cannot be from God, and should be rejected."
   c. In the *Review and Herald* of April 21, 1851, he stated that the Christian should never put the visions ahead of the Bible. "The Word should be in front, and the eye of the church should be placed upon it, as the rule to walk by, and the fountain of wisdom, from which to learn duty in 'all good works.' "
5. Uriah Smith, editor of the *Review and Herald* and apologist for the church, provided a memorable analogy on the role of the prophetic gift in the last days in "Do We Discard the Bible by Endorsing the Visions?" *Review and Herald,* January 13, 1863. He used the illustration of an ocean liner nearing port, where it must stop to allow the harbor pilot to board and ensure a safe journey through the perilous waters near shore. His analogy was clear: "The gifts of the Spirit are given for our pilot through these perilous times, and wherever and in whomsoever we find genuine manifestations of these, we are bound to respect

Authority, Part 1: The Position of the Pioneers

Chapter Summary

them, nor can we do otherwise without in so far rejecting the Word of God, which directs us to receive them. Who now stand upon the Bible, and the Bible alone?"

6. George I. Butler, General Conference president and church leader in various capacities during the latter nineteenth century, responded to criticisms of Ellen White's visions in "The Visions: How They Are Held Among Seventh-day Adventists," *Review and Herald Supplement,* Aug. 14, 1883.
   a. He argued that while Seventh-day Adventists greatly respect and value Ellen White's visions, "We do not hold them to be superior to the Bible, or in one sense equal to it."
   b. "The Scriptures are our rule to test everything by, the visions as well as all other things. That rule, therefore, is of the highest authority; the standard is higher than the thing tested by it. If the Bible should show the visions were not in harmony with it, the Bible would stand, and the visions would be given up."
   c. Thus, he concluded, "this shows plainly that we hold the Bible the highest, our enemies to the contrary, notwithstanding.

7. Mrs. S. M. I. Henry was a prominent figure in the national leadership of the Women's Christian Temperance Union (WCTU) during the late 1800s. She became a Seventh-day Adventist in 1896 while a patient at the Battle Creek Sanitarium.
   a. As a new convert to Adventism, she was perplexed about the relationship of Ellen White's "testimonies" to the Bible.
   b. After wrestling with this issue, Mrs. Henry asked Adventist leaders to pray about the issue with her. After this special season of prayer, she experienced a breakthrough in her understanding, and the result was a most helpful analogy for understanding the relationship between Ellen White's writings and the Bible.
   c. Mrs. Henry saw Ellen White's writings "as simply a lens through which to look at the truth. It at once grew from a lens to a telescope, a perfect, beautiful telescope, directed toward the field of the heavens:—(that field the Bible)."
   d. "If the lens is mistaken for the field we can receive but a very narrow conception of the most magnificent spectacle with which the heavens ever invited our gaze, but in its proper office as a medium

of enlarged and clearer vision, as a telescope, the Testimony has a wonderfully beautiful and holy office. Everything depends upon our relation to it and the use which we make of it."

> e. "The failure," Mrs. Henry concluded, "has been in understanding what the Testimonies are and how to use them. They are not the heavens, palpitating with countless orbs of truth, but they do lead the eye and give it power to penetrate into the glories of the mysterious living word of God."
>
> f. Denton E. Rebok, church administrator and educator, reported that Ellen White "herself said that Mrs. S. M. I. Henry had caught the relationship between the writings of the Spirit of prophecy and the Bible as clearly and as accurately as anyone could ever put it into words."

8. In his book *The Spirit of Prophecy in the Advent Movement* (1937), church administrator and missionary William A. Spicer related his experience of hearing Ellen White's last sermon at the General Conference Session of 1909.

    a. "Mrs. White spoke a few words of good cheer and farewell, and then turned to the pulpit, where lay a Bible. She opened the book, and held it out with hands that trembled with age. And she said: 'Brethren and sisters, I commend unto you this Book.' "

    b. This story beautifully captures Ellen White's lifelong passion to exalt the Bible and point souls to it. She could have held up *The Desire of Ages* or *The Great Controversy*, or any of her other books before that audience, but instead, she held out the Holy Scriptures.

    c. This physical uplifting of the Bible was more than just a respectful gesture, it was an act symbolic of her lifelong conviction that the Bible was the supreme source of authority for the Seventh-day Adventist Church and the individual Christian.

9. In Mrs. White's first book of visions, *A Sketch of the Christian Experience and Views of Ellen G. White* (1851), she concluded with a significant nod to the Bible as the supreme source of authority, setting a tone that would resonate in her writings throughout her life: "I recommend to you, dear reader, the word of God as the rule of your faith and prac-

Authority, Part 1: The Position of the Pioneers

Chapter Summary

tice. By that Word we are to be judged. God has, in that Word, promised to give visions in the 'last days'; not for a new rule of faith, but for the comfort of his people, and to correct those who err from Bible truth."

10. Sixty years later, in the introduction to the 1911 edition of *The Great Controversy*, she affirmed the final authority of Scripture in relationship to the work of the Spirit in her ministry: "In His word, God has committed to men the knowledge necessary for salvation. The Holy Scriptures are to be accepted as an authoritative, infallible revelation of His will. They are the standard of character, the revealer of doctrines, and the test of experience.... The Spirit was not given—nor can it ever be bestowed—to supersede the Bible; for the Scriptures explicitly state that the word of God is the standard by which all teaching and experience must be tested."

11. Throughout her prophetic ministry she repeatedly affirmed the Protestant principle of *sola scriptura*. Many examples can be cited.

12. Ellen White's most memorable analogy of the relationship of her writings to the Bible is found in the often-quoted statement: "Little heed is given to the Bible, and the Lord has given a lesser light to lead men and women to the greater light." The "greater light–lesser light" comparison suggested that just as the moon derives its light from the sun and reflects only what that source emits, so her messages are seen as deriving their authority from Scripture, serving only to mirror the principles presented therein.

13. On April 30, 1871, Ellen White had a dream that led to perhaps her most significant discussion on the relationship of her writings to the Bible. "Additional truth is not brought out," she explained, "but God has through the *Testimonies* simplified the great truths already given and in His own chosen way brought them before the people to awaken and impress the mind with them, that all may be left without excuse."

14. One of the distinguishing characteristics in Ellen White's published books is the scriptural indexes. They show evidence of an author who knew her Bible well and saturated her books with passages from all over the Bible.

15. Without question, anyone who carefully reads Ellen White's writings cannot miss the centrality of the Bible to all of them. She has done more to exalt the Bible and draw minds to it than any other modern claimant to the prophetic gift.

16. Her view of the Bible is best captured in the following statement: "The Bible is

Chapter Summary

God's voice speaking to us, just as surely as though we could hear it with our ears. If we realized this, with what awe would we open God's word, and with what earnestness would we search its precepts! The reading and contemplation of the Scriptures would be regarded as an audience with the Infinite One."

17. Based on the evidence presented in this chapter, it is clear that the pioneers of Seventh-day Adventism all spoke with one voice regarding Ellen White's writings and the Bible. They viewed her prophetic gift as subordinate to the Bible and in no way an addition to it.

CHAPTER 8

Authority, Part 2: Dual Authorities

Do Seventh-day Adventists violate the Reformation principle of *sola scriptura* by having dual authorities—the Bible and Ellen White's writings? Detractors of Ellen White's inspiration claim that, while her statements on the relationship of her writings to the Bible may "give the appearance of orthodoxy," she really "takes away the Reformation teaching of *sola scriptura* by asserting her writings as authoritative."[1] The following statements are considered to be examples of this assertion of authority.

- "God sets no man to pronounce judgment on His Word, selecting some things as inspired and discrediting others as uninspired. The testimonies have been treated in the same way; but God is not in this."[2]

- "The Holy Ghost is the author of the Scriptures and of the Spirit of Prophecy."[3]

- "When I send you a testimony of warning and reproof, many of you declare it to be merely the opinion of Sister White. You have thereby insulted the Spirit of God. You know how the Lord has manifested Himself through the spirit of prophecy. Past, present, and future have passed before me."[4]

- "If you lose confidence in the testimonies you will drift away from Bible truth."[5]

- "The very last deception of Satan will be to make of none effect the testimony of the Spirit of God."[6]

- "In ancient times God spoke to men by the mouth of prophets and apostles. In these days He speaks to them by the testimonies of His Spirit. There was never a time when God instructed His people more earnestly than He instructs them now concerning His will and the course that He would have them pursue."[7]

Based on these statements, critics believe Ellen White's claim that the Bible is the final source of authority is a "pseudo claim." By "making direct and indirect claims to the authoritative nature of her writings, Ellen White tactfully attributed to her writings an aura of authority" and "sparked fear in the hearts of her followers by insisting that her words were from God and that her words were to be heeded." In this sense, then, detractors claim that Seventh-day Adventists have "dual authorities."[8] Or, as Canright put it, "it is the Bible *and something else;* it is the Bible *and the writings of Mrs. White*" (emphasis original).[9]

Another way the argument of dual authorities has been pressed is through the church's Statement of Fundamental Beliefs. Dale Ratzlaff, for example, pointed to Fundamental Belief 18, "The Gift of Prophecy," which reads, "One of the gifts of the Holy Spirit is prophecy. This gift is an identifying mark of the remnant church and was manifested in the ministry of Ellen G. White. As the Lord's messenger, her writings are a continuing and authoritative source of truth which provide for the church comfort, guidance, instruction, and correction. They also make clear that the Bible is the standard by which all teaching and experience must be tested. (Joel 2:28, 29; Acts 2:14–21; Heb. 1:1–3; Rev. 12:17; 19:10).''

Ratzlaff stated that "*the* underlying error of the SDA [Seventh-day Adventist] church" (emphasis original) is the belief that Ellen White's writings, as stated in this Fundamental Belief, "are a continuing and authoritative source of truth." He argues that "SDAs believe the writings of Ellen G. White are inspired on the same level as the Bible." The implication of his argument, of course, is that because Seventh-day Adventists believe Ellen White's writings are inspired on the same level as the Bible, then her writings have the same authority as the Bible.[10] Russell Earl Kelly, author of *Exposing Seventh-day Adventism*, expressed the argument with greater clarity: "Seventh-day Adventists believe that Ellen G. White was inspired by God in exactly the same way that the biblical prophets were inspired, and, as such, her writings are exactly as authoritative and unerring as those of God."[11]

In the mid-twentieth century, Norman Douty argued in his book *Another Look at Seventh-day Adventism* that the Adventist concept of dual authorities is inconsistent and illogical. After he concluded that Adventists equate Ellen White's inspiration with that of the Bible and cited several Adventist authors as evidence, he wrote,

Is it not plain, then, that Seventh-day Adventism, in accepting Mrs. White's assertions about her inspiration and in making such statements as have just been cited, virtually does equate her writings with the Scriptures? Is it not, therefore, extremely inconsistent for Adventists to deny that her works are on a par with the Scriptures? One position or the other has to be given up: either the strong affirmations about her gift or the strong denial that her writings are equal to the Bible. It is logically impossible to hold both positions, for they are diametrically opposed to each other. Adventism must make a choice, and whichever choice it makes will be costly. It must decide between Mrs. White's having no inspiration or having one equal to the Bible's.[12]

Ratzlaff, Kelly, and Douty each make the same assumption: if Ellen White's writings are inspired like the Bible writers, her authority is equal with that of the Bible writers, and, therefore, it is on the same level as Scripture. If this is true, then Adventists are inconsistent when, as Douty argued, they "deny that her works are on a par with the Scriptures."

The problem with Douty's argument is that he created a false dilemma by limiting the issue to one of only two choices: "Mrs. White's having no inspiration or having one equal to the Bible's." There is a third option he failed to recognize: Ellen White's inspiration equals that of the Bible writers, but her prophetic authority is limited because of the nature of its relationship to the Bible.

Is the charge of "dual authorities" valid? A response requires an examination of four issues: (1) the relationship of Ellen White's writings to the Bible canon, (2) Ellen White's place in the pattern of religious authority, (3) Ellen White's authority in doctrinal development, and (4) the meaning of Fundamental Beliefs 1 and 18.

The relationship of Ellen White's writings to the Bible canon

The word *canon* comes from the Hebrew word *qaneh* and the Greek word *kanon*, meaning "measuring rod." Eventually, the term took on the meaning of a rule or standard, and applied to the Christian Scriptures—the standard by which all other religious writings are measured or tested. The canon of Scripture, then, is the collection of biblical books (Genesis to Revelation) that are divinely inspired and therefore authoritative and normative. Christians consider the biblical canon to be all sufficient and closed in the sense that nothing can be added to it.[13]

The development, formation, and closing of the biblical canon make a fascinating story of God's providence. In Jesus' day, the boundaries and divisions of the Old Testament were already known and understood—see, for example, Matthew 23:25 and Luke 24:27, 44, in which Jesus refers to them. In the process of establishing the canonicity of the books that comprise the New Testament, what stood out from the beginning was the self-evidencing quality of the books. The early Christians read the unique witness to Jesus Christ in the apostolic writings and recognized the stamp of divine inspiration. Over time and through the work of God's providence, this unique apostolic witness was acknowledged in the twenty-seven books of the New Testament.

The Bible canon is composed of sixty-six books, written by at least forty authors over a period of approximately fifteen hundred years. Those who wrote the canonical books of the Bible under divine inspiration are canonical or writing prophets. The Bible also mentions prophets who didn't write any books of the canon. This list of noncanonical prophets includes Miriam, Deborah, Huldah, Elijah, Elisha, and Noah in the Old Testament, and John the Baptist, Agabus, Silas, Anna, and Philip's four daughters in the New Testament.[14] Because Scripture indicates no degrees of inspiration, the messages of these prophets were no less inspired than were those of the canonical prophets (2 Kings 17:13; Acts 9:10; 13:2; 21:11).[15]

With regard to the authority of these noncanonical prophets, however, *the same inspiration does not mean the same canonical authority.* This is not to say that the messages of the noncanonical prophets weren't fully authoritative to the people of their day. David, for example, didn't question Nathan's authority for one moment (2 Sam. 12:7–14). Neither did Josiah question the authority of Huldah's message (2 Chron. 34:23–28). "The authority of a prophet is based on his or her inspiration; and the authority of the prophet's writings is based on their inspiration, not on their place in the canon."[16] But if an archaeologist discovered the writings of Nathan, Gad, or any of the other noncanonical prophets, those writings wouldn't be added to the biblical canon. They don't possess the same authoritative status as the canon does. In this sense, the authority of the noncanonical prophets differs from *canonical authority,* even though the quality of inspiration remains the same for all prophets.

A helpful construct for understanding this difference in authority between the noncanonical prophets and the canonical writings is scope and function. First, the scope of the noncanonical prophet's authority covered a shorter time span and targeted only specific individuals or communities. Nathan's prophetic ministry, for example, was limited to the period of David and Solomon, and specifically targeted each of them at crucial turning points during their reign as kings (1 Sam. 12; 2 Sam. 7; 1 Kings 1).

Second, the function of the noncanonical prophet's messages was to apply, intensify, clarify, and amplify the canonical writings, never to add new doctrinal teachings. A good example was the prophetess Huldah, to whom King Josiah turned instead of the contemporary prophet Jeremiah (whose writings would later become part of the canon). The content of her divine revelation was communicated in two oracles: first, a prediction that the curses of Deuteronomy 28 would be poured out on Israel because of their idolatry (2 Chron. 34:24, 25) and second, a divine affirmation of Josiah's humble repentance and promise of a peaceful burial (2 Chron. 34:26, 28).[17] Notice that both oracles were new revelations to Josiah, but they *functioned* as an application of the canonical "book of the law" (2 Chron. 34:14). Huldah's message to Josiah simply reinforced the essential message of the Scripture at hand—namely, punishment for impenitence and reward for obedience. Thus, no new *doctrinal* truth was brought out in her revelation, "but God through the testimony of Huldah simplified the great truths already given."[18]

In contrast to the noncanonical prophets, the canonical writings had no limitations in scope and function. That is, the scope of authority in the canonical Scriptures was timeless and universal, intended to speak to all generations of human history. They functioned as the authoritative, infallible revelation of God's will to humankind and are still "profitable for doctrine, for reproof, for correction, for instruction in righteousness" (2 Tim. 3:16, NKJV). As set forth in the important principle established in Revelation 22:18, 19 (the warning not to take away from the words of Revelation or add to them), none of these canonical books can ever be altered or changed.[19] The closed biblical canon is therefore the final test or measuring rod of what is God's truth and what is not God's truth in all religious writings, inspired or not (Isa. 8:20).

Continuation of the prophetic gift beyond the biblical canon. There is no evidence in the Scriptures that the prophetic gift or any of the other gifts ceased after the closing of the canon.[20] Joel 2:28–32 speaks of the manifestation of the prophetic gift in association with the "great and terrible day of the Lord" at the end of time. Malachi 4:5, 6 speaks of a revival of Elijah's prophetic message at the end of time. Jesus indicated this passage was partially fulfilled in His day (Matt. 17:10–13), but the final fulfillment will come in "the great and dreadful day of the Lord" (Mal. 4:5, NKJV).

In the New Testament, Jesus warned that false prophets would be at work during the time of the end (Matt. 24:11, 24), which indicates that the authentic prophetic gift would be around then too. And Paul clearly indicated in several places that the gifts, including the gift of prophecy, would continue to guide and enrich the church until the end of time. The gifts are bestowed as the Spirit sees fit "until we all attain to the unity of the faith and of the knowledge of the Son of God, to mature manhood, to the measure of the stature of the fullness of Christ" (Eph. 4:13, RSV). Scripture, therefore, clearly teaches the continuation of the gifts of the Holy Spirit until the second coming of Christ.[21]

Adventists believe there is significant evidence for the appearance of the prophetic gift at the end of time in Revelation 12:17: Here are they "who keep the commandments of God and have the testimony of Jesus Christ" (NKJV). In the original Greek, the phrase "testimony of Jesus" means a prophetic message from Jesus that belongs to the remnant at the end of time. When comparing Scripture with Scripture, Revelation 12:17; 19:10; and 22:8, 9 make it clear that the "testimony of Jesus" is the "spirit of prophecy"—the manifestation of the prophetic gift. Detractors, such as Dale Ratzlaff, have challenged this interpretation.[22] But Adventist scholarship has affirmed it, based on a careful linguistic study of these passages.[23] Consequently, we conclude that the prophetic gift will be restored before the second coming of Christ.

The relationship of the postcanonical prophetic gift to the biblical canon. The conclusion we've reached above, that the gift of prophecy is to function during the time of the end, raises another question: how does the authority of the postcanonical prophetic gift relate to the final authority of the closed Bible canon?

Scripture tells us how we are to receive the postcanonical gift. Evangelical scholar Robert Saucy, who takes an "open, but cautious view" on the gift of prophecy today, suggests four scriptural criteria for judging a contemporary prophetic utterance: 1. "It must be totally harmonious with canonical revelation." 2. "It must be judged carefully by the community (1 Cor. 14:29)." 3. "The content of the prophecy should be edifying to the community (1 Cor. 14:3, 4)." 4. "Prophecy must also be done in an orderly manner in accord with the apostle's instructions to the Corinthians (1 Cor. 14:19–33)."[24]

First Thessalonians 5:19–22, a very important passage on receiving the postcanonical gift, reads: "Do not quench the Spirit. Do not despise prophecies. Test all things; hold fast what is good. Abstain from every form of evil" (NKJV). In other words, Paul told the believers not to restrict the Spirit's prophetic activity. Don't disdain prophetic utterances, he commanded, but listen to them and "test all things," holding "fast what is good" and abstain "from every form of evil." In the midst of the many prophetic manifestations in the early church, Paul gave the Thessalonian believers timeless counsel on how to address the manifestation of this gift. Today, whenever the gift of prophecy manifests itself, it should be put to the test—carefully evaluated and proved to be either good or evil.[25]

In 1 Thessalonians 5, Paul didn't provide any criteria for testing prophecy,[26] but in his second letter to the Thessalonians, he indicated that believers should keep in mind at all times the inspired apostolic teaching they had already received (2 Thess. 2:15). Furthermore, his counsel to Timothy regarding Scripture was relevant: "All Scripture," he said, was to be used "for doctrine, for reproof, for correction, for instruction in righteousness" (2 Tim. 3:16, NKJV). These words indicated that Scripture was the final standard, or "test," for everything related to Christian living and church life, including prophecy. So, the fundamental criterion for evaluating the postcanonical manifestation of prophecy is the canon of Scripture.[27]

In light of this biblical teaching, the manifestation of the prophetic gift after the closing of the canon that is a genuine revelation from God doesn't compromise or challenge the authority of the canon. Rather, genuine postcanonical prophecy submits itself to be tested and evaluated by the canon. It always harmonizes with the canon and, like the noncanonical prophets, never adds new doctrine to the previous revelation. "The possibility of God's granting prophetic revelation to his people for specific circumstances in accord with his will," Robert Saucy argues, "need not lead the believer away from the Scripture as his source of spiritual life and canon of belief and practice."[28] The postcanonical prophetic gift, therefore, will lead believers to the canon and will lead them to recognize it as the highest authority.

Adventist theologian Frank Holbrook captured the relationship of the postcanonical prophetic gift to the canon of Scripture:

> Starting with Moses (fifteenth century B.C.) the revelations from God begin to be recorded; over the centuries other prophets record the messages entrusted to them as God saw fit to further the understanding of His people. Finally, God chose to make His ultimate revelation through His Son. Jesus Christ has given the human family the greatest revelation of God possible for man to receive (John 1:18). The New Testament is the inspired apostolic witness and interpretation of Jesus Christ and His teaching. His is an unrepeatable life and disclosure; theirs is an unrepeatable attestation to Him.
>
> Since Christ's life on earth and the apostolic interpretation of it provide the ultimate revelation of God, no function of the prophetic gift (as one of the spiritual gifts) subsequent to the [New Testament] can equal, supersede, or be an addition to its unique witness. But rather, all claims to the prophetic gift must be tested by the Scriptures (1 Thess. 5:19–21; 1 John 4:1–3; Matt. 7:15–20).[29]

Ellen White, a postcanonical prophet. Seventh-day Adventists understand the relationship of Ellen White's writings to the Bible in the terms stated above. She was a postcanonical prophet who posed no threat to the integrity of the scriptural canon. *Like the noncanonical prophets, her inspiration was the same as the canonical prophets, but her authority was not the same as the canon's authority.* She exalted the Bible as the highest authority and endeavored to amplify, clarify, intensify, and apply its teachings.

Ellen White's place in the pattern of religious authority

An understanding of Ellen White's place in the pattern of religious authority[30] will clarify the limitations of her prophetic scope and function. Evangelical theologian Bernard Ramm provided a helpful discussion on religious authority in his book *The Pattern of Religious Authority*.[31] He defined authority as "that right or power to command actions or compliance, or to determine belief or custom, expecting obedience from those under authority, and in turn giving responsible account for the claim to right or power." He then gave a taxonomy of authority as it relates to God's revelatory pattern.

First, he said, there is *imperial authority*—"that power possessed by persons or ruling bodies by reason of superior position such as that of a king, the general of an army, the president of a firm, or the principal of a school."[32] As Creator, Sustainer, and Owner of everything, God is the source and center of imperial authority (Ps. 24:1, 2). In the Christian pattern of authority, according to Ramm, God expressed His authority through His self-revelation.[33] Christians therefore honor and obey Him.

Second, Ramm said, there is *delegated authority*, which he defined as "authority to act, to compel, to have access to, in virtue of right granted by imperial authority." Such authority "is proved by its ability to show its origin from imperial authority."[34] The prophets and apostles showed by their visions, dreams, and teaching that they spoke for God and possessed His delegated authority. Their writings possessed the same kind of authority.[35]

Third, Ramm said, there is *veracious authority*—"that authority possessed by men, books, or principles which either possess truth or aid in the determination of truth."[36] God is the God of truth, "the only true God" (John 17:3, NKJV), and, as such, He is the essence of veracious authority. The prophets possessed veracity because they had experienced revelation-inspiration. The Bible also possesses this veracity: "The entirety of Your word is truth" (Psalm 119:160, NKJV). It is intrinsically true because of its place in God's revelatory pattern and thus has veracious authority.[37] So, Christians obey the Bible because it is true.

The Bible, as the authoritative, infallible revelation of God's will, derives its *veracious authority* from the *delegated authority* of the apostles and prophets who, in turn, expressed the *imperial authority* of God.[38] Because it shares in revelation, therefore, the Bible "possesses delegated imperial authority and veracious authority in all matters in which it intends to teach."[39] For Christians, there are no limits to the authority of the Bible; it is the most authoritative document in the Christian religion, and God means those who receive it to obey it.[40]

Fourth, there is *illumination authority*, or what some Adventists refer to as pastoral authority. This is the inward, illuminatory work of the Holy Spirit that brings understanding and obedience to those who earnestly read the Scriptures. When believers apply a passage of Scripture to their life, the Holy Spirit works with their faith so they understand the external Word—the Scriptures. Thus, "the objective word, the written Scripture, together with the subjective word, the inner illumination and conviction of the Holy Spirit, constitutes the authority for the Christian."[41]

But we mustn't confuse the illuminating work of the Holy Spirit in the mind of the believer with the revelation-inspiration (delegated and veracious) authority designated only for the prophets.[42] Unlike prophetic authority, illumination authority is available to all Christians who come to the Scriptures with open minds and hearts. But there are different degrees of illumination authority because how much of this authority people have depends on the level of their faith, discernment, and aptitude.

The fifth and final kind of authority relevant to this discussion is *circumscribed prophetic authority*.[43] This is prophetic authority that is subject to limits, which is true *only* of the noncanonical and postcanonical prophets. Seventh-day Adventists believe, for example, that Ellen White possessed delegated and veracious revelation-inspiration authority, but this prophetic authority was circumscribed. The table in figure 4 (next page) illustrates Ellen White's place in the pattern of religious authority.

Figure 4: Pattern of religious authority

The reader should note four things about figure 4. First, note that *illumination authority* (or pastoral authority) differs from Ellen White's *circumscribed prophetic authority*. It also differs from the revelation-inspiration-based delegated and veracious authority of the prophets. All Christians can have illumination authority. Significantly, the gift of inspiration wasn't operating in Ellen White during every moment of her life, so, like other Christians, she too experienced illumination authority.

Second, notice that the *Bible* and the *canonical prophets* who wrote the Bible possessed full delegated and veracious authority. This part of the figure demonstrates

Figure 4 Revelatory Pattern of Authority Table

	God	Bible Closed Canon	Prophets Canonical	Prophets Non-Canonical Post-Canonical	Christians
Imperial Authority	God				
Delegated Authority		Bible	Prophets		
Veracious Authority	God	Bible	Prophets		
Circumscribed Prophetic Authority				Non-Canonical Post-Canonical (EGW)	
Illumination Authority					Christians

the power and truth of the Bible as God's Word. It has no equal in terms of its authority.

Third, figure 4 illustrates that the *noncanonical* and *postcanonical prophets (including Ellen White)* have only circumscribed prophetic authority. As recipients of revelation-inspiration, they possessed *delegated* and *veracious authority*, but this authority was circumscribed or limited.

Ellen White claimed to have delegated authority from God: "In all your communications," she was told early in her prophetic ministry, "speak as one to whom the Lord has spoken. He is your authority."[44] In her many communications with individuals, she would first appeal to Scripture in relating her visions. If a person didn't respond to that authority, she would appeal to her own prophetic authority: "It is my first duty to present Bible principles. Then, unless there is a decided, conscientious reform made by those whose cases have been presented before me, I must appeal to them personally."[45] Speaking and writing with this sense of commission, she meant for her admonitions to be obeyed.

Scripture provided the framework for Ellen White's delegated authority, however, which kept it circumscribed. This is what some Adventist theologians mean when they say Ellen White's authority is derived from the Bible. The Bible itself speaks of the prophetic gift continuing to the end of time. Thus, she has delegated authority from the Bible because the basis for her visions and appeals is the Bible. If the writings of Ellen White didn't exist, the Bible would still stand. But if the Bible were taken away, Ellen White's writings would cease to function. There would be nothing to which she could point her readers and hearers.

Ellen White's writings also have circumscribed veracious authority. Her writings contain truth because they are based squarely on the Bible and seek to apply and amplify its truths. But her inspired applications of Scripture aren't the same as a pastor's applying the Bible in a sermon. As a person with revealed-inspired veracious authority, she spoke truth, and this truth should be obeyed. But, as in the case of Huldah, this truth was an inspired *application* of Bible teaching. Mrs. White experienced prophetic visions that provided guidance to the church in specific circumstances, but none of these visions rivaled the Bible as the final rule of faith and practice.

Fourth, the pattern of religious authority in figure 4 illustrates Ellen White's affinity with the noncanonical prophets. Like them, the limitations of her authority consisted in *scope* and *function*. This construct is most helpful for understanding her prophetic authority as circumscribed.

Limitations of Ellen White's scope. The scope of Ellen White's prophetic ministry was limited in its focus to Seventh-day Adventists. J. N. Andrews, considered the most capable scholar among the Adventist pioneers, captured this concept when he wrote that Seventh-day Adventists don't consider the gifts of the Spirit, particularly Ellen White's prophetic gift, to be a "test" to the "world." We do not, he explained, make these gifts a "test of Christian character" in any of "our [social] intercourse with other religious bodies who are striving to walk in the fear of God." He explained, "Upon none of these persons do we urge these manifestations of the Spirit of God, nor test them by their teaching." But for those who "become acquainted with the special work of the Spirit of God, so that they shall acknowledge that their light is clear, convincing, and satisfactory . . . we consider the gifts of the Spirit are clearly a test."[46] This significant statement reflects the understanding of our Adventist pioneers that Ellen White's prophetic gift was directed to the Seventh-day Adventist movement and its people, not to the larger Christian community.

However, this circumscription doesn't mean Ellen White has nothing to say to the larger Christian community. Several of her books, such as *Steps to Christ* and the Conflict of the Ages series, were intended for wider audiences. In *The Great Controversy*, for example, her theological interpretation of the last two thousand years of church history in the framework of the great controversy between Christ and Satan is a relevant paradigm just beginning to be discovered and appreciated by this larger audience.[47] Nevertheless, her major focus was on preparing the Seventh-day Adventist Church for its mission of proclaiming the final message to the world. In this sense her writings focused on the last period of earth's history, which also narrowed her scope in terms of time. That is, her writings were specifically limited to preparing a people for the second coming of Christ. Conversely to these limitations of scope, the Bible possesses no boundaries of time or audience, and it has been relevant to every generation since the closing of the canon, including the present one.

Limitations of Ellen White's function. The other limitation of Ellen White's prophetic ministry is that set by her function as a postcanonical prophet. As shown above, the relationship of the postcanonical prophetic gift to the Bible makes significant the chronological position of Ellen White's gift. *This concept is the key to understanding the relationship of her writings to the Bible.* "No function of the prophetic gift *subsequent* to the New Testament can equal, supersede, or be an addition to its unique witness"[48] (emphasis added). Consequently, Ellen White's writings *cannot be on the same level with the Bible's authority,* even though her inspiration is qualitatively the same. Identical inspiration does not mean identical canonical authority. After the closing of the canon, no manifestation of the prophetic gift—even though it originates from genuine revelation-inspiration—can serve as a new rule of faith or add any new doctrine to the canon. All divinely inspired postcanonical prophecies will submit to the canon for testing and exalt it as the final authority in all matters of faith and practice. Such was the nature of Ellen White's prophetic ministry, so in no sense do her writings violate the *sola scriptura* principle of "the Bible and the Bible alone."[49]

The specific function of these postcanonical inspired writings is defined by their relationship to Scripture:

The postcanonical function of the prophetic gift whenever it shall appear will be similar to its function in the time of the apostles and will carry with it the authority of the Spirit who speaks to the church through it. The function may be summarized as follows: A postcanonical manifestation of the prophetic gift: 1) will point back to Holy Scripture as the basis of faith and practice; 2) will illumine and clarify teachings already present in Scripture; 3) will apply the principles of Scripture to the daily life;

4) may be a catalyst to direct the church to carry out its commission as charged in the Scriptures; 5) may assist in establishing the church; 6) may reprove, warn, instruct, encourage, build up, and unify the church in the truths of Scripture; 7) may function to protect the church from false doctrine and to establish believers in the true.[50]

Several studies have confirmed that Ellen White functioned precisely in this way for the Seventh-day Adventist Church during the seventy years of her prophetic ministry.[51]

Once, after I lectured on this issue in class, an astute student asked me, "If the Bible has the highest degree of authority and Ellen White a lesser degree of authority, then aren't there degrees of obedience? Does this mean that we don't have to obey Ellen White to the same degree we obey the Bible?"

This student certainly raised a valid issue, but the fact that there are degrees of authority doesn't mean that there are corresponding degrees of obedience. In the military, for example, the general of an army carries the highest degree of authority. When a lower-ranked officer, such as a lieutenant, gives an order to a foot soldier, that soldier is obligated to obey the lieutenant's order with no less a degree of obedience than if the general had issued the order personally. The lieutenant is simply carrying out the orders of the highest-ranking authority, the general of the army.

The same is true with regard to inspired canonical and postcanonical writings. Because the authority in these writings lies in their inspiration, they require full, equal obedience. Ellen White's writings, for example, constantly appeal to the Bible as the highest authority. Her appeals and admonitions are *inspired applications* of Scripture, always leading readers back to it. "If the Bible should show the visions were not in harmony with it," George I. Butler correctly argued, "the Bible would stand, and the visions would be given up."[52] But supporters of Mrs. White who carefully study the Bible have never found her to have given an admonition contrary to it. As a postcanonical manifestation of the prophetic gift, then, Ellen White merits full obedience, but this obedience will always lead one into harmony with biblical principles. In this sense, the canon of Scripture is the highest authority (like the general) and Mrs. White's postcanonical writings are a lesser authority (like the lieutenant), but the obedience both deserve is the same.

In sum, Seventh-day Adventists believe Ellen White had circumscribed prophetic authority rather than the authority of the closed canon of Scripture. She was a "lesser light to lead men and women to the greater light" of Scripture.[53] And when Adventism is at its best, it is following

Ellen White's authority in doctrinal development

Two examples in Adventist history illustrate my thesis that Ellen White's revelation-inspiration experience was qualitatively the same as that of the Bible writers, but her prophetic authority was less than that of the Bible. The first example is the role of her visions in early doctrinal formation.

In reflecting on the early Adventist gatherings, Ellen White identified extended Bible study, prayer, and the direct intervention of the Holy Spirit as key factors that led the pioneers to a knowledge of Bible doctrine: "At that time [after the 1844 disappointment] one error after another pressed in upon us; ministers and doctors brought in new doctrines. We would search the Scriptures with much prayer, and the Holy Spirit would bring the truth to our minds. Sometimes whole nights would be devoted to searching the Scriptures and earnestly asking God for guidance. Companies of devoted men and women assembled for this purpose. The power of God would come upon me, and I was enabled clearly to define what is truth and what is error."[54]

The historical context of this narrative is important. The pioneers spent hours and hours of study in the Scriptures until they came to an impasse. This impasse involved "one error after another" and "new doctrines"—in short, confusion. At that point, Ellen White went into vision and "was enabled clearly to define what is truth and what is error" in the array of confusing interpretations. As Herbert Douglass observed, "she was able to affirm the results of Brother C's Biblical study, rather than that of Brethren A, B, or D."[55] Experiences like this brought unity to these gatherings and delivered the pioneers from the mire of endless discussion and debate on the meaning of certain passages.

Based on this narrative, detractors will argue that Ellen White's visions established Adventist doctrine and that she was thus the final arbiter of Bible truth. While it cannot be denied that the visions were a catalyst in this early doctrinal formation, in the end, the Bible was the sole source of the doctrines. What did the pioneers do *before* and *after* they received one of Ellen White's visions that defined "what is truth and what is error"? They studied their Bibles! Did they view Ellen White's visions as establishing a new rule of faith and practice apart from the Bible? Hardly! If her visions did anything, they plunged these people deeper into their Bibles. While the visions provided interpretations of Scripture at crucial junctures, the pioneers continued to study, and ultimately, they based their doctrinal understanding on Scripture alone. James White, a major participant at these meetings, argued that the Word of God, not the visions of his wife, was in the front of the church. "The Bible is a perfect, and complete revelation. It is our only rule of faith and practice," he trumpeted. "True visions are given by God to lead us to God, and his written word; but those that are given for a new rule of faith and practice, separate from the Bible, cannot be from God, and should be rejected."[56]

Nevertheless, the experience of Bible study plus the guidance of the Holy Spirit was the foundation of early Seventh-day Adventist doctrinal formation. But it must be acknowledged that even though Ellen White's prophetic gift was active in helping the pioneers achieve an understanding of Bible teaching, not a single doctrine of the early Adventist church—Sabbath, sanctuary judgment, conditional immortality, Second Coming, spiritual gifts, etc.—was derived from a vision of Ellen White.[57] The visions served to confirm biblical conclusions already reached, guide the pioneers to a correct understanding of biblical passages in the midst of confusion, and lead them back to portions of the Bible for correction when in error. Ellen White's guidance in doctrinal formation can be likened to a compass that pointed the Adventist pioneers in the right direction of biblical truth. But the final conclusions with regard to all the doctrines were based exclusively on Scripture.[58]

The second example is how Ellen White dealt with the case of Albion F. Ballenger, a popular Seventh-day Adventist preacher who worked in England, Wales, and Ireland. Ballenger concluded that the Adventist understanding of Christ's ministry in the sanctuary was unbiblical. After promoting his views, he was eventually dismissed from denominational employment (in 1905), and he left the church shortly thereafter. He then wrote a popular book, *Cast Out for the Cause of Christ* and he edited the anti-Adventist periodical *The Gathering Call* until his death in 1921.[59]

Ellen White spoke pointedly on Ballenger's views. She appealed to the prophetic confirmation given her of the movement's earlier biblical interpretations, declaring that Ballenger was misapplying the Scriptures.[60] Dale Ratzlaff cites one of these statements about Ballenger in his book *Truth About Adventist "Truth,"* and used it as a "proof" of his thesis that Ellen White placed her visions and testimonies above the witness of Scripture.[61] The Ellen White statement reads:

> I have been pleading with the Lord for strength and wisdom to reproduce the writings of the witnesses who were confirmed in the faith and in the early history of the message. After the passing of the time in 1844 they received the light and walked in the light, and when the men claiming to have new light would come in with their wonderful messages regarding various points of Scripture, we had, through

the moving of the Holy Spirit, testimonies right to the point, which cut off the influence of such messages as Elder G [A. F. Ballenger] has been devoting his time to presenting. This poor man has been working decidedly against the truth that the Holy Spirit has confirmed. When the power of God testifies as to what is truth, that truth is to stand forever as the truth. No after suppositions contrary to the light God has given are to be entertained. Men will arise with interpretations of Scripture which are to them truth, but which are not truth. The truth for this time God has given us as a foundation for our faith. He Himself has taught us what is truth. One will arise, and still another, with new light, which contradicts the light that God has given under the demonstration of His Holy Spirit. A few are still alive who passed through the experience gained in the establishment of this truth. God has graciously spared their lives to repeat, and repeat till the close of their lives, the experience through which they passed even as did John the apostle till the very close of his life. And the standard bearers who have fallen in death are to speak through the reprinting of their writings. I am instructed that thus their voices are to be heard. They are to bear their testimony as to what constitutes the truth for this time.

We are not to receive the words of those who come with a message that contradicts the special points of our faith. They gather together a mass of Scripture, and pile it as proof around their asserted theories. This has been done over and over again during the past fifty years. And while the Scriptures are God's word, and are to be respected, the application of them, if such application moves one pillar from the foundation that God has sustained these fifty years, is a great mistake. He who makes such an application knows not the wonderful demonstration of the Holy Spirit that gave power and force to the past messages that have come to the people of God.[62]

After citing this passage, Ratzlaff points to certain phrases and sentences that put the emphasis on Ellen White's prophetic authority, such as the "power of God" testifying "to what is truth"; no "after-suppositions, contrary to the light God has given are to be entertained"; and "we are not to receive the words of those who come with a message that contradicts the special points of our faith." Without question, Ellen White asserted her prophetic authority here regarding Ballenger's interpretation of Scripture. To Ratzlaff, though, this entire statement "demonstrates the cultic heart of Adventism" in "clearly placing" Ellen White's writings "as a 'source of truth' over the witness of Scripture, something no Christian, at least no Protestant Christian, would ever do!"[63]

In the context of the entire document, however, Ellen White affirmed the importance of the Word of God. Early in this letter, written approximately six months after the May 1905 General Conference Session in which Ballenger presented his views, Ellen White asserted that "the Word of God contains the truth, but when this Word is misapplied and made to strengthen error, we must meet this danger without hesitation." We should "reverence the word, but not its misapplication to substantiate error."[64] The above-cited statement comes several paragraphs later. This harmonizes with her other communications regarding the Ballenger charges: "Let Bible truth be presented in our papers. Give the reasons of our faith. In the most cheerful, hopeful, encouraging articles recommend the diligent searching of the Scriptures."[65] Ellen White reinforced this view when she added, "The standard bearers who have fallen in death are to speak through the reprinting of their writings. I am instructed that thus their voices are to be heard. They are to bear their testimony as to what constitutes the truth for this time."[66] Ratzlaff highlights certain phrases in these sentences, but he seems to miss the point.[67]

Earlier that same year Mrs. White wrote in the *Review and Herald* that "we are to repeat the words of the pioneers in our work, who knew what it cost to search for the truth as for hidden treasure, and who labored to lay the foundation of our work. . . . The word given me is, Let that which these men have written in the past be reproduced."[68]

What is she doing in these statements? Clearly, she is calling for the pioneers' exegetical spadework on the sanctuary doctrine to be reprinted for study. Paul Gordon confirmed this in his book *The Sanctuary, 1844, and the Pioneers*.[69] Motivated by Ellen White's call for the church to republish the pioneer writings, Gordon collected approximately four hundred articles published in *The Present Truth* and the *Review and Herald* from 1846 to 1905—everything he could find on the sanctuary judgment message of 1844. He found that all of these articles were based on detailed Bible study and careful exegetical method. In my own reading of this 1,009-page document,[70] I found *not a single instance* in which the authors of these articles used Ellen White as a source of authority. The Bible was the final appeal from beginning to end. This is what Ellen White meant when she called for having the "standard bearers" "speak through the reprinting of their writings."

While it cannot be denied that Ellen White appealed to her prophetic authority in the Ballenger crisis, neither can it be denied that she appealed to previous biblical studies as evidence for the 1844 judgment. She operated on the understanding that during the past fifty years the biblical evidence had already been established in Adventist periodicals. Her role was to remind people that the witness of the Holy Spirit had established the truth of the "passing of the time in 1844" and to call for the reprint of all those articles that contained the biblical evidence. In this light, her statements do not threaten the witness of Scripture or violate the Protestant principle of "the Bible and the Bible alone." Whatever one chooses to believe about the 1844 judgment, the fact that the Seventh-day Adventist pioneers appealed to the Bible alone for evidence of this doctrine is hard to deny in the face of such thorough and well-documented evidence.

Other examples from Adventist history could be given regarding Ellen White's appeals to the Bible—such as in the discussion of the law in Galatians and the debate over the "daily."[71] But the Ballenger issue shows that, even when Ellen White asserted her prophetic authority, she didn't deny the finality of the Bible in all matters of doctrine and teaching.

What value does Ellen White have for Adventists in relation to doctrinal belief? First, she functioned as a corrective authority to the Adventist pioneers in the sense that she spoke authoritatively against heretical teaching. For example, she kept the early pioneers from embracing erroneous ideas on the Communion service, condemned the "holy flesh" teaching that was circulating in Indiana as the nineteenth century drew to a close, and put an end to John Harvey Kellogg's particular brand of pantheism in the early twentieth century.* It is in this sense that Ellen White remarked, "There is one straight chain of truth, without one heretical sentence, in that which I have written."[72] She put the Adventist pioneers back on the right doctrinal track in terms of basic biblical teaching on these subjects.

Second, Ellen White functioned as an authority on the theological framework (worldview) of Seventh-day Adventist beliefs. That is, she expounded on doctrines in the context of the great controversy theme—a theme clearly taught in Scripture (see chapters 11 and 12 of this book). As Luther, Calvin, and Wesley each provided the theological framework for the movements that grew out of their work, so God through Ellen White provided the theological framework for the Adventist worldview. This doesn't mean, however, that she is the source or sole developer of Adventist doctrine. She functioned more as a compass that pointed the way to doctrinal orthodoxy. Put another way, she spoke formatively, not normatively, in the development of Adventist doctrine. Thus, through her guidance, the process of doc-

---

*I will discuss her resistance to these false teachings in more detail in chapter 13.

trinal formation and refinement in the early Seventh-day Adventist Church rested squarely on the normative platform of Scripture.

So far in this chapter I have analyzed Ellen White's authority in terms of the canon, religious authority, and doctrine. Now I will address the "dual authorities" issue in terms of Fundamental Beliefs 1 and 18.

The meaning of Fundamental Beliefs 1 and 18

In promoting the idea that Seventh-day Adventists have two equal authorities, some critics have argued that changes made in 1980 to the wording of two Seventh-day Adventist fundamental beliefs have elevated Ellen White's authority status from what it was before that time. The argument runs thus:

> The wording of the Fundamental Belief concerning the Holy Scriptures was changed from ". . . an all-sufficient revelation of His will to men and are the only unerring rule of faith and practice," to ". . . are the infallible revelation of His will and the authoritative revealer of doctrine. . . ." The wording of the Fundamental Belief concerning the Spirit of Prophecy was changed from ". . . this gift was manifested in the life and ministry of Ellen White" to "This gift was manifested in the ministry of Ellen White. As the Lord's messenger, her writings are a continuing and authoritative source of truth. . . ." It is evident that these revisions to the Fundamental Beliefs have elevated the writings of Ellen White to an authoritative status comparable to that of the Bible, which is no longer the "all-sufficient" and the "only unerring" rule of faith and practice.[73]

The weakness of this argument is evident from the facts. First, Seventh-day Adventists have repeatedly and officially affirmed their belief in Ellen White's prophetic gift over the years, recognizing her writings as having authority for the church. As already shown in this chapter, however, they have never officially viewed her authority as equal with that of the Bible. Second, the change in the two Fundamental Beliefs under consideration at the 1980 General Conference only provided *greater clarity* regarding what Seventh-day Adventists have always believed about the Bible and Ellen White's prophetic ministry. Third, while the wording in Fundamental Belief 18—that Ellen White's writings are a "continuing and authoritative source of truth"—does not mean these writings are on the same level of authority as the Bible, it does mean Seventh-day Adventists believe that God was speaking through Ellen G. White as a postcanonical prophet and her voice should be heeded by the church just as the noncanonical prophetic voices were heeded during biblical times. This in no way compromises the "all-sufficient" nature of Scripture.

What most critics don't recognize, or refuse to acknowledge, is the church's *clarification* of the changes in Fundamental Beliefs 1 and 18 two years after the 1980 changes. A document titled "The Seventh-day Adventist Church's Understanding of Ellen White's Authority" was published in 1982 that presents the church's stand on the relationship of Ellen White's writings to the Bible. It articulates with clarity what the wording of Fundamental Beliefs 1 and 18 means. Because of this document's importance, I have quoted it in its entirety:

> In response to requests, an ad hoc committee of the General conference prepared a preliminary statement on the relationship of the writings of Ellen G. White to the Bible. The statement was published in the July 15 [1982] *Adventist Review* and August [1982] issue of *Ministry* with an invitation to readers to respond to it. Suggestions from readers and from several groups have led to a refinement of the statement to its present form. Although it is not a voted statement, we believe that the worldwide participation in its development makes it a reflection of the views of the church on the topic it addresses.

Biblical Research Institute.

In the Statement of Fundamental Beliefs voted by the General Conference of Seventh-day Adventists at Dallas in April, 1980, the Preamble states: "Seventh-day Adventists accept the Bible as their only creed and hold certain fundamental beliefs to be the teaching of the Holy Scriptures." Paragraph one reflects the church's understanding of the inspiration and authority of the Scriptures, while paragraph eighteen reflects the church's understanding of the writings of Ellen White in relation to the Scriptures. These paragraphs read as follows:

1. The Holy Scriptures

The Holy Scriptures, Old and New Testaments, are the written Word of God, given by divine inspiration through holy men of God who spoke and wrote as they were moved by the Holy Spirit. In this Word, God has committed to man the knowledge necessary for salvation. The Holy Scriptures are the infallible revelation of His will. They are the standard of character, the test of experience, the authoritative revealer of doctrines, and the trustworthy record of God's acts in history. Support is found in these Bible passages: 2 Peter 1:20, 21; 2 Timothy 3:16, 17; Psalm 119:105; Proverbs 30:5, 6; Isaiah 8:20; John

17:17; 1 Thessalonians 2:13; Hebrews 4:12.

18. The Gift of Prophecy

One of the gifts of the Holy Spirit is prophecy. This gift is an identifying mark of the remnant church and was manifested in the ministry of Ellen G. White—as the Lord's messenger. Her writings are a continuing and authoritative source of truth which provide for the church comfort, guidance, instruction, and correction. They also make clear that the Bible is the standard by which all teaching and experience must be tested. Support is found in these Bible passages: Joel 2:28, 29; Acts 2:14–21; Hebrews 1:1–3; Revelation 12:17; Revelation 19:10.

The following affirmations and denials speak to the issues which have been raised about the inspiration and authority of the Ellen White writings and their relation to the Bible. These clarifications should be taken as a whole. They are an attempt to express the present understanding of Seventh-day Adventists. They are not to be construed as a substitute for, or a part of, the two doctrinal statements quoted above.

AFFIRMATIONS

1. We believe that Scripture is the divinely revealed word of God and is inspired by the Holy Spirit.
2. We believe that the canon of Scripture is composed only of the sixty-six books of the Old and New Testaments.
3. We believe that Scripture is the foundation of faith and the final authority in all matters of doctrine and practice.
4. We believe that Scripture is the Word of God in human language.
5. We believe that Scripture teaches that the gift of prophecy will be manifest in the Christian church after New Testament times.
6. We believe that the ministry and writings of Ellen White were a manifestation of the gift of prophecy.
7. We believe that Ellen White was inspired by the Holy Spirit and that her writings, the product of that inspiration, are applicable and authoritative, especially to Seventh-day Adventists.
8. We believe that the purposes of the Ellen White writings include guidance in understanding the teaching of Scripture and application of these teachings, with prophetic urgency, to the spiritual and moral life.
9. We believe that the acceptance of the prophetic gift of Ellen White is important to the nurture and unity of the Seventh-day Adventist Church.

10. We believe that Ellen White's use of literary sources and assistants finds parallels in some of the writings of the Bible.

DENIALS
1. We do not believe that the quality or degree of inspiration in the writings of Ellen White is different from that of Scripture.
2. We do not believe that the writings of Ellen White are an addition to the canon of Sacred Scripture.
3. We do not believe that the writings of Ellen White function as the foundation and final authority of Christian faith as does Scripture.
4. We do not believe that the writings of Ellen White may be used as the basis of doctrine.
5. We do not believe that the study of the writings of Ellen White may be used to replace the study of Scripture.
6. We do not believe that Scripture can be understood only through the writings of Ellen White.
7. We do not believe that the writings of Ellen White exhaust the meaning of Scripture.
8. We do not believe that the writings of Ellen White are essential for the proclamation of the truths of Scripture to society at large.
9. We do not believe that the writings of Ellen White are the product of mere Christian piety.
10. We do not believe that Ellen White's use of literary sources and assistants negates the inspiration of her writings.

We conclude, therefore, that a correct understanding of the inspiration and authority of the writings of Ellen White will avoid two extremes: (1) regarding these writings as functioning on a canonical level identical with Scripture, or (2) considering them as ordinary Christian literature.[74]

Yes, in a sense, Seventh-day Adventists have dual authorities. But one is subordinate to the other, deriving its authority from the other. Ellen White's prophetic authority is thus subject to limits because of its relationship to the Bible. Her prophetic gift is postcanonical and functions as a finger pointing back to the Bible as the highest source of authority for Christian life and doctrine.

Conclusion

On August 13, 1888, D. M. Canright penned the introduction to the first edition of *Seventh-day Adventism Renounced*.[75] In this book he claimed that the Adventists have "another Bible," and "our old Bible" must now be read "in the light of this new Bible."[76] It is not without significance that eight days before Canright penned this introduction, Ellen White wrote a letter to all the church leaders who would attend the upcoming General Conference session in the fall. In this letter, considered an important statement relating to the upcoming 1888 Minneapolis General Conference Session,[77] she appealed to the "brethren" to "search the Scriptures carefully to see what is truth." Let the Bible "speak for itself, let it be its own interpreter, and the truth will shine like precious gems amid the rubbish." Lifting up the Bible to her readers, she exclaimed: "The Word of God is the great detector of error; to it we believe everything must be brought. The Bible must be our standard for every doctrine and preaching." It "is divine authority which is supreme in matters of faith."[78]

Either Canright was totally out of touch with the *real* Ellen White or he refused to acknowledge that she exalted the Bible above her writings and considered it "supreme in matters of faith." It is obvious that he was grossly mistaken on the relationship of Ellen White to the Bible, just as many detractors are today.

One of the arguments critics use to justify discarding Ellen White's inspiration and authority is the so-called gross error in her writings. They cite sentences and paragraphs that seem to contain odd sayings and unbiblical teachings. The next two chapters will address the important issue of the correct interpretation of Ellen White's writings.

Chapter Summary

1. Critics believe Ellen White's claim that the Bible is the final source of authority is a "pseudo claim." By making direct and indirect claims to the authoritative nature of her writings, they argue, "Ellen White tactfully attributed to her writings an aura of authority."

2. Consequently, Seventh-day Adventists violate the Reformation principle of *sola scriptura* by having dual authorities—the Bible and Ellen White's writings.

3. In their arguments against Ellen White, critics make the following assumption: if Ellen White's writings are inspired like the Bible writers', her authority equals that of the Bible writers and therefore is on the same level as Scripture.

4. A valid response to the charge of "dual authorities" requires an examination of four issues.
    a. First, the relationship of Ellen White's prophetic gift to the Bible canon:

Chapter Summary

i. The term *canon* means a rule or standard, and was applied to the Christian Scriptures—the standard by which all other religious writings were measured or tested.

ii. The canon of Scripture, then, is the collection of biblical books—Genesis to Revelation—that are divinely inspired and therefore authoritative and normative. Christians consider the biblical canon to be all-sufficient and closed in the sense that nothing can be added to it.

iii. The Bible canon is composed of sixty-six books written by at least forty authors over a period of approximately fifteen hundred years. The authors who wrote the Bible in the canon under divine inspiration are canonical or writing prophets.

iv. The Bible also speaks of a group of prophets who didn't write any books of the canon. They're called noncanonical prophets. Because Scripture indicates no degrees of inspiration, the messages of these prophets were no less inspired than those of the canonical prophets.

v. With regard to the authority of these noncanonical prophets, however, *the same inspiration does not mean the same canonical authority.*

vi. A helpful construct for understanding the difference in authority between the noncanonical prophets and the canonical writings is *scope* and *function.* As to *scope,* the noncanonical prophet's authority covered a shorter time span and targeted only specific individuals or communities. As to *function,* the noncanonical prophet's messages were to amplify, intensify, clarify, and apply the canonical writings—never to add new doctrinal teachings.

vii. A good example of a noncanonical prophet is the prophetess Huldah, to whom King Josiah turned instead of the contemporary prophet Jeremiah (whose writings would later become part of the canon). Huldah's message to Josiah simply reinforced the essential message of the Scripture at hand—namely, punishment for impenitence and reward for obedience. Thus, her revelation brought out no new *doctrinal* truth.

viii. In contrast to the messages of the noncanonical prophets, the

Chapter Summary

canonical writings had no limitations in scope and authority. That is, the scope of authority in the canonical Scriptures remained timeless and universal; they speak to all generations of human history. And they function as the authoritative, infallible revelation of God's will to humankind and still are "profitable for doctrine, for reproof, for correction, for instruction in righteousness" (2 Tim. 3:16, NKJV).

ix. Scripture clearly teaches the continuation of the gifts of the Holy Spirit until the second coming of Christ (Joel 2:28–32; Malachi 4:5, 6; Matt. 24:11, 24; Eph. 4:13; Revelation 12:17; 19:10; 22:8, 9).

x. In 1 Thessalonians 5:19–21, Paul gave the Thessalonian believers timeless counsel on how to address apparent manifestations of the prophetic gift. Whenever there are claims that the gift of prophecy has been manifested itself, it should be "put to the test," carefully evaluated, and proved to be good or evil.

xi. The genuine manifestation of the prophetic gift after the closing of the canon doesn't compromise or challenge the authority of the canon. Rather, genuine postcanonical prophecy submits itself to be tested and evaluated by the canon. It always harmonizes with the canon, and, like the noncanonical prophets, never adds new doctrine or truth to the previous revelation.

xii. Since Christ's life on earth and the apostolic interpretation of it provide the ultimate revelation of God, no function of the prophetic gift subsequent to the writing of the New Testament can equal, supersede, or be added to its unique witness. Rather, all claims to the prophetic gift must be tested by the Scriptures and so are always subject to them.

xiii. Seventh-day Adventists believe Ellen White's writings relate to the Bible in this way. She was a postcanonical prophet who posed no threat to the integrity of the Scriptural canon.

xiv. Like the noncanonical prophets, her inspiration was the same as the canonical prophets, but her authority was not the same as the canon's authority.

b. Second, Ellen White's place in the pattern of religious authority:

Chapter Summary

i. An understanding of Ellen White's place in the pattern of religious authority will clarify the limitations of her prophet scope and function.

ii. Evangelical theologian Bernard Ramm provided a helpful discussion on religious authority in his significant book *The Pattern of Religious Authority*. Therein he gave a taxonomy of the kinds of authority related to God's revelatory pattern.

iii. First there is *imperial authority,* the kind of authority that stands at the top of the hierarchy. As Creator, Sustainer, and Owner of everything, God has imperial authority—He is the Source and center of all authority (Ps. 24:1, 2). God has expressed His authority through His self-revelation.

iv. Second is *delegated authority*—the authority to act, to compel, to have access in virtue of rights granted by imperial authority. Such authority is derived from and justified by its origin from imperial authority. The prophets and apostles showed by their visions, dreams, and teaching that they spoke for God, that He had delegated authority to them. The canonical writings of these prophets and apostles also have delegated authority.

v. Third is *veracious authority*—"that authority possessed by men, books, or principles which either possess truth or aid in the determination of truth."

vi. The Bible, as the authoritative, infallible revelation of God's will, derives its *veracious authority* from the *delegated authority* of the apostles and prophets who, in turn, expressed the *imperial authority* of God.

vii. A fourth kind of authority important to this discussion is *illumination authority,* or what some Adventists refer to as pastoral authority. This is the inward work of the Holy Spirit to illuminate the mind of people who read the Scriptures, bringing understanding and obedience.

viii. The illumination that the Holy Spirit provides believers shouldn't be confused with the revelation-inspiration—delegated and veracious authority—given only to the prophets.

ix. The fifth and final kind of authority relevant to this discussion is *circumscribed prophetic authority.* This is prophetic authority that is subject to limits, and it applies *only* to the noncanonical and postcanonical prophets.

Chapter Summary

x. Seventh-day Adventists believe that as a postcanonical prophet, Ellen White had both delegated and veracious revelation-inspiration authority, but that this prophetic authority was circumscribed. Ellen White possessed both delegated and veracious authority, but not to the same degree as the canon of Scripture.

xi. Scripture gave Ellen White's prophetic gift the framework for her work.

xii. Thus, she has delegated authority from the Bible because it was the basis for her visions and appeals. If her writings didn't exist, the Bible would still stand. But if the Bible were taken away, Ellen White's writings would cease to function. Her role was to point back to the Bible, so if the Bible no longer existed, her role would be meaningless.

xiii. As a person with revealed-inspired veracious authority, Ellen White spoke truth, and this truth should be obeyed. But, as in the case of Huldah (2 Chronicles 34), this truth was an inspired *application* of Bible teaching. Mrs. White experienced prophetic visions that provided guidance to the church in specific circumstances, but none of these visions replaced the Bible as the final rule of faith and practice for Christians.

xiv. Like the noncanonical prophets, Ellen White's authority was limited in its scope and function.

xv. Her scope was limited to the specific audience to which she ministered—Seventh-day Adventists, and to the period of her ministry—the end times.

xvi. Conversely to these scope limitations, the Bible possesses no time or audience boundaries and has been relevant to every generation since the closing of the canon, including the present one.

xvii. The other limitation of Ellen White's prophetic ministry was that she functioned as a postcanonical prophet. As shown above, the relationship to the Bible that the postcanonical prophetic gift held is intrinsically related to the chronological relationship of that gift to the Bible. *This concept is the key to understanding*

Chapter Summary *the relationship of Ellen White's writings to the Bible.* No function of the prophetic gift *subsequent* to the New Testament can equal, supersede, or be an addition to its unique witness.

xviii. Ellen White's writings, therefore, *cannot be on the same level with the Bible's authority,* even though her inspiration is qualitatively the same. Equal inspiration doesn't mean equal canonical authority. All manifestations of the prophetic gift *after* the closing of the canon, although originating from genuine revelation-inspiration, do not serve as a new rule of faith or add any new doctrine to the canon. Rather, they must submit to it for testing and exalt it as the final authority in all matters of faith and practice.

xix. Such was the nature of Ellen White's prophetic ministry—so in no sense do her writings violate the *sola scriptura* principle of "the Bible and the Bible alone."

xx. While the canon of Scripture has the highest authority and Mrs. White's postcanonical writings a lesser authority, believers must accord them both the same obedience.

xxi. In sum, Seventh-day Adventists believe that in relationship to the closed canon of Scripture, Ellen White held circumscribed prophetic authority. She was a "lesser light to lead men and women to the greater light" of Scripture.

c. Third, Ellen White's authority in doctrinal development:

i. Two examples in Adventist history illustrate that Ellen White's revelation-inspiration experience was qualitatively the same as that of the Bible writers, but her prophetic authority was subservient to the Bible.

ii. The first example is the role of her visions in early doctrinal formation. Ellen White identified extended Bible study, prayer, and the direct intervention of the Holy Spirit as the key factors that led the Adventist pioneers to a knowledge of Bible doctrine.

iii. While it cannot be denied that the visions were a catalyst in this early doctrinal formation, in the end, the Bible was the sole source of the doctrines. Not a single doctrine of the early Adventists—Sabbath, sanctuary judgment, conditional immortali-

Authority, Part 2: Dual Authorities

Chapter Summary

ty, Second Coming, spiritual gifts, etc.—was derived from a vision of Ellen White.

iv. The second example is found in the way Ellen White dealt with the case of Albion F. Ballenger, an Adventist minister who rejected the church's sanctuary doctrine.

v. Ellen White spoke pointedly on Ballenger's views regarding the sanctuary and appealed to the prophetic confirmation given her of the movement's earlier biblical interpretations, declaring that Ballenger was misapplying the Scriptures.

vi. Dale Ratzlaff cites one of these statements about Ballenger in his book *Truth About Adventist "Truth"* and used it to support his thesis that Ellen White placed her visions and testimonies above the witness of Scripture.

vii. In the context of the entire document, however, Ellen White affirmed the importance of the Word of God. She appealed to the wealth of Bible study over the previous fifty years that confirmed the sanctuary message.

viii. While it cannot be denied that Ellen White appealed to her prophetic authority in the Ballenger crisis, neither can it be denied that she appealed to previous biblical studies as evidence for the sanctuary judgment doctrine. Her prophetic opposition to Ballenger's position was based on her understanding that the biblical evidence had already been established, as demonstrated by what had been published during the previous fifty years in Adventist periodicals. All she needed to do was assert the leading of the Holy Spirit in establishing the "passing of the time in 1844" and call for the reprinting of all those articles that contained the biblical evidence.

ix. In this light, her statements don't threaten the witness of Scripture or violate the Protestant principle of "the Bible and the Bible alone."

x. What value does Ellen White have for Adventists in relation to doctrinal belief? First of all, she functioned as a corrective authority to the Adventist pioneers in the sense that she spoke authoritatively against heretical teaching.

xi. Second, she functioned as an authority regarding the theological

Chapter Summary

framework (worldview) of Seventh-day Adventist beliefs. As Luther, Calvin, and Wesley each provided the theological framework for their various movements, so through Ellen White's writings, God provided the theological framework for the Adventist worldview.

    xii. In doctrinal formation, she functioned like a compass that pointed the Adventist pioneers toward biblical truth. The process of doctrinal formation and refinement followed by the early Seventh-day Adventists rested squarely on the normative platform of Scripture.

  d. Fourth, the meaning of Fundamental Beliefs 1 and 18:

    i. In 1982 the important document "The Seventh-day Adventist Church's Understanding of Ellen White's Authority" (accessible online) was published in the *Review and Herald*.

    ii. This document clarifies what Seventh-day Adventists believe with regard to the relationship between Fundamental Belief 1 (the Bible) and Fundamental Belief 18 (the gift of prophecy), which states that Ellen White's writings are "a continuing and authoritative source of truth."

    iii. Most critics never acknowledge the existence of this document.

    iv. The document has ten affirmations and ten denials regarding Ellen White's prophetic ministry that provided clarity on the relationship of her writings to the Bible.

    v. The document concludes that a correct understanding of the inspiration and authority of the writings of Ellen White will avoid two extremes: that of regarding her writings as functioning on a level identical with Scripture or that of considering them as ordinary Christian literature.

    vi. This position represents the official position of the church.

5. In a sense, Seventh-day Adventists have two authorities. But one is subordinate to the other, deriving its authority from the other. Thus, because of the relationship Ellen White's prophetic authority to the Bible, it is subject to limits. Her prophetic gift is postcanonical and functions as a finger pointing back to the Bible as the highest source of authority for Christian life and doctrine.

CHAPTER 9

Interpretation, Part 1: Correct Principles

By the time of her death in 1915, Ellen White had produced more than one hundred thousand pages of written material. With such a voluminous body of writings that were penned during an era (1845–1915) far removed from our twenty-first-century cyberspace world, correct principles of interpretation are essential to understanding her message. And it is here where both her critics and many of her supporters miss the boat. They fail to read Ellen White's writings in their original historical and literary contexts and thus give her a "wax nose" that can be "turned this way, and then that way, and then this way again."[1]

This chapter will address the issue of interpretation in the context of the critics' claim that Ellen White's writings contain many "questionable, unbiblical, or even heretical statements."[2] Since this claim is based on interpretations of these statements, the question should be asked, Are the critics of Ellen White applying *correct principles* of interpretation in their evaluation of her writings? If so, then they are right and Adventist apologists are wrong. But if they are twisting her statements and giving them a meaning contrary to the context, then they are presenting falsehoods.

Principles of interpretation

Hermeneutics is the science and art of interpreting written texts, especially in the areas of literature, law, and religion. Originating from the Greek word *hermeneuō* (to speak plainly, explain, or translate), the term *hermeneutics* took on the meaning of interpretation—principles for obtaining the meaning of a written document.[3] This understanding of the term has been especially important in the discipline of biblical interpretation.[4] Hermeneutics asks what authors mean by what they say. It thus guards the rights of authors and their intended meanings.⁵ An author has the right to be understood, and it is unfair when an interpreter deliberately gives a meaning to a document foreign to the author's intention. When we speak of hermeneutics in relationship to Ellen White, we are speaking about a method of interpreting her writings and guarding the meaning she originally intended.

In recent years, Adventist scholars have pulled together methods and principles of correct interpretation from the discipline of hermeneutics and applied them to the study of Ellen White's writings.⁶ The result is a set of helpful guidelines, such as George Knight's *Reading Ellen White*.⁷ Like any other writer of the nineteenth century, Ellen White has the right to be heard in light of the original context in which she wrote, and it is unfair to her as an author for anyone—friend or foe—to give a meaning to her writings contrary to her original intention. A correct hermeneutic will allow her true voice to be heard. And for those who believe Ellen White's inspiration to be authentic, hearing and understanding her true voice is extremely important.

The principles for interpretation of postcanonical writings will be similar to the principles for interpreting the canon of Scripture itself. Consequently, the vital principles of minding the literary and historical contexts are at the heart of correct interpretation. In this light, Adventist scholars have advocated the following hermeneutical guidelines as the means to understanding the intended meaning in Ellen White's writings:

- Study the Bible first, then go to Ellen White's writings.
- Study all available information on a given topic.
- Study each statement in its immediate and larger literary context.
- Study each statement in its historical context.
- Discover the underlying principles.
- Stay balanced, avoiding extreme interpretations.
- Remember that inspiration is not verbal dictation.
- Maintain a healthy, spiritual mind-set.

Much has been said about each of these guidelines and others, and scholars have supplied numerous helpful illustrations from Adventist history and Ellen White's writings.⁸ This chapter will focus on the guidelines associated with the literary and historical contexts. These two vital principles of hermeneutics are the ones most violated by those who seek to discredit Ellen White.

Literary context

Being "taken out of context" is a frustrating experience. Politicians and public leaders frequently complain of being misquoted by an opponent, and many family quarrels become heated because someone gives words a different slant or emphasis than the original context would justify. The same thing happens in written communication. Misunderstandings occur when people read only part of what was written and base their understanding on that partial reading. This is especially true of the Bible. Take, for example, the statement "there is no God." Because the Bible contains this statement, someone might assert that it endorses atheism. But when the statement is read in its literary context, the original intention is understood: "The fool says in his heart, 'There is no God.' They are corrupt, their deeds are vile; there is no one who does good" (Psalm 14:1, NIV; emphasis added). Clearly, then, wrenching biblical texts from their contexts distorts their intended meaning.[9] The same is true with the writings of Ellen White—or any other author, for that matter, inspired or not.

In the Ellen White corpus, the literary context includes the paragraphs, pages, documents, and books surrounding a particular statement. That is, "the context of a sentence is its paragraph, the context of a paragraph is the series of paragraphs that precede it and follow it."[10] In the case of a letter, manuscript, or published article, one must look at a sentence or paragraph in light of the surrounding paragraphs, and then in light of the entire document. In the case of a book, one must view the statement in light of the surrounding paragraphs and pages in a chapter, and eventually in light of the entire book. Regarding the larger context, every statement should be viewed in light of the Conflict of the Ages series. These five volumes—*Patriarchs and Prophets, Prophets and Kings, The Desire of Ages, The Acts of the Apostles,* and *The Great Controversy*—provide the theological framework for Ellen White's writings. They reflect her most mature theological thought, and thus readers should understand them well and consider their content carefully when they are interpreting themes that appear earlier in her writings.[11]

The following figure sets forth the interrelatedness of the various aspects of the literary context in Ellen White's writings:

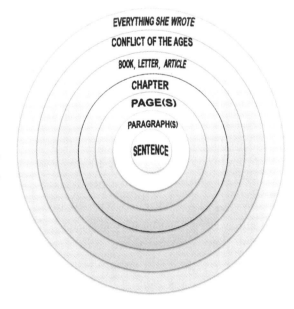

Figure 5: **Circles of Context for Interpreting Ellen White's Writings**

As shown in the "Circles of Context" illustration, a sentence must be understood in the context of the paragraph that contains it, and then in the context of the surrounding paragraphs, which must be understood in the context of the page or pages in the chapter, which must be understood in the context of the entire book, letter, or article, which must be understood in the context of the Conflict of the Ages series, and ultimately, must be understood in the context of everything Ellen White wrote. The concentric circles show the interconnectedness of each component of the literary context. *The point is that any interpretation of a sentence or paragraph that violates any of the other circles is not likely to be correct.*

Another way to put it is that taking a statement made by Ellen White out of its context violates her "flow of thought." Ellen White's flow of thought, like that of any organized writer, was a series of related ideas she organized to communicate a specific concept. This communication involved a logical flow in which one thought led naturally to the next. In this way she communicated like most people communicate, with a series of selected ideas, all linked together in a logical pattern. Thus, each sentence she wrote must be understood in light of the other ideas expressed in the context, which is her train of thought.[12]

Ellen White was very aware of the issue of context. On several occasions she commented on the way her writings were taken out of context:

> Many men take the testimonies the Lord has given, and apply them as they suppose they should be applied, picking out a sentence here and there, taking it from its proper connection, and applying it according to their idea. Thus poor souls become bewildered, when could they read in order all that has been given, they would see the true application, and would not become confused. Much that purports to be a message from Sister White, serves the purpose of misrepresenting Sister White, making her testify in favor of things that are not in accordance with her mind or judgment.[13]

In the same vein, she wrote, "Those who are not walking in the light of the message may gather up statements from my writings that happen to please them, and that agree with their human judgment, and by separating these statements from their connection and placing them beside human reasonings, make it appear that my writings uphold that which they condemn."[14]

In both of these statements she uses the word *connection,* which carries the same meaning as the word *context.* Thus, Ellen White was sensitive to the way her writings were taken out of context by her fol-

Interpretation, Part 1: Correct Principles

lowers. At one point she remarked in frustration, "What I might say in private conversations would be so repeated as to make it mean exactly opposite to what it would have meant had the hearers been sanctified in mind and spirit. I am afraid to speak even to my friends; for afterwards I hear, Sister White said this, or, Sister White said that. My words are so wrested and misinterpreted that I am coming to the conclusion that the Lord desires me to keep out of large assemblies and refuse private interviews."[15]

Dale Ratzlaff's book *Truth About Adventist "Truth"* contains a contemporary example of the citing of one of Ellen White's sentences without its context so that it becomes what Ratzlaff calls one of her "questionable, unbiblical, or even heretical statements." Ratzlaff quotes a line from *The Desire of Ages* that says "Jesus had *older* brothers" (emphasis Ratzlaff's).[16] Notice how he italicized the word "older," which could leave a reader with the impression that Ellen White believed Mary had given birth to children before she bore Jesus. This idea, if that is what Ratzlaff means by his emphasis, destroys the virgin birth and would be considered heretical by most evangelical Christians, the target audience of the book. Although Ratzlaff gives, in a footnote, the page number of the sentence,[17] he doesn't give the context of the sentence quoted, leaving it open for misunderstanding.

On the previous page in *The Desire of Ages,* Ellen White clearly states that these "older" brothers of Jesus were called "the sons of Joseph," indicating she espoused the position that Jesus' older brothers were children from a previous marriage of Joseph's.[18] When we look at the larger context, the whole book, we find that she clearly affirms the virgin birth. She titled the first chapter " 'God With Us,' " which is a reference to Isaiah 7:14, the text that predicted the virgin birth. She also cites this same text in its entirety in the chapter "The Coming of a Deliverer" in *Prophets and Kings,* making clear her belief in the virgin birth.[19] Thus, Ellen White believed Mary was still a virgin when Jesus was born, just as Scripture teaches.[20]

Another statement that critics frequently use against Ellen White is one that says "The man Christ Jesus was not the Lord God Almighty."[21] This statement is perhaps the one most frequently quoted by those who want to prove that Ellen White didn't embrace the full deity of Jesus Christ. The immediate literary context of this statement, however—the paragraph in which it is found—shows at once the fallacious nature of this claim.

> Christ left His position in the heavenly courts, and came to this earth to live the life of human beings. This sacrifice He made in order to show that Satan's charge against God is false—[to show] that it is possible

for man to obey the laws of God's kingdom. Equal with the Father, honored and adored by the angels, in our behalf Christ humbled Himself, and came to this earth to live a life of lowliness and poverty—to be a man of sorrows and acquainted with grief. Yet the stamp of divinity was upon His humanity. He came as a divine Teacher, to uplift human beings, to increase their physical, mental, and spiritual efficiency.

There is no one who can explain the mystery of the incarnation of Christ. Yet we know that He came to this earth and lived as a man among men. *The man Christ Jesus was not the Lord God Almighty, yet Christ and the Father are one.* The Deity did not sink under the agonizing torture of Calvary, yet it is nonetheless true that "God so loved the world, that he gave his only begotten Son, that whosoever believeth in him should not perish, but have everlasting life" [emphasis added].[22]

It becomes obvious, upon a careful reading of this paragraph, that Ellen White is explaining the distinction between God the Father ("the Lord God Almighty") and God the Son ("the man Christ Jesus"). She is in no way diminishing the divinity of Jesus Christ.[23] Her writing is careful: "There is no one who can explain the mystery of the incarnation of Christ. Yet we know that He came to this earth and lived as a man among men." Then comes the statement attempting to explain the unexplainable "mystery of the incarnation": "The man Christ Jesus was not the Lord God Almighty, yet Christ and the Father are one." Notice that critics only cite part of the sentence and leave the rest out. The conjunctive adverb "yet," which begins the latter clause, joins the two contrasting ideas. As such, the two clauses form a unit and should not be separated, which critics often do.

Ellen White is communicating the idea that while Jesus Christ and His Father are distinct in their Persons, they are still One. In the larger literary context of her writings, she wrote: "The Lord Jesus Christ, the divine Son of God, existed from eternity, a distinct person, yet one with the Father."[24] Here she attempts to explain this distinction after the incarnation, without undermining the truth that Christ and the Father are still of "one substance, possessing the same attributes."[25] The "mystery of the incarnation" cannot be fully explained in human words, as she herself acknowledges. It is clear, then, that people who say that the line "the man Christ Jesus was not the Lord God Almighty" shows Ellen White didn't teach Jesus' full divinity have wrenched those words from their literary context—thus revealing that they have no concern for interpreting her writings accurately.

Historical context

Ellen White lived most of her life during the latter half of the nineteenth century. This general historical period, with its rapidly changing religious, political, and cultural landscape, was the historical context of her day-to-day life experience.[26] She lived through such political events as the war with Mexico (1846–1848), the Civil War (1861–1865), reconstruction after the Civil War (1865–1877), the Spanish-American War (1898), and the first decade and a half of a new century.[27] She also observed and experienced the growth of spiritualism, the expansion of evangelicalism, the initiation of numerous social reforms, and the perpetuation of racial tensions.[28] This rich and varied background cannot be ignored in the interpretation of her writings any more than one can ignore the historical context of first-century Palestine when interpreting the teachings of Jesus.

In the more specific historical context of the Seventh-day Adventist Church, time, place, and circumstances are the keys to unlocking the meaning of the many Ellen White statements penned during the seventy years she spent as a prophet.[29] On more than one occasion, she specified the importance of these categories for interpreting her writings. Regarding "time," she wrote in 1875, "That which may be said in truth of individuals at one time may not correctly be said of them at another time."[30] Concerning circumstances in her writings, she stated in 1904 that "circumstances alter conditions. Circumstances change the relation of things."[31] Referring to her writings in 1911, she penned: "Regarding the testimonies, nothing is ignored; nothing is cast aside; but time and place must be considered."[32] Thus, Ellen White expressed concern that her readers keep the historical context of her writings in mind.

Those who ignore the literary context of Ellen White's writings inevitably end up ignoring the historical context. Take, for example, the following statement: "Many carelessly put off blacking their boots, and shaving, until after the beginning of the Sabbath. This should not be. If any neglect to do such work on a working day, they should have respect enough for God's holy time to let their beards remain unshaven, their boots rough and brown, until the Sabbath is past."[33]

Some critics have labeled this statement as Sabbath-keeping legislation that present-day Adventists don't follow. What Seventh-day Adventist preacher today, they argue, would come to church unshaven? This criticism is a classic case of overlooking the historical setting. In 1882, when this statement was penned, shaving consumed much more time than it does today. Men had to mix their own soap lather and sharpen their hand-held straight razors on leather strops. Today, because of disposable blades and canned lather, shaving is a simple process, taking only a few minutes at most. Would Ellen White counsel men never to shave on the Sabbath if she were around today? No. The timeless principle behind this statement is to avoid any unnecessary labor that would interfere with the spirit of the Sabbath. In applying this principle, most Adventist men, depending on their particular culture, see no problem with shaving on the Sabbath before church. Many, however, still polish their shoes or boots preparatory to the Sabbath hours.[34]

Two other historically conditioned statements are often incorrectly applied to the present day. Regarding the wearing of wigs, Ellen White stated in 1871 that "many have lost their reason, and become hopelessly insane." In the context of today's comfortable wigs, this statement sounds crazy and is certainly exploited by critics. Dale Ratzlaff cites it void of its historical context in his *Truth About Adventist "Truth"* as an example of a "questionable" Ellen White statement.[35]

However, present-day wigs are quite different from those of the nineteenth century. Those wigs were "monstrous bunches of curled hair, cotton, seagrass, wool, Spanish moss, and other multitudinous abominations." Some were made from "jute switches"—dark, fibrous bark often infested with "jute bugs." These small insects burrowed under the scalp and caused intense suffering and sometimes death. The press reported stories of people experiencing a level of insanity due to the suffering. Consequently, it's hardly a wonder that Ellen White warned against the dangers of wigs in her day. The principle behind this counsel involved not bowing to fashion at the expense of good health.[36]

The other statement that critics often exploit concerns cosmetics. "Many are ignorantly injuring their health and endangering their life by using cosmetics," Ellen White wrote in 1871. "Many lives have been sacrificed by this means alone." Critics exclaim that we rarely hear of any deaths caused by the wearing of cosmetics. Although this may be true today, in 1871, when Ellen White wrote this statement, "enameling" was the latest cosmetic fad. Enameling was "nothing less than painting the face with lead paint, and for this purpose are used the poisonous salts of lead." Another deadly concoction was vermilion, made from mercuric sulfide. "In such an environment, it is not surprising that Ellen White should warn her readers to the real life and health threats posed by such products."[37]

Conclusion

The above examples show that understanding the literary and historical contexts of Ellen White's writings is essential for understanding her message. Many critics obviously have no use for such contexts, because taking them into account stops people from reading into her writings their own ideas about what she meant. Interestingly, many of these critics, who claim to be evangelical Christians, would never interpret the Bible in the same way they interpret Ellen White's writings. That is, they would never take a verse of Scripture and give it a meaning totally contrary to its obvious meaning in context. With Ellen White, though, they seem to feel they have the right to treat her writings as if they had no context. As we have seen from these few examples, this approach is a violation of the principles of hermeneutics and is unfair to Ellen White as an author. It's one thing to disagree with her regarding matters where her intent is clear—such as in the cases of the Sabbath and the investigative judgment. It is quite another thing to totally misrepresent her intent in her writings.

Chapter 10 will illustrate these interpretive principles in two statements taken out of context by detractors.

Chapter Summary

1. Both those who are critics and those who are supporters of Ellen White often fail to read her writings in their original historical and literary contexts and thus give her a "wax nose" that can be "turned this way, and then that way, and then this way again."

2. This chapter asks, Are the critics of Ellen White applying *correct principles* of interpretation in their evaluation of her writings? If so, then they are right and Adventist apologists are wrong. But if they are twisting her statements and giving them a meaning contrary to the context, then they are presenting falsehoods.

3. Hermeneutics—the science and art of interpreting written texts—asks what writers mean by what they say. It thus guards the rights of authors and their intended meanings. Those who write have the right to be understood, and it's unfair when an interpreter deliberately gives a meaning to a document foreign to the writer's intention.

4. When we speak of hermeneutics in relationship to Ellen White, we are speaking about a method of interpreting her writings and guarding the meaning she originally intended. In recent years, Adventist scholars have pulled together methods and principles of correct interpretation from the discipline of hermeneutics and applied them to the study of Ellen White's writings.

5. Like any other writer of the nineteenth-century, Ellen White has the

> **Chapter Summary**

right to be heard in light of the original context in which she wrote, and it is unfair to her as an author for anyone—friend or foe—to give a meaning to her writings contrary to her original intention. A correct hermeneutic will allow her true voice to be heard. And for those who believe Ellen White's inspiration to be authentic, hearing and understanding her true voice is extremely important.

6. The principles for interpreting postcanonical writings will be similar to those for interpreting the canon of Scripture itself.

7. George Knight, for example, proposed such a set of guidelines for interpreting Ellen White's writings in his *Reading Ellen White*.

8. At the heart of correct interpretation are the vital hermeneutical principles of taking into account the literary and historical contexts of the matter in question. These two vital principles are the ones most violated by those who seek to discredit Ellen White.

9. The literary context:

    a. In the Ellen White corpus, the literary context includes the paragraphs, pages, documents, and books surrounding a particular statement.

    b. The "Circles of Context for Interpreting Ellen White's Writings" illustration teaches that a sentence in Mrs. White's writings must be understood in the context of the paragraph in which it appears, of the surrounding paragraphs, which then must be understood in the context of the page or pages in the chapter, which must be understood in the context of the entire book, letter, or article, which must be understood in the context of the Conflict of the Ages series, and, ultimately, must be understood in the context of everything Ellen White wrote. The concentric circles show the interconnectedness of each component of the literary context. The point is that any interpretation that violates any of these circles is not likely to be true.

    c. Like any organized writer, Ellen White's flow of thought was a series of related ideas that she organized to communicate a specific concept. This meaningful communication involved a logical flow in which one thought led naturally to the next. In this way she communicated like most people communicate, with a series of selected

Interpretation, Part 1: Correct Principles

ideas, all linked together in a logical pattern. Thus each sentence she wrote must be understood in light of the other ideas expressed in the context, which is her train of thought.

Chapter Summary

d. To insert a meaning contrary to her intention is a violation of her rights as an author. Yet, this is what the critics and many supporters do to her writings.
e. Ellen White was very aware of the issue of context in her writings and spoke about it on several occasions.

10. The historical context:
    a. Ellen White lived most of her life during the latter half of the nineteenth century. This general historical period, with its rapidly changing religious, political, and cultural landscape, was the historical context of her day-to-day life experience.
    b. In the more specific historical context of the Seventh-day Adventist Church, time, place, and circumstances are the keys to unlocking the meaning of voluminous writings Ellen White produced over the seventy years of her ministry.
    c. Those who ignore the literary context of Ellen White's writings inevitably end up ignoring the historical context. Examples are plentiful in the literature of her detractors.
11. Understanding the literary and historical contexts of Ellen White's writings is essential for understanding her message. Many critics obviously have no use for such contexts, because to take them into account would stop them from reading into her writings their own ideas about what she meant.

CHAPTER 10

Interpretation, Part 2: Applying Correct Principles

As noted in the introduction, the purpose of this book is not to answer one charge after another but rather to focus on the underlying issues raised by the criticisms of Ellen White's prophetic ministry. In this chapter, however, I will use a contextual study of two Ellen White statements to answer the charges regarding them that critics often make to discredit her writings. The procedure employed here will illustrate how analysis of the literary and historical contexts of Ellen White's writings best answers the charges against her.[1]

Pestilence prophecy

Dirk Anderson and other critics often point to the following statement, penned in 1849, as a prediction that failed:[2] "What we have seen and heard of the pestilence, is but the beginning of what we shall see and hear. Soon the dead and dying will be all around us."[3] The epidemic of which she spoke took place long ago and lasted for only a short time. Was this a failed prediction?

Larger literary context: This statement appeared in *The Present Truth,* the first periodical published by James White, and is the only place in Ellen White's writings where she refers to a local pestilence. The 109 other times she used the word were in either the context of biblical times or of the end of time.[4]

Historical context: The pestilence Mrs. White referred to peaked during the summer of 1849. It was one of the three cholera epidemics that hit the United States, in 1832, 1849, and 1866.[5] This pestilence swept through Europe in 1848 and made it to the United States by April 1849, spreading suffering and death in many cites and villages. By the end of July, the epidemic was so bad in New York that "business had almost ceased: hotels were empty; trains and steamships arrived

Interpretation, Part 2: Applying Correct Principles

without passengers." Dead bodies were literally lying around the city, sometimes for days.[6]

Newspapers informed the public about this epidemic, raising people's anxiety. In response to the crisis, President Zachary Taylor declared Friday, August 3, 1849, as a day of national fasting and prayer.[7] So, when the September issue of *The Present Truth* rolled off the press, the news of the disease was certainly on the minds of its readers. Although the epidemic proportions of the cholera diminished later that fall, the disease would remain active in America until 1854, when it disappeared abruptly, as it had in 1832. It returned after the Civil War in the epidemic of 1866.[8] This is the historical setting in which Ellen White wrote the above statement.

The statement in context:

[1*] O, let us live wholly for the Lord, and show by a well ordered life and godly conversation that we have been with Jesus, and are his meek and lowly followers. We must work while the day lasts, for when the dark night of trouble and anguish comes, it will be too late to work for God. Jesus is in his Holy Temple, and will now accept our sacrifices, our prayers, and our confessions of faults and sins, and will now pardon all the transgressions of Israel, that they may be blotted out before he leaves the Sanctuary. When Jesus leaves the Sanctuary, then he that is holy and righteous, will be holy and righteous still; for all their sins will then be blotted out, and they will be sealed with the seal of the living God. But those that are unjust and filthy, will be unjust and filthy still; for then there will be no Priest in the Sanctuary to offer their sacrifices, their confessions, and their prayers before the Father's throne. Therefore, what is done to rescue souls from the coming storm of wrath, must be done before Jesus leaves the Most Holy Place of the Heavenly Sanctuary.

[2] The Lord has shown me that precious souls are starving, and dying for want of the present, sealing truth, the meat in due season; and that the swift messengers should speed on their way, and feed the flock with the present truth. I heard an Angel say, "speed the swift messengers, speed the swift messengers; for the case of every soul will soon be decided, either for Life, or for Death."

[3] I saw that those who had the means, were required to help speed those messengers, that God had called to labor in his cause, and as they went from place to place, they

---

*To facilitate the explanation that follows, I have numbered the paragraphs.

would be safe from the prevailing pestilence. But if any went that were not sent of God, they would be in danger of being cut down by the pestilence; therefore all should earnestly seek for duty, and be sure and move by the direction of the Holy Spirit.

[4] *What we have seen and heard of the pestilence, is but the beginning of what we shall see and hear. Soon the dead and dying will be all around us.* I saw that some will be so hardened, as to even make sport of the judgements of God. Then the slain of the Lord will be from one end of the earth, to the other; they will not be lamented, gathered, nor buried; but their ill savor will come up from the face of the whole earth. Those only who have the seal of the living God, will be sheltered from the storm of wrath, that will soon fall on the heads of those who have rejected the truth [emphasis added].[9]

The meaning of "soon" in this context: The fact that Ellen White believed the Second Coming was close is clear from the context. In paragraph 2, the angel is quoted as saying, "The case of every soul will soon be decided." Paragraph 4 begins with the words "What we have seen and heard of the pestilence, is but the beginning of what we shall see and hear. Soon the dead and dying will be all around us." This paragraph ends by saying that the "storm of wrath" will "soon fall on the heads of those who have rejected the truth." The repeated use of "soon" indicates that Ellen believed the end of time was near.

How soon is "soon" in this context? Does "soon" mean in the next few months? Does it mean in the next few years? Three and a half decades later, Ellen White explained what she meant by "soon" during those early years. After quoting several New Testament texts that speak of time being short (1 Cor. 7:29, 30; Rom. 13:12; Rev. 1:3; 22:6, 7), she wrote, "The angels of God in their messages to men represent time as very short. Thus it has always been presented to me. It is true that time has continued longer than we expected in the early days of this message. Our Saviour did not appear as soon as we hoped. But has the word of the Lord failed? Never! It should be remembered that the promises and threatenings of God are alike conditional."[10]

While we shouldn't apply the principle of conditional prophecy to everything a prophet says, it does find application in certain utterances, both in the Bible and in Ellen White's writings.[11] This 1849 article in *The Present Truth* is clearly one of those places. At that time Ellen White believed "soon" meant time was short and that the pestilence all around her was a sign that the final pestilence would soon begin. As the years rolled by, she understood "soon" to be conditional. Neverthe-

Interpretation, Part 2: Applying Correct Principles

less, up through the year of her death in 1915, she described the Second Coming as "near" or "soon." The fact that Christ didn't come in Ellen White's lifetime doesn't make her a prophetic failure any more than it does the apostles, who believed Christ was coming in their day.[12]

Detailed analysis of the immediate context: The first paragraph makes it abundantly clear that Ellen White believed the commencement of the final crisis was still forthcoming. "Jesus is still in his Holy Temple," she explained; the "dark night of trouble and anguish" has not come yet. The "storm of wrath" is "coming," but it will commence only when "Jesus leaves the Most Holy Place of the Heavenly Sanctuary." It is at that time, during the "storm of wrath," that the final pestilence will devastate the earth, and the "slain of the Lord will be from one end of the earth, to the other." Thus, when Mrs. White's train of thought is followed through all four paragraphs, the statement under consideration in paragraph 4 cannot mean that the local pestilence was the literal beginning of the final pestilence. *The final global pestilence won't commence until after Jesus leaves the Most Holy Place in heaven.*

Ellen White's statement in paragraph 4, "What we have seen and heard of the pestilence, is but the beginning of what we shall see and hear," *is an application of the local pestilence, rather than a prediction.* Notice that Mrs. White's language in the first clause, "What we have seen and heard," describes what she and her contemporaries had apparently "seen" (in person) and "heard" (from reading the papers or by word of mouth) concerning the cholera epidemic. In the second clause, the "but" functions as a synonym of "only." Accordingly, her statement can be paraphrased as saying, "This pestilence we have seen and heard of is *only the beginning* of what we will see and hear when Jesus leaves the Holy Temple and the storm of wrath commences."

Mark the contrast between "have seen and heard" (related to the current pestilence of 1849) and "shall see and hear" (future final pestilence). The final pestilence is to take place during the "storm of wrath" was still future. The dead lying in the streets of New York during the summer of 1849 were, therefore, only a foreshadowing ("only the beginning") of all the deaths that will take place during the final pestilence. And, as noted above, in Mrs. White's thinking at the time, this final pestilence was near, because the "storm of wrath" was near.

The "I saw" in paragraph 4 demarcates Ellen White's application of the local pestilence (see the first two sentences) from what she saw in vision regarding the final pestilence still in the future (see the remainder of the paragraph after "I saw"). Thus, when Jesus leaves the Holy Temple and the "storm of wrath" commences, some will "make sport of the judgements of God," and "the slain of the Lord will be from one end of the earth, to the other." During that time only those "who have the seal of the living God, will be sheltered from the storm of wrath," which certainly includes protection from the deadly pestilence. This all relates to the time after Jesus leaves the Holy Temple (see paragraph 1). The only specific detail about the local pestilence that Ellen saw in vision was that God's messengers would be protected from it if they were led by the Holy Spirit (see paragraph 3). Therefore, when the literary context is taken into consideration, this statement is an application rather than a prediction.

Meaning of the cholera epidemic of 1849: Was the cholera epidemic of 1849 a sign of the final pestilence that will strike the earth at the end of time? Two years prior to writing this statement, Mrs. White wrote in the context of a discussion about the final crisis, "I saw the sword, famine, pestilence, and great confusion in the land."[13] This statement certainly fits the scenario of the Olivet discourse in Luke 21:10, 11: "kingdom against kingdom [sword]" and "famines and pestilences." Thus, Ellen White understood the final crisis upon the earth to include "pestilence," and in her later writings regarding the end of time, she used this word to describe part of the devastation earth would suffer.[14]

So, what is going on in the statement about the cholera epidemic of 1849? *When Ellen White saw and experienced the pestilence—the suffering, and the death, and the fear they caused—she immediately connected it to what she had seen in vision concerning the final crisis, which included an epidemic of deaths from pestilence.* What Bible-loving Christian today who is looking for Jesus to come would deny that when the end does come and the final pestilence is unleashed on the world, "the dead and dying will be all around us" and "the slain of the Lord will be from one end of the earth to the other"? In other words, for those who believe in Ellen White's prophetic gift, this statement in its context is still relevant, because it gives a glimpse into the future regarding the nature of the final pestilence.

The critics' charges are too simplistic: In light of the above analysis of the historical and literary contexts of this statement, it is too simplistic to call Ellen White's statement about the cholera epidemic of 1849 a false prediction because the end did not come then. The death she had seen and heard about during the summer of 1849 was, in her mind, "only the beginning" of what will take place when the "storm of wrath" commences, which, according to her thinking at the time, was "soon" to occur. The "soon" has taken a lot longer than Ellen or any of us could have ever imagined. The day is yet to come, however (and it will come!), when "the dead and dying will be all around us" and "the slain of the Lord will be from one end of the earth to the other." In that day all true believers in Christ will be able to claim the promise: "I will say of the Lord, 'He is my refuge and my fortress, my God, in whom I trust.' Surely he will save you from the fowler's snare and from the deadly pestilence. He will cover you with his feathers, and under his wings you will find refuge; his faithfulness will be your shield and rampart. You will not fear the terror of night, nor the arrow that flies by day, nor the pestilence that stalks in the darkness, nor the plague that destroys at midday" (Psalm 91:2–6, NIV).

Ellen White communicated with her dead husband

In the article "Do God's Prophets Take Advice From the Dead?"[15] Sidney Cleveland alleged that Ellen White spoke with her dead husband and received guidance from him in a dream. In support of this charge, Cleveland cited a portion of Letter 17, 1881, written by Ellen White to her son Willie on September 12, 1881, five weeks after James White died. In this letter, Mrs. White described a dream about James. Cleveland claims that in this dream, "Ellen White communicated with and received advice from her dead husband, James White—even though God said communicating with the dead (necromancy) is 'detestable' to Him, and worthy of being stoned to death." He cites Isaiah 8:19, 20 and Deuteronomy 18:10–12, which condemns the practice of communicating with the dead and goes on to say, "Don't you think Ellen White should have instantly known that any communication with the dead is prohibited in Scripture—especially when she wrote widely on this topic? If Ellen White was actually inspired by God, why would she take advice from a dead person, thinking it came from the Lord?" Cleveland concludes, "The truth about Ellen White is this: she was a false prophet. There is no light in her whatsoever, because a lie cannot be made into the truth, and a false prophet cannot be made true."[16] He claims that Ellen White violated what she taught about the state of the dead—therefore, she is a false prophet, and none of her dreams or visions can be trusted.

Underlying this charge is the assumption that Ellen White believed she was actually talking with James, who had died five weeks earlier. Does Cleveland offer support for this assumption? Did Mrs. White really believe she conversed with her dead husband and then received guidance from him as this critic charges? I suggest that a careful analysis of this letter in its context will lead to a completely different conclusion.

The published portion of the letter in question:

A few days since, I was pleading with the Lord for light in regard to my duty. In the night I dreamed I was in the carriage, driving, sitting at the right hand. Father was in the carriage, seated at my left hand. He was very pale, but calm and composed. "Why Father," I exclaimed, "I am so happy to have you by my side once more! I have felt that half of me was gone. Father, I saw you die; I saw you buried. Has the Lord pitied me and let you come back to me again, and we work together as we used to?"

He looked very sad. He said, "The Lord knows what is best for you and for me. My work was very dear to me. We have made a mistake. We have responded to urgent invitations of our brethren to attend important meetings. We had not the heart to refuse. These meetings have worn us both more than we were aware. Our good brethren were gratified, but they did not realize that in these meetings we took upon us greater burdens than at our age we could safely carry. They will never know the result of this long-continued strain upon us. God would have had them bear the burdens we have carried for years. Our nervous energies have been continuously taxed, and then our brethren misjudging our motives and not realizing our burdens have weakened the action of the heart. I have made mistakes, the greatest of which was in allowing my sympathies for the people of God to lead me to take work upon me which others should have borne.

"Now, Ellen, calls will be made as they have been, desiring you to attend important meetings, as has been the case in the past. But lay this matter before God and make no response to the most earnest invitations. Your life hangs as it were upon a thread. You must have quiet rest, freedom from all excitement and from all disagreeable cares. We might have done a great deal for years with our pens, on subjects the people need that we have had light upon and can present before them, which others do not have. Thus you can work when your strength returns, as it will, and you can do far more with your pen than with your voice."

He looked at me appealingly and said, "You will not neglect these cautions, will you, Ellen? Our people will never know under what infirmities we have labored to serve them because our lives were interwoven with the progress of the work, but God knows it all. I regret that I have felt so deeply and labored unreasonably in emergencies, regardless of the laws of life and health. The Lord did not require us to carry so heavy burdens and many of our brethren so few. We ought to have gone to the Pacific Coast before, and devoted our time and energies to writing. Will you do this now? Will you, as your strength returns, take your pen and

Interpretation, Part 2: Applying Correct Principles

write out these things we have so long anticipated, and make haste slowly? There is important matter which the people need. Make this your first business. You will have to speak some to the people, but shun the responsibilities which have borne us down."

"Well," said I, "James, you are always to stay with me now and we will work together." Said he, "I stayed in Battle Creek too long. I ought to have gone to California more than one year ago. But I wanted to help the work and institutions at Battle Creek. I have made a mistake. Your heart is tender. You will be inclined to make the same mistakes I have made. Your life can be of use to the cause of God. Oh, those precious subjects the Lord would have had me bring before the people, precious jewels of light!"

I awoke. *But this dream seemed so real.* Now you can see and understand why I feel no duty to go to Battle Creek for the purpose of shouldering the responsibilities in General Conference. I have no duty to stand in General Conference. The Lord forbids me. That is enough [emphasis added].[17]

Historical context: The above description of the dream is part of a five-page letter Ellen White wrote to her son Willie on September 12, 1881 (Letter 17, 1881).

Only portions of the letter have been published.[18] Here is the historical background of this letter: James died on August 6, 1881, five weeks before. Ellen was staying with Mary, Willie's wife, at the cabin they owned in the mountains near Rollinsville, Colorado. Willie, recipient of this letter, remained in Battle Creek to work with his brother, Edson, Ellen White's other son, who was taking care of the financial affairs concerning James White's estate. G. I. Butler, General Conference president at the time, was urging Ellen to attend the General Conference session back in Battle Creek planned for November or December.

Ellen was struggling with illness and the grief of losing her husband. Thus, she was in a weakened condition physically and emotionally. She had been asking the Lord whether she should yield to Butler's request and attend the upcoming General Conference session in spite of her physical and emotional condition. On page one of this letter, before describing the dream, she relates to Willie how much she misses James and intensely feels "his loss while here in the mountains."[19]

Larger literary context: The larger literary context of Ellen White's writings shows that she believed that communicating with the dead violates Scripture and is a satanic deception. A simple search for the words "spiritualism" or "communication with the dead" on the *Ellen G. White Writings Comprehensive Research Edition*

CD-ROM shows that she was adamantly opposed to any form of communication with the dead. From the time when as a youth she first accepted the biblical doctrine of conditional immortality,[20] she consistently taught that death is a state of unconsciousness until the resurrection and that we can't communicate with the dead. Chapter 34 of *The Great Controversy,* "Can Our Dead Speak to Us?"[21] is a classic example of her rejection of belief in the immortality of the soul and that to attempt to speak with the dead is to fall to a satanic deception.

Immediate literary context: When understood in its immediate literary context, the account of this dream doesn't prove Ellen White violated in practice a teaching so basic and fundamental to her thinking. The letter itself shows that Ellen understood this conversation with James was nothing more than a dream. After relating the entire experience to Willie, she exclaimed, "But this dream seemed so real." (See the italicized sentence in the portion of the letter quoted above.) Critics completely overlook this statement, yet it is the key to correctly understanding the entire experience.

Notice the words "seemed so real." When you describe a vivid dream to someone and say, "It seemed so real," your obvious meaning is that the images in the dream had the *feel* of reality but were not reality. It was *only* a dream. In other words, it is obvious from this remark that Ellen White knew she wasn't actually conversing with her husband—in spirit form or "brought back from the grave." Furthermore, if Ellen was supposedly communicating with James in this dream, why did she feel so lonely? On the first page of this letter, before she told the dream to Willie, she remarked, "I miss Father more and more. Especially do I feel his loss while here in the mountains. I find it a very different thing being in the mountains with my husband and in the mountains without him. I am fully of the opinion that my life was so entwined or interwoven with my husband's that it is about impossible for me to be of any great account without him. . . . We have tested the mountains under most unfavorable circumstances."[22]

Based on what she told Willie, Ellen had the dream "a few days" before writing the letter. *If she communicated with her husband in this dream, why did she say in this letter that she misses him "more and more"? Why did she speak as if he were absent in her life? Why didn't this dream console Ellen?* The answer is that in her mind this was only a dream, and James was asleep in the grave, awaiting the resurrection. Naturally, she still missed him. Therefore, the charge of necromancy—consulting the spirits of the departed—doesn't find any support in this dream.

Meaning of the dream: While knowing this conversation with James was only a dream, Ellen still believed it came as

Interpretation, Part 2: Applying Correct Principles

God's answer to her prayer for guidance. When she awoke from the dream and pondered its meaning, she realized that God was conveying a message relevant to her situation in light of the recent death of her husband. As noted above, Butler's urging Ellen to attend the General Conference session and her present state of physical and emotional exhaustion were the issues behind the dream. In this letter, immediately after the section describing the dream, she wrote, "I have stood through two General Conferences to the gratification of my brethren, but ran the risk of my life. What I endured through these meetings, the sufferings of mind, the anxiety, the pain of heart, I know my good brethren knew nothing about. If they did, they would not now put me to the torture and risk to bring me to the general meeting again, and at such a time, when my heart is like a raw sore, bruised and torn. No, no, no. God is too merciful to place upon me any such burden."[23]

Both Willie and Ellen knew the Lord was telling her through this dream not to risk her health by attending the upcoming General Conference session. This is the historical circumstance behind the dream. Thus, she viewed this dream as God's answer to her prayer, relieving her from the burden of attending the General Conference session. In her mind this dream was simply God's medium of communicating His guidance. The fact that the imagery involved her deceased husband intensified the message.

Private letter: This was a private letter written to Willie. Parts of it contained, for example, personal matters, such as descriptions of Ellen's health, the selling of two horses, and the weather conditions, etc., as did many of her letters to family members. Thus, the intended reader of this letter was only her son. The White Estate chose to publish the parts of it that they felt would be beneficial to others, as they have often done with her unpublished letters over the years.

The guidance she received from the dream was intended only for her personal life, not for others. This was no "testimony" for the church. She was writing only to her son Willie, who also missed his father, and thus understood the circumstances of the letter. He knew how much she missed James. He knew that Butler was urging her to come to the General Conference session. He knew his mother was not telling him she actually spoke with his dead father. Ellen, therefore, had no need to clarify to Willie the background and nature of this dream. If this letter had been written for a larger audience, she most likely would have explained the nature and context of this dream in order to avoid any misunderstanding. But Willie needed no such explanation.

Some charge that this letter couldn't be divinely inspired because "nowhere in the Bible do we ever find a prophet receiving a revelation from God through a dead person."[24] The dream is therefore false because it finds no parallel in the Bible.

This argument fails, however, because at least in two instances, the Bible tells of God communicating truth through the imagery of talking dead people. First there's the memorable parable of the rich man and Lazarus that Jesus Himself told (Luke 16:19–31). In the story both of the main characters die, and the rich man engages Abraham—who, of course, was also dead—in conversation (vv. 24–31). The parable was obviously not teaching details about the afterlife, as some have erroneously concluded. Jesus was conveying a powerful spiritual lesson that was contained in the punch line: "If they do not hear Moses and the prophets, neither will they be persuaded though one rise from the dead" (Luke 16:31, NKJV). In other words, "not even a spectacular 'sign,' like one returning from the dead (vss. 27, 30), can change those whose hearts are set against God's Word, as the response of many to the resurrection of Jesus was to show."[25] Jesus thus used a mistaken popular belief about the afterlife, which involved the spirits of the dead talking, to teach a vital truth to His audience.

The second biblical instance of the righteous dead speaking as a means of conveying spiritual truth is found in John's description in Revelation 6:9–11 of souls before the altar. John wrote, "When He opened the fifth seal, I saw under the altar the souls of those who had been slain for the word of God and for the testimony which they held. And they cried with a loud voice, saying, 'How long, O Lord, holy and true, until You judge and avenge our blood on those who dwell on the earth?'"

According to evangelical scholar George Eldon Ladd, "The fact that John saw the souls of the martyrs under the altar has nothing to do with the state of the dead or their situation in the intermediate state; it is merely a vivid way of picturing the fact that they had been martyred in the name of God."[26] Through this vision, God conveyed to John a powerful truth of the persecuted saints crying out for justice.

Thus, as these two examples show, God used the symbolic imagery of dead people talking to communicate spiritual truth. In this light, it is certainly not unbiblical for Ellen White to receive a message from God involving the imagery of a dead person talking. Although the details are different in all three instances, the commonality is that God used the same kind of imagery to convey His message.

False charge: The literary and historical context of this letter demonstrates that the charge that Ellen White actually conversed with her dead husband and received guidance from him is completely false. She believed God conveyed a personal message to her through symbolic imagery relevant to her current situation.

It was God to whom she responded and whom she obeyed, not her dead husband! She believed that James was resting in the grave until the morning of the resurrection. In her mind, contact with him prior to that event was impossible. Furthermore, this dream imagery was within the framework of the rich and varied prophetic imagery in the Bible. We cannot limit how God communicates His will.

Conclusion

Using proof-texts from the Bible, the anti-Christian Web site Evil Bible (http://www.evilbible.com/), accuses God of all sorts of evil, such as murder, rape, slavery, and child abuse. The Skeptic's Annotated Bible (http://www.skepticsannotatedbible.com/), another anti-Christian Web site, also uses biblical proof-texts to portray supposed absurdities and contradictions in the Bible. God, these Web site editors claim, is not a God of love, but a cruel being who tells soldiers to bash babies against rocks and rip open the bellies of pregnant women with the sword (see Psalm 137:9; Hosea 13:16). These atheistic critics of the Bible who accuse it of being narrow-minded, legalistic, and cruel consistently use illegitimate proof-texting to buttress their points. While there is a legitimate use of proof-texting to teach the doctrines of the Bible, illegitimate proof-texting (misusing texts by distorting their contextual meaning and using them to "prove" teachings that those who quote them want to convey)[27] ignores the original intent of the Bible's message and skews the meaning of the texts. Christians and critics of the Bible are both guilty of this practice.

Christians, of course, rightly protest, claiming that the Web site editors have taken the proof-texts they use out of context. They rightly argue that the critics don't read the Bible fairly nor pay attention to the immediate and larger context of the verses they quote.

In a similar way, the critics of Ellen White are guilty of illegitimate proof-texting with her statements to prove their points. As we have seen in this chapter, they ignore the original literary and historical contexts of her writings and give her a "wax nose," turning it any way they choose. Ironically, while most of these critics claim to be Christians who value the Bible, they use the same strategy to discredit Ellen White as the critics at Evil Bible and The Skeptic's Annotated Bible use to denigrate the Bible. They cite her statements void of their contexts to "prove" points contrary to the statements' original intent. These are classic cases of illegitimate proof-texting, and every student of Ellen White should hold the critics who do this accountable for these misguided and unfair practices.

To misrepresent the meaning of Ellen White's writings and present to others a perspective of her words contrary to what she really taught is bearing a false witness.

Moreover, to purposefully and blatantly ignore the original contexts of her writings is a breach of Christian ethics and is patently wrong. Ultimately, those who engage in this unfair activity disqualify themselves as fair and objective interpreters of Ellen White's writings.

The fair and ethical way to assess Ellen White's writings is to look carefully for her message in its immediate and larger contexts. Just as understanding the big picture of the Bible is the key to understanding its parts, so understanding Ellen White's major interlocking themes is the key to understanding the various parts of her writings. Virtually all of Ellen White's critics have either overlooked or ignored the clarity of the big picture in the larger context of her writings, to which we turn in the next chapters.

Chapter Summary

1. This chapter answers charges critics make to discredit Mrs. White's writings based on two of her statements. It does so by presenting a contextual study of those two statements.
2. The procedure employed here illustrated how analysis of the literary and historical contexts in Ellen White's writings best answers the charges made against her.
3. Dirk Anderson and other critics often appeal to the following statement, penned in 1849, as a prediction that failed: "What we have seen and heard of the pestilence, is but the beginning of what we shall see and hear. Soon the dead and dying will be all around us." This epidemic occurred long ago and lasted for only a short time. Was this a failed prediction?
4. Analysis of this statement in its historical and literary contexts shows it is not a prediction.
    a. Historical context: The pestilence Mrs. White referred to peaked during the summer of 1849. It was one of the three cholera epidemics that hit the United States, in 1832, 1849, and 1866. It spread suffering and death in many American cites and villages. By the end of July, the epidemic was so bad in New York that business had almost ceased: hotels were empty; trains and steamships arrived without passengers. Dead bodies were literally lying around the city, sometimes for days.

Interpretation, Part 2: Applying Correct Principles

    b. When the September issue of *The Present Truth* rolled off the press, the news of the disease was on the minds of its readers.

    c. Literary context: According to the literary context of this statement, the final global pestilence won't commence until after Jesus leaves the Most Holy Place in heaven, which has obviously not happened yet.

    d. Her statement, "What we have seen and heard of the pestilence, is but the beginning of what we shall see and hear," *is an application of the local pestilence, rather than a prediction.* Notice that Ellen's language in the first clause, "What we have seen and heard" describes what she and her contemporaries had apparently "seen" (in person) and "heard" (from reading the papers or by word of mouth) concerning the cholera epidemic.

    e. In the second clause, the word *but* functions as a synonym of "only." Accordingly, her statement can be paraphrased as meaning, "This pestilence that we have seen and heard of is *only the beginning* of what we will see and hear when Jesus leaves the Holy Temple and the storm of wrath commences."

    f. Thus, when Ellen White saw and experienced the pestilence—the suffering, the death, and the fear it caused—she immediately connected it to what she had seen in vision concerning the final crisis, which included multitudinous deaths from pestilence.

    g. Calling Ellen White's statement about the cholera epidemic of 1849 a false prediction because the end did not come then is too simplistic.

5. Sidney Cleveland alleged that Ellen White spoke with her dead husband and received guidance from him in a dream. As supposed evidence for this charge, Cleveland cites a portion of Letter 17, 1881, written by Ellen White to her son Willie on September 12, 1881, five weeks after James White died. In this letter, Mrs. White described a dream about James.

6. Cleveland claims that Ellen White violated what she taught about the state of the dead; therefore, she is a false prophet, and none of her dreams or visions can be trusted.

7. Underlying this charge is the assumption that Ellen White believed she

Chapter Summary

Chapter Summary

was actually talking with James, who had died five weeks earlier.

8. Analysis of this statement in its historical and literary contexts shows that Ellen White didn't believe she was communicating with her dead husband.

   a. Historical context: The dream is part of a five-page letter Ellen wrote to her son Willie on September 12, 1881. Only portions of the letter have been published. James had died on August 6, 1881, five weeks earlier. G. I. Butler, General Conference president at the time, was urging Ellen to attend the General Conference session back in Battle Creek that was being planned for November or December. Ellen was struggling with illness and the grief of losing her husband. Thus, she was in a weakened condition physically and emotionally. She had been asking the Lord whether or not she should yield to Butler and attend the upcoming General Conference session despite of her physical and emotional state.

   b. Literary context: The larger literary context of Ellen White's writings shows that she believed that communicating with the dead violates Scripture and is a satanic deception.

   c. When understood in its immediate literary context, the account of this dream doesn't prove Ellen White violated in practice a teaching so basic and fundamental to her thinking.

   d. The letter itself contains evidence that Ellen understood this conversation with James as nothing more than a dream. After relating the entire experience to Willie, she exclaimed, "But this dream seemed so real." Critics completely ignore this sentence, yet it is the interpretive key to understanding the entire experience correctly.

   e. When people say a vivid dream seemed real, their obvious meaning is that the images in the dream had the *feel* of reality but were *not* reality. It was *only* a dream. In other words, it is obvious from this remark that Ellen White knew she was not conversing with her husband in reality—whether in spirit form or somehow "brought back from the grave."

   f. Both Willie and Ellen knew the Lord was telling her through this dream not to risk her health by attending the upcoming General

Interpretation, Part 2: Applying Correct Principles

Conference session. This is the historical circumstance behind the dream. Thus, she viewed this dream as God's answer to her prayer, relieving her from the burden of attending the General Conference session.

g. In her mind, this dream was simply God's medium of communicating His guidance. The fact that the imagery involved her deceased husband intensified the message.

h. Some charge that this letter couldn't be from God because "nowhere in the Bible do we ever find a prophet receiving a revelation from God through a dead person." The dream, they say, is false because it finds no parallel in the Bible.

i. This argument fails, however, because at least twice in the Bible God communicated truth through the imagery of dead people talking. One instance is the memorable parable of the rich man and Lazarus that Jesus Himself told (Luke 16:19–31). The other is John's description of souls before the altar in Revelation 6:9–11.

j. The literary and historical context of this letter demonstrates that the charge that Ellen White actually conversed with her dead husband and received guidance from him is completely false. She believed that James was resting in the grave until the morning of the resurrection. In her mind, contact with him prior to that event was impossible.

9. The critics of Ellen White are guilty of illegitimate proof-texting with her writings to prove their points. As we have seen in this chapter, they ignore the original literary and historical contexts of her writings and give her a "wax nose" that they turn any way they choose.

10. To misrepresent the meaning of Ellen White's writings and present that misrepresentation to others is to bear a false witness. To purposefully and blatantly ignore the original contexts of her writings and twist what she wrote is a breach of Christian ethics and is patently wrong. Ultimately, those who engage in this unfair activity disqualify themselves as fair and objective interpreters of Ellen White's writings.

CHAPTER 11

The Big Picture, Part 1: Understanding Ellen White's Message

"I believe that the critics have missed the boat badly by focusing upon Mrs. White's writings, instead of focusing upon the messages in Mrs. White's writings," stated Attorney Vincent L. Ramik in 1981. Ramik is a specialist in patent, trademark, and copyright law and a Roman Catholic. He had just completed three-hundred-plus hours of research into American literary law and the charge that Ellen White was guilty of plagiarism. "The message is what is crucial," he argued. "The critic reads a sentence, and receives no meaning from it—he may, and often does, even take it out of context. But read the entire message. What is the author's intent? What is the author really saying—where the words come from is really not that important. What is the message of this? If you disregard the message, then even the Bible itself is not worth being read, in that sense of the word."[1]

Ramik was right. The critics of Ellen White fail to hear her message. They isolate a statement, claim that it teaches heresy, and then generalize that the rest of her writings are the same. When viewed collectively, however, these statements that supposedly teach heresy comprise only a tiny part of the vast Ellen White corpus. And those who follow the writings of the critics miss the larger context of her message. This was precisely the case with D. M. Canright, as we saw in chapter 3. He refused to acknowledge to his readers the larger message of Ellen White.

This chapter continues the discussion regarding the importance of context in interpreting Mrs. White's writings, extending that discussion now by focusing on the big picture. If Ellen White was inspired as a postcanonical prophet, as we argued in chapters 5 and 8, then we would expect to see evidences of that inspiration in what she wrote during the seventy-year span of her ministry. This evidence would be most strikingly manifested in the way the details of her message harmonize with the big picture of her message.

What is the big picture in Ellen White's message? What overarching themes blend her various writings over the decades into an intricately woven tapestry? What is the ultimate purpose of her many counsels? The answers to these questions are found only by seeing Ellen White's message in its entirety.

Preliminary considerations

Before we look at the big picture of Ellen White's writings, we must highlight several important considerations.

1. It is important to understand that Ellen White didn't write like a systematic theologian. That is, she didn't organize her writings into theological categories such as the doctrine of Scripture, doctrine of God, doctrine of Christ, doctrine of the Holy Spirit, doctrine of man, doctrine of sin, doctrine of salvation, doctrine of the church, doctrine of last-day events, and so forth. She wrote for the common person rather than the theologian.[2] She wrote to individuals, churches, and institutions with specific spiritual issues in mind, and she sought to give counsel from the framework of her visions and apply biblical principles to the many and varied situations she encountered.[3] Consequently, her writings aren't organized in a dogmatic scheme like that of a systematic theologian.[4] Nevertheless, throughout her ministry, she addressed all of the major doctrines mentioned above and more.

Because of the way Mrs. White wrote, when we want to find her thought on a subject, we must collect her statements on that subject from throughout her writings and then analyze each one in its immediate and larger contexts.[5] Such an approach allows us to see the thematic harmony in her expression of doctrines such as revelation-inspiration, the character of God, the divinity of Christ, the role of the church, the nature of salvation, the power of prayer, etc.[6] When we follow this approach, we see that even though she had no formal training in biblical languages or theological disciplines, her writings reveal that she had significant theological aptitude and discernment. For instance, when she borrowed material from other authors, she generally reformulated it to fit her own theological understanding, often changing significantly what the original source said.[7] As a result, she made an innovative and creative synthesis of theological ideas that extended beyond that of her contemporaries.

2. Readers of Ellen White must understand that over the years of her ministry she experienced growth in her understanding of divine truth. Like Daniel, who didn't understand one of his own visions until years after he had received it (see Daniel 8:27), Ellen White didn't always initially understand every vision. She said, "Often representations are given me which at first I do not understand, but after a time they are made plain by a repeated presentation of those things that I did not at first comprehend, and in ways that make their meaning clear and unmistakable."[8] In another place she commented similarly: "For sixty years I have been in communication with heavenly messengers, and I have been constantly learning in reference to divine things."[9] Thus, Gerhard Pfandl was correct when he wrote, "When comparing earlier writings of Ellen G. White with her later works, we find that she, at times, modified, expanded, or shortened her earlier writings, reflecting deeper insight into God's messages."[10]

A clear example of Ellen White's growth in understanding is the shut-door issue.[11] Shortly after the Great Disappointment of October 22, 1844, Ellen believed William Miller's initial view that the door of salvation was closed to the world. At some point after this, but before her first vision, she adopted the position of Joshua V. Himes, the major leader and promoter of the Millerite movement, who claimed that the October 1844 date was all wrong. Her first vision in December 1844, however, reaffirmed the prophetic significance of the 1844 movement and the shut door. At this point Ellen readopted certain aspects of Miller's shut-door teaching but not her initial, prevision view that all the world was doomed. Her revised view was more in line with the baseline shut-door view that Joseph Turner and Apollos Hale articulated in the January 1845 *Advent Mirror,* which allowed for the salvation of individuals who hadn't heard the 1844 message.[12]

It is in this historical context that we should view the controversial words in the initial presentation of her first vision, when she wrote of the "wicked world which God had rejected."[13] Over the next few years, 1845–1849, Ellen's visions undermined the initial shut-door views and moved her and the other believers to the open-door view of the sanctuary, which can be found in the 1911 *The Great Controversy.*[14]

The evidence shows that Ellen White's understanding of the shut door was modified through her visions and, in the end, revealed significant theological insight. This is a clear case in which the interpreter must read her first vision in light of her later visions. When the historical context is taken into consideration and all her visions on this subject are read together, one can see in the development of her understanding a harmony between the earlier and later statements, rather than the contradiction her critics have so often attempted to read into them.[15] So, when comparing Ellen White's early statements with her later ones on any given subject, we should take into account her progression of thought, her growth in understanding.

3. Readers of Ellen White must understand her limitations. Regarding infallibility, she stated clearly: "I have never claimed it; God alone is infallible."[16] When she claimed that "God's Word is infallible,"[17] however, she didn't mean it is free from error on all points. For example, she openly acknowledged the possibility that the Bible contains errors in factual details:

> Some look to us gravely and say, "Don't you think there might have been some mistake in the copyist or in the translators?" This is all probable, and the mind that is so narrow that it will hesitate and stumble over this possibility or probability would be just as ready to stumble over the mysteries of the Inspired Word, because their feeble minds cannot see through the purposes of God. Yes, they would just as easily stumble over plain facts that the common mind will accept, and discern the Divine, and to which God's utterance is plain and beautiful, full of marrow and fatness. All the mistakes will not cause trouble to one soul, or cause any feet to stumble, that would not manufacture difficulties from the plainest revealed truth.[18]

George Knight provides a helpful comment on this statement:

> The faithful reader's belief is not shaken if he or she discovers that Matthew attributed a Messianic prophecy, written centuries before Christ's birth, to Jeremiah when it was actually Zechariah who inferred that Christ would be betrayed for 30 pieces of silver (see Matt. 27:9, 10; Zech. 11:12, 13). Nor will one be dismayed over the fact that 1 Samuel 16:10, 11 lists David as the eighth son of Jesse, but 1 Chronicles 2:15 refers to him as the seventh. Neither will faith be affected because the prophet Nathan wholeheartedly approved of King David's building of the Temple but the next day had to backtrack and tell David that God didn't want him to build it (see 2 Sam. 7; 1 Chron. 17). Prophets make mistakes.[19]

It is important to note that many of the so-called mistakes in the Scriptures are actually the reader's misunderstandings of the issues. "Despite the existence of some inaccuracies in minor details," however, "sufficient evidence exists to show that those inaccuracies do not distort the basic concept conveyed by the text in which they appear, and they do not break the underlying unity of the Word of God."[20]

"In summary," Knight writes, "it appears that Mrs. White's use of the term *infallibility* has to do with the Bible being completely trustworthy as a guide to salvation. She doesn't mix that idea with the concept that the Bible or her writings are free from all possible errors of a factual nature."[21] In her understanding, the inspired human writers were fallible and prone to minor errors, but the message God conveyed through them was without error. Consequently, the messages delivered by inspired writers are trustworthy; that their writings contain a few minor mistakes doesn't diminish their inspiration and authority.

As is true of the Bible, minor mistakes can be found in the Ellen White writings. For example, she incorrectly attributes Paul's statement in 2 Corinthians 5:14, "the love of Christ constrains us," to Peter, and several numerical and chronological discrepancies can be found in her writings, as well.[22] None of these kinds of minor errors, however, affect her message. The big picture remains intact, and when we view these mistakes in their immediate contexts, these don't pose a problem any more than do the similar mistakes in the Bible. Thus, in the cases of both the Bible writers and Ellen White, God didn't consider minor historical or chronological details "sufficiently important to give a vision for their correction."[23]

Another area of Ellen White's limitation was the fact that she wasn't a historian. "Mother," W. C. White declared, "has never claimed to be an authority on history." Because what she saw in vision didn't always provide the historical context, she made use of history texts to "locate and describe the many figurative representations given to her regarding the development of the great controversy in our day between truth and error."[24]

When the 1888 edition of *The Great Controversy* was being revised, numerous minor errors of a historical nature were found and corrected—with Ellen White's approval.[25] These were only details, however, not historical milestones. The big picture of the great controversy that Ellen White had portrayed remained unchanged. Nevertheless, students of Ellen White "should be careful in using the historical narratives in her books to settle details of history."[26]

Perhaps the most misunderstood limitation of Ellen White is revealed in the need she felt to use the language of others to express the thoughts God inspired within her. Critics exploit this issue and accuse her of blatant plagiarism. While this is not the place to launch into a full-scale response to the plagiarism charge, an abundance of evidence shows that Ellen White engaged in legitimate literary borrowing, not plagiarism.[27] Why did she feel the need to borrow the words of other authors? W. C. White provides the most helpful explanation.

> Notwithstanding all the power that God had given her to present scenes in the lives of Christ and His apostles and His prophets and His reformers in a stronger and more telling way than other historians, yet she always felt most keenly the results of

her lack of school education. She admired the language in which other writers had presented to their readers the scenes which God had presented to her in vision, and she found it both a pleasure, and a convenience and an economy of time to use their language fully or in part in presenting those things which she knew through revelation, and which she wished to pass on to her readers.[28]

According to Vincent Ramik, as cited at the beginning of this chapter, the critics have "missed the boat badly" by focusing on Mrs. White's words and sentences instead of on her message. In concerning themselves with the source of this or that statement, the critics have failed to see the final form of Ellen White's writings—the way they have come to us in her letters, manuscripts, articles, and books. Although she borrowed thoughts, ideas, and phrases from other writers of her day, her message in its final form is what we must hear. To be fair to her as an author, we must see the big picture, her message in its entirety. The remainder of this chapter will attempt to portray just that.

The big picture

As noted above, Ellen White didn't write like a formal theologian who is producing a systematic theology. She did, however, manifest striking theological aptitude and discernment in the way she applied scriptural concepts in her writings. Thus, she was more of a practical or "occasional" theologian, focusing her applications on the "common person."[29] Nevertheless, the careful student can discern a central, controlling principle or organizing theme in her writings, one that ties everything together. Researchers have identified this big picture as "the great controversy theme."[30]

In a nutshell, the great controversy theme advances the idea that throughout history the world has been the field on which the great battle between Christ and His angels and Satan and his angels have fought. While this battle has cosmic implications, it also affects every human being who has ever lived on planet Earth. The Second Coming is the culmination of the controversy. When it occurs, Christ's victory over Satan will be fully realized and all of the evil Satan has caused will be eradicated. The final judgment sets forth the issues before all intelligent beings and vindicates the character of God as displayed in the death of Christ on the cross.[31]

This great controversy theme dominated Ellen White's writings for most of her prophetic ministry. It can be found in embryonic form in her earliest writings, but its shape became clearer and more fully developed after her comprehensive great controversy vision at Lovett's Grove, Ohio, in March of 1858.[32] Six months after this vision, *Spiritual Gifts,* volume 1, was published. This book presented the great controversy story in 219 pages.[33] The second stage of Ellen White's setting forth the great controversy appeared in the series known as the *Spirit of Prophecy*, which she wrote during the years 1870–1884. In this series, what had been contained in the one Spiritual Gifts volume was expanded into four books containing about twelve hundred pages.[34] The third and final stage in setting forth this theme is the five-volume set known today as the Conflict of the Ages series: *Patriarchs and Prophets, Prophets and Kings, The Desire of Ages, The Acts of the Apostles,* and *The Great Controversy.* In these books, the twelve hundred pages of the Spirit of Prophecy series were increased to more than thirty-five hundred pages.[35] This final series was completed during the last two decades of Ellen White's life.

As Mrs. White built each succeeding presentation of the great controversy story upon the previous one, she enlarged and expanded the richness and nuances of the theme. Since the Conflict of the Ages series is the final form of the great controversy theme in Ellen White's writings, it comes the closest to being a formal theological presentation. *Patriarchs and Prophets* and *Prophets and Kings,* for example, cover the great controversy struggle during the Old Testament period. *The Desire of Ages,* considered by some to be Ellen White's greatest book, covers the controversy during the life of Christ as presented in the four New Testament Gospels. *The Acts of the Apostles* addresses the struggle between good and evil from the New Testament book of Acts to Revelation. And the final volume of the series, which carries the formal name of the theme—*The Great Controversy*—develops the battle between Christ and Satan from the destruction of Jerusalem in A.D. 70 through its culmination at the Second Coming and to the earth made new. Ellen White said of this volume that she was "more anxious to see a wide circulation for this book than for any others I have written; for in *The Great Controversy,* the last message of warning to the world is given more distinctly than in any of my other books."[36]

Joseph Battistone produced a significant study of the Conflict of the Ages series, *The Great Controversy Theme in E. G. White Writings.* In that study he wrote, "The 'Conflict of the Ages Series' is in many respects a theological masterpiece. In a unique way Ellen White unfolds the drama of the most significant controversy in human history, identifies the main issues in the conflict, and demonstrates their relevance for each individual. In a [simple] way she provides answers to some of the most vexing questions relating to the human dilemma—those having to do with the problem of evil. One of the major achievements of this work, if not the most important one, is the exoneration of God's character."[37]

Appropriately, as Battistone and many others have observed, *Patriarchs and Prophets,* the first volume in the series, begins with the words " 'God is love.' 1 John 4:16. His nature, His law, is love. It ever has been; it ever will be."[38] And the final volume in the series, *The Great Controversy,* ends with these words: "The great controversy is ended. Sin and sinners are no more. The entire universe is clean. One pulse of harmony and gladness beats through the vast creation. From Him who created all, flow life and light and gladness, throughout the realms of illimitable space. From the minutest atom to the greatest world, all things, animate and inanimate, in their unshadowed beauty and perfect joy, declare that God is love."[39] Thus the "love of God," a distinguishing feature of His character, begins and ends Ellen White's Conflict of the Ages series, exemplifying her purpose to accurately set forth the character of God as displayed in the great controversy story.[40]

In contrast to this theme of God's self-giving, self-sacrificing love, Ellen White exposes Satan's strategy over the ages to deceive the world. She also sets forth Christ as the superior power who is able to overcome evil, and throughout each volume she exalts the gospel of Christ as the only hope for lost sinners.

Because the Conflict of the Ages series presents these themes in the context of the universe-wide controversy between Christ and Satan, we must consider this series to be the theological framework for everything Ellen White wrote.[41] It represents the capstone of her theological thought and should be the starting point for interpreting the rest of her writings. Consequently, students of Mrs. White must return to these volumes repeatedly as a reference point for the study of the rest of her works. Those who approach her writings for the first time should read this series early in their study, for it is here that the big picture of her message is most clearly seen.

John Wood has provided an exceptionally helpful summary of Ellen White's thought on the great controversy. In discussing her writings as a whole, he explains that, while her "interests and writings seem wide-ranging and sometimes unrelated," the system that unites everything is "the great controversy," the "historical facts about the development, history, and resolution of sin." While Ellen White's description of this controversy is "complex and subtle," it "revolves around three basic issues that are fairly simple to state." Behind the simplicity of these statements, however, is "complexity and depth."

The three central issues "are arguments raised by Lucifer against the way the government of God is run." These issues are developed "chronologically and logically as the basis of cosmic rebellion:"[42] (1) "God is a harsh, arbitrary, absolute, unjust, unfair tyrant. The basis for such a view is that God has arbitrarily imposed an absolute law, which He had no intrinsic right to do." (2) "God cannot (or will not) forgive," because "justice and mercy are, by nature, incompatible opposites." (3) "The two arguments having collapsed at the cross, Lucifer then attacks the law by arguing that mercy has now destroyed justice, that the law has been abrogated." For Ellen White, "this is the eschatological issue," and "the very purpose of Christianity is being argued here."[43]

Throughout her writings, Ellen White's use of the great controversy theme pictures God as answering these three charges by the Incarnation, life, death, Resurrection, Ascension, intercession, and second coming of Jesus Christ. Her theology regarding God's character and His law is therefore thoroughly Christ-centered. Wood was right when he stated that "the atonement of Christ is the central aspect of the theological system of Ellen G. White," and the "structure of the 'great controversy' is the unifying theme and controlling principle of that system."[44] In other words, the serpent's crusade against the Son is the framework in which Ellen White sets forth the great sacrifice of Christ for the sins of the world. We must not miss this central feature in her writings.

Notice the following statements, which reveal the centrality of Christ and His sacrifice in her thought:

The sacrifice of Christ as an atonement for sin is the great truth around which all other truths cluster. In order to be rightly understood and appreciated, every truth in the word of God, from Genesis to Revelation, must be studied in the light that streams from the cross of Calvary. I present before you the great, grand monument of mercy and regeneration, salvation and redemption,—the Son of God uplifted on the cross. This is to be the foundation of every discourse given by our ministers.[45]

The atoning sacrifice, the righteousness of Christ, is to us the vital center of all truth. In the cross of Calvary, mercy and truth are met together, righteousness and peace have kissed each other. The law and the gospel are in perfect harmony; they are interwoven as the warp and the woof.[46]

There is one great central truth to be kept ever before the mind in the searching of the Scriptures:—Christ and Him crucified. Every other truth is invested with influence and power corresponding to its relation to this theme. It is only in the light of the cross that we can discern the exalted character of the law of God. The soul palsied by sin can be endowed with life only through the work wrought out upon the cross by the Author of our salvation. The love of Christ constrains man to unite with Him in His labors and sacrifice. The revelation of divine love awakens in them a sense of their neglected obligation to be light-bearers to the world, and inspires them with a missionary spirit. This truth enlightens the mind and sanctifies the soul. It will banish unbelief and inspire faith. It is the one great truth to be constantly kept before the minds of men. Yet how dimly is the love of God understood; and in the teaching of the word it makes but a faint impression.[47]

Thus for Ellen White, the gospel—with Christ's cross at its core—is the Christ-centered story by which God redeems human beings and restores them to His image, thus refuting Satan's charges that God is arbitrary, unforgiving, and unjust. The following statement further clarifies this central theme in her thought.

> The central theme of the Bible, the theme about which every other in the whole book clusters, is the redemption plan, the restoration in the human soul of the image of God. From the first intimation of hope in the sentence pronounced in Eden to that last glorious promise of the Revelation, "They shall see His face; and His name shall be in their foreheads" (Revelation 22:4), the burden of every book and every passage of the Bible is the unfolding of this wondrous theme,—man's uplifting,—the power of God, "which giveth us the victory through our Lord Jesus Christ." 1 Corinthians 15:57.[48]

Here the "redemption plan" is everything God has done in Christ to redeem human beings and assure their place in the earth made new as depicted in the Revelation. It involves all the New Testament concepts of justification, Redemption, adoption, reconciliation, sanctification, Resurrection, and glorification. This is the big picture with the cross at its center. While Ellen White brings into the story the larger picture of the vindication of God's character before the heavenly universe, her main focus is in line with the Bible's—the self-sacrificing love of the Godhead manifested in the redemption of human beings. The great controversy story is thus the framework in which Ellen White sets forth the great theme of God's love in Christ and the redemption plan.

In the following statement, the most concise summary of the great controversy in Ellen White's writings, we see how the central theme—the plan of redemption—and the great controversy framework coalesce in her thought.

> The Bible is its own expositor. Scripture is to be compared with scripture.

The student should learn to view the word as a whole, and to see the relation of its parts. He should gain a knowledge of its grand central theme, of God's original purpose for the world, of the rise of the great controversy, and of the work of redemption. He should understand the nature of the two principles that are contending for supremacy, and should learn to trace their working through the records of history and prophecy, to the great consummation. He should see how this controversy enters into every phase of human experience; how in every act of life he himself reveals the one or the other of the two antagonistic motives; and how, whether he will or not, he is even now deciding upon which side of the controversy he will be found.[49]

Conclusion

In this chapter on the big picture of Ellen White's message, we have seen that her theological thought converges in the Conflict of the Ages series and forms a unified message of redemption through Christ within the framework of the great controversy. This is the final form of her message, which we must keep in mind when we're reading her writings. Failure to see and understand this big picture and to connect the parts to the whole results in misinterpretation, misapplication, and abuse of Mrs. White's writings.

Vincent Ramik used the following analogy to illustrate the way Ellen White used the writings of others and "made them uniquely her own."

The situation is something like the builder who wishes to build a house. There are certain basic, essential units of building materials that are available to him—windows, doors, bricks, and so on. There are even certain recognizable kinds of textures and styles that have been created by various combinations of these different materials by earlier builders. The builder brings together many of these and uses them. Yet the design of the house, the ultimate appearance, the ultimate shape, the size, the feel, are all unique to the immediate, contemporary builder. He individually puts his own stamp upon the final product—and it is uniquely his. (And he doesn't say—or need to say—I got this brick here, that door there, this window there, either!) I think it was that way with Ellen White's use of words, phrases, clauses, sentences, paragraphs, yes, and even pages, from the writings of those who went before her. She stayed well within the legal boundaries of fair use, and all the time created something that was substantially greater (and even more beautiful) than the mere sum of the component parts.[50]

The Big Picture, Part 1: Understanding Ellen White's Message

Chapter Summary

1. This chapter continues the discussion on the importance of context in interpreting Mrs. White's writings, but it extends that discussion by focusing on the big picture.
2. What is the big picture in Ellen White's messages? What overarching themes blend her various writings over the decades into an intricately woven tapestry? What is the ultimate purpose of her many counsels? The answers to these questions are found only by listening to Ellen White's message in its entirety.
3. First, several important considerations must be addressed concerning the issue of harmony in these voluminous writings.
   a. It is important to understand that Ellen White didn't write like a formal, systematic theologian.
   b. Readers of Ellen White must understand that over the years she experienced growth in her understanding of divine truth.
   c. Readers of Ellen White must understand the nature of her limitations.
4. While Mrs. White did not write like a formal theologian producing a systematic theology, she did, however, manifest striking theological aptitude and discernment in the way she applied scriptural concepts in her writings.
5. The careful student can discern in her writings a central, controlling principle or organizing theme that ties everything together.
6. Researchers have identified this big picture as "the great controversy theme." Simply put, this theme advances the idea that throughout its history the world has been and still is the field of the great battle between Christ and His angels and Satan and his angels. While this battle has cosmic implications, it also affects every human being who has ever lived on planet Earth. Ellen White viewed the Second Coming as the culmination of the controversy, when Christ's victory over Satan will be fully realized and all of Satan's evils eradicated. The final judgment sets forth the issues before all intelligent beings and vindicates the character of God as displayed in the death of Christ on the cross.
7. This great controversy theme dominated Ellen White's writings for most of her prophetic ministry. It can be found in embryonic form in her

Chapter Summary earliest writings and takes more discernable shape after her comprehensive vision on the great controversy at Lovett's Grove, Ohio, in March of 1858.

   a. Six months after this vision, *Spiritual Gifts,* volume 1, was published as the first formal presentation of the great controversy story. It was 219 pages long.

   b. The second stage of setting forth the great controversy appeared in the four-volume series known as *The Spirit of Prophecy.* This series, written during the years 1870–1884, expanded the *Spiritual Gifts* volume into about twelve hundred pages.

   c. The third and final stage of Ellen White's setting forth of this theme is the five-volume series known today as the Conflict of the Ages: *Patriarchs and Prophets, Prophets and Kings, The Desire of Ages, The Acts of the Apostles,* and *The Great Controversy.* These books expanded the twelve hundred pages of *The Spirit of Prophecy* series into more than thirty-five hundred pages.

   d. As each stage of Mrs. White's presentation of the great controversy story built upon the previous one, she enlarged and expanded the richness and nuances of the theme.

8. The Conflict of the Ages series is the final form of the great controversy theme in Ellen White's writings and comes the closest to being a formal theological presentation.

9. In the significant study of the Conflict of the Ages series that Joseph Battistone produced, *The Great Controversy Theme in E. G. White Writings,* he wrote, "The 'Conflict of the Ages Series' is in many respects a theological masterpiece."

10. In light of its exposition of these themes in the context of the great controversy between Christ and Satan, the Conflict of the Ages series should be seen as the theological framework for everything Ellen White wrote. It represents the capstone of her theological thought and should be the starting point for interpreting the rest of her writings. Therefore, in studying Mrs. White's works, we must return to these volumes repeatedly as an essential reference point.

11. John Wood has provided an exceptionally helpful summary of Ellen White's thought on the great controversy. He saw three central issues that are arguments raised by Lucifer against the way the government

of God is run and that are developed chronologically and logically as the basis of cosmic rebellion.

Chapter Summary

   a. Lucifer charges that God is a harsh, arbitrary, absolute, unjust, unfair tyrant. He bases this view on his claim that God has arbitrarily imposed an absolute law, which He had no intrinsic right to do.
   b. Lucifer also charges that God cannot (or will not) forgive," because justice and mercy are, by nature, incompatible opposites.
   c. These two arguments having collapsed at the cross, Lucifer then attacks the law by arguing that mercy has now destroyed justice, that the law has been abrogated. For Ellen White, "this is *the* eschatological issue," and "the very purpose of Christianity is being argued here."

12. Throughout her writings, Ellen White uses the great controversy to picture God's answer to these three major charges, which He does by the Incarnation, life, death, Resurrection, Ascension, intercession, and second coming of Jesus Christ.

13. Therefore, Mrs. White's theology regarding God's character and His law is thoroughly Christ-centered. Wood was right when he explained that "the atonement of Christ is the central aspect of the theological system of Ellen G. White," and the "structure of the 'great controversy' is the unifying theme and controlling principle of that system." In other words, the serpent's crusade against the Son is the framework in which Ellen White sets forth the great sacrifice of Christ for the sins of the world. We must not miss this central feature in her writings.

14. For Ellen White, the gospel, with Christ's cross at its core, is the Christ-centered story by which God redeems human beings and restores them to His image, thus refuting Satan's charges that He is arbitrary, unforgiving, and unjust.

15. The "redemption plan," as Ellen White called it, is everything that God has done in Christ to redeem human beings and assure their place in the earth made new. It involves all the New Testament concepts of justification, Redemption, adoption, reconciliation, sanctification, Resurrection, and glorification. This is the big picture with the cross at its center.

16. While Ellen White brings into the story the larger picture of the vindication of God's character before the heavenly universe, her main focus is

Chapter Summary

in line with that of the Bible—the self-sacrificing love of the Godhead manifested in the redemption of human beings.

17. The great controversy story is thus the framework within which Ellen White sets forth the great theme of God's love in Christ and the redemption plan.
18. The big picture of Ellen White's message, therefore, is that her theological thought converges in the Conflict of the Ages series forming a unified message of redemption through Christ in the framework of the great-controversy theme. This is the final form of her message that we must keep in mind when reading her writings.
19. Failure to see and understand this big picture and to connect the parts to the whole results in misinterpretation, misapplication, and abuse of her writings.

CHAPTER 12

The Big Picture, Part 2: Vindicating Ellen White's Message

The critics of Ellen White focus mostly on isolated controversial statements in her writings and fail to hear the larger message. As noted in the previous chapter, these controversial statements comprise only a tiny part of the vast corpus of her writings.[1] Focusing on one small part of these writings and treating them as if they are all Mrs. White said while ignoring the rest of her writings is misleading. Critics who do this have missed the good news, the Christ-centered message that her great controversy theme proclaims.

In recent years, detractors have focused on the great controversy theme and charged that it is unbiblical. They've characterized it as portraying a "hesitating, self-protecting, political God" who is "watching his cosmic popularity polls."[2] The great controversy theme, they argue, "makes God out to protect His integrity," whereas "the gospel declares that God set about to solve the problem created by man, not Himself."[3] The God "who is truly God of all does not have to prove to anyone that He is fair and Satan is lying."[4] It has even been suggested that the Adventist understanding of the great controversy falsely portrays God as "locked in a battle with Satan," and the "outcome" of that battle "is yet to be seen."[5] This chapter will provide a fourfold response to these charges.

1. The biblical evidence for Ellen White's great controversy theme is significant. The fact is that this motif is fundamental to the entire Bible. Here's how Old Testament scholar Richard Davidson summarizes the biblical evidence on the centrality of this theme to Scripture:

> Genesis 1-3 reveals a multifaceted "center" of Scripture, including the following: (1) divine creation and God's original design for His creatures; (2) the character of the Creator,

as the transcendent Elohim and personal Yahweh (in the complementary chapters Genesis 1–2); (3) the rise of cosmic moral conflict concerning the character of God (Genesis 3); and (4) the Gospel solution to this ongoing conflict with the coming of the Promised Seed to bare His heel over the head of the venomous snake, i.e., to voluntarily lay down His life in substitutionary atonement in order to crush the head of that ancient Serpent and bring an end to evil (Gen 3:15). In the final chapters of the book of Revelation (especially 20–22) we find the repetition of this same multifaceted metanarrative, with the wind-up of this cosmic warfare (Revelation 20; 21:6), the creation of a new heavens and earth, and restoration of humanity through the second coming of the Messiah (Revelation 21–22), a final revelation and vindication of the character/name of God (esp. Rev 22:4, 6; cf. 19:1–2), and the Gospel promises of redemption centered in Jesus the Lamb (esp. Rev. 21:6, 22, 23; 22:16–17).[6]

Davidson further explains that he doesn't see this "center" as a kind of "organizing principle" or " 'grid' into which all the other themes, motifs, and concepts of Scripture are to be fitted." Instead, he sees this "center" as more of an "orientation point in light of which the whole of Scripture makes ultimate sense."[7] In other words, the great controversy theme or motif is the framework of Scripture—its "worldview."

Biblical scholars outside of Adventist circles have also pointed to this theme. For example, in his books *God at War: The Bible and Spiritual Conflict* and *Satan and the Problem of Evil: Constructing a Trinitarian Warfare Theodicy,*[8] which has captured the attention of the evangelical community, Gregory A. Boyd recognizes a "warfare worldview" as central to the Bible. And in their book *God Is a Warrior,* Tremper Longman III and Daniel G. Reid propose the thesis that the divine warrior theme is the source of the Bible's organic unity.[9] Thus, although these biblical scholars certainly don't agree with every detail of the Adventist understanding, they recognize that Scripture contains a great controversy theme.

One can clearly see this theme in various places in Scripture, such as in the "enmity" (intense hostility) Genesis 3:15 says there is between the serpent (Satan) and the woman's Seed (Christ), in the antediluvian wickedness, in the development of paganism and idolatry, and in the corrupting of the Hebrew religion. Satan is mentioned by name in Job 1:6–12, 2:1–8; and Zechariah 3:1–10. In the New Testament, the controversy reaches its highest level of intensity during the first advent of Christ. Satan engages Jesus in the wilderness temptations, in His public ministry, and in His sufferings. But Jesus obtains the victory at every step and ultimately defeats Satan at the cross (Rev. 12:10, 11). Jesus also refers to the great controversy in His parables, such as in the parable of the sower (Matt. 13:3–23), the parable of the tares among the wheat (Matt. 13:24–30), the parable of the wedding garment (Matt. 22:1–14), and the parable of the lost son (Luke 15). Paul, in his epistles, refers to Satan as the "prince of the power of the air" (Eph. 2:2, NKJV) and the "god of this age" (2 Cor. 4:4, NKJV). Most notable is his view of the church's warfare with Satan and his angels: "Our struggle is not against flesh and blood, but against the rulers, against the authorities, against the powers of this dark world and against the spiritual forces of evil in the heavenly realms" (Eph. 6:12, NIV). And Peter calls Satan our "adversary the devil" (1 Pet. 5:8, NKJV).

According to Frank Holbrook, "the doctrine of salvation (in Pauline terms, justification, sanctification, glorification) through faith in the merits of Christ and His transforming grace is also described in terms of the moral conflict between God and Satan." Because Adam's fall resulted in the depraving of his own nature and that of his descendants, the "enmity, or hostility, that God places between Satan and the human family is brought about by the function of the Holy Spirit working through the conscience." Consequently, "this condition creates within each individual a microcosm of the same moral controversy that is being fought on the cosmic level." New Testament writers speak of this struggle in terms of the spirit striving against the flesh and the flesh striving against the spirit (Gal. 5:17), the mind oriented to the flesh being hostile to God (Rom. 8:6–8), and desire leading to sin and death (James 1:14, 15).[10]

Ultimately, the book of Revelation pictures the culmination of this great controversy with Christ as the divine warrior destroying the devil and all his followers at the end of time and establishing final peace in the earth made new, where the believers no longer engage in a personal battle with sin (Rev. 19–22). To assert that Ellen White's great controversy theme isn't biblical, then, clearly reveals a failure to pay careful attention to what the Bible says. It's obvious that this theme permeates the Bible from beginning to end and that Mrs. White was simply reflecting this biblical "warfare worldview."

2. The idea that Ellen White viewed the outcome of Christ's battle with Satan as uncertain is the result of a complete failure to hear her message. Joseph Battistone addressed this issue straightforwardly at the outset of his *The Great Controversy in E. G. White Writings*.

> To her [Ellen White's] way of thinking, the conflict between Christ and Satan is not a contest between two powers of equal standing but

between the Creator and a creature. It is incorrect, therefore, to speak of a cosmic dualism in a theological sense, unless one were to qualify from the outset the nature of this dualism. To be sure, Ellen White does understand the controversy to be a contest between two antagonistic powers, but insofar as she is concerned the end of the struggle is never in doubt. The principles of righteousness and truth as exemplified in the life of Christ will ultimately triumph over the principles of sin and error as displayed in the activity of Satan. Then the cancer of sin will be removed from God's creation and will appear no more. This firm conviction in the ultimate triumph of good over evil makes her religious philosophy essentially optimistic.[11]

3. The idea that Scripture doesn't portray a vindication of God's character in the great controversy is mistaken. Notice the evidence. In the narrative of the Fall at the very beginning of the Bible, God's character is the central issue (Genesis 3). The names for God—*Yahweh*, "Lord" (which is used when Scripture is portraying the personal, redeeming God) and *Elohim*, "God" (powerful Creator)—are used together ("Lord God") nine times in verses 1, 8, 9, 13, 14, 21, 22, and 23. Only in verses 1, 3, and 5, when Moses quotes the conversation of the serpent and Eve, is God referred to by the name *Elohim* alone. It appears that the serpent deliberately avoids using God's personal name. So here, at the outset of Scripture, Satan misrepresents God, maligning the loving and redeeming nature that His personal name, *Yahweh*, conveys. This indicates the question of God's character was the great issue in the temptation and the Fall.

Eve accepted Satan's insinuations against God's claims and his maligning of God's character, and she was deceived into doubting the word of God and the goodness of His character, which resulted in her fall.[12] The rest of the Bible points to and tells the story of the vindication of God's character in the context of Genesis 3:15—particularly, the promise of the Redeemer who would crush the head of His venomous foe and redeem the human race.[13]

This vindication continues when God reveals His name—in other words, His character—to Moses (Exodus 3:13–16; 34:5–7). In the larger flow of Scripture, this self-revelation can be viewed as one of God's major responses to Satan's misrepresentation in the Garden of Eden. Throughout the rest of the Old Testament, literally hundreds of texts speak of God's personal name, *Yahweh*. These passages vindicate who He is and what He does. The prophets' writings, the historical narratives, and the psalms all unite in a powerful chorus that proclaims the goodness of God's character—His mercy and justice.

The Big Picture, Part 2: Vindicating Ellen White's Message

The New Testament tells the story of the long-promised Messiah (Genesis 3:15) who has finally arrived. Through His birth, life, and teachings, Jesus Christ entered the world as the ultimate revelation of the loving, self-giving character of God. The Gospels portray Him as One with His Father in life, message, and mission. His life and words rebuked Satan and exposed his deceptions. The wilderness temptations and the many demonic confrontations recorded in the Gospels clearly portray the peak of the great controversy. And Jesus' death on the cross defeated Satan and silenced him once and for all (Rev. 12:7–12).

In the last book of the Bible, Revelation, where all the biblical books converge, there are repeated celebrations of God's mighty actions in behalf of human beings and proclamations of His worthiness, justice, and truthfulness (Rev. 5:9–14; 11:11–15; 15:3, 4; 16:5, 7; 19:1–6). George Knight aptly observes, "Either the heavenly hosts and/or the apostle John has an unhealthy fascination with the topic of God's truthfulness, justice, and worthiness to judge, or it is a central problem in the conflict between good and evil."[14] Clearly, Revelation is concerned with the vindication of God's character and His right to judge—particularly in the context of the battle with evil and the redemption of human beings. So, the Bible, from Genesis to Revelation, substantiates Ellen White's use of the "vindication of the character of God" theme.

4. *The charge that Ellen White's great controversy theme makes God appear to be self-protecting, political, and concerned about His reputation is a gross misunderstanding of her message.* The first chapter of *The Desire of Ages* beautifully sets forth the nature of God's vindication of His character and government. In this chapter she brings to our view the larger picture of the unfallen universe. At the outset of the chapter, she writes,

> By coming to dwell with us, Jesus was to reveal God both to men and to angels. He was the Word of God,—God's thought made audible. In His prayer for His disciples He says, "I have declared unto them Thy name,"—"merciful and gracious, long-suffering, and abundant in goodness and truth,"—"that the love wherewith Thou hast loved Me may be in them, and I in them." But not alone for His earthborn children was this revelation given. Our little world is the lesson book of the universe. God's wonderful purpose of grace, the mystery of redeeming love, is the theme into which "angels desire to look," and it will be their study throughout endless ages. Both the redeemed and the unfallen beings will find in the cross of Christ their science and their song. It will be seen

that the glory shining in the face of Jesus is the glory of self-sacrificing love. In the light from Calvary it will be seen that the law of self-renouncing love is the law of life for earth and heaven; that the love which "seeketh not her own" has its source in the heart of God; and that in the meek and lowly One is manifested the character of Him who dwelleth in the light which no man can approach unto.[15]

Notice how she understands Jesus as declaring God's name, His character, through the words of Exodus 34:6, which portray God's proclamation of His name to Moses. Jesus is understood as the ultimate manifestation of the character of God. One cannot miss the emphasis on the selfless, self-sacrificing, self-renouncing love of God in this statement: "But not alone for His earthborn children was this revelation given." God's revelation of His character is for the entire universe. The statement that both the "redeemed and the unfallen beings will find in the cross of Christ their science and their song" is reminiscent of Colossians 1:20—Christ would "reconcile to himself all things, whether things on earth or things in heaven, by making peace through his blood, shed on the cross" (NIV). This doesn't picture a political God concerned about His reputation in a human sense.

According to Ellen White, Jesus came to "unveil" the "deception" of Satan and show that "God's law of love" is a "law of unselfishness." In stooping to take humanity upon Himself, "Christ revealed a character opposite the character of Satan," the one who is really filled with self-interest and the desire for political gain. Christ "stepped still lower in the path of humiliation" in His death on the cross. By His substitutionary sacrifice, human beings are redeemed and exalted.

Christ was treated as we deserve, that we might be treated as He deserves. He was condemned for our sins, in which He had no share, that we might be justified by His righteousness, in which we had no share. He suffered the death which was ours, that we might receive the life which was His. "With His stripes we are healed."

By His life and His death, Christ has achieved even more than recovery from the ruin wrought through sin. It was Satan's purpose to bring about an eternal separation between God and man; but in Christ we become more closely united to God than if we had never fallen. In taking our nature, the Saviour has bound Himself to humanity by a tie that is never to be broken. Through the eternal ages He is linked with us. "God so loved the world, that He gave His only-begotten

Son." John 3:16. He gave Him not only to bear our sins, and to die as our sacrifice; He gave Him to the fallen race. To assure us of His immutable counsel of peace, God gave His only-begotten Son to become one of the human family, forever to retain His human nature.[16]

God answers Satan's charges by showing all created beings the depth of His love through what He has done in His Son. The love displayed in the gospel is without a parallel. It speaks to each child of humanity, to each angel in heaven, and to all the unfallen beings populating God's perfect universe. "In Christ the family of earth and the family of heaven are bound together."[17] Thus, in Ellen White's understanding, God's interest in vindicating His character bears no resemblance to the human desire for reputation. In the entire process of vindicating Himself and His government, God reveals the depth of His love for His creation. It is a selfless act that intensifies the peace and joy for all the heavenly universe. It reveals that God is more concerned about the welfare and happiness of all His intelligent created beings than about His reputation.

The conclusion to this first chapter of *The Desire of Ages* reveals Ellen White's understanding that Christ's redeeming work is inseparable from the vindication of God's character and His government.

Through Christ's redeeming work the government of God stands justified. The Omnipotent One is made known as the God of love. Satan's charges are refuted, and his character unveiled. Rebellion can never again arise. Sin can never again enter the universe. Through eternal ages all are secure from apostasy. By love's self-sacrifice, the inhabitants of earth and heaven are bound to their Creator in bonds of indissoluble union.

The work of redemption will be complete. In the place where sin abounded, God's grace much more abounds. The earth itself, the very field that Satan claims as his, is to be not only ransomed but exalted. Our little world, under the curse of sin the one dark blot in His glorious creation, will be honored above all other worlds in the universe of God. Here, where the Son of God tabernacled in humanity; where the King of glory lived and suffered and died,—here, when He shall make all things new, the tabernacle of God shall be with men, "and He will dwell with them, and they shall be His people, and God Himself shall be with them, and be their God." And through endless ages as the redeemed walk in the light of the Lord, they will praise Him for His unspeakable Gift,—Immanuel, "God with us."[18]

Such is Ellen White's teaching on the vindication of God's character and His government. God's "reconciling the world to himself in Christ" (2 Cor. 5:19, NIV) is central to her thought regarding this rich motif. Once again, it is clear that the critics have failed to listen to her message.

One other concept relevant to this discussion of the great controversy theme is the nature of the atonement. The word *atonement* ("at-one-ment") is the name of the process by which God reconciles human beings to Himself through the work of Christ. Evangelical theologians often use it in its technical sense as referring to the complete, all-sufficient, once-for-all sacrifice of Christ on Calvary (Rom. 3:25; Heb. 9:12; 10:1; 1 Tim. 2:6). Ellen White also understood the atonement in this biblical sense. She wrote, for example, "He [Christ] planted the cross between Heaven and earth, and when the Father beheld the sacrifice of His Son, He bowed before it in recognition of its perfection. 'It is enough,' He said. 'The atonement is complete' "; and, in the context of the Crucifixion, "No language could convey the rejoicing of heaven or God's expression of satisfaction and delight in His only begotten Son as He saw the completion of the atonement."[19]

But Ellen White also understood the atonement in a wider sense—one found in the New Testament concept of "reconciliation," which includes the effect the atonement has on all of God's creation. For example, Paul declared to the Corinthians, "God was reconciling the world to himself in Christ" (2 Cor. 5:19, NIV), and in Colossians 1:19, 20, he wrote, "God was pleased to have all his fullness dwell in him [Jesus], and through him to reconcile to himself all things, whether things on earth or things in heaven, by making peace through his blood, shed on the cross" (NIV). This wider meaning includes the *application* of the benefits of the sacrificial atonement Christ made on the cross. Ellen White was reflecting this biblical understanding when she wrote, "Our Saviour is in the sanctuary pleading in our behalf. He is our interceding High Priest, making an atoning sacrifice for us, pleading in our behalf the efficacy of His blood."[20]

It is helpful, therefore, as George Knight suggests, to "think of the atonement as a line rather than a single point even though the crucifixion of Christ is the turning point in the conflict between God and Satan."[21] Similarly, Ángel Rodríguez concluded, "The atonement as a sacrificial event on the cross is finished, but . . . the atonement as a process leading to the cleansing of the heavenly temple and the whole cosmos from the impurity of sin remains yet unfinished."[22]

For Ellen White, then, the atonement was a process that involved the different phases of Christ's work—Incarnation, sinless life, vicarious death, Resurrection, Ascension, heavenly intercession, Second Coming, and final judgment.[23] All of these vital works collectively form the atonement process in her thinking. Nevertheless, as noted above, she viewed Christ's death on the cross as central to the atonement—as "the great truth around which all other truths cluster."[24] For, she explained, in looking at the cross, the angels rejoiced "that the destruction of sin and Satan was forever made certain, that the redemption of man was assured, and that the universe was made eternally secure."[25]

A good question at this point is: Which of the five different classical theories on the atonement did Ellen White teach? The five theories are

1. The Example Theory: Rather than being a satisfaction paid to the Father, the death of Christ was an example of the type of dedication we are to possess.

2. The Moral-Influence Theory: Christ's death demonstrated to us the love of God and thus induces us to respond to God's offer of salvation.

3. The Governmental Theory: Christ's death demonstrated the holiness of God's law and the seriousness of transgressing it, thus upholding moral government.

4. The Victory, or Ransom, Theory: The blood of Christ was a ransom paid to Satan to deliver human beings from his control and thus achieved victory over the forces of evil.

5. The Penal-Substitution Theory: Christ was the sinner's Substitute and bore the penalty to satisfy the holy requirements of God's justice.[26] (This is the theory espoused by most evangelicals.[27])

Which of these theories did Ellen White hold? The answer is that she can't be *exclusively categorized* under any *one* theory. Rather, she embraces certain aspects of these theories and rejects others.[28] For instance, while her thought on the great controversy in its cosmic dimensions clearly connects with the governmental theory, she also differed with advocates of this theory in her hearty endorsement of the penal-substitution theory. Like those who hold the moral-influence theory, she saw the cross as a demonstration of the love of God. But again, she clearly moved beyond this theory in her penal-substitution statements, which seem to predominate in her statements regarding the atonement. A good example is the chapter "Calvary" in *The Desire of Ages,* where she spells out the substitutionary work of Christ in a moving depiction of His sufferings.

> Upon Christ as our substitute and surety was laid the iniquity of us all. He was counted a transgressor, that He might redeem us from the condemnation of the law. The guilt of every descendant of Adam was pressing upon His heart. The wrath of God against sin, the terrible manifestation of His displeasure because of iniquity,

filled the soul of His Son with consternation. . . .

Christ felt the anguish which the sinner will feel when mercy shall no longer plead for the guilty race. It was the sense of sin, *bringing the Father's wrath upon Him as man's substitute,* that made the cup He drank so bitter, and broke the heart of the Son of God.

The spotless Son of God hung upon the cross, His flesh lacerated with stripes; those hands so often reached out in blessing, nailed to the wooden bars; those feet so tireless on ministries of love, spiked to the tree; that royal head pierced by the crown of thorns; those quivering lips shaped to the cry of woe. And all that He endured—the blood drops that flowed from His head, His hands, His feet, the agony that racked His frame, and the unutterable anguish that filled His soul at the hiding of His Father's face—speaks to each child of humanity, declaring, *It is for thee that the Son of God consents to bear this burden of guilt;* for thee He spoils the domain of death, and opens the gates of Paradise. He who stilled the angry waves and walked the foam-capped billows, who made devils tremble and disease flee, who opened blind eyes and called forth the dead to life,—*offers Himself upon the cross as a sacrifice, and this from love to thee. He, the Sin Bearer, endures the wrath of divine justice, and for thy sake becomes sin itself.* [29]

Those critics who accuse Ellen White of teaching legalism have failed to understand the larger context of her message on the atonement.[30]

Misunderstanding Ellen White's message of salvation

Ellen White's teaching on the salvation experience[31] is often misunderstood due to a lack of understanding of the Wesleyan-Arminian influence on her thought.[32] Wesleyan Arminianism is a combination of the theological concepts of Jacob Arminius (1560–1609),[33] professor of theology at Leiden, Holland, known for his rejection of the strict Calvinistic doctrine of predestination and emphasis on the freedom of the will;[34] and John Wesley (1703–1791),[35] the renowned revivalist and founder of Methodism. Numerous studies have confirmed that Wesley and Arminius were thoroughly evangelical and biblical in their theology.[36]

Impressed with the theological concepts of Arminius, Wesley developed his own theological system with an emphasis on grace and the human response, justification and assurance, sanctification and perfection.[37] One of his hallmark teachings was that sanctification and perfection are indispensable to the Christian experience.[38] Wesley taught that if believers quench the convictions of the Holy Spirit and fall into a habitual pattern of unconfessed sin, they could make a shipwreck of their faith and lose salvation.[39] Thus, while Wesley believed that assurance of salvation was a vital part of Christian experience, he believed as well that the Christian must still "take heed, lest he fall."[40]

Ellen White was raised as a Wesleyan, and she stood in the American Holiness Methodist tradition regarding sanctification,[41] although she didn't follow Wesley in all of his ideas about sanctification and perfection.[42] Nevertheless, George Knight correctly asserts that "we cannot really understand Ellen White's use of terminology and concepts related to perfection until we examine the Wesleyan background that she grew up in. Her writings are permeated with those Wesleyan usages that are in harmony with the biblical teachings on sin, perfection, and sinlessness."[43]

It is also important that we realize that Ellen White followed Wesley in his teaching on free will and the conditional perseverance of the saints—the possibility that Christians can fall from grace if they choose to live in sin without repenting. This background is essential for correctly understanding Ellen White's "never say, 'I am saved' " statements. Critics cite these statements as proof that she is robbing the Christian of assurance of salvation by "arguing for salvation by works" and "claiming that a person must be perfect and sinless before he can claim that he is saved."[44]

Careful analysis of these statements, however, reveals that the critics have not done their homework. In each instance, Ellen White is responding from the background of her Wesleyan-Arminian understanding of conditional perseverance of the saints and emphasizing the biblical mandate/principle: "If you think you are standing firm, be careful that you don't fall!" (1 Cor. 10:12, NIV). To her, the finality of the statement "I am saved" encouraged the presumptuous "once saved, always saved" attitude and influenced Christians to "rest in a satisfied condition and cease to make advancement" in Christian growth. "When this idea is entertained," she said, "the motives for watchfulness, for prayers, for earnest endeavor to press onward to higher attainments, cease to exist."[45] In saying this, however, she wasn't trying to undermine the encouragement and motivation that comes from the biblical assurance of salvation.[46]

In fact, throughout her long life Ellen White believed and taught that Christians can have assurance of salvation. The following statements, listed in chronological order, reveal a person who trusted in the merits of Jesus Christ and encouraged others to do the same.

1843—from Ellen's description of her conversion experience: "Faith now took possession of my heart. I felt an inexpressible love for God, and *had the witness of His Spirit that my sins were pardoned.* My views of the Father were changed. I now looked upon

Him as a kind and tender parent, rather than a stern tyrant compelling men to a blind obedience. My heart went out toward Him in a deep and fervent love. Obedience to His will seemed a joy; it was a pleasure to be in His service. No shadow clouded the light that revealed to me the perfect will of God. I felt the *assurance of an indwelling Saviour,* and realized the truth of what Christ had said: 'He that followeth Me shall not walk in darkness, but shall have the light of life.' John 8:12."[47]

1851—*from her first book,* A Sketch of the Christian Experience and Views of Ellen G. White: "If the enemy can lead the desponding to take their eyes off from Jesus, and look to themselves, and dwell upon their own unworthiness, *instead of dwelling upon the worthiness of Jesus, His love, His merits, and His great mercy,* he will get away their shield of faith and gain his object; they will be exposed to his fiery temptations. *The weak should therefore look to Jesus, and believe in Him; they then exercise faith.*"[48]

1864—*from her description of her understanding of the plan of salvation:* "Angels held communication with Adam after his fall, and informed him of the plan of salvation, and that the human race was not beyond redemption. Although a fearful separation had taken place between God and man, yet provision had been made through the offering of his beloved Son by which man might be saved. But *their only hope was through a life of humble repentance,* and *faith in the provision made.* All those who could *thus accept Christ as their only Saviour, should be again brought into favor with God through the merits of his Son.*"[49]

1869—*from remarks she made at a tent meeting:* "Eternal things should awaken our interest, and should be regarded, in comparison with temporal things, as of infinite importance. God requires of us to make it our first business to attend to the health and prosperity of the soul. *We should know that we are enjoying the favor of God, that he smiles upon us, and that we are his children indeed,* and in a position where he can commune with us, and we with him. . . . When a Christian draws his life from above, and strengthens his soul with the contemplation of things that are unseen, God is honored, because he takes him at his word. *He believes the promise, and it is accounted unto him for righteousness.*"[50]

1876—*from a camp meeting sermon by James White that Mrs. White approvingly quoted:* "My husband then spoke a few words to those who were seeking the Lord. . . . Go forward in faith, you that have taken your position upon these front seats, and thereby acknowledge your desire to serve your Heavenly Father. *Expect that you will be saved, if you comply with the conditions laid down in the word of God.* Take advance steps in faith. Make efforts in and through Jesus, *relying upon the merits of his blood.* You must have repentance toward God, because it is the Father's law which you have transgressed; and *you must exercise faith in our Lord and Saviour Jesus Christ as the sinner's advocate, to plead in his behalf. Come, sinner, to the Father and the Son! All Heaven invites you to come and gain eternal life. Jesus wants you to come.* If you stumble once and again, do not give up in despair. If you are brought into trial, if you are overcome and do wrong, repent sincerely before God, but do not despair. *Try again, laying hold more firmly of the merits and strength of Christ. When sinful man has no righteousness of his own to rely upon, Christ becomes his righteousness.* When he feels that he has no strength, Jesus offers to put his arm beneath him. The sinner may then indeed say, Christ died for me, and his blood cleanseth me from all sin."[51]

1878—from assurance she found through considering Christ's ministry in heaven: "He who considered it not robbery to be equal with God, once trod the earth, bearing our suffering and sorrowing nature, and tempted in all points like as we are; and now he appears in the presence of God as our great High Priest, *ready to accept the repentance, and to answer the prayers of his people,* and, *through the merits of his own righteousness, to present them to the Father.* He raises his wounded hands to God, and *claims their blood-bought pardon. I have graven them on the palms of my hands, he pleads.* Those memorial wounds of my humiliation and anguish secure to my church the best gifts of Omnipotence."[52]

1883—*from a talk she gave at a General Conference session:* "We must not trust at all to ourselves nor to our good works; but when as erring, sinful beings we come to Christ, we may find rest in His love. God will accept every one that comes to Him trusting wholly in the merits of a crucified Saviour."[53]

1890—*from a manuscript on the "Danger of False Ideas on Justification by Faith":* "There is not a point that needs to be dwelt upon more earnestly, repeated more frequently, or established more firmly in the minds of all, than the *impossibility of fallen man meriting anything by his own best good works. Salvation is through faith in Jesus Christ alone.* . . .

"Christ has given me words to speak: 'Ye must be born again, else you will never enter the kingdom of heaven.' Therefore all who have the right understanding of this matter should put away their controversial spirit and seek the Lord with all their hearts. Then they will find Christ and can give distinctive character to their religious experience. They should keep this matter—the simplicity of true godliness—distinctly before the people in every discourse. This will come home to the heart of every hungering, thirsting soul who is longing to come into the *assurance of hope and faith and perfect trust* in God through our Lord Jesus Christ.

"Let the subject be made distinct and plain that it is not possible to effect anything in our standing before God or in the gift of God to us through creature merit. Should faith and works purchase the gift of salvation for anyone, then the Creator is under obligation to the creature. Here is an opportunity for falsehood to be accepted as truth. *If any man can merit salvation by anything he may do, then he is in the same position as the Catholic to do penance for his sins.* Salvation, then, is partly of debt that may be earned as wages. *If man cannot, by any of his good works, merit salvation, then it must be wholly of grace, received by man as a sinner because he receives and believes in Jesus. It is wholly a free gift.* Justification by faith is placed beyond controversy. And all this controversy is ended, as soon as the matter is settled that the merits of fallen man in his good works can never procure eternal life for him."[54]

1891—from a camp-meeting sermon: "Now, some will tell you, and they will begin to reckon, and reckon, and reckon when the latter rain is coming. I would rather that you would reckon right now whether you have brought eternity into your reckoning concerning your individual self. Consider whether you have brought eternity daily to view. *If you are right with God today, you are ready if Christ should come today.* What we need is Christ formed within, the hope of glory. We want that you should have a deep and earnest longing for the righteousness of Jesus Christ. *Your old, tattered garments of self-righteousness will not give you an entrance into the kingdom of God, but that garment that is woven in the loom of heaven—the righteousness of Jesus Christ—will.* It will give you an inheritance among the sanctified. That is what we want. It is worth more than all the worldly gain; it is worth more than all your farms; it is worth more than all the honor that finite beings can bestow upon you."[55]

The Big Picture, Part 2: Vindicating Ellen White's Message

***1894**—from a letter of comfort and assurance to an afflicted woman:* "The message from God to me for you is 'Him that cometh unto me, I will in no wise cast out' (John 6:37). If you have nothing else to plead before God but this one promise from your Lord and Saviour, you have the assurance that you will never, never be turned away. It may seem to you that you are hanging upon a single promise, but appropriate that one promise, and it will open to you the whole treasure house of the riches of the grace of Christ. Cling to that promise and you are safe. 'Him that cometh unto me I will in no wise cast out.' Present this assurance to Jesus, and you are as safe as though inside the city of God."[56]

***1898**—from* The Desire of Ages: "Jesus bade His disciples, 'Fear not them which kill the body, but are not able to kill the soul.' Those who are true to God need not fear the power of men nor the enmity of Satan. *In Christ their eternal life is secure.* Their only fear should be lest they surrender the truth, and thus betray the trust with which God has honored them."[57]

***1900**—from* Christ's Object Lessons: "By the messengers of God are presented to us the righteousness of Christ, justification by faith, the exceeding great and precious promises of God's word, free access to the Father by Christ, the comfort of the Spirit, the well-grounded *assurance of eternal life in the kingdom of God.*"[58]

"When Christ reigns in the soul, there is purity, freedom from sin. The glory, the fullness, the completeness of the gospel plan is fulfilled in the life. The acceptance of the Saviour brings a glow of perfect peace, perfect love, *perfect assurance.* The beauty and fragrance of the character of Christ revealed in the life testifies that God has indeed sent His Son into the world to be its Saviour."[59]

***1901**—from a* General Conference Bulletin: "Our Saviour is not in Joseph's tomb. He has risen, and has proclaimed over the rent sepulchre, 'I am the resurrection and the life.' Let us show by our actions that we are living by faith in him. We can call upon him for assistance. He is at our right hand to help us. Each one of you may know for yourself that you have a living Saviour, that he is your helper and your God. *You need not stand where you say, 'I do not know whether I am saved.'* Do you believe in Christ as your personal Saviour? If you do, then rejoice."[60]

1905—from a letter to a dying woman: "Our precious Saviour has given His life for the sins of the world, and has pledged His word that He will save all who come to Him. *'God so loved the world, that he gave his only begotten Son, that whosoever believeth in him should not perish, but have everlasting life'* (John 3:16). *These are the conditions of gaining eternal life. Comply with them, and your hope is secured, whether you live or die.* Trust in the soul-saving Redeemer. Cast your helpless soul upon Him, and He will accept and bless and save you. *Only believe.* Receive Him with all your heart, and know that He wants you to win the crown of life."[61]

1915—from a conversation with her son shortly before her death: "I know in whom I have believed."[62]

The harshest critics don't know what to do with these statements, so they assert that Mrs. White contradicted herself. Close examination of the contexts in all of her writings on this topic, however, will cause the apparent contradictions to dissolve like vapors in the sun.[63] Like John Wesley, Ellen White taught that Christians must be faithful to the end, but they can have assurance of salvation along the journey. Such is the larger picture of Ellen White's teaching on salvation. The "never say, 'I am saved' " statements and the like should be read with this context in mind.

One additional point should be made regarding Ellen White and the assurance of salvation. In *The Great Controversy,* she gives the following description of the judgment process: "Every man's work passes in review before God and is registered for faithfulness or unfaithfulness. Opposite each name in the books of heaven is entered with terrible exactness every wrong word, every selfish act, every unfulfilled duty, and every secret sin, with every artful dissembling. Heaven-sent warnings or reproofs neglected, wasted moments, unimproved opportunities, the influence exerted for good or for evil, with its far-reaching results, all are chronicled by the recording angel."[64]

This is often presented as a fear-inducing statement that militates against the assurance of salvation Christianity offers. But analysis of the context gives a different picture. After explaining that the righteous won't be raised to life until after the judgment is completed and thus aren't "present in person at the tribunal when their records are examined and their cases decided," Mrs. White wrote, "Jesus will appear as their advocate, to plead in their behalf before God. 'If any man sin, we have an advocate with the Father, Jesus Christ the righteous.' 1 John 2:1. 'For Christ is not entered into the holy places made with hands, which are the figures of the true; but into heaven itself, now to appear in the presence of God for us.' 'Wherefore He is able also to save them to the uttermost that come unto God by Him, seeing He ever liveth to make intercession for them.' Hebrews 9:24; 7:25."⁶⁵

Here, on the *same page* of the solemn statement about the judgment, we find a word of encouragement that comes from two promises in Scripture. Thus, Ellen White says that the righteous will be judged—but not without their Advocate, Jesus Christ, pleading their case. On the next page we find the following statement: "All who have truly repented of sin, and by faith claimed the blood of Christ as their atoning sacrifice, have had pardon entered against their names in the books of heaven; as they have become partakers of the righteousness of Christ, and their characters are found to be in harmony with the law of God, their sins will be blotted out, and they themselves will be accounted worthy of eternal life."⁶⁶

And on the next page comes this assurance:

> The divine Intercessor presents the plea that all who have overcome through faith in His blood be forgiven their transgressions, that they be restored to their Eden home, and crowned as joint heirs with Himself to "the first dominion." Micah 4:8. Satan in his efforts to deceive and tempt our race had thought to frustrate the divine plan in man's creation; but Christ now asks that this plan be carried into effect as if man had never fallen. He asks for His people not only pardon and justification, full and complete, but a share in His glory and a seat upon His throne.
>
> While Jesus is pleading for the subjects of His grace, Satan accuses them before God as transgressors. The great deceiver has sought to lead them into skepticism, to cause them to lose confidence in God, to separate themselves from His love, and to break His law. Now he points to the record of their lives, to the defects of character, the unlikeness to Christ, which has dishonored their Redeemer, to all the sins that he has tempted them to commit, and because of these he claims them as his subjects.
>
> Jesus does not excuse their sins, but shows their penitence and faith, and, claiming for them forgiveness, He lifts His wounded hands before the Father and the holy angels, saying: I know them by name. I have graven them on the palms of My hands. "The sacrifices of God are a broken spirit: a broken and a contrite heart, O God, Thou wilt not despise." Psalm 51:17. And to the accuser of His people He declares: "The Lord rebuke thee, O Satan; even the Lord that hath chosen Jerusalem rebuke thee: is not this a brand plucked out of the fire?" Zechariah 3:2. Christ will clothe His faithful ones with His own righteousness, that He may present them to His Father "a

glorious church, not having spot, or wrinkle, or any such thing." Ephesians 5:27. Their names stand enrolled in the book of life, and concerning them it is written: "They shall walk with Me in white: for they are worthy." Revelation 3:4.[67]

Clifford Goldstein correctly observed that these kinds of Ellen White statements never seem to make it into the books that the critics write.[68] But one shouldn't miss the themes that these paragraphs contain—themes of forgiveness, justification, hope, and assurance for all those who trust in Jesus Christ, their Redeemer-Intercessor. The righteous can, indeed, experience assurance of salvation during the investigative judgment as long as they remain in union with Christ and "afflict their souls before God by sorrow for sin and true repentance."[69] Thus, the chapter "Facing Life's Record" in *The Great Controversy*, although indeed solemn, affirms rather than undermines Christian assurance.

Of no small significance is the fact that the evangelical John Wesley also believed and taught that the righteous would be judged in the final judgment. In his sermon "The Great Assize," based on Paul's statement in Romans 14:10, "We shall all stand before the judgment seat of Christ" (NKJV). Wesley clearly taught that the judgment will be exact and precise, detailing "every inward working of every human soul," and that the righteous will be judged with all their good and evil deeds exposed. But in the end, it will "be abundantly sufficient for them [the righteous], that all the transgressions which they had committed shall not be once mentioned unto them to their disadvantage; that their sins and transgressions, and iniquities shall be remembered no more to their condemnation."[70] While John Wesley and Ellen White differed on details regarding the final judgment, they were in agreement that the righteous will be judged and acquitted in "the great assize." So, when read in its immediate and larger literary contexts, Ellen White's teaching on the investigative judgment harmonizes with her larger message of salvation.[71]

Adventist theologian Samuele Bacchiocchi captured the dynamic relationship between faith and works during the investigative judgment that resonates with Ellen White's teaching.

> The final judgment "according to works" will be in a sense a judgment about faith. It will reveal if the professed faith was indeed genuine. If the faith was genuine, then works will be there as evidence. If the works are not there, then the faith was not real. James expresses this truth very strikingly: "But some one will say, 'You have faith and I have works.' Show me your faith apart from your works, and I by my works will show you my faith" (James 2:18).

The Big Picture, Part 2: Vindicating Ellen White's Message

The final judgment is not a judgment of our own merits, but of our faith-response to God's grace extended to us freely through Jesus Christ. God will not ask: What works have you done to deserve eternal life? But He will ask: What are your "fruits of righteousness which come through Jesus Christ" (Phil. 1:11)? To put it differently, God will ask for the "proof" of a living, active faith (Rom. 5:4; 2 Cor. 9:13). The task of the Christian is not to perform daily an adequate amount of works to pass the final judgment, but rather to verify daily that his faith is alive, "working through love" (Gal. 5:6).[72]

Ultimately, the big picture of Ellen White's understanding of salvation and the Christian life is found in her bestseller *Steps to Christ*. In this little book, she set forth her vision of the Christian life in thirteen Christ-centered "steps": (1) understanding God's love for man, (2) understanding the sinner's need of Christ, (3) repentance, (4) confession, (5) consecration, (6) experiencing faith and acceptance, (7) understanding the test of discipleship, (8) understanding how to grow up into Christ, (9) understanding the nature of Christian work and life, (10) gaining a knowledge of God, (11) experiencing the privilege of prayer, (12) learning how to handle doubt in the Christian life, and (13) rejoicing in the Lord.[73] Here the warmth of the Wesleyan-Arminian assurance of salvation and the concept of works of faith comes through clearly; yet in *Steps to Christ*, Ellen White adds an emphasis on the character of God as revealed and vindicated in the life and death of Jesus Christ.[74] Particularly evident is the idea of the freedom of the will. Mrs. White wrote, for example, that we are "always free" to "*choose* another master"[75] than Christ.

Steps to Christ is thoroughly evangelical and thoroughly biblical and has blessed countless readers over the years. The fact, then, that it was compiled from Mrs. White's previous writings that ranged from 1857 to 1890, demonstrates that this Christ-centered emphasis spanned at least that much of her writing career.[76] The critics' refusal to acknowledge this should point us to the realization that the only way to hear her real message is to interpret her writings fairly and honestly.

George Knight has identified seven themes that "integrate the various strands of [Ellen White's] thinking into a unified network of concepts that provide an interpretive framework for not only single documents but for entire sectors of her writings (such as health, education, and family living)." While there are more than seven major themes, these seven "seem to be among her most basic," and "represent ideas that help us understand her theology and her burden for individuals and the church."[77] They are (1) the love of God, (2) the great controversy, (3) Jesus, the cross, and salvation through Him, (4) the centrality of the Bible, (5) the Second Coming, (6) the third angel's message and Adventist mission, and (7) practical Christianity and the development of Christian character.[78]

While themes 2 and 3 are all-encompassing themes that run throughout all of Ellen White's writings, as we have shown in this chapter, all seven themes are woven beautifully into a rich tapestry that expresses her true message. When we see and understand this message in its immediate and larger contexts, the critics' wrenching of Ellen White's writings loses its power, and we see it for what it is.

Conclusion

Ellen White's primary call to Christians was to give themselves in radical discipleship to Jesus Christ. Her longing was for all her readers to love God with all their physical and mental powers and to be completely sold out to Jesus. The following statement in *Steps to Christ* beautifully sums up her message.

A life in Christ is a life of restfulness. There may be no ecstasy of feeling, but there should be an abiding, peaceful trust. Your hope is not in yourself; it is in Christ. Your weakness is united to His strength, your ignorance to His wisdom, your frailty to His enduring might. So you are not to look to yourself, not to let the mind dwell upon self, but look to Christ. Let the mind dwell upon His love, upon the beauty, the perfection, of His character. Christ in His self-denial, Christ in His humiliation, Christ in His purity and holiness, Christ in His matchless love—this is the subject for the soul's contemplation. It is by loving Him, copying Him, depending wholly upon Him, that you are to be transformed into His likeness.[79]

The final section of this book discusses how to respond in a positive way to the criticisms of Ellen White. One way to do this is to provide evidence that she was an evangelical at heart—a fact that most critics ignore.

Chapter Summary

1. The critics of Ellen White focus mostly on isolated controversial statements in her writings and fail to hear the good news in her larger message.
2. In recent years, detractors have focused on the great controversy theme, and charging that it is not a biblical concept. They have characterized it as portraying a "hesitating, self-protecting, political God"

The Big Picture, Part 2: Vindicating Ellen White's Message

who is "watching his cosmic popularity polls." The great controversy theme, they argue, portrays God focusing on Himself—on protecting His integrity—whereas "the gospel declares that God set about to solve the problem created by man, not Himself." The God "who is truly God of all does not have to prove to anyone that He is fair and Satan is lying." It has even been suggested that the Adventist understanding of the great controversy falsely portrays God as "locked in a battle with Satan," the outcome of which "is yet to be seen." This chapter provided a fourfold response to these charges:

Chapter Summary

a. First, the biblical evidence supporting Ellen White's great controversy theme is significant.

　i. This motif is fundamental to the entire Bible, and in her writings, Mrs. White was simply reflecting this worldview.

　ii. Evangelical scholar Gregory A. Boyd has captured the attention of the evangelical community with his books *God at War: The Bible and Spiritual Conflict* and *Satan and the Problem of Evil: Constructing a Trinitarian Warfare Theodicy*. These books recognize a "warfare worldview" as central to the Bible.

　iii. One can clearly see the great controversy theme at work throughout Scripture—in the Old Testament, in the "enmity" Genesis 3:15 says would exist between the serpent, Satan, and of the woman's Seed, Christ; in the wickedness of the antediluvians; in the development of paganism and idolatry; and in the corrupting of the Hebrew religion.

　iv. In the New Testament, the controversy reached its highest level of intensity at the first advent of Christ. Satan engaged Him in the wilderness temptations, in His public ministry, and in His sufferings. But He obtained the victory at every step and ultimately defeated Satan at the cross (Rev. 12:10, 11). Jesus also referred to the great controversy in His parables.

　v. Paul referred to Satan as the "prince of the power of the air" (Eph. 2:2, NKJV) and the "god of this world" (2 Cor. 4:4). Most notable is his view of the church's warfare with Satan and his angels: "Our struggle is not against flesh and blood, but against the rulers, against the authorities, against the powers of this

Chapter Summary

      dark world and against the spiritual forces of evil in the heavenly realms" (Eph. 6:12, NIV).

   vi. Ultimately, the book of Revelation describes the culmination of this great controversy, picturing Christ as the Divine Warrior who destroys the devil and all his followers at the end of time and establishes eternal peace on the earth made new where the believers no longer engage in battles with sin (Rev. 19–22).

   vii. To assert that Ellen White's great controversy theme is not biblical, then, is clearly a failure to listen carefully to Scripture.

b. Second, the idea that Ellen White viewed the outcome of Christ's battle with Satan as uncertain is evidence of a complete failure to hear her message.

   i. In his *The Great Controversy Theme in E. G. White Writings*, Joseph Battistone stated that it is incorrect "to speak of a cosmic dualism" in Ellen White's writings.

   ii. "To be sure," he argued, "Ellen White does understand the controversy to be a contest between two antagonistic powers, but insofar as she is concerned the end of the struggle is never in doubt. The principles of righteousness and truth as exemplified in the life of Christ will ultimately triumph over the principles of sin and error as displayed in the activity of Satan."

c. Third, the idea that Scripture doesn't portray a vindication of God's character in the great controversy is mistaken.

   i. The character of God is a major theme that runs throughout the Bible from Genesis to Revelation.

   ii. The character of God is the central issue in the narrative of the Fall (Genesis 3). Satan misrepresents God, maligning His loving and redeeming nature, which is summed up in His personal name, *Yahweh*. This indicates the centrality of God's character as the great issue in earth's first temptation and Fall.

   iii. Throughout the rest of the Old Testament, literally hundreds of texts speak of God's personal name, *Yahweh*, vindicating who He is and what He does. The prophets' writings, the historical narratives, and the psalms all unite in a powerful chorus to praise God's character—His goodness, mercy, and justice.

   iv. By the time we get to the New Testament, the Messiah, first promised way back in the Garden (see Genesis 3:15), has finally arrived. Through His birth, life, and teachings, Jesus Christ gave the world the ultimate revelation of God's good character, His loving, self-giving nature.

Chapter Summary

  v. The last book of the Bible, Revelation, where all the biblical books converge, contains repeated celebrations of God's mighty actions in behalf of human beings and proclamations of His worthiness, justice, and truthfulness.
d. Fourth, the charge that the great controversy theme portrays God as self-protecting, political, and focused on His reputation is a gross misunderstanding of Ellen White's message.
  i. The first chapter of *The Desire of Ages* beautifully sets forth the nature of God's vindication of His character and government.
  ii. There, Ellen White presents Jesus as declaring God's name and His character through the words of Exodus 34:6, God's proclamation of His name to Moses.
  iii. According to Ellen White, Jesus came to "unveil" the "deception" of Satan and show that "God's law of love" is a "law of unselfishness." In stooping to take humanity upon Himself, "Christ revealed a character opposite of the character of Satan," the one who is really filled with self-interest and the lust for political gain. Christ "stepped still lower in the path of humiliation" in His death on the cross.
  iv. God answers Satan's charges to show all created beings the depth of His love by what He has done in His Son. Such love as is displayed in the gospel is without a parallel. It speaks to each child of humanity, to each angel in heaven, and to all the unfallen beings that populate God's perfect universe.
  v. In Ellen White's understanding, God's interest in vindicating His character bears no resemblance to the human desire to build one's own reputation. In the entire process of vindicating Himself and His government, God reveals a deeper level of His love for His creation. He acts in selfless ways that intensify the peace and joy experienced throughout the universe. God is more concerned about the welfare and happiness of all His

Chapter Summary

intelligent created beings than about His reputation—at least in the sense that humans are selfishly concerned about theirs.

3. The nature of the atonement is another concept relevant to this discussion of the great controversy theme. *Atonement* ("at-one-ment") is the process by which God reconciles human beings to Himself through the work of Christ. Evangelical theologians often use this word in its technical sense of designating the complete, all-sufficient, once-for-all sacrifice of Christ on Calvary. Ellen White also understood the atonement in this biblical sense.

   a. But Ellen White also understood the atonement in its wider biblical sense as found in the New Testament concept of "reconciliation," which includes the effect the atonement has on all of God's creation.

   b. It is helpful, as George Knight suggests, to "think of the atonement as a line rather than a single point even though the crucifixion of Christ is the turning point in the conflict between God and Satan."

   c. For Ellen White, then, the atonement was a process that involved the different phases of Christ's work—Incarnation, sinless life, vicarious death, Resurrection, Ascension, heavenly intercession, Second Coming, and final judgment. In her thinking, all of these vital works collectively form the atonement process. Nevertheless, she viewed Christ's death on the cross as central to the atonement—"the great truth around which all other truths cluster."

4. Which of the five classical theories on the atonement did Ellen White teach?

   a. The five theories are example, moral influence, governmental, ransom, and penal substitution.

   b. The answer to the question is that Ellen White's writings cannot be categorized as being *exclusively* under any *one* theory. Rather, her writings reflect different aspects of four of these theories.

   c. For instance, while her thought on the great controversy in its cosmic dimensions clearly connects with the governmental theory, she also differed with advocates of this theory in her hearty endorsement of the penal-substitution theory.

   d. In relation to the moral-influence theory, she saw the Cross as a

The Big Picture, Part 2: Vindicating Ellen White's Message

demonstration of the love of God but, again, she clearly parted from this theory in her penal-substitution statements, which seem to predominate in her expressions of the atonement.

Chapter Summary

e. Those critics who accuse Ellen White of teaching legalism have failed to understand the larger context of her message on the atonement.

5. Ellen White's teaching on the salvation experience is often misunderstood, due to a lack of understanding of the Wesleyan-Arminian influence on her thought.

    a. Wesleyan Arminianism is a combination of the theological concepts of Jacob Arminius (1560–1609), a professor of theology at Leiden, Holland, known for his rejection of the strict Calvinistic doctrine of predestination and emphasis on the freedom of the will, and John Wesley (1703–1791), the renowned revivalist and founder of Methodism.

    b. Impressed with the theological concepts of Arminius, Wesley developed his own theological system, emphasizing both grace and human response: justification and assurance on the one hand, and sanctification and perfection on the other.

    c. Wesley believed that while a believer can have assurance of salvation, if that believer quenches the convictions of the Holy Spirit and falls into a habitual pattern of unconfessed sin, he or she can lose salvation.

    d. Ellen White followed Wesley in his teaching on free will and the conditional perseverance of the saints—the possibility that Christians can fall from grace if they choose to live in sin without repenting.

    e. This background is essential for correctly understanding Ellen White's "never say, 'I am saved' " statements. Critics cite these statements as proof that she robs Christians of the assurance of salvation by "arguing for salvation by works" and "claiming that a person must be perfect and sinless before he can claim that he is saved."

    f. A careful analysis of these statements, however, reveals that the critics haven't done their homework. In each instance, Ellen White is responding from her Wesleyan-Arminian understanding of the

> **Chapter Summary**

conditional perseverance of the saints, and she is emphasizing the biblical mandate/principle: "If you think you are standing, be careful that you don't fall!" (1 Cor. 10:12, NIV).

    g. To her, the finality of the statement "I am saved" encourages the presumptuous "once saved, always saved" attitude and influences Christians to "rest in a satisfied condition and cease to make advancement" in Christian growth. However, she did not undermine the encouragement and motivation that comes from the biblical assurance of salvation.

    h. That Ellen White believed in and taught assurance of salvation for Christians throughout her long life is evident from the abundance of statements she made to that effect.

    i. When Ellen White's teaching on the investigative judgment is read in context, it harmonizes with her larger message of salvation. She viewed the judgment in light of the dynamic relationship between faith and works as found in Scripture.

    j. Of no small significance is the fact that John Wesley, whose theology was thoroughly evangelical, also believed and taught that the righteous would be judged and acquitted in the final judgment, "The Great Assize"—though Ellen White differed from Wesley regarding details of that judgment.

6. Ultimately, the big picture of Ellen White's understanding of salvation and the Christian life is found in her bestseller, *Steps to Christ*.

    a. Here the warmth of the Wesleyan-Arminian assurance of salvation and its agreement of the importance of works of faith come through clearly. Yet *Steps to Christ* moves beyond this tradition by emphasizing the character of God as revealed and vindicated in the life and death of Jesus Christ.

    b. This little book is both thoroughly evangelical and thoroughly biblical. It has blessed countless readers over the years.

    c. The fact that it was compiled from previous writings of Mrs. White, ranging in date from 1857 to 1890, indicates the Christ-centered emphasis spanned at least that much of her writing career.

    d. The fact that critics refuse to acknowledge this should alert their readers to the fact that one can hear Ellen White's real message only when one interprets her writings fairly and honestly.

Part III

RESPONDING IN THE AFFIRMATIVE

CHAPTER 13

An Evangelical at Heart

Throughout Ellen White's life and in the century following her death, critics claimed that she was legalistic, harsh, judgmental, untruthful, defensive, revengeful, eccentric, self-contradictory, dishonest, and deceptive. Today's critics also argue that she taught aberrant theological ideas and therefore cannot be called an evangelical in any sense of the term. On top of that, they say, she can't be trusted because she lied about her use of the works of other authors, so Christians should stay away from her writings.

A point-by-point analysis of the historical data regarding the person of Ellen White refutes each of these charges. We'll focus particularly on whether she was a genuine evangelical, arguing that, yes, she was a true evangelical at heart. Contrary to what the critics say, Mrs. White lived and articulated a warm, vibrant, evangelical spirituality with Christ at its center and the Bible as its foundation.

Like the evangelicalism of today,[1] the evangelical Christianity that existed during Ellen White's lifetime had distinctive characteristics that set it apart from the rest of Christendom. Its adherents were orthodox in the sense that they shared with other Christians an acceptance of the doctrines articulated in the ancient Christian creeds. But they "usually preferred to dwell on what, as a package, distinguished them from other orthodox Christians."[2] According to historian David Bebbington, this package included four major emphases: the Bible as the Word of God, Christ and Him crucified, the necessity of conversion (i.e., a changed life), and Christian missionary activity.[3] Additional emphases were the efficacy of daily prayer and intimate fellowship with Jesus.[4]

A reading of *Steps to Christ, Christ's Object Lessons, Thoughts From the Mount of Blessing,* and the Conflict of the Ages series shows that Ellen White clearly fits within this theological framework. She took a different path, however, when it came to certain traditional, evangelical doctrines such as Sunday sacredness, immortality of the soul, predestination, an eternal burning hell, postmillennialism, and premillennial dispensationalism. She advocated instead a unique doctrinal package that included the obligation to observe the seventh-day Sabbath; the cleansing of the heavenly sanctuary with the antitypical Day of Atonement beginning on October 22, 1844; the personal, visible, premillennial return of Christ; the validity of the gift of prophecy; the conditional nature of immortality; and a distinctive understanding of final events on planet Earth—all integrated into two biblical ideas: the sanctuary and the three angels' messages of Revelation 14:6–12.

This unique and original theological system set Ellen White and her followers apart from other evangelical Christians.[5] Nevertheless, the framework for her presentation of these unique doctrines was basic evangelical Christianity. Her prophetic ministry was bathed in its warm and unmistakable piety, with a personal, living Savior, Jesus Christ, at its center.

To demonstrate that Ellen White was an evangelical at heart, I will present in this chapter three lines of evidence that her life and teaching fit within the basic theological framework of evangelicalism.[6]

A person of integrity

The first evidence that Ellen White was an evangelical at heart is that the historical records confirm that she was a person of integrity and worthy Christian influence in her personal and professional life. While Ellen White wasn't perfect and never claimed infallibility, her life revealed a consistent pattern of devotion to God and love for her neighbors. When read in context, her writings display an uncommon depth of evangelical spirituality permeated with the grace and goodness of God.

The nine volumes of the *Testimonies*, for example, are often cited by contemporary critics as an illustration of her legalistic, harsh, and judgmental attitude. Yet, when one reads through these volumes in their entirety, a different picture emerges. No doubt she called sin by its right name and delivered strong rebukes to the disobedient, but she delivered these rebukes in the context of grace-filled statements on Christ's love and strong appeals to embrace His salvation.[7]

For instance, Ellen White wrote a testimony to a man who had committed adultery. But rather than simply condemn him as unworthy of salvation, the words of reproof that she uttered were laced with grace. She clearly pointed out that he had sinned—"You forgot to watch and pray always lest you should *enter into* temptation," she wrote. "Your soul was marred by a crime. You stamped your life record in heaven with a fearful blot." But instead of continuing to dwell on the man's sin, she wrote him words of encouragement: "Yet deep humiliation and repentance before God will be acceptable to Him. The blood of Christ can avail to wash these sins away." And throughout the testimony, she repeatedly emphasized the mercy and forgiveness of God: "It is now your privilege, by humble confession and sincere repentance, to take words and return unto the Lord. The precious blood of Christ can cleanse you from all impurity, remove all your defilement, and make you perfect in Him. The mercies of Christ are still within your reach if you will accept them." In this grace-filled context she pled, "For the sake of your wronged wife, and your children, the fruit of your own body, cease to do evil, and learn to do well."[8] This pattern of admonition laced with grace is typical of the *Testimonies*.

Indeed, Geoffrey Garne's assessment of these nine volumes is correct: "That there is hope and mercy when we stumble is a message that falls like refreshing showers of rain from the pages of the *Testimonies*." He correctly concludes that "every counsel, admonition, instruction, and reproof is directed toward this supreme end, that Christ might reign in the hearts of His people and in every sphere of His church's life, operation, and endeavor." Far from being legalism, "this is true Christianity."[9]

Some will object, of course, and argue that Ellen White made many harsh and exacting demands. But the same could be said about Paul and Jesus when *they* aren't read in context. Paul's appeal to "mortify the deeds of the body" (Rom. 8:13, KJV), for example, sounds harsh without its context. Even some of Jesus' words are chilling out of context: "If anyone comes to me and does not hate his father and mother, his wife and children, his brothers and sisters—yes, even his own life—he cannot be my disciple" (Luke 14:26, NIV). And Peter, Jude, and John can sound demanding, as well. But when all of these New Testament demands are studied in their larger literary contexts, they fit perfectly into the balance of faith and works in the gospel. The same is true of Ellen White. When her apparent harsh and exacting demands are read in their immediate and larger literary contexts, grace always shines through.

The great evangelical writers, such as the Puritan Richard Baxter and the founder of Methodism John Wesley, provide other examples. Anyone who reads parts of Baxter's *Christian Directory*[10] without looking at the larger message could easily get bogged down in some of his detailed and apparent legalistic applications of divine truth. But when this magisterial work is read widely and deeply, the Christianity of Baxter's message comes through with great clarity. It is the same with the works of both Wesley and Ellen White. They must be seen in their entirety, in their literary context. When this is done, Ellen

White's evangelical spirit is hard to miss.

Concerning Ellen White's personal qualities, several statements can be found outside of the Adventist community, such as the following published in the *American Biographical History of Eminent and Self-Made Men of the State of Michigan* (1878): "Mrs. White is a woman of singularly well-balanced mental organization. Benevolence, spirituality, conscientiousness, and ideality are the predominating traits. Her personal qualities are such to win for her the warmest friendship of all with whom she comes in contact, and to inspire them with the utmost confidence. . . . Notwithstanding her many years of public labor, she has retained all the simplicity and honesty which characterized her early life."[11]

Within the Adventist community, several witness statements were published over the years with regard to the charges that Mrs. White and her husband engaged in fanaticism. The following one, published in 1860, was signed by twenty-nine people.

> In view of the slanderous reports circulated by a few individuals against Bro. and sister White, we feel called upon to testify that we have been personally acquainted with them and their course since 1844, and therefore know that any statements that would represent them as being in any wise connected with, or countenancing in any degree, those fanatical abominations into which some in Maine and elsewhere were drawn during the years 1844–1846, are wicked and malicious falsehoods. We have never known them to be in the least infected with the spirit or works of fanaticism, but on the contrary, as the untiring and unflinching opposers of the same.[12]

Of special interest is an affirmation of Ellen White's Christian experience from her most significant detractor, Dudley M. Canright. Dudley's brother, Jasper Canright, who remained faithful to the Seventh-day Adventist Church all of his life, recalled Dudley's words at the time of her funeral: "As he stood at Sister White's casket with one hand on my arm and the other hand on her coffin with tears streaming down his cheeks, he said: 'There's a noble Christian woman gone.' "[13]

When all of the evidence is placed on the table, the *real* Ellen White of history emerges as a person of integrity, humility, simplicity, sincerity, determination, humor, happiness, balance, and devotion.[14] This view of her can be verified in her own writings and in the testimonies of those who worked with her—all of which is documented in the historical records housed at the Ellen G. White Estate and its research centers around the world and is gradually being put online for the public to access.[15]

The cardinal doctrines

The second evidence that Ellen White was an evangelical at heart is that she affirmed the cardinal doctrines of the historic Christian church. The cardinal doctrines are those biblical teachings central in the teaching of the Christian church over the centuries: the Bible as the inspired-revealed Word of God and thus the final authority for Christian life and teaching; the Trinity, or Godhead (God the Father, God the Son, and God the Holy Spirit); the person and work of Jesus Christ in His incarnation, perfect life, atoning death, bodily resurrection, ascension, intercession, and second coming; and the experience of salvation through justification and sanctification.[16] There are others, of course, but the focus in this chapter is on Ellen White's relation to these particular doctrines so important to evangelicals.

1. Ellen White affirmed the Bible as the revealed-inspired Word of God and thus the final authority for Christian life and teaching. As we saw in chapter 7, Ellen White repeatedly exalted the Bible as the final authority for Christian life and teaching. Not once in her seventy-year-long prophetic ministry did she present her writings as equal to or above the Bible. The Bible was first, last, and best in all of her teaching. Even in those places in her writings where she doesn't directly cite the Bible, it is clearly the framework for her counsels.[17] To Mrs. White, the Bible was the inspired-revealed Word of God, "the guidebook to the inhabitants of a fallen world, bequeathed to them that, by studying and obeying the directions, not one soul would lose its way to heaven."[18]

If I felt for one instant that Ellen White's writings posed a threat to the final authority of Scripture, her claim to the prophetic office would lose its significance for me. However, reading her writings over the years has increased my appreciation of and desire for the Bible as the authoritative Word of God and guidebook for my life and ministry. In fact, her writings have influenced the type of preaching students learn in my homiletics classes—expository preaching, which explains and applies the original meaning of a biblical text to the contemporary audience.[19]

2. Ellen White affirmed the biblical teaching of the Godhead (God the Father, God the Son, and God the Holy Spirit). Her teaching was clear on the full deity of each Member of the Godhead.[20] For example, she referred to "the Father, the Son, and the Holy Spirit" as the "three living persons of the heavenly trio," the "eternal heavenly dignitaries," and the "three highest powers in heaven."[21] Using the language of Colossians 2:9, she unequivocally declared,

> The Father is *all the fullness of the Godhead* bodily, and is invisible to mortal sight.

The Son is *all the fullness of the Godhead* manifested. The Word of God declares Him to be "the express image of His person." "God so loved the world, that He gave His only-begotten Son, that whosoever believeth in Him should not perish, but have everlasting life." Here is shown the personality of the Father.

The Comforter that Christ promised to send after He ascended to heaven, is the Spirit in *all the fullness of the Godhead,* making manifest the power of divine grace to all who receive and believe in Christ as a personal Saviour.[22]

Over the years I have studied different works on systematic theology and enjoyed the Trinitarian insights of the various theologians. But none of these writers has made the concept of the Trinity more clear, meaningful, personal, and powerful to me than has Ellen White.[23]

3. Ellen White affirmed the person and work of Jesus Christ in His incarnation, perfect life, atoning death, bodily resurrection, ascension, intercession, and second coming. That Ellen White fits within the historic Christian teaching on these aspects of the person and work of Jesus Christ is abundantly clear from a reading of her classic, Christ-centered works *The Desire of Ages, The Acts of the Apostles,* and *Steps to Christ.* Furthermore, scholarly studies confirm her evangelical position on Christ's incarnation and atoning death. For example, Eric Claude Webster's engaging study *Crosscurrents in Adventist Christology* documents Ellen White's biblical approach to the Incarnation, and John Wood's insightful study "Mighty Opposites: The Atonement of Christ in the Writings of Ellen G. White" sets forth her broad view of the atonement and shows her careful navigation away from the heresy of perfectionism.[24]

The second coming of Christ was central to Ellen White's thought and experience from the time of her conversion in the Millerite experience during the 1840s to the end of her life in 1915. She earnestly believed in the premillennial return of Christ following the Tribulation, and she consistently taught this view throughout her ministry. It is in *The Great Controversy* that her writing on the second coming of Christ becomes most pointed. There she describes the hope of the ages—the day when Christ comes—in the most moving language. For example, she writes that at the moment of the resurrection,

amid the reeling of the earth, the flash of lightning, and the roar of thunder, the voice of the Son of God calls forth the sleeping saints. He looks upon the graves of the righteous, then, raising His hands to heaven, He cries: "Awake, awake, awake, ye that sleep in the dust, and arise!" Throughout the length and breadth of the earth the dead shall hear that voice, and they that hear shall live. And the whole earth shall ring with the tread of the exceeding great army of every nation, kindred, tongue, and people. From the prison house of death they come, clothed with immortal glory, crying: "O death, where is thy sting? O grave, where is thy victory?" 1 Corinthians 15:55. And the living righteous and the risen saints unite their voices in a long, glad shout of victory.[25]

Christ and His works of salvation were major emphases in her counsels to preachers of the gospel.

O that I could command language of sufficient force to make the impression that I wish to make upon my fellow-laborers in the gospel. My brethren, you are handling the words of life; you are dealing with minds that are capable of the highest development. Christ crucified, Christ risen, Christ ascended into the heavens, Christ coming again, should so soften, gladden, and fill the mind of the minister that he will present these truths to the people in love and deep earnestness. The minister will then be lost sight of and Jesus will be made manifest.

Lift up Jesus, you that teach the people, lift Him up in sermon, in song, in prayer. Let all your powers be directed to pointing souls, confused, bewildered, lost, to "the Lamb of God." Lift Him up, the risen Saviour, and say to all who hear, Come to Him who "hath loved us, and hath given Himself for us." [Ephesians 5:2.] Let the science of salvation be the burden of every sermon, the theme of every song. Let it be poured forth in every supplication. Bring nothing into your preaching to supplement Christ, the wisdom and power of God. Hold forth the word of life, presenting Jesus as the hope of the penitent and the stronghold of every believer. Reveal the way of peace to the troubled and the despondent, and show forth the grace and completeness of the Saviour.[26]

4. Ellen White affirmed the historic Protestant understanding of justification and sanctification. Research has verified that Ellen White followed Martin Luther's understanding on justification and John Wesley's understanding on sanctification, but that she synthesized these two concepts in her own unique way. After examining her writings and comparing them with the writings of the two reformers, W. R. Lesher concluded that she agrees with Luther on justification and, for the most part, with Wesley on sanctification. "Luther's emphasis is on justification and he holds a stronger view of it than Wesley," Lesher explained. And "Wesley's emphasis is on sanctification and he holds a stronger view of it than Luther." But, Lesher emphasized, Ellen White "holds the strong view of each and synthesizes them." Thus, it "must be concluded that in the relationship between justification and sanctification neither Luther or Wesley agrees fully with White but a synthesis of their views approximates her position."[27] Mrs. White's understanding best captured the dynamic relationship between justification and sanctification portrayed in Scripture.[28]

Ellen White's harmony with the Lutheran-Protestant position is further documented in Gunnar Pedersen's groundbreaking doctoral dissertation "The Soteriology of Ellen G. White Compared with the Lutheran Formula of Concord: A Study of the Adventist Doctrine of the Final Judgment of the Saints and Their Justification Before God." In the conclusion to his careful analysis, he writes,

> Ellen White understood the terms *justification* and *pardon* essentially as a forensic declaration of acceptance and forgiveness pronounced by the highest legal and judicial authority in the universe, based exclusively on Christ's merits and righteousness imputed to the believer. An essential agreement thus exists between Ellen White and the Lutherans regarding the basic meaning of justification as a forensic-relational reality that refers to a restored relationship with God on the basis of the divine pardon and forgiveness in Christ. She accordingly agreed with the Lutherans that the divine verdict of justification would be based exclusively on divine grace, manifested in the merits and righteousness of Christ, and received by the believer exclusively through a faith relationship with Christ—as the imputation of Christ's righteousness was seen as providing a complete satisfaction of the ultimate demands of the divine moral law. The penitent believer was likewise seen as existentially receiving and possessing a full and complete salvation as a present reality at the very moment that faith in Christ was born. The two traditions thus appear to be in essential accord with regard to the manner and time that a believer existentially receives and possesses a full and complete salvation.[29]

Concerning Ellen White's teaching on the pre-Advent investigative judgment, Pedersen notes that "none of her references to the function of the divine records in the judgment seem to indicate that sanctification has any meritorious function." That is, "the theological content and context of these statements reflect the idea that the celestial records basically serve as evidence with respect to the presence or absence of true justifying and sanctifying faith."[30]

Where Lutheran-Protestant theology and Ellen White's theology differ regarding forensic justification, according to Pedersen, is Ellen's introduction of the sanctuary doctrine. It "provides a dual, temporal perspective in which salvation may be viewed from the point of view of either its existential reception or from its eschatological, judicial ratification." He continues:

> In this salvation-historical perspective, she used the terms *pardon* and *justification* not only as a designation of the present existential reception and possession of salvation but also as a designation of its eschatological, judicial ratification in the judgment. In both temporal usages these terms carry the same forensic meaning expressive of divine forgiveness granted by the highest legal and judicial authority in the universe based exclusively on the provisions of Christ. The Lutherans, however, did not have a real temporal distinction between the existential reception and the forensic ratification of salvation: both aspects were seen basically as a present timeless reality.[31]

Pedersen concludes, therefore, that Ellen White's "assertion that the believer will instantly receive and possess a full and complete salvation as a present reality fully concurs with the Lutheran tradition," while "the eschatological dimension, implying that the forensic confirmatory aspect of salvation will be eschatological, constitutes a new feature in Protestant theology."[32]

Hans K. LaRondelle elaborates on Pedersen's conclusion regarding Ellen White and Adventism.

> Theologically speaking, Adventism has integrated the eschatological dimension of the final judgment in its soteriology, while Protestant theology has excluded it. Protestantism does not have a real temporal distinction between existential reception and the final ratification of salvation, because it views both aspects basically as a present reality. Adventist theology is thus characterized by its dual temporal dimension of justification. The sanctuary doctrine includes the eschatological dimension in its soteriology, without denying the assurance of a present salvation. The ongoing mediatorial work of Christ during the last judgment resolves the seeming paradox and tension that Protestant theology experiences when it faces the twofold revelation that humanity is saved by faith as a present reality, while judged ultimately according to works as a future reality.[33]

To simplify these theological statements: When read in context, Ellen White taught that the believer can, at the moment of conversion and throughout the Christian life, experience assurance of salvation based exclusively on Christ's merits and imputed righteousness. The fact that the pre-Advent judgment is taking place doesn't deny this assurance of present salvation. Furthermore, the decision God makes regarding every believer in the final judgment ratifies their prior experience of justification and sanctification. This final judicial ratification during the pre-Advent investigative judgment is the unique contribution of Adventism.[34]

Avoiding unbiblical, heretical teachings

The third evidence that Ellen White was an evangelical at heart is that she repeatedly directed the Seventh-day Adventist Church pioneers away from unbiblical, heretical teachings.

1. She directed the church away from strange, unbiblical ideas about the millennium, the 144,000, and the Lord's Supper. As early as 1848, long before the Seventh-day Adventist Church was organized, Ellen White led these early believers away from several strange unbiblical teachings. Ellen recalled,

Our first general meeting in western New York, beginning August 18, was held at Volney, in Brother David Arnold's barn. About thirty-five were present,—all the friends that could be collected in that part of the State. But of this number there were hardly two agreed. Some were holding serious errors, and each strenuously urged his own views, declaring that they were according to the Scriptures.

One brother held that the one thousand years of the twentieth chapter of Revelation were in the past, and that the one hundred and forty-four thousand mentioned in the seventh and fourteenth chapters of Revelation, were those raised at Christ's resurrection.

As we had before us the emblems of our dying Lord, and were about to commemorate His sufferings, this brother arose and said that he had no faith in what we were about to do; that the Lord's supper was a continuation of the Passover, and should be partaken of but once a year.

She went into vision and pointed out the errors of those present. "My accompanying angel," she wrote, "presented before me some of the errors of those present, and also the truth in contrast with their errors. These discordant views, which they claimed were in harmony with the Scriptures, were only according to their opinion of Bible teaching; and I was bidden to tell them that they should yield their errors, and unite upon the truths of the third angel's message. Our meeting closed triumphantly. Truth gained the victory. Our brethren renounced their errors and united upon the third angel's message, and God greatly blessed them and added many to their numbers."[35]

This type of prophetic guidance was typical of Ellen White's early ministry to the founders of Seventh-day Adventist theology. Rather than draw those Adventist pioneers away from sound biblical teaching, her visions moved them toward it.

2. She directed the church away from an unbiblical view of Jesus Christ. Most of Adventism's early pioneers held an Arian or semi-Arian position on the person of Jesus Christ. How then did the church move into its present position that the orthodox Christian doctrine of the Trinity, including Christ's full equality with the Father, is correct? The story is told in a most helpful way in the important book *The Trinity: Understanding God's Love, His Plan of Salvation, and Christian Relationships* written by three Adventist scholars: Woodrow Whidden, Jerry Moon, and John W. Reeve. In chapter 13 of that book, Moon provides a concise and penetrating overview of the history of the Trinity debate in Adventism, and in chapter 14, he sets forth Ellen White's view. He shows that the publication of Ellen White's *The Desire of Ages* in 1898 became the "continental divide for the Adventist understanding of the Trinity," and that its definitive statement that "in Christ is life, original, unborrowed, underived," set forth Jesus Christ as the "self-existent God."[36]

And, according to Moon, Ellen White had more to say regarding the subject of the Godhead.

> While *The Desire of Ages* set in motion a shift in the Adventist understanding of the Godhead, it was not her last word on the subject. Later, during the Kellogg crisis of 1902–1907, Ellen White repeatedly used expressions such as "three living persons of the heavenly trio," while continuing to maintain the essential unity of the Godhead. Thus she affirmed the plurality and the unity—the threeness and the one-ness—the foundational elements of a simple, biblical understanding of the Trinity.[37]

As such, Ellen White clearly set the stage for further Bible study by Seventh-day Adventist leaders. This fostered a steady decline in anti-Trinitarianism (1915–1946) and eventually resulted in the triumph of Trinitarianism (1946 to the present) in Seventh-day Adventism.

3. She directed the church away from crass legalism. As we saw in chapter 3, it was Ellen White who plainly identified the legalism of the 1870s and 1880s and admonished church leaders to depend on Christ rather than on themselves for righteousness. Her endorsement of the Christ-centered message of A. T. Jones and E. J. Waggoner during the 1888 General Conference Session set the church on a trajectory that eventually put righteousness by faith at the center of its theology. In other words, she put "Christian" back into Adventism. The following memorable statement sums up her appeal to dispense with a legalistic use of the law: "Let the law take care of itself. We have been at work on the law until we get as dry as the hills of Gilboa. . . . Let us trust in the merits of Jesus."[38]

4. She directed the church away from the heretical "holy flesh" teaching. The "holy flesh" movement asserted itself in the Indiana Conference during the years 1899–1900 and became "one of the most troubling doctrinal trends among Seventh-day Adventists during the post-1888 period." The leaders of this movement claimed it was a "cleansing message." The worship services of this movement were "characterized by forceful music and clapping of hands, shouting, and leaping" in order to obtain the anointing of the Holy Spirit. "Worshipers frequently fell prostrate, and after further tumultuous celebration by the congregation, they were declared to have passed 'through the garden experience,' which Christ had in Gethsemane." As a result, the "newly born person was now free from the power of death because he or she had received 'holy flesh' and therefore could sin no more."[39]

At the opening of the 1901 General Conference Session, when the cleansing message was about to spread to adjoining conferences, Ellen White unequivocally pronounced the holy flesh movement to be unbiblical and its goal a mistake. She said, "To those who have tried so hard to obtain by faith so-called holy flesh, I would say, You cannot obtain it. Not a soul of you has holy flesh now. No human being on the earth has holy flesh. It is an impossibility." She pointed out the satanic influence in this type of emotional excitement and admonished these people to seek true sanctification and to "keep within the bounds of the Bible."[40] Consequently, as the conference leaders accepted the reproof and resigned their offices, the movement ended.[41]

5. She directed the church away from John Harvey Kellogg's special brand of pantheism. In *The Living Temple,* the book the influential Adventist physician John Harvey Kellogg wrote on human physiology, he blended Christian teaching with pantheism. Church leaders, such as A. G. Daniells and W. W. Prescott, were alarmed at certain statements in the book. They objected to Kellogg's assertion that "God is the explanation of nature,—not a God outside of nature, but in nature, manifesting himself through and in all of the objects, movements, and varied phenomena of the universe," and especially Kellogg's claim that "God enters into our bodies in the taking of food."[42] Kellogg's views were posing a distinct threat to the church because some of its leading constituents—physicians, nurses, ministers, and church members in Battle Creek—were embracing them.

In response to this situation, Ellen White penned some strong warnings against Kellogg's pantheistic teachings, calling on church leaders to "meet it firmly, and without delay."[43] Arthur White describes the intensity of her efforts to steer the church away from this heresy.

> To sound a warning to the church throughout the land, Ellen White hurried the production of *Testimonies for the Church,* volume 8, with its section on "The Essential Knowledge," dealing with God and nature and a personal God. She dwelt at length on the danger of speculative knowledge, her message buttressed with abundant scripture evidence of a personal God. The book *The Ministry of Healing* was in preparation at this time; there was included in it also a section entitled "The Essential Knowledge," dealing with speculative knowledge and the false and true in education. Thus Ellen White went on record with warnings that would continue to sound.[44]

Conclusion

In light of these three lines of evidence, when she is read in context, the *real* Ellen White of history cannot be easily excluded from evangelical Christianity. While she didn't unite with the evangelicals of her day in all of their doctrinal positions, in terms of practical Christianity and the core doctrines of salvation, she was an evangelical at heart, as the following statement beautifully shows.

> O precious, loving, long-suffering, long-forbearing Jesus, how my soul adores Thee! That a poor, unworthy, sin-polluted soul can stand before the Holy God, complete in the righteousness of our Substitute and Surety! Wonder, O Heavens, and be astonished, O earth, that fallen man is the object of His infinite love and delight. He rejoices over them with celestial songs, and man defiled with sin, having become cleansed through the righteousness of Christ, is presented to the Father free from every spot and stain of sin, "not having spot, or wrinkle, or any such thing" (Eph. 5:27).[45]

This chapter has provided one way to respond affirmatively to the many charges against Ellen White. The realization that she was in harmony with the great themes of the biblical, evangelical faith and that she rejected all teachings that are contrary to the gospel undermines the charges of legalism and dishonesty. The final chapter of this book will wrap things up by offering proactive strategies for defending and advocating the prophetic ministry of Ellen White.

An Evangelical at Heart

Chapter Summary

1. Throughout her life and in the century following her death, critics claimed Ellen White was legalistic, harsh, judgmental, untruthful, defensive, revengeful, eccentric, self-contradictory, dishonest, and deceptive. Today's critics continue the same arguments and encourage Christians to stay away from her writings.
2. While a point-by-point analysis of the historical data regarding the person of Ellen White refutes each of these charges, this chapter argued instead that she was an evangelical at heart.
3. Contrary to what the critics say, Mrs. White lived and articulated a warm, vibrant, evangelical spirituality with Christ at its center and the Bible as its foundation.
4. Nineteenth-century evangelicalism possessed distinctive characteristics that set it apart from the rest of Christendom. It was characterized by four major emphases: the Bible as the Word of God, Christ and Him crucified, the necessity of conversion (i.e., a changed life), and Christian missionary activity. Additional emphases were the efficacy of daily prayer and intimate fellowship with Jesus.
5. A reading of *Steps to Christ, Christ's Object Lessons, Thoughts From the Mount of Blessing,* and the Conflict of the Ages series shows that Ellen White clearly fits within this theological framework.
6. She took a different path, however, when it came to certain traditional, evangelical doctrines such as Sunday sacredness, immortality of the soul, predestination, an eternal burning hell, postmillennialism, and premillennial dispensationalism.
7. Ellen White's unique and original theological system set her and her followers apart from other evangelical Christians. Nevertheless, the framework for her teaching on these unique doctrines was basic evangelical Christianity. Her prophetic ministry was bathed in its warm and unmistakable piety, which had a personal, living Savior, Jesus Christ, at its center.
8. This chapter presented three lines of evidence that Ellen White's life and teaching fit within the basic theological framework of evangelicalism.
    a. First, the historical records confirm that in her personal and

Chapter Summary

professional life Ellen White was a person of integrity and worthy Christian influence.

i. While Ellen White was not perfect and never claimed infallibility, her life revealed a consistent pattern of devotion to God and love for her neighbor. When read in context, her writings display an uncommon depth of evangelical spirituality permeated with the grace and goodness of God.

ii. The nine volumes of the *Testimonies* are often cited by contemporary critics as demonstrating her legalistic, harsh, and judgmental attitude. Yet, when one reads through these volumes in their entirety, a different picture emerges. No doubt she called sin by its right name and delivered strong rebukes to the disobedient, but she delivered these rebukes in the context of grace-filled statements on Christ's love and strong appeals to embrace the salvation He has made available. Geoffrey Garne's assessment of these nine volumes is correct: "That there is hope and mercy when we stumble is a message that falls like refreshing showers of rain from the pages of the *Testimonies*."

iii. Concerning Ellen White's personal qualities, several statements can be found outside of the Adventist community affirming her as a person of integrity.

iv. Even her most significant detractor, Dudley M. Canright, remarked at her funeral: "There's a noble Christian woman gone."

v. Many statements affirming her Christian character come from those who knew her.

vi. When all of the evidence is placed on the table, the *real* Ellen White of history emerges as a person of integrity, humility, simplicity, sincerity, determination, humor, happiness, balance, and devotion. This view of her can be verified in her own writings and in the testimonies of those who worked with her—all of which is documented in the historical records housed at the Ellen G. White Estate and its research centers around the world and is gradually being put online for the public to access.

An Evangelical at Heart

    b. Second, Ellen White affirmed the cardinal doctrines of the historic Christian church. The cardinal doctrines are those biblical teachings central in the teaching of the Christian church over the centuries.

Chapter Summary

       i. She affirmed the Bible as the revealed-inspired Word of God and thus the final authority for Christian life and teaching.

      ii. She affirmed the biblical teaching of the triune Godhead (God the Father, God the Son, and God the Holy Spirit).

     iii. She affirmed the person and work of Jesus Christ in His incarnation, perfect life, atoning death, bodily resurrection, ascension, intercession, and second coming.

     iv. She affirmed the historic Protestant understanding of justification and sanctification. Where Lutheran-Protestant theology and Ellen White's theology differ regarding forensic justification is in Ellen's introduction of the sanctuary doctrine. The fact that the pre-Advent judgment is taking place doesn't negate this assurance of present salvation.

    c. Third, Ellen White repeatedly directed the Seventh-day Adventist Church pioneers away from unbiblical, heretical teachings.

       i. She directed the church away from strange, unbiblical ideas about the millennium, the 144,000, and the Lord's Supper.

      ii. She directed the church away from an unbiblical view of Jesus Christ.

     iii. She directed the church away from crass legalism in the 1870s and 1880s.

     iv. She directed the church away from the heretical "holy flesh" teaching.

      v. She directed the church away from John Harvey Kellogg's special brand of pantheism.

9. In light of these three lines of evidence, when the *real* Ellen White of history is read in context, her standing within evangelical Christianity becomes clear. While she didn't unite with the evangelicals of her day in all of their doctrinal beliefs, in terms of practical Christianity and the core doctrines of salvation she was an evangelical at heart.

CHAPTER 14

The Best Defense Is a Good Offense

"Sanctify Christ as Lord in your hearts," counseled the apostle Peter, "always being ready to make a defense to everyone who asks you to give an account for the hope that is in you, yet with gentleness and reverence" (1 Pet. 3:15, NASB). We noted in chapter 1 that responding to criticisms of Ellen White's prophetic gift in the light of this text takes us beyond defensiveness. There is no need for us to be touchy and reactive to every criticism against our faith. We can exercise simple trust in Christ as Lord and give a reasoned defense at the appropriate time with "gentleness and reverence." Responding to criticisms with this kind of attitude leads us to do our best and leave the results in God's hands.

In chapter 2 we saw that the pioneers of our church passed a resolution in 1855 to protect themselves from being consumed by the task of answering their critics. In this important resolution, they voted to keep the "defense" of truth—the act of defending it against attacks—and the "advocacy" of truth—the act of arguing in favor of truth and presenting positive evidence for it—together in their work of spreading the everlasting gospel. This is a smart, God-given approach that we are wise to continue today. Accordingly, this chapter proposes eight proactive strategies for defending and advocating the prophetic ministry of Ellen White. As the old saying goes, "the best defense is a good offense."

1. We should acknowledge that we have made mistakes and correct them.

The fact that there are so many former Adventists who say that leaving Adventism was like "freedom from bondage" or a "journey out of legalism" dramatically alerts us to the fact that there are still pockets of legalism within the Adventist Church—in some cases, sometimes large pockets. While the testimonies posted on the Internet by those who have left the church don't reflect the true nature of Seventh-day Adventism, many of the individuals who left had a legalistic experience while they were still Adventists.[1] It is no small wonder that criticisms of Adventism appealed to them. To deny this reality would be a gross mistake.

In this context, we need to ask ourselves what we as a people have done wrong to create such strong negative feelings in those who have left us. Is it all their fault, or are we to blame, as well? Is our local church warm, loving, and friendly? Or is it cold, harsh, and unforgiving? Does our local Adventist community "shoot its wounded"? The old saying "we have found the enemy, and he is us" may be true for too many of us.

Adventists have all too often created a climate that squelches genuine Christian spirituality and fosters legalism. Sometimes we have even been downright mean-spirited in our Adventism. Many can relate to George Knight when he writes that he has known "Sabbath-keepers" and "vegetarians" who "are meaner than the Devil." Unfortunately, he is right—it "is all too easy to be an Adventist without being a Christian." God "has chosen to use quite fallible human instruments to finish His work," so we all need genuine humility.[2] I suggest, therefore, that we acknowledge the following mistakes and make the necessary corrections:

We allow some Adventists to place Ellen White on a pedestal—something that she never would have allowed to happen. Roger Coon stated the case humorously when he said that some Adventists portray Ellen White as a "Vegetarian Virgin Mary." They take every word she wrote literally, often without the literary context, and promote it as though it were equal with or above the Bible. Sometimes they espouse extreme interpretations and press them on others as the only correct view. While the rest of us may never have participated in such distortions and abuses of Ellen White's writings, if we have allowed them to happen on our watch—whether it be in our church, Sabbath School class, small group, or home—we are part of the problem. It is now time for us to take a stand and hold those accountable who misrepresent and misapply these writings. Neither Ellen White nor the pioneers were silent about these kinds of abuses. Ellen White herself said,

> There is a class of people who are always ready to go off on some tangent, who want to catch up something strange and wonderful and new; but God desires us all to move calmly, considerately, choosing our words in harmony with the solid truth for this time. The truth should be presented to the mind as free as possible from that which is emotional, while still

bearing the intensity and solemnity befitting its character. We must guard against encouraging extremists, those who would be either in the fire or in the water.

I beseech you to weed out of your teachings every extravagant expression, everything that unbalanced minds, and those who are inexperienced, will catch up, and which will lead them to make wild, immature movements. It is necessary for you to cultivate caution in every statement, lest you start some on a wrong track, and make confusion that will require much sorrowful labor to set in order, thus diverting the strength of the laborers into lines which God does not design shall be entered. One manifestation of fanaticism among us will close many doors against the soundest principles of truth.[3]

In 1868, James White described some of the challenges his wife faced with her readers:

She works to this disadvantage, namely: she makes strong appeals to the people, which a few feel deeply, and take strong positions, and go to extremes. Then to save the cause from ruin in consequence of these extremes, she is obliged to come out with reproofs for extremists in a public manner. This is better than to have things go to pieces; but the influence of both the extremes and the reproofs are terrible on the cause, and brings upon Mrs. W. a three-fold burden. Here is the difficulty: What she may say to urge the tardy, is taken by the prompt to urge them over the mark. And what she may say to caution the prompt, zealous, incautious ones, is taken by the tardy as an excuse to remain too far behind.[4]

The situation hasn't changed much in this regard. People still misread these writings. In the spirit of our pioneers, then, let us each take a personal stand against the abuses of Ellen White's writings in our churches that serves only to discredit the prophetic gift.

We allow "Ellen White missiles" to whistle through the church corridors and strike the unsuspecting victim, exploding into pain and frustration. This forceful use of Ellen White quotes to put others in their place has happened all too often in Adventist history and has never helped the prophetic gift. There is a definite place for using appropriate Ellen White statements to encourage and give loving correction, but the indiscriminate and insensitive "Sister White says!" has proven harmful to the cause. This abuse of her statements must stop. We must hold each other accountable as to how we cite Ellen White. Listen to her own concern about this matter, written as early as 1857.

I saw that many have taken advantage of what God has shown in regard to the sins and wrongs of others. *They have taken the extreme meaning of what has been shown in vision, and then have pressed it until it has had a tendency to weaken the faith of many in what God has shown, and also to discourage and dishearten the church.* With tender compassion should brother deal with brother. Delicately should he deal with feelings. It is the nicest [most exacting] and most important work that ever yet was done to touch the wrongs of another. With the deepest humility should a brother do this, considering his own weakness, lest he also should be tempted.[5]

We allow too many individuals or groups with legalistic interpretations of Ellen White's writings to hold us or our local churches hostage. They keep us from appreciating the real worth of these writings and from doing the work that we should be doing. These individuals and their views have caused many a person to become discouraged or angered and leave the church. Every Seventh-day Adventist should work with his or her local church pastor in establishing a congregational atmosphere of love, compassion, and truth so that this spirit of legalism cannot flourish. Ellen White said it best herself.

It is the desire and plan of Satan to bring in among us those who will go to great extremes—people of narrow minds, who are critical and sharp, and very tenacious in holding their own conceptions of what the truth means. They will be exacting, and will seek to enforce rigorous duties, and go to great lengths in matters of minor importance, while they neglect the weightier matters of the law—judgment and mercy and the love of God. Through the work of a few of this class of persons, the whole body of Sabbathkeepers will be designated as bigoted, Pharisaical, and fanatical. The work of the truth, because of these workers, will be thought to be unworthy of notice.

God has a special work for the men of experience to do. They are to guard the cause of God. They are to see that the work of God is not committed to men who feel it their privilege to move out on their own independent judgment, to preach whatever they please, and to be responsible to no one for their instructions or work. Let this spirit of self-sufficiency once rule in our midst, and there will be no harmony of action, no unity of spirit, no safety for the work, and no healthful growth in the cause. There will be false teachers, evil workers who will, by insinuating error, draw away souls from the truth. Christ prayed that his followers might be one as he and the Father were one. Those who desire to see this prayer answered, should seek to discourage the slightest tendency to division, and try to keep the spirit of unity and love among brethren.[6]

Yes, some supporters of Ellen White have acted as much like her enemies as have those who have left the church and now oppose it. We as a people still have a lot of self-educating and growing to do. There are other mistakes we need to work on, as well. To those who once were a part of us but who got discouraged because of an oppressive use of Ellen White's writings, all I can say is that I'm sorry. What you experienced was not right or fair to you as a human being made in the image of God. This is not true Adventism, nor is it how the church officially views Ellen White.

So, indeed, the first step in launching a good offense for Ellen White's prophetic ministry is to acknowledge our mistakes and correct them.

2. We should read and study our Bibles first and then read the writings of Ellen White.

"If we are hearing Ellen White correctly," wrote George Knight in *Reading Ellen White: How to Understand and Apply Her Writings*, "we should begin with the Bible rather than with her works."[7] In my view, no other statement in this excellent book on how to read Ellen White's writings is as important as this one. Those Seventh-day Adventists who really understand Ellen White's message will start with the Bible and drink deeply of its divine contents every day. They will develop a systematic reading plan that will take them through the entire Bible each year.[8] It will be their number one priority for study and meditation every day. This kind of Adventist, who knows his or her Bible through and through and breathes in its atmosphere daily, will be a powerful testimony for the validity of Ellen White's prophetic gift. Surely this kind of Adventist understands the subtle distinction between "the Book *and* the books" and "the Book, *then* the books" and chooses the latter.

After we've studied and meditated on the Bible, we'll find that the writings of Ellen White have much to offer us. The best way to read her writings is in the form in which she wrote them—as books, articles, and manuscripts.[9] Start with the Conflict of the Ages series, and then move on to her other books, such as *Steps to Christ*, *Christ's Object Lessons*, *Thoughts From the Mount of Blessing*, *Education*, and *The Ministry of Healing*. Don't neglect the *Testimonies*, for they, too, have much to offer when read in context. The key is to read *widely* in Ellen White, not in bits and pieces.[10] I agree with George Knight that Frederick E. J.

Harder provided good advice for reading Ellen White:

> Be fair to yourself and to the author. Don't confine your reading to proof-text excerpts, "striking statements," isolated counsels, or illuminating paragraphs, but read her books *as she wrote them*. Of course, the compilations are excellent for reference. However, for getting acquainted with the real Ellen White, for learning what she actually taught, for appreciating what the impact of her insights can mean for your understanding, and for nurturing an experience in life enrichment, few activities can match the force of reading the inspired and inspiring writings of Ellen G. White in the literary context and form in which they came from her pen.[11]

In his campaign against Ellen White, Dale Ratzlaff has made the claim that "one cannot understand the Bible correctly while continuing to study the writings of Ellen White." By this he means that Ellen White, like Joseph Smith to the Mormons, is a "veil" that "lies" over the eyes of Adventists and "keeps them from seeing the real *biblical* truth."[12] Behind this statement, of course, is the belief that his interpretation of Scripture is the only right one, and that Ellen White can't be a true prophet because she doesn't espouse his interpretation.

I suggest that one cannot understand the Bible correctly while continuing to study the writings of Ellen White *incorrectly*. That is, when her writings are studied more than the Bible, viewed as equal with the Bible, interpreted literalistically, and read out of context, a person's entire spiritual and theological outlook will be deficient and sometimes warped. But many Adventists past and present have found that Ellen White's writings, when read correctly, influence them to love their Bible more, to be more diligent in comparing Scripture with Scripture, and to base their doctrinal understanding on the Bible. Many, many Adventists have told me that this has been their experience when they have read Ellen White's writings carefully. It is my conviction that most of the individuals who have left Adventism and who now fight Ellen White never really understood how to read her correctly *while they were Adventists*.

There have been and still are those in Adventism who abuse Ellen White's writings and make them out to be something they were never meant to be. This has happened repeatedly throughout Adventist history, evidenced in Ellen White's own statements, as we saw above. To restate Ratzlaff's words differently, these individuals believe and practice the idea that "one cannot understand the Bible correctly *without* continuing to study the writings of Ellen White." These are the Adventists who know more about Ellen

White's writings than they know about the Bible, and it shows in the way they use her writings at church. Their understanding of Adventist doctrine and spiritual life derives from reading Ellen White, not the Bible. They find their "thus saith the Lord" in Ellen White's writings. It is statements from Ellen White rather than from the Bible that ends all discussion.

Robert Olson, former director of the White Estate, was right when he wrote regarding the relationship of Ellen White's writings to Adventist doctrine that "to give an individual complete interpretive control over the Bible would, in effect, elevate that person above the Bible."[13] Ellen White never endorsed such an approach to her writings, and neither does the Adventist Church. In the context of great appreciation for the prophetic gift in its midst, true Adventism values the Bible as the supreme authority for Christian teaching and living.

3. When studying Ellen White's writings, we should apply correct principles of interpretation.

In reading Ellen White's writings, the greatest failure by any person—supporter or critic—is the failure to apply correct principles of interpretation. As we saw in chapters 9 and 10, critics ignore these principles and give Ellen White a "wax nose" that they can bend this way and that way to suit their ideas. But when read correctly and widely, her writings cannot be bent any which way. They have an overarching purpose. And, as discussed in chapters 11 and 12, understanding this big picture will bring many insights and blessings to the reader of these writings.

In *Reading Ellen White: How to Understand and Apply Her Writings*, George Knight proposed fifteen principles of correct interpretation. Knight's book should be on the required reading list for every new convert to Adventism, and every veteran Adventist should also review it regularly. The fifteen principles are

- Read with a plan.
- Begin with a healthy outlook.
- Focus on the central issues.
- Emphasize the important.
- Account for problems in communication.
- Study all available information on a topic.
- Avoid extreme interpretations.
- Take time and place into consideration.
- Study each statement in its literary context.
- Recognize Ellen White's understanding of the ideal and the real.
- Use common sense.
- Discover the underlying principles.
- Realize that inspiration is not infallible, inerrant, or verbal.
- Avoid making the counsels "prove" things they were never intended to prove.
- Make sure Ellen White said it.[14]

If as readers of Ellen White we will carefully apply these principles to her writings, not only will we gain a tremendous blessing, but we'll be inoculated against the extreme interpretations of misguided supporters and the twisting tactics of the critics. *Reading Ellen White in context is one of the strongest actions we can take as individuals to vindicate her writings—to show they're beneficial.*

4. We should fortify our minds with the facts about Ellen White and her prophetic ministry.

Over the years, much has been written about the life and ministry of Ellen White. The more you know of the facts about the genuine person, the less impact the spin of her critics will have on you. After many years of studying the life of Ellen White, I find many of the charges and negative spin about her not only to be false but also tired and worn out.

The best place to start learning about Ellen White's life and prophetic ministry is the four helpful, easy-to-read books by George Knight: *Meeting Ellen White, Reading Ellen White, Walking With Ellen White,* and *Ellen White's World*.[15] For those who want to go deeper, the six-volume set *Ellen G. White* by her grandson Arthur White contains a plethora of information in biographical form.[16] It should be noted that this lengthy biography has been condensed into one volume, *Ellen G. White: Woman of Vision*.[17] Herbert Douglass's *Messenger of the Lord: The Prophetic Ministry of Ellen G. White* is a must read for detailed information about Ellen White and her prophetic gift.[18] Another excellent resource for gaining facts about Ellen White is the current *Ellen G. White Writings Comprehensive Research Edition* CD-ROM.[19] This CD-ROM contains a wealth of resources available at the click of a mouse. Finally, the *Ellen G. White Encyclopedia* from the Review and Herald® will be a resource that those interested in her will want to have in their personal libraries.[20] And we mustn't forget to read the apologetic books and Web sites as well.[21] They provide information on Ellen White's life and prophetic ministry in the context of answering criticisms.

5. When we encounter criticisms of Ellen White, we should use them as opportunities to learn more about her prophetic ministry.

Ellen White herself believed that all arguments for any doctrine of the Seventh-day Adventist Church, including that of the prophetic gift, should be able to "bear the closest and most searching scrutiny."[22] If there is a troubling question on your mind about Ellen White, then don't hesitate to search it out with "the most searching scrutiny." Never be afraid of honest, open investigation of these writings. Listen to all sides of an argument, and carefully examine the evidence. You'll be amazed at what you learn when you do your homework well. I haven't yet found a charge on any of the critical Web sites that can withstand "the most searching scrutiny." So, no earnest supporter of Ellen White needs to be afraid of the critics' challenges.

It is helpful to keep in mind the wise counsel from Ellen White herself: "There is no excuse for doubt or skepticism. God has made ample provision to establish the faith of all men, if they will decide from the weight of evidence. But if they wait to have every seeming objection removed before they believe, they will never be settled, rooted, and grounded in the truth. God will never remove all seeming difficulties from our path. Those who wish to doubt may find opportunity; those who wish to believe will find plenty of evidence upon which to base their faith."[23]

We shouldn't feel that we have to find an answer for every difficulty in Ellen White's writings. As Clifford Goldstein noted in the foreword to this book, we can't explain everything perfectly; questions remain. But the weight of evidence is sufficient to establish confidence in her prophetic gift.

6. We should avoid being overly clever and arrogant in responding to criticisms.

As I listen to both sides of the debate on Ellen White, I hear plenty of strong rhetoric that focuses more on emotional appeal (anger, sarcasm, scorn of those who disagree, etc.) and on being clever than on presenting the facts in a persuasive way. Not that there is anything wrong with being clever, but cleverness shouldn't be the main focus in an argument.[24] Christian apologist James Sire was right when he wrote that "valid, well substantiated arguments presented with arrogance, aggression, or an overly clever attitude are often not heard clearly enough to attract the attention they deserve."[25] So, we should learn the arguments that offer the strongest support to Ellen White's having the prophetic gift and present those arguments in the most persuasive way, free of questionable rhetoric that adds nothing of value.

7. We should learn how to detect fallacies and avoid using them ourselves.

Fallacious reasoning is everywhere, and all of us should be aware of its deceptive nature. The arguments of the critics against Ellen White certainly contain plenty of fallacies. Of course, they also argue that Seventh-day Adventist defense literature contains plenty of fallacies too.[26] It behooves all of us, therefore, to learn how to detect informal fallacies in the Ellen White debate.

A fallacy is "a type of argument that may seem to be correct but that proves, upon examination, not to be so." It is unsound in its content and "dangerous because most of us are, at one time or another, fooled by some of them."[27]

Fallacies have been studied for centuries and are classified in various ways. Several well-known kinds of fallacies are *ad hominem* (attacking the person rather than addressing the argument), "accent" (certain words or entire sentences and paragraphs are taken out of context and given an emphasis they were not meant to have), "loaded language" (mocking or distorting the position of the other side), "false dilemma" (reducing the options to just two when there are other alternatives), "poisoning the well" (using loaded language to disparage an argument before it's ever heard), and "straw man" (caricaturing an opposing view in a false way and then refuting the false image of that view).[28] One can learn about many other types of fallacies through the Internet and in books on logic.[29]

While all the fallacies mentioned above can be found in the writings of the critics, the fallacy of accent is the most prevalent one. In this fallacy, a false meaning is given to a single statement void of its literary context.[30] That is, the single statement is given an "accent" different from what its author intended. We looked at several examples of this fallacy in chapter 9. In addition to the kinds of fallacies mentioned above, one will find others in the arguments against Ellen White, such as the "appeal to hostile witnesses" or "appeal to the crowd."

Supporters of Ellen White aren't immune to using fallacies. One fallacy that tends to show up in our arguments is the *ad hominem,* or "attack on the man." This fallacy often occurs when someone points to a personal problem in a critic's life—such as marriage troubles or anger at the church—and says that problem has motivated the critic's attack on the church or Ellen White. Many Adventists, for example, have tended to use the *ad hominem* fallacy against D. M. Canright, emphasizing his character flaws rather than addressing his arguments.[31] However, personal problems, even if true, don't invalidate the arguments of the critic. To avoid this fallacy, we must focus on the arguments of the critics rather than on the critics themselves. When we allow fallacies to creep into our own arguments, we not only lose our credibility, but we weaken our ability to advance the truth about Ellen White's prophetic ministry.

8. We should remember that the best argument for Ellen White's prophetic ministry is the positive fruits it produces in our life.

I am convinced that we can present good, rational arguments in favor of the prophetic ministry of Ellen White—arguments that start from true premises, avoid logical fallacies, marshal a great body of evidence, answer objections, clarify the issues, and draw valid, true conclusions.[32] The best arguments, however, are not the *ultimate* proof that Ellen White was God's messenger to the Seventh-day Adventist Church. The ultimate proof is the positive fruits her prophetic ministry produces in our lives. If she leads us to the Bible as we say she does, then we should be exceptionally earnest Bible students. If her writings are as inspiring as we say they are, then that inspiration should flow through us to all those whose lives we touch. If her writings are as Christ-centered as we say they are, then our lives should show how much we love Jesus. Remember, it was Ellen White herself who said, "The strongest argument in favor of the gospel is a loving and lovable Christian."[33]

If the love of God is not in our hearts and we don't live the truth we profess, then our case for Ellen White will ultimately fail no matter how sound our arguments may be. People must see that the principles in these writings actually work. This is our best argument. Then, and only then, will other arguments work effectively.

Conclusion

Ultimately, when all is said and done, the strategy that impacts all of the others and makes them most effective is prayer. This is the missing link in how we deal with the attacks on Ellen White and Seventh-day Adventism. The greatest need today is that we offer intercessory prayer on behalf of those who are caught in the web of the anti-Adventist campaign, those who are studying to become Seventh-day Adventist Christians, and those who are discouraged in the Advent hope. Prayer can make a difference! When one of the anti-Adventist groups comes to your city or a city near you to discredit Adventism and Ellen White—and most likely one will come[34]—the best and most powerful strategy is earnest prayer. Pray for God to intervene in the lives of the people in your city! Pray for the advancement of gospel truth! Pray that those who misrepresent our message (from both inside and outside the Adventist community) won't prevail!

It is important to remember that we are often dealing with former Adventist Christians who believe Seventh-day Adventism is wrong. They are praying for victory in their cause, as well. In light of this situation, I keep one of God's natural laws in mind—one called the "law of noncontradiction." This law teaches that things in God's universe do not contradict one another, that "no two contradictory statements can both be true at the same time and in the same sense."[35] Thus, when opponents of Seventh-day Adventism are praying for its demise, and at the same time, supporters of Seventh-day Adventism are praying for its advancement, God won't say Yes to both prayers. He'll fulfill only those prayers that are in harmony with His will.

If you believe that Adventism carries God's last-day message to a dying world, then please pray like you believe it! Pray in organized intercessory prayer groups, and pray individually. Never forget the promise in 2 Chronicles 7:14: "If My people who are called by My name will humble themselves, and pray and seek My face, and turn from their wicked ways, then I will hear from heaven, and will forgive their sin and heal their land" (NKJV). Let us pray for healing, then—healing in our own hearts and healing in the hearts of former Adventists. Faith-filled, earnest prayer will do more than anything else to burst through barriers and advance the proclamation of the three angels' messages of Revelation 14:6–12. "Ask and you will receive, and your joy will be complete" (John 16:24, NIV).

Chapter Summary

1. In chapter 2 we saw that the pioneers of our church passed a resolution to protect them from being consumed by the task of answering their critics. In this important resolution, they voted to keep the "defense" of truth (the act of defending it against attacks) and the "advocacy" of truth (the act of arguing in favor of truth and presenting positive evidence for it) together in their work of spreading the everlasting gospel.
2. The Adventist pioneers' approach was a smart, God-given one that we would be wise to continue today. Accordingly, this chapter proposed eight proactive strategies for defending and advocating the prophetic ministry of Ellen White. As the old saying goes, "the best defense is a good offense."
    a. First, we should acknowledge that we have made the following mistakes and correct them.
        i. We have allowed some Adventists to place Ellen White on a pedestal—something that she never would have allowed to happen.
        ii. We have allowed "Ellen White missiles" to whistle through the church corridors and strike unsuspecting victims, causing them pain and frustration.
        iii. We have allowed too many individuals and groups with legalistic interpretations of Ellen White's writings to hold us and our local churches hostage.
        iv. Some supporters of Ellen White have been as truly her enemies as those who have left and who now oppose the church. We as a people still have a lot of self-educating and growing to do.

Chapter Summary

    b. Second, we should read and study our Bibles first and only then read the writings of Ellen White.

        i. "If we are hearing Ellen White correctly," wrote George Knight in *Reading Ellen White: How to Understand and Apply Her Writings,* "we should begin with the Bible rather than with her works."

        ii. After we have studied and meditated on the Bible, the writings of Ellen White have much to offer us. The best way to read her writings is in the final form in which she wrote them—as books, articles, and manuscripts.

        iii. Dale Ratzlaff has made the claim that "one cannot understand the Bible correctly while continuing to study the writings of Ellen White." Behind this statement, of course, is the belief that his interpretation of Scripture is the only right one and that Ellen White cannot be a true prophet because she doesn't espouse his interpretation.

        iv. I believe that one cannot understand the Bible correctly while continuing to study the writings of Ellen White *incorrectly.*

        v. Some misguided Adventists think that one cannot understand the Bible correctly *without* continuing to study the writings of Ellen White.

        vi. Every Seventh-day Adventist should understand the subtle distinction between "the Book *and* the books" and "the Book, *then* the books" and choose the latter.

    c. Third, we should apply correct principles of interpretation when studying Ellen White's writings.

        i. The greatest failure in reading Ellen White that any person—supporter or critic—can make is the failure to apply correct principles of interpretation.

        ii. In *Reading Ellen White: How to Understand and Apply Her Writings,* George Knight proposed fifteen basic principles for reading and interpreting Ellen White's writings.

        iii. Reading Ellen White in context is one of the strongest positive actions we can take as individuals to vindicate her writings, to show that they are beneficial.

The Best Defense Is a Good Offense

Chapter Summary

d. Fourth, we should fortify our minds with the facts about Ellen White and her prophetic ministry.
   i. Read the books by George Knight: *Meeting Ellen White, Reading Ellen White, Walking With Ellen White,* and *Ellen White's World;* the six-volume set *Ellen G. White* by her grandson Arthur White; and Herbert Douglass's *Messenger of the Lord.*
   ii. Two other excellent resources for gaining facts about Ellen White are the *Ellen G. White Writings Comprehensive Research Edition* CD-ROM and the *Ellen G. White Encyclopedia.*
   iii. The apologetic books and Web sites are helpful, as well.
e. Fifth, when we encounter a criticism of Ellen White, we should use it as an opportunity to learn more about her prophetic ministry.
   i. Ellen White herself believed that all arguments for any doctrine of the Seventh-day Adventist Church, including the prophetic gift, should be able to "bear the closest and most searching scrutiny.
   ii. If there is a question about Ellen White troubling you, don't hesitate to search it out with the "the most searching scrutiny."
   iii. Listen to all sides of an argument and carefully examine the evidence.
   iv. We shouldn't feel it necessary to find an answer for every difficulty in Ellen White's writings. The weight of evidence is sufficient to establish confidence in her prophetic gift.
f. Sixth, we should avoid being overly clever and arrogant in responding to criticisms.
   i. Christian apologist James Sire was right when he wrote that "valid, well substantiated arguments presented with arrogance, aggression or an overly clever attitude are often not heard clearly enough to attract the attention they deserve."
   ii. Thus, we should learn the best arguments for Ellen White and present them in the most persuasive way, free of questionable rhetoric that lends nothing to a good argument.
g. Seventh, we should learn how to detect fallacies and avoid using them ourselves.
   i. A fallacy is "a type of argument that may seem to be correct but that proves, upon examination, not to be so." It is unsound in its

Chapter Summary

content and "dangerous because most of us are, at one time or another, fooled by some of them."

  ii. Several well-known kinds of fallacies are *ad hominem* (attacking the person rather than addressing the argument), "accent" (certain words or entire sentences and paragraphs are taken out of context and given an emphasis they weren't meant to have), "loaded language" (mocking or distorting the other side), "false dilemma" (reducing the options to just two when there are others), "poisoning the well" (using loaded language to disparage an argument before it is ever heard), and "straw man" (caricaturing an opposing view in a false way and then refuting the false view).

  iii. While all the fallacies mentioned above can be found in the writings of the critics, the fallacy of accent is the most prevalent one. In this fallacy, a false meaning is given to a single statement void of its literary context.

  iv. Supporters of Ellen White aren't immune to using fallacies. One that tends to show up in our arguments is *ad hominem*, or "attack on the man."

  v. Many Adventists, for example, have tended to use the *ad hominem* fallacy with D. M. Canright, emphasizing his character flaws rather than addressing his arguments.

  vi. When we allow fallacies to creep into our arguments, we lose not only our credibility but our ability to advance the truth about Ellen White's prophetic ministry.

h. Eighth, we should remember that the greatest argument for Ellen White's prophetic ministry is the positive fruit it produces in our life.

  i. If she leads us to the Bible as we say she does, then we should be exceptionally earnest Bible students. If her writings are as inspiring as we say they are, then we should be conduits of inspiration to all those whose lives we touch. If her writings are as Christ-centered as we say they are, then our lives should show how much we love Jesus.

  ii. Ellen White said it best: "The strongest argument in favor of the gospel is a loving and lovable Christian."

The Best Defense Is a Good Offense

Chapter Summary

3. Ultimately, when it is all said and done, the strategy that impacts all of the others and makes them most effective is prayer.
4. Prayer is the missing link in how we deal with the attacks on Ellen White and Seventh-day Adventism.
5. Faith-filled, earnest prayer will do more than anything else on earth to burst through barriers and advance the proclamation of the three angels' messages of Revelation 14:6–12.

CONCLUSION

Why I Believe in Ellen White's Prophetic Ministry

In bringing this study of Ellen White and the charges made against her to a close, I will condense its contents to a formal argument with premises and a conclusion. There are many more arguments that could be made from the contents in this volume and beyond it, but the twenty premises that follow summarize the basic reasons why I believe in Ellen White's prophetic ministry.

1. True postcanonical manifestations of the prophetic gift operate within the proper limitations of the scope and function of this gift, pointing to the Bible as the highest source of authority for Christian faith and practice. Ellen White met this requirement with precision (chapter 8).
2. Ellen White's experience of revelation-inspiration involved the same vertical-horizontal work of the Holy Spirit as that found in the biblical prophets. Thus her inspiration was qualitatively the same as theirs (chapter 5).
3. The whole-person model of inspiration as found in the Bible is also found in Ellen White's experience (chapter 6).
4. As a postcanonical manifestation of the prophetic gift, Ellen White's inspiration was the same as that of the canonical prophets, but her authority was not the same as that of the canon. It was circumscribed in its relationship to the canon, the Bible. In this sense, her revelations never competed with the Bible; rather, they applied it (chapter 8).
5. Throughout Ellen White's seventy-year prophetic ministry, as a true postcanonical prophet should, she repeatedly exalted the Bible as the highest authority for the Christian (chapter 7).

6. The pioneers all spoke with one voice regarding the relationship of Ellen White's writings to the Bible: her prophetic gift was subordinate to the Bible and in no way an addition to it (chapter 7).
7. Ellen White's one hundred thousand-plus pages of writing are permeated with allusions to and citations from Scripture (chapter 7) and are intended to attract the reader to the Word of God.
8. When people interpret Ellen White's writings using the correct principles of interpretation, the charges that false teachings permeate her writings cannot be sustained. Her message is consistent and rings true to the Bible and the gospel of Jesus Christ (chapters 9 and 10).
9. The organizing theme that ties everything together in Ellen White's writings is the great controversy between Christ and Satan, which sets forth the gospel, with Christ's cross at its core, as the story by which God redeems human beings and restores them to His image, thus refuting Satan's charges that God is arbitrary, unforgiving, and unjust (chapter 11). The force with which Mrs. White set forth this theme cannot be found anywhere else in the literature of her day.
10. The great controversy theme as Ellen White articulated it runs throughout the Bible itself, from Genesis to Revelation (chapter 12). Her application of this theme provides a good example of how her theology resonates with the Bible.
11. Throughout Ellen White's long life, she believed and taught that Christians can and should have the assurance of salvation. She taught this doctrine in the context of the biblical mandate/principle: "If you think you are standing, be careful that you don't fall!" (1 Corinthians 10:12, NIV. See chapter 12.)
12. In Ellen White's classic book *Steps to Christ,* the warmth of the Wesleyan-Arminian assurance of salvation and works of faith come through clearly, yet her book moves beyond this tradition by emphasizing the biblical idea of the character of God as revealed and vindicated in the life and death of Jesus Christ (chapter 12).
13. Ellen White lived and articulated a warm, vibrant, evangelical spirituality with Christ at its center and the Bible as its foundation (chapter 13). All of her prophetic counsel is presented against the backdrop of this framework, thus fulfilling the biblical tests for a prophet: loyalty to the teaching of the Bible (Isaiah 8:20), and the proclamation of

Jesus Christ as God's Son who came in the flesh to redeem humanity (1 John 4:1–3).

14. The historical records confirm that Ellen White was a person of integrity and worthy influence in her personal and professional life (chapter 13), thus fulfilling the biblical test for a prophet: "by their fruit you will recognize them" (Matthew 7:15–20).

15. Ellen White affirmed the cardinal doctrines of the historic Christian church: the Bible as the inspired-revealed Word of God and thus the final authority for Christian life and teaching; the Trinity, or Godhead (God the Father, God the Son, and God the Holy Spirit); the person and work of Jesus Christ in His incarnation, perfect life, atoning death, bodily resurrection, ascension, intercession, and second coming; and the experience of salvation through justification that leads to sanctification. These cardinal biblical doctrines permeated her counsel and admonition to the Seventh-day Adventist Church in particular and to all Christians in general (chapter 13).

16. Ellen White repeatedly directed the Seventh-day Adventist Church pioneers away from unbiblical, heretical teachings. She used her prophetic authority to contend for the faith (Jude 3). As such, her prophetic ministry was free from heresy and fanaticism (chapter 13).

17. During the first forty years of Ellen White's prophetic ministry, the critics failed to produce irrefutable arguments against her work, as is obvious from the response of church leaders like Uriah Smith (chapter 2).

18. During the last thirty years of Ellen White's prophetic ministry, D. M. Canright's campaign against her failed to produce an irrefutable argument against her work, as demonstrated in Francis D. Nichol's massive *Ellen G. White and Her Critics,* published in 1951 (chapters 3 and 4).

19. When Ellen White borrowed material from other authors' writings, she generally reformulated it to fit her own inspired understanding, which often differed significantly from that of the original source. As a result, she contributed an innovative and creative synthesis of theological ideas beyond those of her contemporaries (chapters 11 and 12).

20. Uriah Smith's list of four major fruits of Ellen White's prophetic ministry, first penned in 1866, remains true to this day: her work tends to the purest morality, leads us to Christ, leads us to the Bible,

and brings comfort and consolation to many hearts (chapter 2 and appendix B).

In light of these twenty premises, I conclude that:

1. The life and work of Ellen G. White was a genuine manifestation of the prophetic gift as presented in Joel 2:28–32; 1 Corinthians 12:4, 10; and Ephesians 4:8–13.
2. She fulfilled the role of a postcanonical prophet, subjecting all of her visions and prophetic writings to the final authority of the Bible.
3. Her prophetic counsel is an authoritative source for the Seventh-day Adventist Church and should be heeded.
4. Her critics have not proven her to be a false prophet.
5. Her voice deserves to be heard among the larger Christian community.

A personal testimony

I became a Seventh-day Adventist at the age of seventeen through an evangelistic series that Kenneth Cox conducted in the winter of 1976.[1] I was a youth wandering aimlessly through my high-school years, and these meetings brought a focus to my life that I had never before experienced. The new truths of the Sabbath, fulfilled prophecy, and the imminent return of Jesus Christ awakened new spiritual desires and set me on a life-altering course.

I remember reading the book *Steps to Christ* after I joined the Adventist Church. While poring over those pages during my lunch break in the shade of the cedar trees next to the gymnasium at J. O. Johnson High School in Huntsville, Alabama, Jesus spoke to my heart. The potential of a life given completely over to God thrilled my soul, and I committed myself to whatever God wanted. From this reading of *Steps to Christ,* the joy of living for Jesus as a personal Savior and Friend captured my imagination. After this experience, I never desired to return to my former life, and I have been a disciple of Jesus Christ now for more than thirty years.

In my years as a student at Southern Missionary College (now Southern Adventist University), I spent many hours reading Ellen White's writings, sometimes instead of studying for class. During those years I read through the Conflict of the Ages series, much of the *Testimonies,* and several of Ellen White's "great" books: *Education, The Ministry of Healing, Thoughts From the Mount of Blessing, Christ's Object Lessons, Gospel Workers,* and *Testimonies to Ministers.* Like many others who have read widely in Ellen White's writings, the three books which affected me the most were *The Desire of Ages, The Great Controversy,* and, of course, *Steps to Christ.*

Reading Ellen White during these formative years had a lasting influence on my life that continues to this day. Her writings blessed me in three ways: first, they presented Jesus Christ to me as a personal Savior and the core of Christianity as a relationship with Him; second, they drew me into my Bible and presented it as the voice of God to my soul, which motivated me to study it with great vigor; third, reading her writings shaped my Christian worldview in terms of the great controversy between Christ and Satan. The clear message of Christ's victory over the devil filled my young soul with hope and with the importance of being on the Lord's side.

Over the years since then, Ellen White's writings have been a most helpful guide through pastoral ministry, graduate study, and teaching. Her influence on my life has been profound. In terms of my professional life as an Adventist theologian, her writings continually remind me to keep Christ at the center of my theology and the Bible as the supreme source of truth and the inspired guide to Christian living. They have kept the blessed hope of Christ's return uppermost in my mind and provided helpful parameters for engagement with the ideas of contemporary culture.

In the same way, her writings have enriched my personal life. They have brought hope and courage when I needed them most and helped me to love Jesus more and more as my best Friend. And yes, these writings often have stepped on my toes and rebuked my sins. As I reflect on my life, it strikes me that my personal successes have resulted from following these counsels, and my personal failures issued from not following them. But, thank the Lord, Ellen White's strong admonitions are grounded in the grace and mercy of God. In the end, the fact that her writings have pushed me repeatedly into Scripture has made *it* the most influential book in my life. For that, I am grateful!

Why do I believe in Ellen White's prophetic ministry? Ultimately, because her writings are self-authenticating. That's why many first-time readers exclaim, "This woman must be inspired!" The deep spirituality that permeates her writings speaks to the heart and brings the reader into contact with God. Waves of spiritual insight splash upon the soul, and a conviction wells up from within that nothing is more important than being a disciple of Jesus Christ.

The promises of Scripture sprinkled across her pages sparkle, attracting the reader to the voice of God sounding in His Word, the Bible. Jesus Christ is exalted as Lord, Savior, and Friend in such a way that the reader's devotion to Him grows and expands into an intimate relationship filled with faith, hope, and courage. I've heard the voice of Jesus speak to my own heart in her writings, and that experience is to me evidence of her inspiration. Taste and see for yourself!

After Francis D. Nichol completed his *magnum opus, Ellen G. White and Her Critics,* he stood before a special committee set up by the church to examine the manuscript. Earnestly peering into the faces of the listeners, he made a statement revelatory of his deep convictions. His words perfectly capture my own thoughts and feelings as this book comes to a close.

> I have examined all the major criticisms of Mrs. White that I could find in any book or pamphlet, checking back on all the alleged historical declarations and going to the original sources for the accurate text of all statements by Mrs. White. I have also examined many facts regarding her life. Having completed my task by preparing the extended manuscript now before you, I wish to offer this testimony: I end this work fully and irrevocably persuaded in my mind and heart that Mrs. White was what she claimed to be, a humble handmaiden of God, to whom He gave revelations, authoritative and unique, to guide and direct the Advent people in these last days.[2]

APPENDIX A

Seven Contemporary Views of Ellen White: A Taxonomy

Below are seven basic contemporary views of Ellen White both inside and outside of the Seventh-day Adventist community. This taxonomy is not meant to be prescriptive but simply descriptive. That is, it provides an overview of the contemporary landscape of Ellen White perceptions. No attempt has been made to identify individuals who represent the views, except to note that the official position of the church is view 3 (my own position), and the position specifically critiqued in this book is view 6 (although issues in some of the other views are critiqued in this book). It is understood that there is some overlapping of characteristics in these views. The purpose of this taxonomy is to foster the reader's understanding of Ellen White perceptions today and where he or she fits in relationship to the church's official view.

Five Views Within the Seventh-day Adventist Community

1. Perfect Prophet
- Affirm Ellen White's prophetic status
- Maintain a high view of Ellen White's prophetic ministry
- Espouse a strict verbal model of inspiration
- Value the entire corpus of the EGW writings
- Emphasize the divine side: espouse inerrancy—the Ellen White writings are free of any theological and historical error
- Give her writings almost a canonical authority; place them on a level of authority equal with the Bible, at least in practice if not in theory

Appendix A: Seven Contemporary Views of Ellen White

- Often results in a critical spirit toward those with a different understanding

2. Human Prophet
- Affirm Ellen White's prophetic status
- Maintain a middle-to-high view of Ellen White's prophetic ministry
- Espouse the thought model of inspiration
- Value much, but not all, of the corpus of Ellen White's writings—not all of it applies to us today
- Emphasize the human side of the Ellen White writings and thus view them as containing some error, especially in the earlier writings
- View the later writings of Ellen White as more authoritative than the earlier writings

3. Postcanonical Prophet (official view of the Seventh-day Adventist Church)
- Affirm Ellen White's prophetic status
- Maintain a high view of Ellen White's prophetic ministry
- Espouse a comprehensive or whole person view of inspiration
- Value the entire corpus of her work
- Emphasize both the human and divine side: seek to balance the human side of Ellen White with her gift of inspiration
- Espouse the idea that while the Ellen White writings are free of any major error, they do contain minor discrepancies
- View the Ellen White writings as authoritative for the church but always subordinate to the Bible's authority because she is a post-canonical prophet

4. Irrelevant Prophet
- Not concerned about Ellen White's prophetic status
- Have some vague idea that Ellen White is important but know little about her
- May have a somewhat negative attitude from what they have heard from others but are generally uninformed and largely uninterested
- Consist mostly of Adventist youth, young adults, and new converts who have not been taught much, if anything, about Ellen White
- There is much work to do for this group by the official church view

5. Erroneous Prophet
- Have mixed beliefs about Ellen White's prophetic status
- Maintain a low view of Ellen White's prophetic ministry

- Espouse the encounter model of inspiration
- Discard much of Ellen White's earlier writings and value only certain later writings
- View the Ellen White writings as error-prone throughout the entire corpus
- Want the Ellen White writings to have less prophetic authority in the future church
- May want to throw out all belief in the prophetic authority of Ellen White's writings

Two Views Outside the Seventh-day Adventist Community

6. False Prophet
- Comprised chiefly of former Seventh-day Adventists who reject Ellen White's prophetic status
- Believe she taught false doctrine and made untruthful claims
- Maintain an aggressive campaign against Ellen White's prophetic ministry on the Internet and in books
- Line of argument closely follows that of the late nineteenth- and early twentieth-century critic Dudley M. Canright, who was at one time an Adventist
- Serve as the chief source of information regarding Ellen White for evangelicals who criticize her

7. Historical Figure
- Recognize Ellen White as a gifted person who made a significant contribution in some areas
- Don't view her as inspired or having any prophetic status
- May view her as a genuine and devoted Christian or may be critical of her life and work
- Comprised chiefly of non-Adventists who have researched Ellen White's writings, many with scholarly interest, and many of whom consider Ellen White to be an important figure in American religious history
- View her as having a positive influence on the development of the Seventh-day Adventist Church

APPENDIX B

Uriah Smith's Defense of Ellen White's Prophetic Ministry

Ellen G. White's prophetic ministry was under intense attack in the late 1860s. In 1868, Uriah Smith (1832–1903), longtime editor of the Review and Herald *and apologist for the church, published a book in defense of the prophetic gift:* The Visions of Mrs. E. G. White: Manifestation of Spiritual Gifts According to the Scriptures *(Battle Creek, Mich.: Seventh-day Adventist Publishing, 1868). The following excerpt comes from pages 5–8. It's a classic expression of what Seventh-day Adventists believe about the prophetic ministry of Mrs. White.*

Every test which can be brought to bear upon such manifestations [Ellen White's visions], proves these genuine. The evidence which supports them, internal and external, is conclusive. They agree with the word of God, and with themselves. They are given, unless those best qualified to judge are invariably deceived, when the Spirit of God is especially present. They are free from the disgusting contortions and grimaces which attend the counterfeit manifestations of Spiritualism. Calm, dignified, impressive, they commend themselves to every beholder, as the very opposite of that which is false or fanatical. The instrument is herself above jugglery or deceit.

The influence is not mesmeric; for this people, reprobating the use of that agency, studiously refuse to learn the principles of its application, or to have aught to do with its practical workings; besides, the hallucinations of a mesmerized subject embrace only such facts and scenes as previously exist in the mind of the mesmerizing power; but the visions take cognizance of persons and things, and bring to light facts known, not only by no person present, but not even by the one through whom the visions are given.

They are not the effect of disease; for no disease has ever yet been known to have the effect of repeatedly suspending the functions of the lungs, muscles, and every bodily sense, from fifteen to one hundred and eighty minutes, while in obedience to some influence which evidently has supreme possession of the mind, and in obedience to that alone, the eyes would see, the lips speak, and the limbs move. Further, their fruit is such as to show that the source from which they spring is the opposite of evil.

1. They tend to the purest morality.

They discountenance every vice, and exhort to the practice of every virtue. They point out the perils through which we are to pass to the kingdom. They reveal the devices of Satan. They warn us against his snares. They have nipped in the bud scheme after scheme of fanaticism which the enemy has tried to foist into our midst. They have exposed hidden iniquity, brought to light concealed wrongs, and laid bare the evil motives of the false-hearted. They have warded off dangers from the cause of truth upon every hand. They have aroused and re-aroused us to greater consecration to God, move zealous efforts for holiness of heart, and greater diligence in the cause and service of our Master.

2. They lead us to Christ.

Like the Bible, they set him forth as the only hope and only Saviour of mankind. They portray before us in living characters his holy life and his godly example, and with irresistible appeals they urge us to follow in his steps.

3. They lead us to the Bible.

They set forth that book as the inspired and unalterable word of God. They exhort us to take that word as the man of our counsel, and the rule of our faith and practice. And with a compelling power, they entreat us to study long and diligently its pages, and become familiar with its teaching, for it is to judge us in the last day.

4. They have brought comfort and consolation to many hearts.

They have strengthened the weak, encouraged the feeble, raised up the despondent. They have brought order out of confusion, made crooked places straight, and thrown light on what was dark and obscure. And no person, with an unprejudiced mind, can read their stirring appeals for a pure and lofty morality, their exaltation of God and the Saviour, their denunciations of every evil, and their exhortations to everything that is holy and of good report, without being compelled to say, "These are not the words of him that hath a devil."

Negatively, they have never been known to counsel evil or devise wickedness. No instance can be found in which they have lowered the standard of morality. No one of their adherents has ever been led by them into paths of transgression and sin. They do not lead men to serve God less faithfully or to love him less fervently. They do not lead to any of the works of the flesh nor make less devoted and faithful Christians of those who be-

Appendix B: Uriah Smith's Defense of Ellen White's Prophetic Ministry

lieve them. In not a single instance can any of the charges here mentioned be sustained against them; and, concerning them, we may emphatically ask the question which Pilate put to the Jews in reference to the Saviour, "Why, what evil hath he done?"

Yet with all this array of good fruit which they are able to present, with all this innocency of any charge of evil that can be brought against them, they everywhere encounter the bitterest opposition. They are the object of the blindest prejudice, the intensest hate, and most malignant bitterness. Worldlings and formal professors of all denominations, join in one general outcry against them of vituperation and abuse. Many will go a long distance out of their way for the purpose of giving them an uncalled-for and malicious thrust. And false-hearted brethren in our own ranks make them the butt of their first attacks, as they launch off into apostasy and rebellion. Why is all this? Whence all this war against that of which no evil can be said? From the example of Cain who slew his brother, of the Jews who clamored for the blood of the innocent Saviour, of the infidel who storms with passion at the very name of Jesus, and from the principle of the carnal heart which is at enmity with everything that is holy and spiritual, we leave the reader to answer.

APPENDIX C

"Our Use of the Visions of Sr. White," by John Nevins Andrews

John Nevins Andrews (1829–1883), first Seventh-day Adventist missionary outside of America and respected biblical scholar, penned this important article, "Our Use of the Visions of Sr. White," in the Review and Herald, *February 15, 1870, 64, 65. It serves as a classic expression of what Seventh-day Adventists believe about spiritual gifts and the function of Ellen White's prophetic ministry in the church. The twenty points set forth with clarity the biblical rationale for the prophetic gift and speak afresh to issues raised by today's critics.*

It is quite generally understood that the Seventh-day Adventists are believers in the perpetuity of spiritual gifts. It is also understood that we regard the visions of Sr. White as given by the Spirit of God. But the use which we make of the doctrine of spiritual gifts, and particularly of the visions of Sr. White, are very generally misunderstood.

1. We understand that the Holy Scriptures are divinely inspired, and that they contain the truth of God which is able to make us wise unto salvation.

2. But we do not understand that the gift of the Scriptures to mankind, supersedes the gift of the Holy Spirit to the people of God.

3. On the contrary, we do believe that the Scriptures plainly reveal the office and work of the Holy Spirit; which office and work can never cease while man remains upon probation.

4. This work of the Holy Spirit is revealed to us in the Bible doctrine of spiritual gifts.

5. While therefore we do heartily accept the Scriptures as teaching man's whole duty toward God, we do not deny the Holy Spirit that place in the church which the Scriptures assign to it.

6. The office of the Holy Spirit is to reprove men of sin (John 16:8); to take away the carnal mind, and to change our evil nature by removing guilt from the conscience to make us new creatures (Rom. 8:1–9); and to shed abroad in our hearts the love of God (Rom. 5:5); and to bear witness with our spirits that we are the children of God (Rom. 8:16); and to lead into all truth (John 16:13); and finally to change the saints to immortality at the last day. Rom. 8:11; 2 Cor. 5:4, 5.

7. The Scriptures contain the truth of God, as the precious metals are contained in a mine. The work of the Spirit of God in leading men into all truth is to search out, lay open, bring to light, and vindicate the truth of God. And in reproving sin, it has not only the work of impressing the conscience of the sinner by powerful convictions of guilt, but also in showing to chosen servants of God the guilt of others; and revealing wrongs which otherwise would remain hidden to the great detriment of the church, and to the ruin of the sinner.

8. The work of the Holy Spirit may be divided into two parts: First, that which is designed simply to convert and to sanctify the person affected by it. Second, that which is for the purpose of opening the truth of God, and of correcting error, and of reproving and rebuking secret sins. This part of the work is wrought by what the Scriptures term spiritual gifts. These exist, not for the especial good of the person to whose trust they are committed, but for the benefit of the whole body of the church.

9. Now it is plain that those who reject the work of the Spirit of God under the plea that the Scriptures are sufficient, do deny and reject all that part of the Bible which reveals the office and work of the Holy Spirit.

10. Thus 1 Cor. 12 and Eph. 4, which define the gifts of the Spirit of God, cannot really form a part of the rule of life of those who affirm that the Scriptures are so sufficient in themselves that the gifts of the Spirit are unnecessary.

11. The Spirit of God gave the Scriptures. But it is plain that it did not give them for the purpose of shutting itself out from all participation in the work of God among men. And what the Bible says of the gifts of the Spirit shows just what relation the Spirit of God sustains to the work of the gospel.

12. Thus Paul states the matter in two of his epistles: 1 Cor. 12:4–11 "Now there are diversities of gifts, but the same Spirit. And there are differences of administrations, but the same Lord. And there are diversities of

operations, but it is the same God which worketh all in all. But the manifestation of the Spirit is given to every man to profit withal. For to one is given by the Spirit the word of wisdom; to another the word of knowledge by the same Spirit; to another, faith by the same Spirit; to another, the working of miracles; to another, prophecy; to another, discerning of spirits; to another, divers kinds of tongues; to another, the interpretation of tongues: but all these worketh that one and the selfsame Spirit, dividing to every man severally as he will."

13. Now the Bible expressly teaches that the existence of these gifts is as necessary to the church of Christ, as the different members are necessary to the well-being of the body. While, therefore, the Bible recognizes the gifts of the Spirit, these are not given to supersede the Bible, nor yet to fill the same place as the Bible.

14. The object of spiritual gifts is to maintain the living work of God in the church. They enable the Spirit of God to speak in the correction of wrongs, and in the exposure of iniquity. They are the means whereby God teaches his people when they are in danger of taking wrong steps. They are the means by which the Spirit of God sheds light upon church difficulties, when otherwise their adjustment would be impossible. They also constitute the means whereby God preserves his people from confusion by pointing out errors, by correcting false interpretations of the Scriptures, and causing light to shine out upon that which is in danger of being wrongly understood, and therefore of being the cause of evil and division to the people of God. In short, their work is to unite the people of God in the same mind and in the same judgment upon the meaning of the Scriptures. Mere human judgment, with no direct instruction from Heaven, can never search out hidden iniquity, nor adjust dark and complicated church difficulties, nor prevent different and conflicting interpretations of the Scriptures. It would be sad indeed if God could not still converse with his people.

15. But here it is proper to say that those uses of the gifts of the Spirit pertain almost wholly to the household of faith. Men who have no acquaintance with them cannot be affected by them. And also, where men have had little opportunity to be acquainted with the manifestations of the Spirit of God, they cannot be asked to accept such work as specially wrought by God. It is but just that they should have clear and convincing evidence for

Appendix C: "Our Use of the Visions of Sr. White," by John Nevins Andrews

themselves that the Spirit of God is in the work.

16. For this purpose we hold that all the tests presented in the Bible should be applied to the gifts, and that they should be found to sustain the test of such examination.

17. We therefore do not test the world in any manner by these gifts. Nor do we in our intercourse with other religious bodies who are striving to walk in the fear of God, in any way make these a test of Christian character. Upon none of these persons do we urge these manifestations of the Spirit of God, nor test them by their teaching.

18. There is such a thing, however, as men having in the providence of God an opportunity to become acquainted with the special work of the Spirit of God, so that they shall acknowledge that their light is clear, convincing, and satisfactory. To such persons, we consider the gifts of the Spirit are clearly a test. Not only has God spoken, but they have had opportunity to ascertain that fact, and to know it for themselves. In all such cases, spiritual gifts are manifestly a test that cannot be disregarded except at the peril of eternal ruin.

19. One of the chief gifts of the Spirit of God that he has placed in the New Testament church is the gift of prophecy. Joel 2:28; Acts 2:1–4, 17, 18; I Cor. 12:1–31; 14:1–5; Eph. 4:11–13. This gift the Bible connects with the closing work of this dispensation. Rev. 12:17; 14:12; 19:10. Spiritual gifts do not, therefore, cease to be of importance in the sight of God, nor in that to his true people. And that message which is to accomplish the perfecting of the saints and to fit them for translation, has the Spirit of God connected with it, and speaking out in the management of its work.

20. Finally, in the reception of members into our churches, we desire on this subject to know two things: 1. That they believe the Bible doctrine of Spiritual gifts; 2. That they will candidly acquaint themselves with the visions of Sr. White, which have ever held so prominent place in this work. We believe that every person standing thus and carrying out this purpose will be guided in the way of truth and righteousness. And these who occupy this ground, are never denied all the time they desire to decide in this matter.

APPENDIX D

Resources for Answering the Critics of Ellen White

The following lists of Web sites and books are recommended resources for finding answers to the charges against Ellen White. Please keep in mind that the URLs and the content of the Web sites can change due to the fluidity of the Internet.

Web sites:

The official Ellen G. White Estate Web site: http://www.whiteestate.org

Adventist Biblical Research Web site: http://www.adventistbiblicalresearch.org

The Ellen White Information Web site: http://www.ellenwhite.info

Ellen-White.com: http://ellen-white.com

Adventist Defense League: http://adventist-defense-league.blogspot.com

The Truth About Ellen White: http://dedication.www3.50megs.com/egw.html

The Literary Dependency of Ellen White: http://dedication.www3.50megs.com/David/index.html

Defending SDA Beliefs: http://sdaforme.com/index.html

Answering Ellen White Criticisms: http://ellenwhiteanswers.org

Books:

Brand, Leonard, and McMahon, Don S. *The Prophet and Her Critics: A Striking New Analysis Refutes the Charges That Ellen G. White "Borrowed" the Health Message.* Nampa, Idaho: Pacific Press® Publishing Association, 2005.

Douglass, Herbert E. *Messenger of the Lord: the Prophetic Ministry of Ellen G. White.* Nampa, Idaho: Pacific Press®, 1998. Full manuscript accessible online at http://www.whiteestate.org.

Fagal, William. *101 Questions About Ellen White and Her Writings.* Nampa, Idaho: Pacific Press®, 2010.

Fortin, Denis, and Moon, Jerry, eds. *The Ellen G. White Encyclopedia.* Hagerstown, Md.: Review and Herald® Publishing Association, 2010.

Nichol, Francis D. *Ellen G. White and Her Critics: An Answer to the Major Charges That Critics Have Brought Against Mrs. Ellen G. White.* Washington, D.C.: Review and Herald®, 1951. Full manuscript accessible online at http://www.whiteestate.org.

Goldstein, Clifford. *Graffiti in the Holy of Holies: An Impassioned Response to Recent Attacks on the Sanctuary and Ellen White.* Nampa, Idaho: Pacific Press®, 2003.

McMahon, Don S. *Acquired or Inspired: Exploring the Origins of the Adventist Lifestyle.* Victoria, Australia: Signs Publishing, 2005.

ELLEN WHITE UNDER FIRE

(Chapter 1)
Ellen White Under Fire

1. Several notable examples are http://www.ratzlaf.com, http://www.exadventist.com, http://www.truthorfables.com, http://ex-sda.com, and http://www.nonsda.org. Their sole purpose is to discredit Adventist teachings, such as the investigative judgment, seventh-day Sabbath keeping, perpetuity of the Ten Commandments, conditional immortality of the soul, Sunday laws, papal dominance at the end of time, and just about anything associated with the Seventh-day Adventist Church.

2. Numerous books perpetuate the criticisms of Seventh-day Adventism: Wallace D. Slattery, *Are Seventh-day Adventists False Prophets? A Former Insider Speaks Out* (Phillipsburg, N. J.: Presbyterian & Reformed, 1990); Russell Earl Kelly, *Exposing Seventh-day Adventism* (New York: Universe, Inc., 2005); Teresa Beem and Arthur Beem, *It's Okay NOT to Be a Seventh-day Adventist: The Untold History and the Doctrine That Attempts to Repair the Temple Veil* (North Charleston, S. C.; BookSurge, 2008); and Dale Ratzlaff, *The Cultic Doctrine of Seventh-day Adventists* (Glendale, Ariz.: LAM Publications, 1996); Ratzlaff, *Sabbath in Christ* (Glendale, Ariz.: LAM Publications, 2003); Ratzlaff, *Truth About Adventist "Truth,"* 2nd rev. ed. (Glendale, Ariz.: LAM Publications, 2007). Sources for helpful responses to the issues raised in these books include the Biblical Research Institute at the General Conference: http://www.adventistbiblicalresearch.org; Raoul Dederen, ed., *Handbook of Seventh-day Adventist Theology* (Hagerstown, Md.: Review and Herald® Publishing Association, 2000); and Gerhard Pfandl, ed., *Interpreting Scripture: Bible Questions and Answers*, Biblical Research Institute Studies, vol. 2 (Silver Spring, Md.: Biblical Research Institute General Conference of Seventh-day Adventists, 2010). Specific responses to Ratzlaff's books include Clifford Goldstein, *Graffiti in the Holy of Holies: An Impassioned Response to Recent Attacks on the Sanctuary and Ellen White* (Nampa, Idaho.: Pacific Press® Publishing Association, 2003); Skip MacCarty, *In Granite or Ingrained? What the Old and New Covenants Reveal About the Gospel, the Law, and the Sabbath* (Berrien Springs, Mich.: Andrews University Press, 2007); Hans K. LaRondelle, *Our Creator Redeemer: An Introduction to Biblical Covenant Theology* (Berrien Springs, Mich.: Andrews University Press, 2005); Jud Lake, "Dale Ratzlaff," http://ellenwhiteanswers.org/critics/Daleratzlaff; and Herbert Douglass, *Messenger of the Lord: The Prophetic Ministry of Ellen G. White* (Nampa, Idaho: Pacific Press®, 1998), 478–511, 549–569.

3. One anti-Adventist Web site, for example, is translated into at least twelve languages (http://www.ellenwhiteexposed.com/egw4.htm [accessed 9/29/08]).

4. Also at the core of all criticisms of Seventh-day Adventism is the doctrine of the investigative judgment. Critics often attribute this doctrine to Ellen White rather than to the Bible. The historical evidence, however, shows that it came from Bible study—see George Knight, *The Search for Identity: The Development of Seventh-day Adventist Beliefs* (Hagerstown, Md.: Review and Herald®, 2000), 58, 59; Paul A. Gordon, *The Sanctuary, 1844, and the Pioneers* (Silver Spring, Md.: Ministerial Association, General Conference of Seventh-day Adventists, 2000); and Gordon, *Pioneer Articles on the Sanctuary, Daniel 8:14, the Judgment, 2300 Days, Year-day Principle, Atonement: 1846–1905* (Silver Spring, Md.: Ellen G. White Estate, 1983).

5. The anti-Adventist Web sites and books mentioned in endnotes 1 and 2, for example, have a special place for criticisms of Ellen White's prophetic ministry.

6. At the time of this writing, the material in http://www.ellenwhiteexposed.com (founding editor, Dirk Anderson) is being transferred to a fairly

new site: http://www.nonsda.org (editor, also Dirk Anderson). This site may become the main place for Ellen White criticisms. The Internet is fluid, and Web sites are constantly changing.

7. See http://www.ellenwhiteexposed.com/egw4.htm (accessed 9/29/08).

8. Dirk Anderson, *White Out: An Investigation of Ellen G. White* (Glendale, Ariz.: LAM Publications, 2001). A new edition of this book is forthcoming; Anderson, *More Than a Profit, Less Than a Prophet* (Jacksonville, Fla.: Via Del Agape, 2008); Anderson, *Prophet? Or Pretender? Does Ellen White Pass the Tests of a Prophet?* (Jacksonville, Fla.: Via Del Agape, 2008); Anderson, *The Fake Controversy* (Jacksonville, Fla.: Via Del Agape, 2009); and Sidney Cleveland, *White Washed: Uncovering the Myths of Ellen G. White* (Glendale, Ariz.: LAM Publications, 2000).

9. Walter T. Rea, *The White Lie* (Turlock, Calif.: M & R Publications, 1982); D. M. Canright, *The Life of Mrs. E. G. White, Seventh-day Adventist Prophet, Her False Claims Refuted* (Salt Lake City: Sterling Press, 1998; originally published 1919).

10. See, for example, the personal testimonies of former Seventh-day Adventists at http://www.ellenwhiteexposed.com/guests.htm (accessed 10/7/08) and http://truthorfables.com/Readers_Testimony.htm (accessed 10/7/08).

11. Roy Graham correctly divided Ellen White criticisms into two headings: charges discrediting her person, and charges accusing her of false doctrine (*Ellen G White: Co-Founder of the Seventh-day Adventist Church* [New York: Peter Lang, 1985], 382–388).

12. Anderson, *Prophet? Or Pretender?* 38.

13. See, for example, Anderson, "Ellen White's Plagiarism," http://www.ellenwhiteexposed.com/egw4.htm (accessed 9/29/08); and ibid., http://www.nonsda.org/egw/plagiarism.html (accessed 9/29/08).

14. For a full explanation of the shut-door theory and Ellen White, see Merlin Burt, "Shut Door," in *The Ellen G. White Encyclopedia,* Denis Fortin and Jerry Moon, eds. (Hagerstown, Md.: Review and Herald®, 2011).

15. See, for example, Anderson, "The Shut Door," http://www.ellenwhiteexposed.com/egw15.htm (accessed 9/29/08); "Did Ellen White's Visions Teach a Shut Door Falsehood?" http://www.nonsda.org/egw/shutdoor.html (accessed 9/29/08).

16. Robert K. Sanders, "Ellen White Contradicts the Bible Over 50 Times," http://truthorfables.com/EGW_Contradicts.htm. (accessed 9/29/08); see also Dirk Anderson, "Do Ellen G. White's Writings Contradict the Bible?" http://www.nonsda.org/egw/bible.html (accessed 9/29/08).

17. See, for example, Anderson, "Ellen White's Contradictory Writings and Behavior," http://www.nonsda.org/egw/contras.html (accessed 9/30/08); and Anderson, "Ellen White's Contradictions," http://www.ellenwhiteexposed.com/contras.htm (accessed 9/30/08).

18. See Ratzlaff, *Truth About Adventist "Truth,"* 29–31.

19. See, for example, Sanders, "Visions That Failed by EGW," http://truthorfables.com/SUBJECTS.htm (accessed 9/30/08).

20. See Anderson, *Prophet? Or Pretender?* 9–16.

21. See Anderson, "Sources of Her Health Writings," http://www.ellenwhiteexposed.com/health.htm (accessed 9/30/08); and Anderson, *More Than a Profit, Less Than a Prophet*, 6–35.

22. See Anderson, *White Out: An Investigation of Ellen G. White*, 150, where he recommends the Ronald L. Numbers' book. Because of its scholarly nature, Numbers's book, *Prophetess of Health: A Study of Ellen G. White,* 3rd ed. (Grand Rapids, Mich.: Wm. B. Eerdmans, 2008), is in a different category than the other books against Ellen White. Although a critical study, its purpose was to analyze her health teaching without a supernatural presupposition. In addition, Numbers provides a helpful history of nineteenth-century health reform. For a response to Numbers' book, see

Leonard Brand and Don S. McMahon, *The Prophet and Her Critics: A Striking New Analysis Refutes the Charges That Ellen G. White "Borrowed" the Health Message* (Nampa, Idaho: Pacific Press®, 2005), 34–47; and the Ellen G. White Estate's "Critique of the Book *Prophetess of Health*" at http://www.whiteestate.org/issues/prophetess-of-health.pdf.

23. "Was Ellen White an Epileptic?" *Ministry* (August 1984), 24.

24. See, for example, Anderson, "Mrs. White's Health Problems," http://www.ellenwhiteexposed.com/health.htm (accessed 9/30/08); Molleurus Couperus, "The Significance of Ellen White's Head Injury," *Adventist Currents*, vol. 1, no. 6 (June 1985), 17–33.

25. See, for example, Anderson, *White Out: An Investigation of Ellen G. White*.

26. See Ratzlaff, *Cultic Doctrine of Seventh-day Adventists*, 43–82.

27. See, for example, Anderson, "Ellen White: The Odd, the Weird, and the Absurd," http://www.nonsda.org/egw/shockers.html (accessed 9/30/08).

28. Anderson, "Cover-up of Ellen White's Original Writings?" http://www.ellenwhiteexposed.com/egw5.htm (accessed 9/30/08).

29. For testimonies of those who have left Seventh-day Adventism, see, for example, http://www.ellenwhiteexposed.com/guests.htm (accessed 10/7/08) and http://truthorfables.com/Readers_Testimony.htm (accessed 10/7/08).

30. The word *apologia* occurs eight times in the Greek New Testament, several times in Paul's letters (Acts 22:1; 25:16; 1 Cor. 9:3; 2 Cor. 7:11; Phil. 1:7, 16; 2 Tim. 4:16; 1 Pet. 3:15). It is generally translated "defense" or "answer," but it can carry other meanings (see the context). The basic idea behind the word is a formal defense in court.

31. J. P. Moreland and William Lane Craig, *Philosophical Foundations for a Christian Worldview* (Downers Grove, Ill.: InterVarsity Press, 2003), 14. For several other major treatments of Christian apologetics, see W. C. Campbell-Jack and Gavin McGrath, eds., *New Dictionary of Christian Apologetics* (Downers Grove, Ill.: InterVarsity Press, 2006); Norman Geisler, *Baker Encyclopedia of Christian Apologetics* (Grand Rapids, Mich.: Baker Books, 1999); Josh McDowell, *The New Evidence That Demands a Verdict* (Nashville, Tenn.: Thomas Nelson Publishers, 1999); and James E. Taylor, *Introducing Apologetics: Cultivating Christian Commitment* (Grand Rapids, Mich.: Baker Academic, 2006). For the debate on the different approaches to Christian apologetics, see Steven B. Cowan, *Five Views of Apologetics* (Grand Rapids, Mich.: Zondervan, 2000).

32. See, for example, Lee Strobel's classic, *The Case for Christ: A Journalist's Personal Investigation of the Evidence for Jesus* (Grand Rapids, Mich.: Zondervan, 1998), 191–272.

33. See, for example, William Lane Craig, *Reasonable Faith: Christian Truth and Apologetics*, 3rd ed. (Wheaton, Ill.: Crossway Books, 2008), 93–204.

34. See, for example, Craig L. Blomberg, *The Historical Reliability of the Gospels*, 2nd ed. (Downers Grove, Ill.: IVP Academic, 2007).

35. R. C. H. Lenski, *The Interpretation of I and II Epistles of Peter, the three Epistles of John, and the Epistle of Jude* (Minneapolis, Minn.: Augsburg Publishing House, 1966), 151.

36. J. Ramsey Michaels, *1 Peter, Word Biblical Commentary*, vol. 49 (Waco, Tex.: Word, 1988), 189.

37. Ellen G. White to Uriah Smith, July 31, 1883 (Letter 3, 1883).

38. E. G. White to Stephen McCullagh, April 9, 1897 (Letter 98a, 1897). See the context of this letter in Arthur L. White, *Ellen G. White*, vol. 4, *The Australian Years, 1891–1900* (Washington, D.C.: Review and Herald®, 1983), 275–286; see also Lester D. Devine, "Stephen McCullagh," *The Ellen G. White Encyclopedia*.

39. See E. G. White, *Selected Messages* (Washington, D.C.: Review and Herald®, 1980), 3:348–352, for statements about the criticisms of her prophetic ministry.

(Chapter 2)
Nothing New Under the Sun

1. Ellen G. White, *Selected Messages* (Hagerstown, Md.: Review and Herald®, 1958), 1:69.

2. Prior to the formal organization of the General Conference in 1863, the sabbatarian Adventists were not the official Seventh-day Adventist Church yet.

3. For more detail on the charges against Ellen White's prophetic gift during this period, see chapters 2 and 3 of Theodore N. Levterov, "The Development of the Seventh-day Adventist Understanding of Ellen G. White's Prophetic Gift: 1844–1889" (forthcoming PhD dissertation, Andrews University).

4. For a discussion on opposition to Ellen White's prophetic ministry prior to the Messenger party, see Ellen G. White, *Spiritual Gifts* (Battle Creek, Mich.: James White, 1860), 2:69, 70; Merlin Burt, "The Historical Background, Interconnected Development, and Integration of the Doctrines of the Sanctuary, The Sabbath, and Ellen G. White's Role in Sabbatarian Adventism from 1844–1849," (PhD dissertation, Andrews University, 2002), 215–217; Burt, "Joseph Turner," in *The Ellen G. White Encyclopedia,* Denis Fortin and Jerry Moon, eds. (Hagerstown, Md.: Review and Herald®, 2011); and Jud Lake, "John Howell," in ibid.

5. For the full story, see *Seventh-day Adventist Encyclopedia* (1996 ed.), s.v. "Messenger party," 11: 51, 52; Richard W. Schwarz and Floyd Greenleaf, *Light Bearers: A History of the Seventh-day Adventist Church* (Nampa, Idaho: Pacific Press® Publishing Association, 2000), 89, 613; Arthur L. White, *Ellen G. White: The Early Years, 1827–1862* (Washington D.C.: Review and Herald®, 1985), 306–315; and Dennis Pettibone, "The Messenger Party," *Review and Herald*, January 23, 1975, 8, 9; Paul Gordon, "Messengers of Error," *Review and Herald*, March 5, 1992, 14, 15; J. N. Loughborough, *Rise and Progress of the Seventh-day Adventists* (Battle Creek, Mich.: General Conference Association of the Seventh-day Adventists), 188–192; Loughborough, *The Great Second Advent Movement: Its Rise and Progress* (Washington, D.C.: Review and Herald®, 1909), 325, 326; and E. G. White, *Spiritual Gifts*, 2:181, 182.

6. James White, "Mark Them Which Cause Divisions," *Review and Herald*, August 22, 1854, 14.

7. There are only three known extant issues housed at the Ellen G. White Estate: *Messenger of Truth*, vol. 1, no. 3, October 19, 1854; *Messenger of Truth*, vol. 1, no. 4, November 2, 1854; and *Messenger of Truth*, vol. 1, no. 5, November 30, 1854. For detailed discussion on the content of these extant issues, see Levterov, chapter 2.

8. See the *Review and Herald Extra*, April 1855, where later issues of the *Messenger of Truth* are cited.

9. J. N. Andrews, R. F. Cottrell, and Uriah Smith, "To the Readers of the Advent Review," *Review and Herald*, November 7, 1854, 101.

10. J. N. Loughborough, *The Great Second Advent Movement: Its Rise and Progress* (Washington, D.C.: Review and Herald®, 1905, 1909), 325.

11. J. N. Loughborough, "Sketches of the Past," No. 99, *Pacific Union Recorder*, June 30, 1910, 1.

12. E. G. White, *Testimonies for the Church* (Nampa, Idaho: Pacific Press®, 1948), 1:122.

13. Ibid., 123. The statement, "We are doing a great work, and cannot come down," reflects the biblical imagery of Nehemiah's refusal to come down from building the walls of Jerusalem; see Nehemiah 6:3: "So I sent messengers to them, saying, 'I am doing a great work, so that I cannot come down. Why should the work cease while I leave it and go down to you?' " (NKJV).

14. Loughborough, "Sketches of the Past," 1. By the fall of 1855, two other ministers from

Wisconsin, recent converts to Sabbatarianism, J. M. Stephenson and D. P. Hall, temporarily joined the Messenger party. See E. G. White, *Testimonies*, 1:116, 117 for her view of this volatile situation. In 1855, she was shown in vision that the Messenger party would fall apart and the church would grow (*Testimonies*, 1:122, 123). Loughborough, who was present during this vision, recalls: "Mrs. White was given a vision in which she was shown that if we would keep at our work, preaching the truth, regardless of any such as the 'Messenger party,' they would go to war among themselves and their paper would go down, and when that should happen we would find that our ranks had doubled" (*The Great Second Advent Movement*, 325, 326). By 1858, the party had fallen apart. James White wrote, "The faction has crumbled and disappeared, and the body has risen in union and strength. And where one destitute of moral worth has left the ranks, four of real worth have joined the ranks of Sabbath-keepers. At the time of the disaffection, when the effort was to break down the *Review*, the church property at the office was only $700; since, it has increased to $5000. Then there were but about 1000 paying subscribers, now there are near 2000" (James White, "A Sketch of the Rise and Progress of the Present Truth," *Review and Herald*, January 14, 1858, 77, 78).

15. Joseph Bates and Uriah Smith, "Business Proceedings of the Conference at Battle Creek, Mich.," *Review and Herald*, December 4, 1855, 76.

16. E. G. White, *Testimonies*, 1:123.

17. In one publication—Uriah Smith, *Defense of Eld. James White and Wife: Vindication of Their Moral and Christian Character* (Battle Creek, Mich.: Steam Press, 1870)—the focus was on defending the characters of church leaders. This publication may seem to disregard Ellen White's vision recorded in 1T, 122, 123, where she speaks against "coming down" and answering the personal attacks of the Messenger party. But it is important to note that this vision was specifically focused on the situation facing the church during 1854–55. By 1870, the church had grown significantly, and resources were such that energy devoted to answering personal attacks on leaders' characters wouldn't distract from advocating present truth. The lesson, however, is still relevant today: don't let answering the critics get in the way of spreading the gospel.

18. For an overview of this movement, see *Seventh-day Adventist Encyclopedia* (1996 ed.), s.v. "Marion Party,"11:32; Schwarz and Greenleaf, 130, 131, 613; A. White, *Ellen G. White: The Progressive Years, 1862–1876* (Washington D.C.: Review and Herald®, 1985), 2: 145–153; Loughborough, *Rise and Progress of Seventh-day Adventists*, 267–269; and G. I. Butler, "A Brief History of the 'Marion' Movement," *Review and Herald Supplement*, August 14, 1883, 7, 8.

19. See B. F. Snook, "From Bro. Snook"; and W. H. Brinkerhoff, "From Bro. Brinkerhoff," *Review and Herald*, July 25, 1865, 62, 63.

20. See Butler, "A Brief History of the 'Marion' Movement," 7; and U. Smith, G. W. Amadon, and J. M. Aldrich, "Remarks," *Review and Herald*, January 23, 1866, 63.

21. J. N. Loughborough, "Sketches of the Past—No. 132," *Pacific Union Recorder*, November 21, 1912, 2.

22. B. F. Snook and Wm. H. Brinkerhoff, *The Visions of E. G. White, Not of God* (Cedar Rapids, Iowa: Cedar Valley Times Book and Job Print, 1866).

23. The objections in this book had already been circulating before 1866. A letter to Thomas Hare from J. N. Loughborough, dated October 29, 1865, speaks of Hare's concern for the need of "an answer to the objections." See File 349, E. G. White Estate. It is possible that Snook and Brinkerhoff's book could have been circulating in mimeographed form before it was published in

Cedar Rapids.

24. Snook and Brinkerhoff's original book was twenty-seven pages of small print.

25. Snook and Brinkerhoff, 1.

26. The entire manuscript of *The Visions of E. G. White, Not of God* is published on one of the anti-Ellen White Web sites: http://www.ellenwhiteexposed.com/snook/visionsc.htm.

27. Uriah Smith, "Objections to the Visions," *Review and Herald*, June 12, 1866, 16.

28. Ibid.

29. Ibid., "The Visions—Objections Answered," 9, 10; and Smith, "The Visions—Objections Answered," *Review and Herald*, July 31, 1866, 66, 67.

30. Ibid., June 19, 1866, 17–19. Part of Smith's answer to the shut door has been used to support a controversial document entitled "The Camden Vision," an alleged vision of Ellen White that contains terminology uncommon to her writings. For a comprehensive treatment of this issue and careful analysis of Smith's statements, see Glyn Parfitt, "The Camden Vision: Is It Genuine or Spurious?" (Glyn Parfitt: January, 2004), document, Ellen G. White Estate. Parfitt provides comprehensive evidence that the vision is spurious and that Smith's wording reflects this conclusion.

31. Ibid., July 31, 1866, 65, 66.

32. For discussion of this statement and Smith's answer to the objection, see Gordon Shigley, "Amalgamation of Man and Beast: What Did Ellen White Mean?" *Spectrum*, June, 1982, 10–19; and Michael W. Campbell and Timothy G. Standish, "Amalgamation," in *The Ellen G. White Encyclopedia*. For other responses to the issue, see Lake, http://ellenwhiteanswers.org/answers/answershardsayings ; and the insightful discussion sensitive to the historical context of Ellen White's statements on amalgamation in David G. Read, *Dinosaurs: An Adventist View* (Keene, Tex.: Clarion Call Books, 2009), 483–539.

33. E. G. White's *A Sketch of the Christian Experience and Views of Ellen G. White* (Saratoga Springs, N.Y.: James White, 1851) was her first published book, containing her early visions. Its contents have been reprinted in the book *Early Writings* (Washington, D.C.: Review and Herald®, 1945; originally published, 1882). *Testimonies for the Church* at this time included only Testimonies 1–10 (which can be found in today's *Testimonies for the Church*, 1:113–455). *Spiritual Gifts*, vols. 1–4, came out during the years 1858–1864. These books, then, were the only published account of Ellen White's visions in 1866.

34. Smith, "The Visions—Objections Answered," *Review and Herald*, June 12, 1866, 9.

35. Ibid.

36. See Michael W. Campbell, "John Nevins Andrews," in *The Ellen G. White Encyclopedia*.

37. J. N. Andrews, "Answers to the Objections Against the Visions," *Review and Herald*, August 14, 1866, 88.

38. See Denis Fortin, "Charles O. Taylor," *The Ellen G. White Encyclopedia*.

39. C. O. Taylor, "The Visions, Objections Answered," *Review and Herald*, September 11, 1866, 120.

40. Uriah Smith, *The Visions of Mrs. E. G. White: A Manifestation of Spiritual Gifts According to the Scriptures* (Battle Creek, Mich.: Seventh-day Adventist Publishing, 1868).

41. Smith added answers to other objections presented by the first published non-Sabbatarian critic, William Sheldon. Influenced by the Snook and Brinkerhoff book, Sheldon wrote a series of articles against Ellen White in the January and February 1867 editions of *Voice of the West* and used them as a basis for a sixty-four-page book titled *The Visions and Theories of the Prophetess Ellen G. White in Conflict With the Bible* (Buchanan, Mich.: W.A.C.P. Association, 1867).

42. Smith, *The Visions of Mrs. E. G. White*, 129–143.

43. According to J. N. Loughborough, Snook

left the group and became a Universalist minister, and Brinkerhoff returned to his previous profession in law (*Pacific Union Recorder*, January 9, 1913, 1). For more discussion on their personal history, see Arthur White, *Ellen G. White: The Progressive Years, 1862–1876*, 150, 151.

44. For a concise history of this branch of the Church of God, see *Seventh-day Adventist Encyclopedia* (1996 ed.), s.v. "Marion Party," 11:32; Arthur White, *Notes and Papers Concerning Ellen G. White and the Spirit of Prophecy* (Washington, D.C.: Ellen G. White Estate, 1974), 223–230.

45. Henry E. Carver, *Mrs. E. G. White's Claims to Divine Inspiration Examined* (Marion, Iowa: Published at the "Hope of Israel" Office), 1870; rev. ed., 1877.

46. James White, "Mutual Obligations," *Review and Herald*, June 13, 1871, 204.

47. Carver, 89–100.

48. Ibid., 89–91. On the "Camden Vision," see the Parfitt study.

49. James White, "Mutual Obligations," 204.

50. H. C. Blanchard, *The Testimonies of Mrs. E. G. White Compared With the Bible* (Marion, Iowa: Advent and Sabbath Advocate, 1877).

51. A. C. Long, *Comparison of the Early Writings of Mrs. White With Later Publications* (Marion, Iowa: Advent and Sabbath Advocate, 1883). On page 16, Long tells the reader that the contents of his sixteen-page book was "reprinted from the columns of the 'Advent and Sabbath Advocate,' Marion, Iowa, 1883."

52. Ibid., 12.

53. Dirk Anderson, *White Out: An Investigation of Ellen G. White* (Glendale, Ariz.: LAM Publications, 2001). A new edition is forthcoming.

54. E. G. White, *A Sketch of the Christian Experience and Views of Ellen G. White*; E. G. White, *Supplement to Experience and Views* (Saratoga Springs, N.Y.: James White, 1854); E. G. White, *Spiritual Gifts: The Great Controversy Between Christ and His Angels and Satan and His Angels*, vol. 1 (Battle Creek, Mich.: James White, 1858).

55. E. G. White, *Early Writings* (Washington, D.C.: Review and Herald®, 1882; 1945).

56. G. I. Butler, "A Book Long Desired," *Review and Herald*, December 26, 1882, 792.

57. Arthur White, *Ellen G. White: The Lonely Years, 1876–1891*, 208.

58. Long, 12.

59. Arthur White, *Ellen G. White: The Lonely Years*, 222.

60. J. H. Waggoner, "Suppression and the Shut Door," *Review and Herald Supplement*, August 14, 1883, 1, 2.

61. G. I. Butler, "'Early Writings' and 'Suppression,'" ibid., 4.

62. Butler, "A Venerable Document," ibid., 5.

63. See, for example, Dale Ratzlaff, *The Cultic Doctrine of Seventh-day Adventists* (Glendale, Ariz.: Life Assurance Ministries, 1996), 146–149; and Dirk Anderson, *White Out: An Investigation of Ellen G. White* (Glendale, Ariz.: Life Assurance Ministries, 2001), 46–50. Interestingly, in his coverage of the *Early Writings* episode, Anderson makes no reference to the church's response in the *Review and Herald Extra*, August 14, 1883.

64. *A Word to the Little Flock* has been in and out of print over the last century and is presently in circulation. See, for example, Francis D. Nichol, "Appendix D," *A Word to the Little Flock*, in *Ellen G. White and Her Critics* (Washington, D.C.: Review and Herald®, 1951), 560–584; George Knight, ed., "Part I. *A Word to the "Little Flock*," May 1847, in *Earliest Seventh-day Adventist Periodicals*, Adventist Classic Library (Berrien Springs, Mich.: Andrews University Press, 2005), 24; and on the Internet, http://www.earlysda.com/flock/lflockcontents.html .

65. E. G. White, "Our Present Position," *Review and Herald*, August 28, 1883, 545.

66. E. G. White, "Notes of Travel," *Review and Herald*, October 16, 1883, 642.

67. E. G. White, *Selected Messages* (Hagerstown, Md.: Review and Herald, 1958), 1:60.

68. See ibid., 59–73.

69. Denis Fortin, "Miles Grant," in *The Ellen G. White Encyclopedia*; F. L. Piper, *Life and Labors of Miles Grant* (Boston: Advent Christian Publication Society, 1914). Grant was the second published non-Sabbatarian critic; William Sheldon, the first.

70. Miles Grant, *The True Sabbath: Which Day Shall We Keep? An Examination of Mrs. Ellen White's Visions* (Boston, Mass.: Advent Christian Publication Society, 1874). The book was reprinted twice, in 1877 and 1890.

71. Ibid., 68 (1874).

72. The *Extra* began with these words in the preface: "The object of this sheet is to express the dishonest and unjust course which Eld. Miles Grant, editor of the *World's Crisis*, has pursued toward Seventh-day Adventists for a number of years past. Though often corrected in his misstatements, he still persists in repeating them in the most barefaced and reckless manner, as will appear from what is herewith presented. The facts speak for themselves" (J. N. Andrews and U. Smith, "To the Reader," *Review and Herald Extra*, April 14, 1874, 1).

73. E. G. White to J. N. Loughborough, August 24, 1874, Letter 2, 1874; see also *Manuscript Releases* (Silver Spring, Md.: E. G. White Estate, 1990), 8:228–243; and *Selected Messages*, 1:74.

74. Arthur White, *Ellen G. White: The Lonely Years*, 335.

75. E. G. White, "Notes of Travel," in *Historical Sketches of Foreign Missions*, Adventist Classic Library (Berrien Springs, Mich.: Andrews University Press, 2005), 236, 237.

76. Ibid., 237.

(Chapter 3)
Dudley M. Canright: Father of Ellen White Criticisms

1. Biographical information on Canright can be found in the following sources: D. M. Canright, *Seventh-day Adventism Renounced: After an Experience of Twenty-Eight Years by a Prominent Minister and Writer of That Faith,* 14th ed. (New York: Fleming H. Revell, 1914), 37–39 (numerous reprints of this book are available); Norman F. Douty, *The Case of D. M. Canright: Seventh-day Adventist Charges Examined* (Grand Rapids, Mich: Baker Book House, 1964), 32–41; and Carrie Johnson, *I Was Canright's Secretary* (Washington, D.C.: Review and Herald®, 1971), 10–19.

2. D. M. Canright, "From Bro. Canright," *Review and Herald,* January 26, 1860, 78.

3. A helpful summary of some of these articles is found in Johnson, 13–17.

4. D. M. Canright, "From Bro. Canright," *Review and Herald,* November 8, 1864, 191.

5. I am indebted to I. Barry Burton, "Dudley M. Canright: Articles and News Items, SDA Publications, 1860–1887," CD-ROM, 2009, who specialized in finding all of Canright's writings throughout the early Adventist periodicals and shared his research with me. Canright's literary output was quite impressive.

6. I will base this narrative of Canright's in-and-out experience of the Adventist ministry on his own account, which corresponds with George I. Butler's account in "Brief History of Eld. Canright's Connection With This People," *Review and Herald Extra,* November 22, 1887, 2, 3. Butler remembered three times in which Canright experienced "doubts" and "ceased to preach": 1873, 1880, and 1882. He added one other time that Canright experienced doubts in 1870 but did not cease preaching.

7. Canright's relationship with Ellen White was similar to that of A. T. Jones, whose relationship with her has been described as "love and hate." See George Knight, chapter 15: "Love and Hate: A. T. Jones's Relationship to Ellen White," in *From 1888 to Apostasy: The Case of A. T. Jones* (Hagerstown, Md.: Review and Herald®, 1987), 226–239.

8. Dudley M. Canright, "To My Brethren, The S. D. Adventists," *Review and Herald,* October 7, 1884, 633, 634.

9. The letter is published in Ellen G. White, "To a Young Minister and His Wife," *Testimonies for the Church* (Nampa, Idaho: Pacific Press®, 1948), 3: 304–329.

10. Canright, "To My Brethren," 633.

11. D. M. Canright, "A Plain Talk to the Murmurers: Some Facts for Those Who Are Not in Harmony With the Body," *Review and Herald,* March 15, 1877, 84, 85; Canright, "Continued," *Review and Herald,* April 12, 1877, 116, 117; Canright, "Continued," *Review and Herald,* April 19, 1877, 124, 125; Canright, "Continued," *Review and Herald,* April 26, 1877, 132; Canright, "Continued," *Review and Herald,* May 10, 1877, 148, 149; Canright, "Continued," *Review and Herald,* May 17, 1877, 156, 157; Canright, "Continued," *Review and Herald,* May 24, 1877, 165; Canright, "Continued," *Review and Herald,* May 31, 1877, 173; Canright, "Continued," *Review and Herald,* June 7, 1877, 181; Canright, "Continued," *Review and Herald,* June, 14, 1877, 188, 189.

12. Canright, "A Plain Talk to the Murmurers," ibid., April 26, 1877, 132.

13. This letter (E. G. White to D. M. Canright, Letter 1, 1880) is published in E. G. White, "An Appeal to D. M. Canright," *Selected Messages* (Hagerstown, Md.: Review and Herald®, 1958), 2:162. 170, "An Appeal to D. M. Canright."

14. Canright, "To My Brethren," 633.

15. Canright, "Danger of Giving Way to Dis-

couragement and Doubts," *Review and Herald*, September 13, 1881, 185.

16. Ibid.

17. Ibid.

18. Canright, "To My Brethren," 633.

19. D. M. Canright to A. C. Long, December 8, 1883; Document File 351, Center for Adventist Research, Andrews University.

20. Ibid. As we saw in the last chapter, A. C. Long was an opponent of Ellen White and had published his book *Comparison of the Early Writings of Mrs. White with Later Publications* earlier that year. Long was trying to learn what Canright's relationship was to Seventh-day Adventism, since he wasn't preaching for them anymore. This letter is Canright's response to Long, evidently an old friend. Although Canright spoke frankly about his concerns with Ellen White and Seventh-day Adventism, he also expressed concern for Long's cause: "I see no light in that direction." He ended the letter with these words: "Well, I have given you my position frankly and freely as an old friend. I have always thought much of you since we were acquainted and now hope we may reach the kingdom together" (ibid.).

21. Canright, "To My Brethren," 633.

22. Ibid.; emphasis added.

23. Ibid., 634.

24. Ibid.

25. D. M. Canright, "Items of Experience," *Review and Herald*, December 2, 1884, 764.

26. See Johnson, 73–80, for details of Canright's ministry during this period.

27. D. M. Canright, "To Those in Doubting Castle," *Review and Herald*, February 10, 1885, 85.

28. There were exceptions, though, such as Joseph Bates, a legalist from the beginning. See George Knight, *Joseph Bates: The Real Founder of Seventh-day Adventism* (Hagerstown, Md.: Review and Herald®, 2004), 83–88. Bates's tendency toward legalism doesn't diminish his profound contributions to Seventh-day Adventism, as Knight points out in this biography.

29. Arthur W. Spalding, *Origin and History of Seventh-day Adventists*, vol. 2 (Washington, D.C.: Review and Herald®, 1961), 286.

30. Arnold Valentin Wallenkampf, *What Every Adventist Should Know About 1888* (Washington, D.C.: Review and Herald®, 1988), 10.

31. Richard W. Schwarz and Floyd Greenleaf, *Light Bearers: A History of the Seventh-day Adventist Church* (Nampa, Idaho: Pacific Press®, 2000), 175, 176.

32. George Knight, *The Search for Identity: The Development of Seventh-day Adventist Beliefs* (Hagerstown, Md.: Review and Herald®, 2000), 104, 105.

33. Canright, "Our Mission," *Signs of the Times*®, July 9, 1874, 29.

34. E. G. White, *Spiritual Gifts*, (Battle Creek, Mich.: Steam Press of the Seventh-day Adventist Publishing Association, 1864), 3:46, 47, 52.

35. First published as a small pamphlet—E. G. White, "The Sufferings of Christ" (Battle Creek, Mich.: Seventh-day Adventist Publication Association, 1869)—and housed at the Ellen G. White Estate as Pamphlet 169. It was later published that same year in *Testimonies for the Church*, 2:200, 215. The pamphlet was edited and published several more times: E. G. White, "Sufferings of Christ," *Signs of the Times*®, August 7, 1879, 233, 234; E. G. White, "Sufferings of Christ, *Signs of the Times*®, August 14, 1879, 241; E. G. White, "Sufferings of Christ," *Signs of the Times*®, August 28, 1879; also in the *Bible Echo*: E. G. White, "Sufferings of Christ," *Bible Echo*, August 1, 1892, 234; E. G. White, "Sufferings of Christ," *Bible Echo*, August 15, 1892, 242; and "The Great Sacrifice," *Bible Echo*, September 15, 1892, 274. It was also enlarged and expanded for *The Desire of Ages*, chapters 74–78. Its repeated exposure to the church over the years demonstrates its importance to Ellen White.

36. E. G. White, *Testimonies for the Church*, 2:201.

37. Ibid., 215.

38. E. G. White, "Christ and the Law," sermon given at Rome, New York, June 19, 1889, *The Ellen G. White 1888 Materials*, vol. 1 (Washington, D.C.: Ellen G. White Estate, Silver Spring, Md., 1987), 348.

39. Ibid. For a discussion on the time reference "forty-five years," see Woodrow W. Whidden, "The Soteriology of Ellen G. White: The Persistent Path to Perfection, 1836–1902," (PhD dissertation, Drew University, 1989), 289–292.

40. E. G. White, *Testimonies for the Church*, 4:313.

41. Ibid., 374, 375.

42. E. G. White, "Christ Prayed for Unity Among His Disciples," *Review and Herald*, March 11, 1890, 146.

43. E. G. White, "Our Duties and Obligations," *Review and Herald*, December 18, 1888, 794.

44. E. G. White, "Preparation for the Camp Meeting," *Review and Herald*, August 15, 1882, 522.

45. The history of Adventists and the law has been discussed in George Knight, *A User-Friendly Guide to the 1888 Message* (Hagerstown, Md.: Review and Herald®, 1998), 36–46; Woodrow W. Whidden, *E. J. Waggoner: From the Physician of Good News to Agent of Division* (Hagerstown, Md.: Review and Herald®, 2008), 98–104; and Bert Haloviak, "From Righteousness to Holy Flesh: Judgment at Minneapolis," research paper, Archives and Statistics Research Papers, Office of Archives and Statistics, General Conference of Seventh-day Adventists, chapter 2, "World of the Pioneers," 1–26; and chapter 2a, "Pioneers on Exhibit," 1–22, http://www.adventistarchives.org/docs/AST/JAM1987/index.djvu.

46. Dudley M. Canright, *The Two Laws, As Set Forth in the Scriptures of the Old and New Testaments* (Battle Creek, Mich.: Steam Press of the Seventh-day Adventist Publishing Association, 1876).

47. Knight, *A User-Friendly Guide*, 37.

48. George Knight correctly points out in *Angry Saints: Tensions and Possibilities in the Adventist Struggle Over Righteousness by Faith* (Hagerstown, Md.: Review and Herald®, 1989), 38, note 28, that the "1886 printing of Canright's *Two Laws* carries an 1882 introduction and imprint. Since the 1876 edition was also published in 1882, there is some question as to whether the new edition first came out in 1882 or 1886. It appears that the denomination didn't advertise the second edition until 1886. The fact that Canright temporarily left the Adventist ministry in 1882 somewhat clouds the picture."

In a letter dated February 29, 1886, W. C. White mentioned that the press had just "run a large edition of Canright's *Two Laws*" although it was condemned about "two years ago." This "large edition" leads me to believe that the 1886 printing was the version already enlarged by Canright in 1882 (W. C. White to C. H. Jones, February 19, 1886; and W. C. White to F. E. Belden, July 3, 1888). At any rate, Canright's expanded discussion on Galatians 3 was considered by church leaders G. I. Butler and U. Smith to be the correct position.

49. Dudley M. Canright, *The Two Laws, As Set Forth in the Scriptures of the Old and New Testaments* (Battle Creek, Mich.: Seventh-day Adventist Publishing Association, 1886), 62.

50. Ellet J. Waggoner, "Comments on Galatians 3," *Signs of the Times*®, August 26, 1886, 518; see also Waggoner, "Under the Law," *Signs of the Times*®, September 11, 1884, 553, 554.

51. Knight, *User-Friendly Guide*, 40, 59.

52. Ibid., 58–61.

53. George I. Butler, *The Law in the Book of Galatians* (Battle Creek, Mich.: Review and Herald®,) 1886.

54. Knight, 41.

55. Haloviak, Chapter 2, "World of the Pioneers," 17.

56. See Knight, *User-Friendly Guide*, 41; and G. I. Butler, "General Conference Proceedings:

Twenty-fifth Annual Session," *Review and Herald*, December 14, 1886, 779.

57. Several denominational historians have recognized the significant role of this theological committee debate in Canright's departure from Adventism: Knight, 41, 42; Haloviak, "Pioneers on Exhibit," chapter 2a, 14, 15; and Paul Ernest McGraw, "Born in Zion? The Margins of Fundamentalism and the Definition of Seventh-day Adventism" (PhD dissertation, George Washington University, 2004), 77–83.

58. D. M. Canright, *Seventh-day Adventism Renounced After an Experience of Twenty-Eight Years: By a Prominent Minister and Writer of that Faith*, 14th ed. (New York: Fleming H. Revell, 1914), 50, 51.

59. Ibid., 382, 389.

60. Ibid., 51.

61. Knight, 42, 43.

62. E. G. White to G. I. Butler, October 14, 1888, *The Ellen G. White 1888 Materials*, 8, 12.

63. Ibid.

64. Canright, 51.

65. G. I. Butler to E. G. White, February 17, 1887.

66. G. I. Butler, "Why This Extra Is Issued," *Review and Herald Extra*, November 22, 1887, 1.

67. G. I. Butler to E. G. White, February 17, 1887.

68. G. I. Butler, "Why This Extra Is Issued," 1.

69. G. I. Butler, "Eld. Canright's Change of Faith," *Review and Herald*, March 1, 1887, 138.

70. See, for example, ibid.

71. "A Few Words More Concerning Eld. Canright," *Review and Herald*, March 22, 1887, 185. Canright wrote in *Seventh-day Adventism Renounced* that "though I went out quietly and peaceably, they immediately attributed to me all sorts of evil motives, base sins, and ambitious designs.... 'Apostate' was the epithet all applied to me" (55, 56). What he failed to mention was Butler's published rebuke to those individual Adventists writing to Canright and saying those kinds of things ("A Few Words More Concerning Eld. Canright," 185).

72. Douty argues that the Adventists broke the truce by applying "apostasy" to Canright's experience (93–98), whereas Johnson argues that Canright "began to wage war" on the Adventists "quite contrary to his declared intentions" (91). Analysis of the evidence behind both arguments is beyond the purview of this book. Both sides appear to have played a role in the breaking of the truce.

73. E. G. White to G. I. Butler and U. Smith, April 3, 1887, *The Ellen G. White 1888 Materials*, 35.

74. From G. I. Butler's description of Canright's activity in "Why This Extra Is Issued," *Review and Herald Extra*, Nov. 22, 1887, 1.

75. "Reply to Eld. Canright's Attacks on S. D. Adventists," *Review and Herald Extra*, November 22, 1887, and "Our Rejoinder," *Review and Herald Extra*, no. 2, February 21, 1888; *Replies to Elder Canright's Attacks on Seventh-day Adventists* (Battle Creek, Mich.: Review and Herald®, 1888); *Replies to Elder Canright's Attacks on Seventh-day Adventists* (Battle Creek, Mich.: Review and Herald®, 1895).

76. "Reply to Eld. Canright's Attacks on S. D. Adventists," 10–13.

77. Ibid., 7, 8.

78. D. M. Canright, *Seventh-day Adventism Renounced After an Experience of Twenty-Eight Years: By a Prominent Minister and Writer of That Faith* (Kalamazoo, Mich.: Kalamazoo Publishing, 1888); 14th ed. (New York: Fleming H. Revell, 1914).

79. Canright, *Seventh-day Adventism Renounced*, 1888, 43–55; 1914 ed., 129–165.

80. Ron Graybill, "D. M. Canright in Healdsburg, 1889: The Genesis of the Plagiarism Charge," *Insight*, October 21, 1980, 7–10; McGraw's dissertation also deals with the Healdsburg debates in considerable detail and provides a list of all the newspaper articles in the bibliography, 62–75, 330, 331.

81. Graybill, 9.

82. D. M. Canright, *Adventism Refuted in a Nutshell*, ten-tract series (n.p., 1889); Canright, *The Lord's Day From Neither Catholics Nor Pagans: An Answer to Seventh-day Adventism on This Subject*, 2nd ed. (New York: Fleming H. Revell, 1915); Canright, *The Complete Testimony of the Early Fathers: Proving the Universal Observance of Sunday in the First Centuries* (New York: Fleming H. Revell, 1916).

83. D. M. Canright, *Life of Mrs. E. G. White, Seventh-day Adventist Prophet: Her False Claims Refuted* (Cincinnati: Standard Publishing, 1919).

84. Presently, both of these books circulate on the Internet, and reprinted versions are sold at Amazon.com.

85. This definitive statement is considered to be the best summary of the 1888 message: E. G. White, *Testimonies to Ministers and Gospel Workers* (Mountain View, Calif.: Pacific Press®, 1923), 91–93; see Knight's helpful summary of this statement in *A User-Friendly Guide*, 19–22.

86. E. G. White, "Meetings at South Lancaster, Mass.," *Review and Herald*, March 5, 1889, 146.

87. E. G. White, "Camp Meeting at Ottawa, Kansas," *Review and Herald*, July 23, 1889, 466.

88. W. W. Prescott, "Report of the Educational Secretary," *Review and Herald Extra*, "Daily Bulletin of the General Conference," February 23, 1893, 350; Knight, *A Brief History of Seventh-day Adventists*, 2nd ed. (Hagerstown, Md.: Review and Herald®, 2004), 96, 97; Floyd Greenleaf, *In Passion For the World: A History of Seventh-day Adventist Education* (Nampa, Idaho: Pacific Press®, 2005), 41, 42.

89. Knight, 92, 93.

90. Canright, *Adventism Renounced*, 14th ed., 305.

91. See, for example, ibid., 305–394.

92. Ibid., 51.

93. Woodrow Whidden was right when he wrote: "For Ellen White, Minneapolis represented a great turning point in the intensity and further clarity of her expression of justification by faith. There were, however, no landmark advances or major reversals in her basic understanding" (Whidden, "The Soteriology of Ellen G. White," 284ff).

94. Schwarz and Greenleaf, *Light Bearers: A History of the Seventh-day Adventist Church*, 187.

95. For discussion on the church's promotion of Ellen White's books during this period, see LeRoy E. Froom, *Movement of Destiny* (Washington, D.C.: Review and Herald®, 1971), 444, 445.

96. Alberto R. Timm, "Issues on Ellen G. White and Her Role in the Seventh-day Adventist Church," unpublished paper presented at the Ellen White Conference, Battle Creek, Michigan, 2002, 3.

97. For an example of how Canright dismissed evidence contrary to his claims, compare his book *Life of Mrs. E. G. White, Seventh-day Adventist Prophet: Her False Claims Refuted* with Francis D. Nichol's response in *Ellen G. White and Her Critics: An Answer to the Major Charges That Critics Have Brought Against Mrs. Ellen G. White* (Washington D.C.: Review and Herald®, 1951).

98. E. G. White, *Testimonies for the Church*, 5:663–670.

99. Ibid, 665.

100. While Adventism moved beyond the legalistic charges of Canright, it has not been without its struggles on righteousness by faith. See, for example, George Knight, *The Search for Identity*, 144–152; and Martin Weber, *Who's Got the Truth?* (Silver Spring, Md.: Home Study International Press, 1994).

101. The term *cult* is generally used to describe a fundamental departure from established Christian teaching, particularly conservative Christianity. See Sydney E. Ahlstrom, *A Religious History of the American People*, 2nd ed. (New Haven and London: Yale University Press, 2004), 474, for an insightful explanation of the term.

102. Timm, 3.

(Chapter 4)
Canright's Legacy and the Church's Response

1. Juhyeok Nam covered the work of these two writers in his doctoral dissertation, "Reactions to the Seventh-day Adventist Evangelical Conferences and *Questions on Doctrine*, 1955–1971" (PhD dissertation, Andrews University, 2005), 15–21.

2. Nam's dissertation, ibid., is the most thorough study to date on the background to the book *Questions on Doctrine*; see also George Knight's "Historical and Theological Introduction to the Annotated Edition," in Knight, ed. *Questions On Doctrine: Annotated Edition*, Adventist Classic Library (Berrien Springs, Mich.: Andrews University Press, 2003), xiii–xxxvi; two other studies worthy of attention include: Leroy Moore, *Questions on Doctrine Revisited!* (Ithaca, Mich.: AB Publishing, 2005); and Herbert Douglass, *A Fork in the Road "Questions on Doctrine": The Historic Adventist Divide of 1957* (Coldwater, Mich.: Remnant Publications, 2008).

3. Walter Martin, *The Truth About Seventh-day Adventism* (Grand Rapids, Mich.: Zondervan, 1960), 98.

4. Alberto R. Timm, "Issues on Ellen G. White and Her Role in the Seventh-day Adventist Church," unpublished paper presented at the Ellen White Conference, Battle Creek, Michigan, 2002, 3–6.

5. Ronald L. Numbers, *Prophetess of Health: A Study of Ellen G. White* (New York: Harper and Row, 1976). When this book was first published in 1976, it was on the crest of a wave generated in the Adventist academic community. The Autumn 1970 issue of *Spectrum*, published by the Association of Adventist Forums, had explicitly encouraged Adventist scholars to study Ellen White's writings from a historical-critical perspective, which discounted the supernatural element in her visions. Numbers thus approached Ellen White without a presupposition of supernaturalism or divine inspiration in her experience. His purpose was not to destroy her credibility as Canright and many critics of today seek to do but to understand her in the cultural milieu on the nineteenth century. Nevertheless, his book was critical of her visionary experience in a way similar to that of Canright. Consequently, it elicited various critical responses from supporters of Ellen White's divine inspiration (see chapter 1, note 22). It is important to note that Numbers's book transformed Ellen White from a person "largely hidden in the shadows of American religious history" to a "fixture in accounts of women and religion in America" (see Numbers, *Prophetess of Health: A Study of Ellen G. White*, 3rd ed. [Grand Rapids, Mich.: Wm. B. Eerdmans, 2008], xix–xxi, for documentation). Considered the "standard biography of Ellen White" (ibid., xix), the influence of *Prophetess of Health* shouldn't be underestimated. Although supporters of Ellen White's prophetic gift will not agree with the various accounts of her life and work based upon Numbers's book, the fact that she is receiving such attention in academic circles opens the door for believing scholars to join the discussion and contribute their research to the appraisal of her prophetic credentials.

6. Walter T. Rea, *The White Lie* (Turlock, Calif.: M & R Publications, 1982).

7. Recently changed to http://www.ellenwhite-exposed.com.

8. There are, of course, many more manifestations of Canright's influence in the flurry of anti-Ellen White writing from the 1980s up to the present. This section is intended only as a brief survey. For more detail, see Timm, 2–7.

9. D. M. Canright, *Life of Mrs. E. G. White, Seventh-day Adventist Prophet: Her False Claims Refuted* (Cincinnati: Standard Publishing, 1919); the republished edition used in this book is Canright, *Life of Mrs. E. G. White, Seventh-day*

Adventist Prophet: Her False Claims Refuted (Salt Lake City, Utah: Grant Shurtliff, 1998).

10. "Correspondence between Elder A. G. Daniells and F. E. Dufty over *The Life of Mrs. E. G. White* by D. M. Canright, October 15, 1919, to July 17, 1922," Office of Archives and Statistics, General Conference of Seventh-day Adventists. During this period approximately twenty letters passed between the two, mostly short, regarding delays and inquiries as to when answers could be expected. This document contains copies of the two longest and most significant letters, which may be considered the concluding communications in this lengthy correspondence: Daniells to Dufty, 1921 (Daniells's letter to Dufty was not dated but written sometime in mid to late 1921); Dufty to Daniells, January 11, 1922.

11. Both letters refer to the previous correspondence, Daniells to Dufty, 1, 2; Dufty to Daniells, 1.

12. Daniells to Dufty, 2.

13. Ibid., 8.

14. Ibid., 7.

15. Ibid., 11; Canright, 59.

16. Ibid.

17. Ibid.

18. Ibid., 12.

19. Ibid., 22, 23.

20. Dufty to Daniells, 1.

21. Ibid., 8, 9.

22. "Correspondence Between Elder A. G. Daniells and F. E. Dufty," 2.

23. Daniells's conclusion on Ellen White and the shut door has been confirmed by recent research: Merlin Burt, "The Historical Background, Interconnected Development, and Integration of the Doctrines of the Sanctuary, the Sabbath, and Ellen G. White's Role in Sabbatarian Adventism from 1944 to 1849" (PhD dissertation, Andrews University, 2002); see also Bert's article, "The 'Shut Door' and Ellen White's Visions," in the forthcoming *Ellen G. White Letters: 1846–1859* (Review and Herald® Publishing Association).

24. Arthur G. Daniells, "The Shut Door and the Close of Probation: The Position of the Spirit of Prophecy Between 1844 and 1851, as Revealed in Original Sources of Our Early Documents and Periodicals," *Review and Herald*, November 25, 1926, 3–8.

25. Wilcox's series ran in the following dates of the *Review and Herald* under the title "The Shut Door and the Close of Probation; Faith of the Early Believers Regarding These Questions": "Part One," December 19, 1929, 3–5; "Part Two," December 26, 1929, 4, 5; "Part Three," January 2, 1930, 9, 10; "Part Four," January 9, 1930, 7–9; "Part Five," January 16, 1930, 27–29; "Part Six," January 23, 1930, 7, 8; "Part Seven," January 30, 1930, 6–8.

26. Ibid., "Part Seven," January 30, 1930, 8.

27. Daniells's series ran in the following dates of the *Review and Herald* under the title "The Shut Door and the Close of Probation: The Position of the Spirit of Prophecy Between 1844 and 1851, as Revealed in Original Sources of Our Early Documents and Periodicals": "Second Series—No. 1," February 6, 1930, 4, 5; "Second Series—No. 2," February 13, 1930, 4, 5; "Second Series—No. 3," February 20, 1930, 6–8; "Second Series—No. 4," February 27, 1930, 7, 8.

28. According to Daniells in "The Shut Door and the Close of Probation: An Important Statement From Mrs. E. G. White," *Review and Herald*, January 14, 1932, 6.

29. Francis M. Wilcox and Arthur G. Daniells, *The Faith of the Pioneers: Relating to the Shut Door and the Close of Probation* (Washington, D.C.: Review and Herald®, n.d.). Published sometime in 1930 or 1931.

30. Arthur G. Daniells, "The Shut Door and the Close of Probation: An Important Statement From Mrs. E. G. White," *Review and Herald*, January 14, 1932, 6–8.

31. Ibid., 6; part of the letter Daniells published is found in Ellen G. White, *Selected Messages*

(Hagerstown, Md.: Review and Herald®, 1958), 1:74. The letter in its entirety is published in *Manuscript Releases* (Silver Spring, Md.: E. G. White Estate, 1990), 8:228–243; Letter 2: E. G. White to J. N. Loughborough, August 24, 1874.

32. Daniells, 7.

33. Arthur G. Daniells, *The Abiding Gift of Prophecy* (Mountain View, Calif.: Pacific Press® Publishing Association, 1936). In this comprehensive volume, Daniells set forth the operation of the prophetic gift during biblical times and its continuation in history. In the latter part of the book, he related his own experience as he observed the gift guiding the Seventh-day Adventist Church.

34. Ibid., 368.

35. Canright, 2.

36. The complete stenographic transcript of the 1919 Bible Conference has been put online and can be accessed at http://www.adventistarchives.org/DocArchives.asp; see also Molleurus Couperus, "The Bible Conference of 1919," *Spectrum: Journal of the Association of Adventist Forums* (March 1979), 23–57, for the transcript of the July 30 and August 1 discussions pertaining to Ellen White. For a major study on this important conference, see Michael W. Campbell, "The 1919 Bible Conference and Its Significance for Seventh-day Adventist History and Theology" (PhD dissertation, Andrews University, 2008).

37. See http://www.adventistarchives.org/DocArchives.asp for the July 30 and August 1 transcripts online; and Campbell, 151–169. In one of the discussions, E. R. Palmer refers to Canright's charge of plagiarism: "Report of Bible Conference, Held in Takoma Park, D.C., July 1–19, 1919," July 19, 1919, 1075.

38. Canright, 22, 46, 47, 129, 130.

39. Meeting held at Elmshaven Office, August 15–17, 1930: "To Answer D. M. Canright's Misrepresentations" (DF 351, E. G. White Estate). "Elmshaven" is the name of the home in St. Helena, California, where Ellen White spent the last years of her life. She provided for the establishment of the Ellen G. White Estate in her will. The Estate is responsible for the continued publication and dissemination of her writings.

40. Ibid., 1.

41. W. C. White and D. A. Robinson, *Brief Statements Regarding the Writings of Ellen G. White* (St. Helena, Calif.: Elmshaven Office, 1933).

42. W. C. White and D. A. Robinson, *Brief Statements Regarding the Writings of Ellen G. White*, insert, *Adventist Review*, June 4, 1981.

43. For example, Walter Rea, *Los Angeles Times*, October 23, 1980.

44. William H. Branson, *In Defense of the Faith, The Truth About Seventh-day Adventists: A Reply to Canright* (Washington, D.C.: Review and Herald®, 1933).

45. See Nam, 15–17.

46. Branson, 338, 339.

47. Although this book was written at the request of the General Conference Committee, not all of the committee members were happy with it. Some felt it was an "inadequate treatment" of the sanctuary question, it didn't deal with serious issues, and its tone of irony and sarcasm was embarrassing. According to Gilbert M. Valentine, "in spite of the negative assessment, the manuscript was published in 1933 but what changes were required in the manuscript before publication are not clear" (Valentine, *The Struggles for the Prophetic Heritage: Issues in the Conflict for Control of the Ellen G. White Publications 1930–1939* [Muak Lek, Thailand: Institute Press, 2006], 62, 63, 69, 70, note 23).

48. Francis D. Nichol, *Ellen G. White and Her Critics: An Answer to the Major Charges That Critics Have Brought Against Mrs. Ellen G. White* (Washington D.C.: Review and Herald®, 1951).

49. Nichol, *Ellen G. White and Her Critics*, 16, 17.

50. Francis D. Nichol, ed. *The Seventh-day Adventist Bible Commentary*, vols. 1–7 (Washington, D.C.: Review and Herald®, 1953–57).

51. Francis D. Nichol, *Answers to Objections: An Examination of the Major Objections Raised Against the Teachings of Seventh-day Adventists* (Washington, D.C.: Review and Herald®, 1932, 1847, 1952); Nichol, *The Midnight Cry: A Defense of William Miller and the Millerites* (Takoma Park, Md.: Review and Herald®, 1944). For more details on Nichol, see Miriam and Kenneth Wood, *His Initials Were F.D.N.: A Life Story of Elder F. D. Nichol* (Washington, D.C.: Review and Herald®, 1967).

52. Merlin Burt, "Bibliographic Essay of Publications about Ellen G. White," in *Ellen White and Current Issues Symposium*, vol. 3 (Berrien Springs, Mich.: Center for Adventist Research Andrews University, 2007), 16.

53. Norman F. Douty in his *The Case of D. M. Canright: Seventh-day Adventist Charges Examined* (Grand Rapids, Mich.: Baker Book House, 1964); Carrie Johnson, *I Was Canright's Secretary* (Washington, D.C.: Review and Herald®, 1971).

54. Norman F. Douty, *Another Look at Seventh-day Adventism* (Grand Rapids, Mich.: Baker Book House, 1962),184, 188.

55. Douty, *The Case of D. M. Canright*, 11, 173, 174.

56. To my knowledge, there is no major critique of Douty's work, and such a critique is beyond the purview of this book.

57. Douty, 160–162.

58. See, for example, Johnson, 120–150.

59. It is my belief that the *real* D. M. Canright lies somewhere between the Douty and Johnson biographies.

60. Arthur L. White, *Notes and Papers Concerning Ellen G. White and the Spirit of Prophecy* (Washington, D.C.: Ellen G. White Estate, 1974), 231–247.

61. For example, from my own files: Roger Coon, Lecture Notes, "The Writings of Ellen G. White," Winter Quarter, Andrews University Theological Seminary, 1984.

62. At the Adventist seminary, the classes on Ellen White's prophetic ministry are presently taught by Denis Fortin, Jerry Moon, and Merlin Burt and continue in the tradition of Roger Coon's apologetics. This same tradition also continues at other Adventist universities, such as Southern Adventist University, where Ellen White criticisms are addressed in a class for ministerial students taught by Jud Lake.

63. Robert W. Olson, *One Hundred and One Questions on the Sanctuary and on Ellen White*, accessible on the *Ellen G. White Writings Comprehensive Research Edition CD-ROM* (Silver Spring, Md.: Ellen G. White Estate); first published by the Ellen G. White Estate in 1981.

64. For a concise introduction to Desmond Ford and the issues he raised, see Richard W. Schwarz and Floyd Greenleaf, *Light Bearers: A History of the Seventh-day Adventist Church* (Nampa, Idaho: Pacific Press®, 2000), 633, 634; see also Desmond Ford, *Daniel 8:14, the Day of Atonement, and the Investigative Judgment* (Casselberry, Fla.: Euangelion Press, 1980), 350–361.

65. Arthur White, *Ellen G. White*, vol. 1, *The Early Years, 1827–1862* (Washington, D.C.: Review and Herald®, 1985); Arthur White, *Ellen G. White*, vol. 2, *The Progressive Years, 1863–1876* (Washington, D.C.: Review and Herald®, 1986); Arthur White, *Ellen G. White*, vol. 3, *The Lonely Years, 1876–1891* (Washington, D.C.: Review and Herald®, 1984); Arthur White, *Ellen G. White*, vol. 4, *The Australian Years, 1891–1900* (Washington D.C.: Review and Herald®, 1983); Arthur White, *Ellen G. White*, vol. 5, *The Early Elmshaven Years, 1900–1905* (Washington D.C.: Review and Herald®, 1981); Arthur White, *Ellen G. White*, Vol. 6, *The Later Elmshaven Years, 1905–1915* (Washington D.C.: Review and Herald®, 1982).

66. Vincent L. Ramik, "Memorandum of Law Literary Property Rights, 1790–1915" (Washington, D.C.: Diller, Ramik & Wight, Ltd., Aug. 14, 1981); accessible online at http://ellenwhiteanswers

.org/answers/plagarism; and Fred Veltman, "Full Report of the Life of Christ Research Project," 4 vols. (Washington, D.C.: Ellen G. White Estate, 1988); accessible online at http://www.adventistarchives.org/DocArchives.asp.

67. Herbert E. Douglass, *Messenger of the Lord: The Prophetic Ministry of Ellen G. White* (Nampa, Idaho.: Pacific Press®, 1998).

68. T. Housel Jemison, *A Prophet Among You* (Boise, Idaho: Pacific Press®, 1955).

69. Douglass, "Section VII: How to Evaluate Criticism," 468–512.

70. Clifford Goldstein, *Graffiti in the Holy of Holies: An Impassioned Response to Recent Attacks on the Sanctuary and Ellen White* (Nampa, Idaho.: Pacific Press®, 2003).

71. Don S. McMahon, *Acquired or Inspired: Exploring the Origins of the Adventist Lifestyle* (Victoria, Australia: Signs Publishing, 2005).

72. Leonard Brand and Don S. McMahon, *The Prophet and Her Critics: A Striking New Analysis Refutes the Charges That Ellen G. White "Borrowed" the Health Message* (Nampa, Idaho: Pacific Press®, 2005).

73. Ibid., 88. Ronald Numbers responded to Brand and McMahon in the third edition of *Prophetess of Health*, xxiii–xxiv.

74. Alden Thompson, *Escape From the Flames: How Ellen White Grew From Fear to Joy—and Helped Me to Do It Too* (Nampa, Idaho: Pacific Press®, 2005); Thompson, *Inspiration: Hard Questions, Honest Answers* (Hagerstown, Md.: Review and Herald®, 1991).

75. Thompson, *Escape From the Flames*, 151. It should also be mentioned that a theme throughout the book is unity amid diversity, which Thompson expands in his *Beyond Common Ground: Why Liberals and Conservatives Need Each Other* (Nampa, Idaho: Pacific Press®, 2009).

76. Graeme S. Bradford, *Prophets Are Human* (Victoria, Australia: Signs Publishing, 2004); Bradford, *People Are Human: Look What They Did to Ellen White* (Victoria, Australia: Signs Publishing, 2005); Bradford, *More Than a Prophet: How We Lost and Found Again the Real Ellen White* (Berrien Springs, Mich.: Biblical Perspectives, 2006); Bradford, "Books and Articles on CD-ROM including a live lecture" (Berrien Springs, Mich.: Biblical Perspectives, 2006).

77. See William Fagal, "New Testament Prophets—Are They Less Reliable?" accessible at http://whiteestate.org/issues/NTProphets.htm; and Campbell, "Review of *More Than a Prophet*, by Graeme Bradford," *Ministry* (February 2007), 29; Campbell, "Review of *More Than a Prophet*, by Graeme Bradford," *BRI Newsletter #18* (April 2007), 9, 10.

78. Denis Fortin and Jerry Moon, eds. *The Ellen G. White Encyclopedia* (Hagerstown, Md.: Review and Herald®, 2011).

79. William Fagal, *101 Questions About Ellen White and Her Writings* (Nampa, Idaho: Pacific Press®, 2010).

80. Dirk Anderson's testimonial against Ellen White on his Web site will be used for the information in this biographical sketch. See http://www.ellenwhiteexposed.com/archive/testimony.htm (accessed 11/19/09).

81. See chapter 1, note 8, for the references.

82. George Knight, *I Used to Be Perfect: A Study of Sin and Salvation*, 2nd ed. (Berrien Springs, Mich.: 2001), 70, 79.

83. See Woodrow W. Whidden, "The Soteriology of Ellen G. White: The Persistent Path to Perfection, 1836–1902" (PhD dissertation, Drew University, 1989).

84. Ellen G. White, *Counsels on Diet and Foods* (Mountain View, Calif.: Pacific Press®, 1938), 202.

85. Knight, *Reading Ellen White: How to Understand and Apply Her Writings* (Hagerstown, Md.: Review and Herald®, 1997).

86. Anderson has recently launched a new Web site, http://dirkanderson.com (accessed 9/9/09),

which expresses his general philosophy of life, personal interests, and spiritual journey.

87. The main source of information about Dale Ratzlaff is found in his own autobiography, *Truth Led Me Out: A Seventh-day Adventist Pastor Courageously Studies His Way to Biblical Truth* (Glendale, Ariz.: LAM Publications, 2008), 1.

88. Ibid., 71–78.

89. Ibid., 1.

90. Ibid.

91. Ibid., 142.

92. "Dale Ratzlaff," in *Historical Dictionary of the Seventh Day Adventists*, Gary Land, ed. (Lanham, Md.: Scarecrow Press, 2005), 242, 243.

93. See chapter 1, note 2, for references.

94. See http://www.ratzlaff.com/page3.html.

95. Ratzlaff, *Truth Led Me Out*, 142.

96. Dale Ratzlaff, "New Editor of ellenwhiteexposed.com," http://www.ellenwhiteexposed.com/mystory2.htm (accessed 11/19/09).

97. Ratzlaff, *Truth Led Me Out*, 33.

98. Ibid., 33, 59, 84.

99. Ibid., 84.

100. Ibid., 84, 89–98.

101. Ibid., 103ff.

102. Ibid., 40; here he mentions "*Selected Messages*, book 2, which has the best material on this topic" and then states, "Whoever combed the writings of Ellen White to pull out the quotations for this section did a good job." Evidently, he meant *Selected Messages* (Washington, D.C.: Review and Herald®, 1958), 1:350–400, which contains several of Ellen White's key addresses on righteousness by faith not found in book 2. Although, it's possible he meant *Selected Messages*, 2:246–256, where excerts from Ellen White's letters to those facing death contain assurance in Christ. He doesn't give page numbers in his reference to *Selected Messages*.

103. Ibid., 40, 65, note 2.

104. George Knight, *A User-Friendly Guide to the 1888 Message* (Hagerstown, Md.: Review and Herald®, 1998); Woodrow Whidden, *Ellen White on Salvation* (Hagerstown, Md.: Review and Herald®, 1995); E. G. White, *The Ellen G. White 1888 Materials*, vols. 1–4 (Washington, D.C.: Ellen G. White Estate, 1987).

105. See Herbert Douglass, *Should We Ever Say, "I Am Saved"? What It Means to Be Assured of Salvation* (Nampa, Idaho: Pacific Press®, 2003).

106. Ratzlaff, 145–148.

107. Anderson, "Spiritual Journey," http://dirkanderson.com (accessed 9/9/09).

(Chapter 5)
Revelation-Inspiration: The Foundation of God's Communication With Us

1. For helpful discussions of general revelation, see Millard J. Erickson, *Christian Theology*, 2nd ed. (Grand Rapids, Mich.: Baker, 1998), 177–199; and Norman Gulley, *Systematic Theology*, vol. 1, *Prolegomena* (Berrien Springs, Mich.: Andrews University Press, 2003), 189–225.

2. Erickson, 201; see his entire discussion on special revelation, 200–223.

3. Raoul Dederen, "Toward a Seventh-day Adventist Theology of Revelation-Inspiration," unpublished paper in *North American Bible Conference* (General Conference of Seventh-day Adventists, 1974), 7, 8.

4. Gordon R. Lewis and Bruce A. Demarest, *Integrative Theology*, vol. 1 (Grand Rapids, Mich.: Zondervan, 1987), 100; see also the excellent study on Genesis 3:15, Afolarin Olutunde Ojewole, "The Seed in Genesis 3:15: An Exegetical and Intertextual Study" (PhD dissertation, Andrews University, 2002), which shows the significance of this *protoevangelium* throughout Scripture.

5. See Bernard Ramm, *Special Revelation and the Word of God* (Grand Rapids, Mich.: Eerdmans, 1961), 31–52; and René Pache, *The Inspiration and Authority of Scripture*, Helen I. Needham, trans. (Salem, Wis.: Sheffield Publishing Company, 1992), 20–24.

6. Erickson, 225, 226.

7. For further discussion on the oral delivery and transmission of the prophetic oracles and Jesus' teaching, see G. V. Smith, "Prophet, Prophecy," in Geoffrey W. Bromiley, ed., *The International Standard Bible Encyclopedia*, rev. ed. (Grand Rapids, Mich.: Wm. B. Eerdmans, 1986), 3:998, 999; and Willem A. Vangemeren, *Interpreting the Prophetic Word* (Grand Rapids, Mich.: Zondervan, 1990), 76–78; Birger Gerhardsson, *The Reliability of the Gospel Tradition* (Peabody, Mass.: Hendrickson, 2001); and Craig L. Blomberg, *The Historical Reliability of the Gospels*, 2nd ed. (Downers Grove, Ill.: IVP Academic, 2007), 50–66.

8. Clark H. Pinnock, *Biblical Revelation: The Foundation of Christian Theology* (Chicago, Ill.: Moody Press, 1971), 35.

9. See "Chapter Six: Scripture As Revelation," in Gulley, 227–289.

10. For a constellation of texts on the Bible's testimony to its inspiration, see Wayne A. Grudem, "Scripture's Self-Attestation and the Problem of Formulating a Doctrine of Scripture," in *Scripture and Truth*, D. A. Carson and John D. Woodbridge, eds. (Grand Rapids: Zondervan, 1983), 19–59; and Gerhard Hasel, "Divine Inspiration and the Canon of the Bible, *Journal of the Adventist Theological Society*, vol. 5, no.1 (1994), 76–89.

11. For a concise discussion of these two texts by Adventist theologians, see Peter M. van Bemmelen, "Revelation and Inspiration," in *Handbook of Seventh-day Adventist Theology*, Raoul Dederen, ed. (Silver Spring, Md.: Review and Herald® and the General Conference of Seventh-day Adventists, 2000), 34–37; Fernando Canale, "Revelation and Inspiration," in *Understanding Scripture: An Adventist Approach*, George W. Reid, ed. (Silver Spring, Md.: Biblical Research Institute, General Conference of Seventh-day Adventists, 2006), 48, 49; and Gerhard Hasel, *Understanding the Living Word of God* (Mountain View, Calif.: Pacific Press®, 1980), 66–68.

12. "While Peter and Paul unequivocally affirm God's direct involvement in the generation of Scripture, neither explains the concrete ways in which the divine and human agencies interfaced, nor details their specific modus operandi" (Canale, 49). To understand this human-divine interfacing, one must investigate the data throughout Scripture itself. For a thorough discussion of this scriptural data, see Canale, *Understanding Revelation-Inspiration*

in a Postmodern World (Fernando L. Canale, 2001), 363–470.

13. The important book *Understanding Scripture: An Adventist Approach*, edited by George W. Reid, was dedicated to Dederen, who is considered to be "one of the most important and influential theologians in Seventh-day Adventist history" (Silver Spring, Md.: Biblical Research Institute, 2001), v.

14. Reid, 8.

15. Ibid.

16. Ellen G. White, *Education* (Mountain View, Calif.: Pacific Press®, 1952), 170.

17. E. G. White, "Who Will Keep the Way of the Lord," *Bible Echo*, July 20, 1892.

18. Dederen, "Revelation-Inspiration Lecture Notes," Andrews University Theological Seminary, Fall Quarter, 1983.

19. For a classic discussion on illumination, see John Calvin, *Institutes of the Christian Religion*, book 1, chapters 7 and 9; and more recently, the helpful discussion by Pache, 199–212.

20. E. G. White, *Testimonies for the Church* (Nampa, Idaho: Pacific Press®, 1948), 4:441.

21. E. G. White, "How to Gain Spiritual Strength," *Review and Herald*, October 1, 1901, 631.

22. Pache, 55.

23. George I. Butler, "Inspiration," 10-part series in the *Review and Herald*, "no. 1," January 8, 1884, 24; "no. 2," January 15, 1884, 41; "no. 3," January 22, 1884, 57, 58; "no. 4," January 29, 1884, 73, 74; "no. 5," February 5, 1884, 89, 90; "no. 6," April 15, 1884, 249, 250; "no. 7," April 22, 1884, 265–267; "no. 8," May 6, 1884, 296, 297; "no. 9," May 27, 1884, 344–346; "no. 10," June 3, 1884, 361, 362. For the historical setting of these articles and Butler's motivation for writing them, see Emmett K. Vande Vere, *Rugged Heart: The Story of George I. Butler* (Nashville, Tenn.: Southern Publishing Association, 1979), 62–68; and Alberto Timm, "A History of Seventh-day Adventist Views on Biblical and Prophetic Inspiration (1844–2000)," *Journal of the Adventist Theological Society* 10/1–2 (1999): 491–493. This article can be accessed online at http://www.atsjats.org.

24. Butler, "Inspiration—No. 2," *Review and Herald*, January 15, 1884, 41.

25. Roy Graham states in his dissertation, *Ellen G White: Co-Founder of the Seventh-day Adventist Church* (New York: Peter Lang, 1985), 159, that Butler was obviously influenced by Thomas H. Horne, who advocated the "degrees of inspiration" theory in his *An Introduction to the Critical Study and Knowledge of the Holy Scriptures* (London: Longman, Brown, Green, and Longmans, 1846), 1:474ff.

26. Butler, "Inspiration—no. 7," *Review and Herald*, April 22, 1884, 265.

27. Ibid., "Inspiration—no. 6," *Review and Herald*, April 15, 1884, 250.

28. Ibid., "Inspiration—no. 7," *Review and Herald*, April 22, 1884, 266.

29. Ibid.

30. See M. H. Brown's motion in "General Conference Proceedings," *Review and Herald*, Nov. 25, 1884, in which he moved that Butler's articles on inspiration be published in pamphlet form. See also Ellen G. White to R. A. Underwood, January 18, 1889, Ellen G. White Estate.

31. Ellen White to R. A. Underwood, January 18, 1889, Lt. 22 in *The Ellen G. White 1888 Materials*, vol. 1 (Washington, D.C.: Ellen G. White Estate, Silver Spring, Md., 1987), 238; see also E. G. White, *Selected Messages* (Hagerstown, Md.: Review and Herald®, 1958), 1:23.

32. E. G. White, *Selected Messages*, 1:19–21; E. G. White, *The Great Controversy* (Mountain View, Calif.: Pacific Press®, 1911), v–xii (first published in the 1888 edition); E. G. White, *Selected Messages*, 1:15–18; E. G. White, *Testimonies for the Church*, 5:698–711.

33. E. G. White, "The Discernment of Truth," Ms., 16, 1889, in *The Ellen G. White 1888 Materials*, vol. 1 (Silver Spring, Md.: Ellen G. White Estate, 1987), 259; emphasis added.

34. E. G. White to John Harvey Kellogg, letter 92, 1900; see *Manuscript Releases* (Silver Spring, Md.: E. G. White Estate, 1990), 2:189.

35. E. G. White, *Spiritual Gifts: My Christian Experience, Views and Labors: In Connection With the Rise and Progress of the "Third Angel's Message"* (Battle Creek, Mich.: James White, 1860), 2:293.

36. Herbert Douglass, *Messenger of the Lord: The Prophetic Ministry of Ellen G. White* (Nampa, Id.: Pacific Press®, 1998), 138.

37. For a partial list of Ellen White's visions, see ibid., "Appendix D," 546–549.

38. E. G. White, *Spiritual Gifts*, 2:292.

39. For this section, I am indebted to Arthur White's discussion on how Ellen White delivered her messages in *Ellen G. White: Messenger to the Remnant* (Washington, D.C.: Review and Herald®, 1969), 12–14.

40. E. G. White, *Early Writings* (Washington, D.C.: Review and Herald®, 1945), 20.

41. A. White, 12.

42. E. G. White, *Spiritual Gifts*, 2:292, 293.

43. A. White, 12.

44. E. G. White, *Testimonies for the Church* (Nampa, Idaho: Pacific Press®, 1948), 5: 678.

45. A. White, 12.

46. See George Knight, *Meeting Ellen White: A Fresh Look at Her Life, Writings, and Major Themes* (Hagerstown, Md.: Review and Herald®, 1996), 91–106, for a concise and helpful overview of the different divisions of Ellen White's writings and the facts regarding her literary output.

47. Ibid., 104.

48. Ibid., 43, 44.

49. Ibid., 44, 45.

50. E. G. White, *Testimonies for the Church*, 4:147, 148. Ellen White repeated this statement again in 1889, ibid., 5:661, in a context where she made it clear that the *Testimonies* were not to take the place of the Bible, ibid., 5:663–668.

51. For an insightful discussion on the many claimants to visions and spiritual communications during the nineteenth century from the perspective of the interplay between religion and psychology, see Ann Taves, *Fits, Trances, and Visions: Experiencing Religion and Explaining Experience from Wesley to James* (Princeton, N.J.: Princeton University Press, 1999).

(Chapter 6)
Ellen White and Models of Inspiration

1. D. M. Canright, *Seventh-day Adventism Renounced: After an Experience of Twenty-Eight Years by a Prominent Minister and Writer of That Faith*, 14th ed. (New York, N.Y.: Fleming H. Revell, 1914), 138, 139.

2. See, for example, Donald K. Mckim, ed., *The Authoritative Word: Essays on the Nature of Scripture* (Grand Rapids, Mich.: Eerdmans, 1983). For evangelical perspectives, see, for example: Millard J. Erickson, *Christian Theology*, 2nd ed. (Grand Rapids, Mich.: Baker, 1998). Erickson classified the models of inspiration thusly: intuition theory, illumination theory, dynamic theory, verbal theory, and dictation theory, 231–233. David S. Dockery, *Christian Scripture: An Evangelical Perspective on Inspiration, Authority, and Interpretation* (Nashville, Tenn.: Broadman and Holman, 1995). Dockery employed the following terms in his classification: dictation view, illumination view, encounter view, dynamic view, and plenary view. Gerhard Maier (*Biblical Hermeneutics*, Robert W. Yarbrough, trans. [Wheaton, Ill.: Crossway, 1994]) used the following terms: personal inspiration, inspiration of ideas, verbal inspiration, and entire inspiration.

Three Seventh-day Adventist theologians have also contributed to the classification of inspiration theories or models: In his *Systematic Theology*, vol. 1, *Prolegomena* (Berrien Springs, Mich.: Andrews University Press, 2003), Norman Gulley employed terms similar to Erickson. Frank Hasel ("Ellen White and Inspiration," unpublished paper) discussed four theories or models of inspiration relevant to the present discussion in Adventism. And Fernando Canale ("Revelation and Inspiration," in George W. Reid, ed., *Understanding Scripture: An Adventist Approach*, Biblical Research Institute Studies [Silver Spring, Md.: Biblical Research Institute, 2006]) discussed three theories—encounter, verbal, and thought—in the context of what he called the "Biblical Model of Revelation-Inspiration" (52–68). Of course, there are other evangelical classifications too numerous to mention in this note. Suffice it to say that evangelicals and Adventists have given much thought to the subject of inspiration.

3. For an article related to the issues in this chapter, see Nicholas P. Miller, "Divided by Visions of the Truth: The Bible, Epistemology, and the Adventist Community," *Andrews University Seminary Studies* (Autumn 2009): 241–262. This article provides an insightful discussion on different views of the Bible in the Adventist community and supplements the contents in this chapter.

4. Paul J. Achtemeier, *Inspiration and Authority: Nature and Function of Christian Scripture* (Peabody, Mass.: Hendrickson Publishers, 1999), 102.

5. Ibid., 151.

6. See James Barr, *Holy Scripture: Canon, Authority, Criticism* (Philadelphia: Westminster Press, 1983); and Barr, *The Scope and Authority of the Bible* (London: SCM, 1980). Barr has been an outspoken critic of the evangelical view of the inspiration of the Bible.

7. Erickson, 231, 232.

8. Encounter theology, also called the "neo-orthodox view," is represented by the well-known German theologians Karl Barth and Emil Brunner. For a helpful overview of the philosophical background to this view and a critique of its presuppositions, see Ronald Nash, *The Word of God and the Mind of Man* (Phillipsburg, N.J.: Presbyterian and Reformed Publishing Company, 1982), 25–54. For a concise but helpful discussion of the theological issues, see Erickson, 216–222. See also Fernando Canale's important assessment in *Back to Revelation-Inspiration: Searching for a Cognitive Foundation of Christian Theology in a Postmodern*

World (Lanham, Md.: University Press of America, 2001), 97–125.

9. Brunner, *Truth as Encounter*, a new edition, much enlarged (Philadelphia: Westminster Press, 1964), 87.

10. Gerhard Pfandl, "Emil Brunner on Truth as Encounter," unpublished paper.

11. Alberto Timm, "A History of Seventh-day Adventist Views on Biblical and Prophetic Inspiration" (1844–2000)," *Journal of the Adventist Theological Society* 10/1–2 (1999): 514–516. This article can be accessed online at http://www.atsjats.org.

12. Raoul Dederen, "Toward a Seventh-day Adventist Theology of Revelation-Inspiration," unpublished paper in *North American Bible Conference* (General Conference of Seventh-day Adventists, 1974), 1–17.

13. Canale, "Revelation and Inspiration," in Reid, *Understanding Scripture: An Adventist Approach*, 53, 54, 60, 61.

14. For more lists of texts and discussion on this subject, see R. Dederen, "Revelation-Inspiration Phenomenon," in *Issues in Revelation and Inspiration*, Adventist Theological Society Occasional Papers, vol. 1, Frank Holbrook and Leo Van Dolson, eds. (Berrien Springs, Mich.: 1992), 13–15.

15. Benjamin B. Warfield, *The Inspiration and Authority of the Bible* (Philadelphia: Presbyterian and Reformed Publishing Company, 1970). For a more recent evangelical work advocating the verbal theory, see the monumental multivolume series by Carl F. H. Henry, *God, Revelation, and Authority*, 6 vols. (Waco, Tex.: Word, 1979–1983).

16. See I. S. Rennie, "Verbal Inspiration," in Walter A. Elwell, ed., *Evangelical Dictionary of Theology*, 2nd ed. (Grand Rapids, Mich.: Baker Book House, 2001), 1242–1244; John Barton, "Verbal Inspiration," in R. J. Coggins and J. L. Houlden, eds., *A Dictionary of Biblical Interpretation* (Philadelphia: Trinity Press International, 1990), 719–722.

17. Erickson, 232.

18. See, for example, J. I. Packer, *Fundamentalism and the Word of God* (London: InterVarsity, 1958), 78ff; Warfield, 95; and Peter Maarten van Bemmelen, *Issues in Biblical Inspiration: Sunday and Warfield*, Andrews University Seminary Doctoral Dissertation Series, vol. 13 (Berrien Springs, Mich.: Andrews University Press, 1988), 361ff.

19. Packer, 80.

20. Fernando Canale, "Revelation and Inspiration," in Reid, *Understanding Scripture: An Adventist Approach*, 52. See also Canale's groundbreaking study, *A Criticism of Theological Reason: Time and Timelessness as Primordial Presuppositions*, Andrews University Seminary Doctoral Dissertation Series, vol. 10 (Berrien Springs, Mich.: Andrews University Press, 1983), which shows the indebtedness of theology to Greek philosophy; and his two important volumes on revelation-inspiration that grew out of his initial study: *Understanding Revelation-Inspiration in a Postmodern World* (Berrien Springs, Mich.: Fernando L. Cnale, 2001); and Canale, *Back to Revelation-Inspiration*. For a helpful summary of Canale's *Back to Revelation-Inspiration* in its original article form, see Gulley, 116–126.

21. For a concise overview of the timeless view of God in philosophy and theology, see Gulley, 4–11.

22. Canale, *Back to Revelation-Inspiration*, 37, 38.

23. Canale, "Revelation and Inspiration," 52.

24. Canale, *Back to Revelation-Inspiration*, 87.

25. Timm, 503–505. See Canale, "Revelation and Inspiration," 55, 73: note. 10, for a recent example.

26. See Packer, 78, 79, who rejects this view.

27. For a thorough discussion of this account, see Jerry Allen Moon, *W. C. White and Ellen G. White: The Relationship Between the Prophet and Her Son*, Andrews University Seminary Doctoral Dissertation Series, Vol. 19 (Berrien Springs, Mich.: Andrews University Press, 1993), 122–129. See also Arthur L. White, *Ellen G. White: The Lonely Years*,

1876–1891 (Washington, D.C.: Review and Herald®, 1984), 217–219; Herbert Douglass, *Messenger of the Lord: The Prophetic Ministry of Ellen G. White* (Nampa Idaho: Pacific Press®, 1998), 118, 119; and Alden Thompson, "Adventists and Inspiration–2: Improving the *Testimonies* through Revisions," *Review and Herald*, Sept. 12, 1985, 13–15.

28. A. White, 218.

29. G. I. Butler and O. B. Oyen, "General Conference Proceedings (Concluded)," *Review and Herald*, Nov. 27, 1883, 741, 742.

30. Moon, 125.

31. Thompson, 14.

32. Earlier in 1883, critic A. C. Long had already been circulating the charge that Ellen White deleted sentences from her writings. See chapter 2, where Long is discussed.

33. E. G. White to U. Smith, February 19, 1884 (Letter 11, 1884); cited in Moon, 127, 128.

34. Moon, 128, 129.

35. See Timm, 494–496, 502–509. Timm has documented the cases of belief in the dictation model and verbal-plenary model of inspiration in Adventism during the late nineteenth and early twentieth centuries. It should be pointed out that Seventh-day Adventists didn't use the term *dictation*. Instead, the term *verbal inspiration* was used, but with the more mechanical/dictation understanding in mind, as in the statement of W. C. White regarding the 1911 edition of *The Great Controversy*: "Mother has never laid claim to verbal inspiration" (*Selected Messages* [Washington, D.C.: Review and Herald®, 1980], 3:437). By the early twentieth century, some Adventists evidently understood verbal inspiration in the sense of the verbal-plenary model rather than the dictation model (Timm, 503). Either way, the focus of those who espoused verbal inspiration was more on the words.

36. D. M. Canright, *Seventh-day Adventism Renounced After an Experience of Twenty-Eight Years by a Prominent Minister and Writer of That Faith* (Kalamazoo, Mich.: Kalamazoo Publishers, 1888), 44, 45.

37. A comparison of the 1888 edition, 44, 45, with the 14th edition, published in 1914, 138–141, reveals that Canright perpetuated this same six-part argument in the last edition with only minor changes.

38. E. G. White to Dr. Paulson, June 14, 1906; Letter, 206, 1906; E. G. White, *Selected Messages* (Washington, D.C.: Review and Herald®, 1958), 1:24–31.

39. E. G. White, *Selected Messages*, 3:437. See also George R. Knight, "The Case of the Overlooked Postscript: A Footnote on Inspiration," *Ministry* (August 1997): 9–11, for the story behind an October 31, 1912, letter W. C. White wrote to S. N. Haskell, who espoused a rigid verbal, inerrantist view of inspiration. White told Haskell about the "danger" of such a view, and Ellen White added a postscript on her son's letter that read: "I approve of the remarks made in this letter."

40. During the early part of the twentieth century, fundamentalists reacted to liberalism by espousing a strict view of verbal inspiration and biblical inerrancy. Because Adventists were facing the same challenges, many followed the fundamentalist approach in defending the Bible and Ellen White thus emphasizing the words in their view of inspiration. See Knight, *A Search for Identity: The Development of Seventh-day Adventist Beliefs* (Hagerstown, Md.: Review and Herald®, 2000), 129–138; and Gary Land, "Shaping the Modern Church 1906–1930," in *Adventism in America: A History*, rev. ed., Gary Land, ed. (Berrien Springs, Mich.: Andrews University Press, 1998), 113–137. On Fundamentalism, see George M. Marsden, *Fundamentalism and American Culture*, 2nd ed. (New York: Oxford University Press, 2006).

41. Douglass, 437.

42. See Richard W. Schwarz and Floyd Greenleaf, *Light Bearers: A History of the Seventh-day Adventist Church* (Nampa, Idaho: Pacific Press®,

2000), 627–631; Knight, 128–138.

43. See Michael W. Campbell, "The 1919 Bible Conference and Its Significance for Seventh-day Adventist History and Theology" (PhD dissertation, Andrews University, 2008), 89, 90, 152, 153.

44. Douglass, 461.

45. Roger Coon, "Continuing Education of Church Members and Providing Bases of Confidence," unpublished paper presented at the International Prophetic Guidance Workshop, Washington, D.C., April 11–15, 1982.

46. Douglass, 461.

47. Douglass, 437.

48. C. S. Longacre to W. A. Colcord, Dec. 10, 1929; cited in Knight, *Reading Ellen White* (Hagerstown, Md.: Review and Herald®, 1997), 112.

49. Millard J. Erickson, *Christian Theology*, 2nd ed. (Grand Rapids, Mich.: Baker, 1998), 232. He labels it the "dynamic theory."

50. See the article in the *Seventh-day Adventist Encyclopedia* (1996 ed.), s.v. "Inspiration of Scripture," 10:770, 771, where it is stated that Seventh-day Adventists "do not believe in verbal inspiration," but "in what may properly called thought inspiration."

51. E. G. White, *Selected Messages*, 1:21.

52. G. I. Butler and O. B. Oyen, 741.

53. Fernando Canale, "Revelation and Inspiration," in Reid, *Understanding Scripture: An Adventist Approach*, 56.

54. Ibid., 58.

55. Ibid, 56–58.

56. Ratzlaff, *Truth Led Me Out* (Glendale, Ariz.: LAM Publications, 2008), 82, note 3 continued.

57. Norman F. Douty, *Another Look at Seventh-day Adventism* (Grand Rapids, Mich: Baker Book House, 1962), 18.

58. The problem with the thought-word dichotomy is twofold. First, numerous passages of Scripture indicate that in the process of inspiration, biblical authors were writing and speaking God's words (see, for example, the many times "Thus says the Lord" produces the word of God; also Josh. 24:26; 2 Sam. 23:2; Jer. 30:2). Yet, their human contribution was not violated in any way, and they expressed themselves with their total personality. Second, philosophical reflection suggests that "thought and words belong together"—that is, "a thought with no word or words to be communicated perishes in the mind of the thinker." Thus, "the Holy Spirit guided the prophets in the writing process, ensuring that the prophets' own words expressed the message they received in a trustworthy and reliable form" (Canale, 59).

59. See, for example, Frank Hasel, "Ellen White and Inspiration," unpublished paper, 15; Canale, *Back to Revelation-Inspiration*, 127–153; Canale, "Revelation and Inspiration," 66–71.

60. Gulley, 325.

61. Gulley, 315.

62. Gulley, 325.

63. Peter M. van Bemmelen, "Revelation and Inspiration," in Raoul Dederen, ed., *Handbook of Seventh-day Adventist Theology* (Silver Spring, Md.: Review and Herald® and the General Conference of Seventh-day Adventists, 2000), 39.

64. As expressed in the book *Understanding Scripture: An Adventist Approach*, George W. Reid, ed., in which all the articles passed the Biblical Research Institute Committee (BRICOM), composed of thirty-six Seventh-day Adventist theologians. Although some might use a term other than "whole person" to describe it, the understanding is the same.

65. E. G. White, *Selected Messages*, 1:21.

66. Ángel Manuel Rodríguez, "Issues on Revelation and Inspiration," http://biblicalresearch.gc.adventist.org/documents/issuesrevelationinspiration.htm.

67. Ibid.

68. E. G. White, *Manuscript Releases* (Silver Spring, Md.: Ellen G. White Estate, 1987), 2:156, 157.

69. E. G. White, *Selected Messages*, 1:37.

70. E. G. White, *Special Testimonies to Our Ministers* (n.p.: Ellen G. White Estate, 1892), 17.

71. Rodríguez. For the charge that Ellen White contradicted herself on thought inspiration by using terms such as "words" of Scripture or "dictated," see Jud Lake, "Did Ellen White Contradict Herself on Thought Inspiration?" http://ellenwhiteanswers.org/dyn/media/pdf/dictation-or-verbal.pdf.

72. Dederen, "Toward a Seventh-day Adventist Theology of Revelation-Inspiration," 11–13.

73. Canale, "Revelation and Inspiration," 65.

74. Canale, 66.

75. E. G. White, *Selected Messages*, 1:21.

76. Canale, 65, 66.

77. E. G. White, *Selected Messages*, 1:16–18. For examples of discrepancies of minor consequence in the Bible and in Ellen White's writings, see Roger Coon, "Infallibility, Inerrancy, and the Prophets: Does a True Prophet Ever Make a Mistake?" http://ellenwhiteanswers.org/dyn/media/pdf/Coon-in-fall-inerr.pdf.

78. Canale, 63.

79. Juan Carlos Viera, *The Voice of the Spirit: How God Has Led His People Through the Gift of Prophecy*; Viera, "The Dynamics of Inspiration," http://www.whiteestate.org/issues/dynamics.html.

80. For evidence, see for example, van Bemmelen's important article, "Revelation and Inspiration," in the *Handbook of Seventh-day Adventist Theology*, 22–57.

81. See Robert W. Olson, *One Hundred and One Questions on the Sanctuary and On Ellen White*, 105, 106 (accessible on the *Ellen G. White Writings Comprehensive Research Edition* CD-ROM [Silver Spring, Md.: Ellen G. White Estate]); examples borrowed from Olson. See also Tim Crosby, "Does Inspired Mean Original? *Ministry*, February 1986, 4–7, accessible at http://www.adventistarchives.org.

82. For a significant study on the research model of inspiration in the Gospel of Luke, called "The Lucan Model" by the author, see George E. Rice, *Luke, A Plagiarist?* (Mountain View, Calif.: Pacific Press®, 1983).

83. Canale, *Understanding Revelation-Inspiration*, 460, 461.

84. Viera, *The Voice of the Spirit*, 86, 87. The entire book can be accessed at http://www.whiteestate.org.

85. W. C. White to L. E. Froom, January 8, 1928, *Selected Messages*, 3:460.

86. As to the charges of plagiarism and Ellen White's denying it, the church has straightforwardly responded to these charges and continues to research the issue of Ellen White's literary borrowing. See, for example, the recent study by E. Marcella Anderson King and Kevin L. Morgan, *More Than Words: A Study of Inspiration and Ellen White's Use of Sources in* The Desire of Ages (Berrien Springs, Mich.: Honor Him Publishers, 2009), which provides a helpful summary of Fred Veltman's "Life of Christ Research Project" (available at www.adventistarchives.org) and addresses the many issues related to the plagiarism charge and literary borrowing. See also Jud Lake, "Answers to the Plagiarism Charge," at http://ellenwhiteanswers.org/answers/plagarism.

87. See, for example, the entire issue of *Proclamation!* (May–June 2006) that is devoted to the issue of inspiration and inerrancy. Especially see Verle Streifling, "The Bible: Inerrant? Adventist Claims of Bible Contradictions and Errors," ibid., 5–11.

88. Due to the importance of interpretation, chapters 9 through 11 of this book are devoted to its principles and practices.

(Chapter 7)
Authority, Part 1: The Position of the Pioneers

1. D. M. Canright, *Life of Mrs. E. G. White, Seventh-day Adventist Prophet: Her False Claims Refuted* (Cincinnati: Standard Publishing, 1919; republished, Salt Lake City: Grant Shurtliff, 1998), 18.

2. Ibid., 21.

3. See Gerald Wheeler, "James Springer White," in *The Ellen G. White Encyclopedia,* Denis Fortin and Jerry Moon, eds. (Hagerstown, Md.: Review and Herald®, 2011); and Wheeler, *James White: Innovator and Overcomer* (Hagerstown, Md.: Review and Herald®, 2003).

4. For the historical setting and content analysis of this important early publication, see George Knight, "Historical Introduction," in George Knight, *Earliest Seventh-day Adventist Periodicals* (Berrien Springs, Mich.: Andrews University Press, 2005), xxiv–xxvi.

5. James White, *A Word to the Little Flock* (May 1847), in Knight, *Earliest Seventh-day Adventist Periodicals*, 13.

6. Ellen G. White, *A Sketch of the Christian Experience and Views of Ellen G. White* (Saratoga Springs, N.Y.: James White, 1851), 2.

7. James White, "The Gifts of the Gospel Church," *Review and Herald*, April 21, 1851, 70.

8. George Knight, *A Brief History of Seventh-day Adventists,* 2nd ed. (Hagerstown, Md.: Review and Herald®, 2004), 37, 38.

9. James White, "Time to Commence the Sabbath," *Review and Herald*, February 25, 1868, 168.

10. See E. F. Durand, "Uriah Smith," in *The Ellen G. White Encyclopedia*; and Durand, *Yours in the Blessed Hope, Uriah Smith* (Washington, D.C.: Review and Herald, 1980).

11. Uriah Smith, "Do We Discard the Bible by Endorsing the Visions?" *Review and Herald*, January 13, 1863, 52.

12. See Michael W. Campbell, "George Ide Butler," in *The Ellen G. White Encyclopedia*; and Emmett K. Vande Vere, *Rugged Heart: The Story of George I. Butler* (Nashville, Tenn.: Southern Publishing Association, 1979).

13. George I. Butler, "The Visions: How They Are Held Among Seventh-day Adventists," *Review and Herald Supplement*, Aug. 14, 1883, 12.

14. See Douglas Morgan, "Sarepta Myrenda Irish Henry," in *The Ellen G. White Encyclopedia*.

15. S. M. I. Henry, "My Telescope," *The Gospel of Health*, January 1898, 25.

16. Although Mrs. Henry and Ellen White never met face to face, the two women later connected through mail and maintained an extensive correspondence across the Pacific Ocean until Mrs. Henry's untimely death in 1900. See Arthur White, *Ellen G. White*, vol. 4, *The Australian Years, 1891–1900* (Washington, D.C.: Review and Herald®, 1983), 346–348.

17. Henry, 26.

18. Ibid., 27, 28.

19. See Herb Ford, "Denton E. Rebok," in *The Ellen G. White Encyclopedia*.

20. Denton E. Rebok, *Believe His Prophets* (Washington, D.C.: Review and Herald, 1956), 181.

21. See D. E. Rebok, "Biographical Sketch of W. A. Spicer," *Review and Herald*, November 13, 1952, 14.

22. William A. Spicer, *The Spirit of Prophecy in the Advent Movement* (Washington, D.C.: Review and Herald®, 1937), 30.

23. Based on a word search of the words *Bible, Scripture, Scriptures,* and *Word of God* on the "Domain Search Template: 1845–1917" in the *Ellen G. White Writings Comprehensive Research Edition* CD-ROM (Silver Spring, Md.: Ellen G. White Estate). This search didn't include the many other terms she used to describe the Bible.

24. E. G. White, *A Sketch of the Christian Experience and Views of Ellen G. White*, 64. For lists of other statements listed in this section, see "The Primacy of the Word," chapter 4, in *Selected Messages* (Washington, D.C.: Review and Herald®, 1980), 3:29–33.

25. E. G. White, *The Great Controversy* (Mountain View, Calif.: Pacific Press®, 1950), vii.

26. E. G. White, "A Missionary Appeal," *Review and Herald*, December 15, 1885, 770.

27. E. G. White, "Bible Religion," *Review and Herald*, May 4, 1897, 273.

28. E. G. White, *Prophets and Kings* (Mountain View, Calif.: Pacific Press®, 1943), 626. The context of this statement doesn't forbid preachers from citing sources outside of the Bible while in the pulpit. Her emphasis is on making the Bible central to the sermon rather than "tradition and human theories and maxims." Thus, "let the word of God speak to the heart" through exposition of its text, and the congregants will "hear the voice of Him who can renew the soul unto eternal life" (ibid.).

29. E. G. White, *The Great Controversy*, 204, 205.

30. Ibid., 595.

31. E. G. White, Letter 105, 1903; *Manuscript Releases* (Silver Spring, Md.: E. G. White Estate, 1990), 8:341.

32. E. G. White, Letter 130, 1901; *Selected Messages*, 3:29.

33. E. G. White, *Testimonies for the Church* (Nampa, Idaho: Pacific Press®, 1948), 4:246.

34. E. G. White, "An Open Letter From Mrs. E. G. White to All Who Love the Blessed Hope," *Review and Herald*, January 20, 1903, 15; *Colporteur Ministry*, 125.

35. Tim Poirier, "Contemporary Prophecy and Scripture: The Relationship of Ellen G. White's Writings to the Bible in the Seventh-day Adventist Church, 1845–1915" (Research Paper, Wesley Theological Seminary, 1986), 16.

36. E. G. White, *Testimonies for the Church*, 2:605, 606; see also *Testimonies*, 5:663–668, where Ellen White provides another very important discussion on the relationship of her writings to the Bible.

37. E. G. White, Manuscript 43, 1901; *Selected Messages*, 3:33.

38. I am grateful to Merlin Burt, who provided me with a copy of the lecture notes he used for the class "The Writings of Ellen G. White," Spring Semester 2008, Andrews University Theological Seminary. This particular lecture was "Ellen G. White's Writings and the Bible."

39. This fact was first brought to my attention in a conversation with Adventist theologian E. Edward Zinke at Andrews University, October 2007.

40. E. G. White, *Testimonies for the Church*, 6:393.

41. Uriah Smith, "Mrs. White and Her Work," *Review and Herald Extra*, November 22, 1887, 11. This entire *Extra* was reprinted in book form twice: *Replies to Elder Canright's Attacks on Seventh-day Adventists* (Battle Creek, Mich.: Review and Herald®, 1888); and *Replies to Elder Canright's Attacks on Seventh-day Adventists* (Battle Creek, Mich.: Review and Herald®, 1895).

(Chapter 8)
Authority, Part 2: Dual Authorities

1. Dennis L. Palmer, "Whose Authority Shall We Follow?" *Proclamation!* (September–December 2003), 20, 21. While this article is certainly problematic, it is helpful in the sense that it raises the issue of "dual authorities," an issue that all Adventists should be aware of and know how to explain.

2. Ellen G. White, *Selected Messages* (Washington D.C.: Review and Herald®, 1958), 1:23.

3. E. G. White, *Selected Messages*, 3:30.

4. E. G. White, *Testimonies for the Church* (Nampa, Idaho: Pacific Press®, 1948), 5:64.

5. Ibid., 5:98.

6. E. G. White, *Selected Messages*, 1:48.

7. E. G. White, *Testimonies for the Church*, 5:661.

8. Palmer, 22.

9. D. M. Canright, *Life of Mrs. E. G. White, Seventh-day Adventist Prophet: Her False Claims Refuted* (Cincinnati: Standard Publishing, 1919; republished, Salt Lake City: Grant Shurtliff, 1998), 18.

10. Dale Ratzlaff, *Truth About Adventist "Truth,"* 2nd rev. ed. (Glendale, Ariz.: LAM Publications, 2007), 15.

11. Russell Earl Kelly, *Exposing Seventh-day Adventism* (New York: iUniverse, Inc., 2005), 11. Some Seventh-day Adventists today mistakenly argue that Ellen White's authority equals that of Scripture. But as will be pointed out below, this has never been the official position of the church.

12. Norman F. Douty, *Another Look at Seventh-day Adventism* (Grand Rapids, Mich.: Baker Book House, 1962), 22.

13. For discussion on the meaning and formation of the biblical canon, see Gerald A. Klingbeil, "The Text and the Canon of Scripture," in *Understanding Scripture: An Adventist Approach*, George W. Reid, ed. Biblical Research Institute Studies (Silver Spring, Md.: Biblical Research Institute, General Conference of Seventh-day Adventists, 2006), 91–110; G. L. Robinson, "Canon of the OT," in *The International Standard Bible Encyclopedia*, rev. ed., Geoffrey W. Bromiley, ed. (Grand Rapids, Mich.: Wm. B. Eerdmans, 1979), 1:591, 592; John McRay, "Canon of the Bible," in *Evangelical Dictionary of Biblical Theology*, Walter A. Elwell, ed. (Grand Rapids, Mich.: Baker Books, 1996), 58–60, 155, 156; David G. Dunbar, "The Biblical Canon," in *Hermeneutics, Authority, and Canon*, rev. ed., D. A. Carson and John D. Woodbridge, eds. (Grand Rapids, Mich.: Baker Books, 1995), 299–360; F. F. Bruce, *The Canon of Scripture* (Leicester and Downers Grove, Ill.: InterVarsity Press, 1988); Bruce M. Metzger, *The Canon of the New Testament: Its Origin, Development, and Significance* (New York: Oxford University Press, 1987). For a helpful study in nontechnical language, see Neil R. Lightfoot, *How We Got the Bible*, 3rd ed. (Grand Rapids, Mich.: Baker Books, 2003).

14. For a more complete but not exhaustive listing, see *Seventh-day Adventists Believe: An Exposition of the Fundamental Beliefs of the Seventh-day Adventist Church*, 2nd ed. (Silver Spring, Md.: Ministerial Association, General Conference of Seventh-day Adventists, 2005), 253. For insightful discussions on noncanonical prophets, see the following studies and their bibliographies: Willem A. Vangemeren, *Interpreting the Prophetic Word* (Grand Rapids, Mich.: Zondervan Publishing House, 1990), 18–103; K. Moller, "Prophets and Prophecy," in *Dictionary of the Old Testament Historical Books*, Bill T. Arnold and G. G. M. Williamson, eds. (Downers Grove, Ill.: InterVarsity Press, 2005), 825–829; G. F. Hawthorne, "Prophets, Prophecy," in *Dictionary of Jesus and the Gospels*, Joel B. Green, Scot McKnight, and I. Howard Marshall, eds. (Downers Grove, Ill.: InterVarsity Press, 1992), 636–642; C. M. Robeck Jr.,

"Prophecy, Prophesying," in *Dictionary of Paul and His Letters*, Gerald F. Hawthorne, Ralph P. Martin, and Daniel G. Reid, eds. (Downers Grove, Ill.: InterVarsity Press, 1993), 755–762; and K. N. Giles, "Prophecy, Prophets, False Prophets," in *Dictionary of the Later New Testament and Its Developments*, Ralph P. Martin and Peter H. Davids, eds. (Downers Grove, Ill.: InterVarsity Press, 1997), 970–973.

15. In the New Testament, note how Luke describes the Holy Spirit as speaking through the prophets, such as Agabus in Acts 21:11. Agabus's prophecy concerning Paul is clearly fulfilled: Paul is bound by the Jews (Acts 21:30–33) and delivered into the hands of the Gentiles (Acts 23; see also 28:17). Agabus doesn't say how Paul will be delivered into the hands of the Gentiles, just that he will be.

16. Gerhard Pfandl, *The Gift of Prophecy: The Role of Ellen White in God's Remnant Church* (Nampa, Idaho: Pacific Press®, 2008), 75.

17. See Eric Livingston, "Inquire of the Lord," *Ministry* (April 1981): 4–6. For a helpful discussion of Huldah in relationship to Ellen White; see also Herbert Douglass, *Messenger of the Lord* (Nampa, Idaho: Pacific Press®, 1998), 17–19; and A. G. Daniells, *The Abiding Gift of Prophecy* (Mountain View, Calif.: Pacific Press®, 1936), 36–172.

18. Livingston, 6. I concur with this author that "Ellen White parallels Huldah the prophetess."

19. The context of this passage specifically prohibits adding to or deleting from the words of the prophecies in the book of Revelation. But over the centuries, Christians have applied this principle to all the books in the New Testament canon as well as to the Old Testament canon.

20. Evangelical Christianity is divided on this issue, with views ranging from cessationist (all miraculous gifts of the Holy Spirit have ceased today) to charismatic (all miraculous gifts of the Holy Spirit are functioning today). A very helpful articulation and comparison of the different views is found in Wayne Grudem, ed., *Are Miraculous Gifts for Today? Four Views* (Grand Rapids, Mich.: Zondervan, 1996). Based on the evidence in Scripture, Adventists believe the spiritual gifts of the Holy Spirit will be around until Jesus comes, but they question the claims of some people regarding the gifts today. See George Rice, "Spiritual Gifts," in *Handbook of Seventh-day Adventist Theology*, Raoul Dederen, ed. (Hagerstown, Md.: Review and Herald®, 2000), 613–620.

21. For more discussion on Scripture's teaching regarding the continuation of spiritual gifts, T. Housel Jemison, *A Prophet Among You* (Mountain View, Calif.: Pacific Press, 1955), 135–146.

22. Dale Ratzlaff, "The Christ Event and the Spirit of Prophecy," *Proclamation!* March–April 2007, 16–19.

23. The evidence indicates that "the testimony of Jesus" is a subjective genitive in Greek, meaning the testimony is a prophetic message from Jesus, not a person's testimony about Him (objective genitive). For linguistic evidence, see Gerhard Pfandl, "The Remnant Church and the Spirit of Prophecy," *Symposium on Revelation*, Daniel and Revelation Committee Series, Frank B. Holbrook, ed. (Silver Spring, Md.: Biblical Research Institute, 1992), 7:305–315; Pfandl, "The Testimony of Jesus," unpublished paper presented at the International Bible Conference in Turkey, July 2006.

24. Robert L. Saucy, "An Open but Cautious View," in Grudem, 128.

25. For a helpful commentary on this passage, see F. F. Bruce, *1 and 2 Thessalonians,* Word Biblical Commentary, vol. 45 (Waco, Tex.: Word, 1982), 121–127.

26. One other important issue relevant to the context of 1 Thessalonians 5:19–22 is whether this passage involves levels of prophecy or true versus false prophets. Some interpret this passage and others to mean that Paul counsels believers to discern what part of a prophet's message is true and

what part of it is false—as though a New Testament prophet or postcanonical prophet can have a mixture of true and false messages. Evangelical scholar Wayne Grudem is the best-known advocate of this view in *The Gift of Prophecy in the New Testament and Today*, rev. ed. (Wheaton, Ill.: Crossway Books, 2000). Graeme S. Bradford, *More Than a Prophet* (Berrien Springs, Mich.: Biblical Perspectives, 2006), provides an Adventist adaptation of it. But nowhere in the context of 1 Thessalonians 5—or anywhere else in the New Testament, for that matter—is there evidence for this claim. Because Scripture recognizes all manifestations of the prophetic gift as fully inspired, the testing is not between truth or error in a single prophet's message but between true and false prophets. See Saucy, 127, 128; Gerhard Pfandl, "Ellen White and Modern Prophets," in the forthcoming *Ellen White Issues*, Merlin Burt, ed.; and the references in note 14 above.

27. For more discussion on biblical tests for determining a genuine prophet, see Douglass, 28–32; Rice, 629–631; and Saucy, 146–148.

28. Saucy, 70.

29. Frank Holbrook, "The Biblical Basis for a Modern Prophet"; accessible at http://www.adventistbiblicalresearch.org.

30. A helpful reading that will supplement this section is Gerhard Pfandl's discussion on the authority of prophets in *The Gift of Prophecy: The Role of Ellen White in God's Remnant Church*, 73–80.

31. Bernard Ramm, *The Pattern of Religious Authority* (Grand Rapids, Mich.: Wm. B. Eerdmans, 1959).

32. Ibid., 10.
33. Ibid., 20, 21.
34. Ibid., 11.
35. Ibid., 26, 27.
36. Ibid., 12.
37. Ibid., 21–23.
38. See Kwabena Donkor, "The Authority of Ellen White's Writings," in the forthcoming *Ellen White Issues*.

39. Ramm, 38.

40. Ramm's discussion of personal reception of authority in the Christian religion is worth pursuing but beyond the scope of this chapter. See Ramm, 40–44.

41. Millard J. Erickson, *Christian Theology*, 2nd ed. (Grand Rapids, Mich.: Baker Books, 1998), 277. Ramm discusses this concept of authority and calls it "the Protestant principle." He says, "There is an external principle (the inspired Scripture) and an internal principle (the witness of the Holy Spirit)," and continues by saying this "is the principle of an objective divine revelation, with an interior divine witness," 29. See Ramm for further discussion, see 28–33; see also Ramm, *The Witness of the Spirit: An Essay on the Contemporary Relevance of the Internal Witness of the Holy Spirit* (Grand Rapids, Mich.: Wm. B. Eerdmans, 1959).

42. In a sense, the more a Christian studies the Bible with the illumination of the Holy Spirit and aligns his or her life up with the teaching in the Bible, the more delegated and veracious authority he or she will experience. Nevertheless, whatever amount of delegated and veracious authority he or she might have, it will never be on the same level with the delegated and veracious authority of the prophets who participated in the revelation that produced the Scriptures. See Pfandl's discussion on pastoral authority versus prophetic authority, 78, 79.

43. Donkor's paper contributed to my thinking regarding this kind of authority.

44. Ellen White to Edson and Willie White, December 2, 1902; Letter 186, 1902; *Manuscript Releases* (Silver Spring, Md.: E. G. White Estate, 1993), 17:63.

45. E. G. White, Letter 69, 1896; *Selected Messages*, 3:30.

46. J. N. Andrews, "Our Use of the Visions of Sr. White," *Review and Herald*, February 15,

1870, 65. Appendix C contains the entire article.

47. See Ángel Manuel Rodríguez, "Ellen White's Inaugural Vision: Prophetic Call, Commission, and Role," in *Ellen White and Current Issues Symposium*, vol. 4 (Berrien Springs, Mich.: Center for Adventist Research Andrews University), 61–82. Rodriguez believes Ellen White provides a theological interpretation of the history of Christianity within the larger framework of the great controversy theme. As we approach the close of the cosmic conflict, we should thus expect to see an increasing interest in her ministry to the Christian world. "This would require," Rodriguez says, "our Christian friends to give Ellen White a fair chance to be heard by herself and not through the voices of her critics," 75. Already, evangelical Gregory A. Boyd has written several widely read books on the cosmic conflict theme, such as *God at War: The Bible and Spiritual Conflict* (Downers Grove, Ill.: InterVarsity Press, 1997); and *Satan and the Problem of Evil: Constructing a Trinitarian Warfare Theodicy* (Downers Grove, Ill.: InterVarsity Press, 2001).

48. Holbrook; accessible at http://www.adventistbiblicalresearch.org.

49. See Merlin Burt, "Ellen White and Sola Scriptura"; accessible at http://www.adventistbiblicalresearch.org.

50. Holbrook; accessible at http://www.adventistbiblicalresearch.org.

51. See, for example, Roy Graham's doctoral dissertation, published as *Ellen G. White: Co-founder of the Seventh-day Adventist Church* (New York: Peter Lang, 1985); and Herbert Douglass, *Messenger of the Lord: The Prophetic Ministry of Ellen G. White* (Nampa, Idaho: Pacific Press®, 1998).

52. George I. Butler, "The Visions: How They Are Held Among Seventh-day Adventists," *Review and Herald Supplement*, Aug. 14, 1883, 12.

53. E. G. White, *Colporteur Ministry* (Mountain View, Calif.: Pacific Press®, 1953), 125.

54. E. G. White, *Selected Messages*, 3:31, 32.

55. Douglass, 171.

56. See the statements by James White in the previous chapter on pages 133, 134.

57. For detailed discussions on the role of Bible study and Ellen White's visions in early Adventist doctrinal development, see George Knight, *A Brief History of Seventh-day Adventists*, 2nd ed. (Hagerstown, Md.: Review and Herald®, 2004), 28–50; Knight, *A Search for Identity: The Development of Seventh-day Adventist Beliefs* (Hagerstown, Md.: Review and Herald®, 2000), 55–89; Richard W. Schwarz and Floyd Greenleaf, *Light Bearers: A History of the Seventh-day Adventist Church* (Nampa, Idaho: Pacific Press®, 2000), 64–67; and Douglass, 170–172.

58. See Denis Fortin, "Ellen G. White and the Development of Seventh-day Adventist Doctrines," forthcoming *Ellen White Issues*, Merlin Burt, ed.

59. See Calvin W. Edwards and Gary Land, *Seeker After Light: A. F. Ballenger, Adventism, and American Christianity* (Berrien Springs, Mich.: Andrews University Press, 2000) for a detailed account of Ballenger's life and work.

60. For an overview of Ellen White's statements on Ballenger, see Arthur L. White, *Ellen G. White*, vol. 5, *The Early Elmshaven Years* (Washington, D.C.: Review and Herald®, 1981), 404–413; and especially, the Ellen White comments in "The Integrity of the Sanctuary Truth," Manuscript Release, no. 760, Ellen G. White Estate, accessible on the *Ellen G. White Writings Comprehensive Research Edition* CD-ROM (Silver Spring, Md.: Ellen G. White Estate).

61. Dale Ratzlaff, *Truth About Adventist "Truth,"* 2nd rev. ed. (Glendale, Ariz.: LAM Publications, 2007), 19, 20.

62. Ibid., 18, 19. I am citing from the original letter; see Ellen White, "The Integrity of the Sanctuary Truth," 15–20.

63. Ibid., 19, 20.

64. E. G. White, "The Integrity of the Sanctuary Truth," 16.

65. Ibid., 24.

66. Ibid., 19.

67. Ratzlaff, 19.

68. E. G. White, "The Word for This Time: Address by Mrs. E. G. White Before the Conference, Tuesday Afternoon, May 16," *Review and Herald*, May 25, 1905, 17.

69. Paul A. Gordon, *The Sanctuary, 1844, and the Pioneers* (Silver Spring, Md.: Ministerial Association, General Conference of Seventh-day Adventists, 2000); originally published in 1983 by Review and Herald®.

70. Gordon, *Pioneer Articles on the Sanctuary, Daniel 8:14, the Judgment, 2300 Days, Year-Day Principle, Atonement: 1846–1905* (Silver Spring, Md.: Ellen G. White Estate, 1983).

71. On the law in Galatians, see George Knight, *Angry Saints* (Hagerstown, Md.: Review and Herald®, 1989), 104–109; on the "daily," see Gilbert M. Valentine, *W. W. Prescott: Forgotten Giant of Adventism's Second Generation*, 214–235; and Bert Haloviak, "In the Shadow of the Daily: Background and Aftermath of the 1919 Bible and History Teachers Conference" (unpublished paper, 1979).

72. E. G. White, *Selected Messages*, 3:52; Letter, 329, 1905.

73. Richard Goyne, "A Word (or Two) From God," *Proclamation!* (September–October 2004), 11, 12; see also Kelly, *Exposing Seventh-day Adventism*, 8, 9.

74. Accessible at http://www.whiteestate.org/issues/scripsda.html.

75. D. M. Canright, *Seventh-day Adventism Renounced* (Kalamazoo, Mich.: Kalamazoo Publishing Co., 1888), iii–v.

76. Ibid., 43.

77. George R. Knight, "Crisis in Authority," *Ministry*, February 1991, 10.

78. Ellen White to "brethren who shall assemble in General Conference," August 5, 1888. To read the document in its entirety, see the *Ellen G. White Writings Comprehensive Research Edition* CD-ROM.

(Chapter 9)
Interpretation, Part 1: Correct Principles

1. J. Paxton Geoffrey, *The Shaking of Adventism* (Grand Rapids, Mich.: Baker Book House, 1978), 156.

2. Dale Ratzlaff, *Truth About Adventist "Truth,"* 2nd rev. ed. (Glendale, Ariz.: LAM Publications, 2007), 17.

3. See A. C. Thiselton, "hermeneuo," in *The New International Dictionary of New Testament Theology,* 4 vols., Colin Brown, ed. (Grand Rapids, Mich.: Zondervan, 1975–78), 1:579–584; D. G. Burke, "Interpret; Interpretation," in *The International Standard Bible Encyclopedia,* 4 vols., rev. ed., Geoffrey W. Bromiley, ed. (Grand Rapids, Mich.: William B. Eerdmans, 1982), 861–863. I am using the term *hermeneutics* here in its more traditional sense of principles and methods of interpretation, such as those found in Milton S. Terry's *Biblical Hermeneutics: A Treatise on the Interpretation of the Old and New Testaments* (New York: Phillips & Hunt, 1890; reprint, Grand Rapids, Mich.: Zondervan, 1974). For discussions on the broader meaning of hermeneutics regarding the complex issue of reader versus text, see Anthony C. Thiselton, *The Two Horizons: New Testament Hermeneutics and Philosophical Description With Special Reference to Heidegger, Bultmann, Gadamer, and Wittgenstein* (Grand Rapids, Mich.: Eerdmans, 1980); Thiselton, *New Horizons in Hermeneutics* (Grand Rapids, Mich.: Zondervan, 1992); and Kevin J. Vanhoozer, *Is There a Meaning in This Text?* (Grand Rapids, Mich.: Zondervan, 1998).

4. See, for example, the following excellent evangelical studies: William W. Klein, Craig L. Blomberg, and Robert L. Hubbard, Jr., *An Introduction to Biblical Interpretation,* rev. ed. (Nashville, Tenn.: Thomas Nelson Publishers, 2004); Grant Osborn, *The Hermeneutical Spiral: A Comprehensive Introduction to Biblical Interpretation* (Downers Grove, Ill.: InterVarsity, 1991); Henry A. Virkler and Karelynne Gerber Ayayo, *Hermeneutics, Principles and Processes of Biblical Interpretation,* 2nd ed. (Grand Rapids, Mich.: Baker Academic, 2007); and Walter Kaiser, *Toward an Exegetical Theology: Biblical Exegesis for Preaching and Teaching* (Grand Rapids, Mich.: Baker Books, 1981). For Adventist studies in the same vein, see Gordon M. Hyde, ed., *A Symposium on Biblical Hermeneutics* (Washington, D.C.: Review and Herald®, 1974); Gerhard F. Hasel, *Understanding the Living Word of God* (Mountain View, Calif.: Pacific Press®, 1980); Lee J. Gugliotto, *Handbook for Bible Study* (Hagerstown, Md.: Review and Herald®, 1995). See especially Richard Davidson, "Biblical Interpretation," in *Handbook of Seventh-day Adventist Theology,* Raoul Dederen, ed. (Hagerstown, Md.: Review and Herald®, 2000), 58–104; George W. Reid, ed., *Understanding Scripture: An Adventist Approach* (Silver Spring, Md.: Biblical Research Institute, General Conference of Seventh-day Adventists, 2005); and Norman R. Gulley, *Systematic Theology,* vol. 1, *Prolegomena* (Berrien Springs, Mich.: Andrews University Press, 2003), 640–716.

5. E. D. Hirsch's concept of authorial intention in his *Validity in Interpretation* (New Haven, Conn.: Yale University Press, 1967) and *The Aims of Interpretation* (Chicago: University of Chicago, 1976) has been influential in my thinking. Vanhoozer's thoughtful dialogue with contemporary hermeneutical thought in *Is There a Meaning in This Text?* and Millard J. Erickson's emphasis on the Holy Spirit as author in *Evangelical Interpretation: Perspectives on Hermeneutical Issues* (Grand Rapids, Mich.: Baker Books, 1993) provides a helpful balance to Hirsch.

6. See, for example, Roger Coon, "Hermeneutics: Interpreting a 19th Century Prophet in the Space Age," *Journal of Adventist Education,* Sum-

mer 1988, 16–31; George Knight, *Myths in Adventism* (Hagerstown, Md.: Review and Herald®, 1985); Knight, *Reading Ellen White: How to Understand and Apply Her Writings* (Hagerstown, Md.: Review and Herald®, 1997); Jon Paulien, "The Interpreter's Use of the Writings of Ellen G. White," in *Symposium on Revelation,* Frank B. Holbrook, ed., Daniel and Revelation Committee Series (Silver Spring, Md.: Biblical Research Institute, General Conference of Seventh-day Adventists, 1991) 6:163–174; Herbert Douglass, *Messenger of the Lord: The Prophetic Ministry of Ellen G. White* (Nampa, Idaho: Pacific Press®, 1998), 372–443; Gerhard Pfandl, "Ellen G. White and Hermeneutics," in *Understanding Scripture: An Adventist Approach,* 309–328; Pfandl, *The Gift of Prophecy: The Role of Ellen White in God's Remnant Church* (Nampa, Idaho: Pacific Press®, 2008), 96–104.

7. Knight, *Reading Ellen White.*

8. See note 6.

9. I am borrowing from the excellent discussion of the biblical literary context in Klein, Blomberg, and Hubbard Jr., 214.

10. Ibid.

11. Knight, *Meeting Ellen White: A Fresh Look at Her Life, Writings, and Major Themes* (Hagerstown, Md.: Review and Herald®, 1996), 94, 95.

12. Again, I borrow from Klein, Blomberg, and Hubbard Jr., 215, and apply their discussion to Ellen White studies. Their effective discussion resonated with me as I thought not only of how the Bible books were put together but also how Ellen White wrote her articles, manuscripts, and books.

13. E. G. White, *Selected Messages* (Washington, D.C.: Review and Herald®, 1958), 1:44.

14. Letter 208: Ellen White to G. C. Tenney, June 29, 1906.

15. E. G. White, *Selected Messages,* 3:82.

16. Dale Ratzlaff, *Truth About Adventist "Truth,"* 2nd rev. ed. (Glendale, Ariz.: LAM Publications, 2007), 17.

17. E. G. White, *The Desire of Ages* (Nampa, Idaho: Pacific Press®, 1941), 87.

18. This position is one of three views articulated in the early (fourth century) church regarding the brothers of Jesus (Mark 6:3; Matt. 13:55, 56): (1) that they were younger brothers born to Joseph and Mary after Jesus, (2) that they were the sons of Joseph by a previous marriage, and (3) that they were not true brothers, but cousins. In all three of these views, the virgin birth of Christ is maintained. Ellen White espouses the second view, evangelical scholars generally take the first view, and Catholic scholars take the third view. See Robert H. Stein, *Jesus the Messiah: A Survey of the Life of Christ* (Downers Grove, Ill.: InterVarsity Press, 1996), 82–84, for an insightful discussion on the three views concerning Jesus' brothers and sisters. Also see Mark L. Strauss, *Four Portraits, One Jesus: An Introduction to Jesus and the Gospels* (Grand Rapids, Mich.: Zondervan, 2007), 419, 420, who takes the first view, but acknowledges that the second view is possible.

19. E. G. White, *The Desire of Ages,* 19–26; E. G. White, *Prophets and Kings* (Mountain View, Calif.: Pacific Press®, 1943), 695.

20. Interestingly, Ellen White used the phrase "virgin Mary" only in reference to the Catholic veneration of Mary. She was careful not to confuse Catholic and Protestant ideas regarding Mary. That she affirmed the virgin birth of Christ is unmistakable from the larger context of her writings; see Eric Claude Webster's *Crosscurrents in Adventist Christology* (Berrien Springs, Mich.: Andrews University Press, 1984), 74–88, for a helpful discussion on Ellen White's understanding of the incarnation.

21. E. G. White, Manuscript 140, 1903; *Seventh-day Adventist Bible Commentary* (Washington, D.C.: Review and Herald®, 1952–1957), 5:1129.

22. Ibid., 5:1129, 1130.

23. For more discussion on Ellen White and the divinity of Christ, see my apologetic piece, "Ellen White and Arianism" at http://ellenwhiteanswers

.org/answers/mischarges/egwandarianism; and especially the excellent study by Woodrow Whidden, Jerry Moon, and John W. Reeve, *The Trinity: Understanding God's Love, His Plan of Salvation, and Christian Fellowship* (Hagerstown, Md.: Review and Herald®, 2002).

24. E. G. White, "The Word Made Flesh," *Review and Herald,* April 5, 1906, 8.

25. E. G. White, "The True Sheep Respond to the Voice of the Shepherd," *Signs of the Times,* Nov. 27, 1893, 54.

26. See the following helpful studies on the nineteenth-century world in which Ellen White lived: Gary Land, *The World of Ellen G. White* (Hagerstown Md.: Review and Herald®, 1987); George Knight, *Ellen White's World: A Fascinating Look at the Times in Which She Lived* (Hagerstown, Md.: Review and Herald®, 1998); Otto L. Bettmann, *The Good Old Days—They Were Terrible!* (New York: Random House, 1974); Jack Larkin, *The Reshaping of Everyday Life, 1790–1840* (New York: Harper & Row, 1988); Daniel E. Sutherland, *The Expansion of Everyday Life, 1860–1876* (Fayetteville, Ark.: University of Arkansas Press, 2000); Thomas J. Schlereth, *Victorian America: Transformations in Everyday Life, 1876–1915* (New York: HarperPerennial, 1991); Louise L. Stevenson, *The Victorian Homefront: American Thought and Culture, 1860–1880* (New York: Cornell University Press, 1991); Daniel Walker Howe, *What Hath God Wrought: The Transformation of America, 1815–1848* (New York: Oxford University Press, 2007); George Knight, *Millennial Fever and the End of the World: A Study of Millerite Adventism* (Nampa, Idaho: Pacific Press®, 1993); Ronald L. Numbers and Jonathan M. Butler, *The Disappointed: Millerism and Millenarianism in the Nineteenth Century* (Knoxville, Tenn.: University of Tennessee Press, 1993); David L. Rowe, *God's Strange Work: William Miller and the End of the World* (Grand Rapids, Mich.: William B. Eerdmans, 2008); James McPherson, *Battle Cry of Freedom: The Civil War* (New York: Oxford University Press, 1988); and James M. Volo and Forthy Denneen Volo, *Family Life in 19th-Century America* (Westport, Conn.: Greenwood Press, 2007). Because many excellent studies abound, this list is far from exhaustive.

27. See any reliable history or encyclopedia of the United States for details.

28. See, for example, Mark A. Noll, *A History of Christianity in the United States and Canada* (Grand Rapids, Mich.: William B. Eerdmans, 1992); Noll, *America's God: From Jonathan Edwards to Abraham Lincoln* (New York: Oxford University Press, 2002); the following volumes in the series A History of Evangelicalism: People, Movements, and Ideas in the English-Speaking World: Noll, *The Rise of Evangelicalism: The Age of Edwards, Whitefield, and the Wesleys,* vol. 1 (Downers Grove, Ill.: InterVarsity Press, 2003); John Wolffe, *The Expansion of Evangelicalism: The Age of Wilberforce, More, Chalmers, and Finney,* vol. 2 (Downers Grove, Ill.: InterVarsity Press, 2007); David W. Bebbington, *The Dominance of Evangelicalism: The Age of Spurgeon and Moody,* vol. 3 (Downers Grove, Ill.: InterVarsity Press, 2005). See also George M. Marsden, *Fundamentalism and American Culture* (New York: Oxford University Press, 2006); Nathan O. Hatch, *The Democratization of American Christianity* (New Haven, Conn., and London: Yale University Press, 1989); Ann Taves, *Fits, Trances, and Visions: Experiencing Religion and Explaining Experience from Wesley to James* (Princeton, N.J.: Princeton University Press, 1999); Bret E. Carroll, *Spiritualism in Antebellum America* (Indianapolis, Ind.: Indiana University Press, 1997); Barbara Wiesberg, *Talking to the Dead: Kate and Maggie Fox and the Rise of Spiritualism* (New York: HarperSanFransisco, 2004); Timothy L. Smith, *Revivalism & Social Reform: American Protestantism on the Eve of the Civil War* (Baltimore, Md., and London: Johns Hopkins University Press, 1980); and William G.

McLoughlin, *Revivals, Awakenings, and Reform* (Chicago: University of Chicago Press, 1978). Although there are many other helpful studies in this area, these works are a good place for the interested student to begin.

29. Helpful for understanding the historical context of Ellen White's experience with the Seventh-day Adventist Church is Arthur L. White, *Ellen G. White*, vol. 1, *The Early Years, 1827–1862* (Washington, D.C.: Review and Herald®, 1985); Arthur White, *Ellen G. White*, vol. 2, *The Progressive Years, 1863–1875* (Washington, D.C.: Review and Herald®, 1986); Arthur White, *Ellen G. White*, vol. 3, *The Lonely Years, 1876–1891* (Washington, D.C.: Review and Herald®, 1984); Arthur White, *Ellen G. White*, vol. 4, *The Australian Years, 1891–1900* (Washington, D.C.: Review and Herald®, 1983); Arthur White, *Ellen G. White*, vol. 5, *The Early Elmshaven Years, 1900–1905* (Washington, D.C.: Review and Herald®, 1981); Arthur White, *Ellen G. White*, vol. 6, *The Later Elmshaven Years, 1905–1915* (Washington, D.C.: Review and Herald®, 1982). See also Richard W. Schwarz and Floyd Greenleaf, *Light Bearers: A History of the Seventh-day Adventist Church* (Nampa, Idaho: Pacific Press®, 2000); George Knight, *A Brief History of Seventh-day Adventists*, 2nd ed. (Hagerstown, Md.: Review and Herald®, 2004); Knight, *Myths in Adventism*; Gary Land, ed., *Adventism in America: A History*, rev. ed. (Berrien Springs, Mich.: Andrews University Press, 1998); *Seventh-day Adventist Encyclopedia* (1996 ed.); and Denis Fortin and Jerry Moon, eds., *The Ellen G. White Encyclopedia* (Hagerstown, Md.: Review and Herald®, 2011).

30. E. G. White, *Testimonies for the Church* (Nampa, Idaho: Pacific Press®, 1948), 3:471.

31. E. G. White, *Selected Messages*, 3:217.

32. Ibid., 1:57.

33. E. G. White, "At the Southern Camp Meeting," *Signs of the Times*, May 25, 1882.

34. For guidelines on keeping the Sabbath, see "Guidelines for Sabbath Observance" at the official Seventh-day Adventist Web site: http://www.adventist.org/beliefs/other_documents/other_doc6.html.

35. Ratzlaff, 18.

36. See "Wigs and Insanity?" at http://www.whiteestate.org/issues/faq-unus.html#unusual-section-c7.

37. See "Death From Cosmetics" at http://www.whiteestate.org/issues/faq-unus.html#unusual-section-c3.

(Chapter 10)
Interpretation, Part 2: Applying Correct Principles

1. The two examples of contextual analysis in this chapter come from my Web site, http://ellenwhiteanswers.org, where many other responses to the charges against Ellen White can be found, as well as links to other Web sites.

2. Dirk Anderson, *Prophet? Or Pretender?* (Jacksonville, Fla.: Via Del Agape, 2008), 13; and Teresa and Arthur Beem, *It's Okay NOT To Be a Seventh-day Adventist* (North Charleston, S.C.: BookSurge Publishing, 2008), 90.

3. E. G. White, "Dear Brethren and Sisters," *The Present Truth*, September, 1849, 32, in *Earliest Seventh-day Adventist Periodicals*, Adventist Classic Library, George Knight, ed. (Berrien Springs, Mich.: Andrews University Press, 2005).

4. See the *Ellen G. White Writings Comprehensive Research Edition* CD-ROM (Silver Spring, Md.: Ellen G. White Estate).

5. Charles E. Rosenbert, *The Cholera Years: The United States in 1832, 1849, and 1866* (Chicago: University of Chicago Press, 1987).

6. Ibid., 112, 114.

7. Ibid., 121, 122.

8. Ibid., 172.

9. E. G. White, 32.

10. E. G. White, *Selected Messages* (Washington D.C.: Review and Herald®, 1958), 1:67.

11. See William G. Johnsson, "Conditionality in Biblical Prophecy With Particular Reference to Apocalyptic," in *70 Weeks, Leviticus, Nature of Prophecy*, Daniel and Revelation Committee Series, Frank Holbrook, ed. (Washington, D.C.: Biblical Research Institute, 1986), 3:259–287.

12. For studies on Ellen White and the delay of Christ's coming, see Ralph E. Neall, *How Long, O Lord?* (Washington, D.C.: Review and Herald®, 1988); Arnold Wallenkampf, *The Apparent Delay: What Role Do We Play in the Timing of Jesus' Return?* (Hagerstown, Md.: Review and Herald®, 1994); and Herbert Douglass, *Why Jesus Waits*, rev. ed. (Nampa, Idaho: Pacific Press®, 2001).

13. E. G. White, "Dear Brother Bates," *A Word to the Little Flock*, May 1847, 19, in *Earliest Seventh-day Adventist Periodicals*.

14. E. G. White, *The Great Controversy* (Mountain View, Calif.: Pacific Press®, 1950), 649.

15. Sidney Cleveland, "Do God's Prophets Take Advice From the Dead?" http://www.ellenwhiteexposed.com/egw61.htm, accessed August 10, 2009.

16. Ibid.

17. Letter 17, 1881; Ellen White to W. C. White, September 12, 1881, 2–4.

18. Parts of the letter are published in *Ellen G. White, The Retirement Years* (Hagerstown, Md.: Review and Herald®, 1990), 161, 162; and *Manuscript Releases* (Silver Spring, Md.: E. G. White Estate, 1990), 10:38–40.

19. See Arthur L. White, *Ellen G. White*, vol. 3, *The Lonely Years, 1876–1891* (Washington D.C.: Review and Herald®, 1984), 182, 183.

20. E. G. White, *Testimonies for the Church* (Nampa, Idaho: Pacific Press®, 1948), 1:39, 40.

21. E. G. White, *The Great Controversy*, 552, 562.

22. E. G. White, Letter 17, 1881, 1.

23. Ibid., 4.

24. Web site editor (Dirk Anderson), http://www.ellenwhiteexposed.com/egw61.htm (accessed August 10, 2009).

25. Walter Liefeld, "Luke," in *Expositor's Bible Commentary*, vol. 8, Frank E. Gabelein, ed. (Grand Rapids, Mich.: Zondervan, 1984), 992.

26. George Eldon Ladd, *A Commentary on the Revelation of John* (Grand Rapids, Mich.: Eerdmans, 1979), 103.

27. A helpful discussion on the topic of "proof-texts" can be found in Reformed theologian John M. Frame's *The Doctrine of the Knowledge of God* (Phillipsburg, N.J.: Presbyterian and Reformed Publishing, 1987), 197.

(Chapter 11)
The Big Picture, Part 1: Understanding Ellen White's Message

1. Roger W. Coon, "There Simply Is No Case: Interview With Attorney Vincent L. Ramik," *Review and Herald,* September 17, 1981, 3; accessible at http://www.adventistbiblicalresearch.org/documents/plagiarist.pdf.

2. Ellen White was more of a "practical theologian" like John Wesley. See Randy L. Maddox, *Responsible Grace: John Wesley's Practical Theology* (Nashville, Tenn.: Kingswood Books, 1994), 16.

3. Because of this approach, Ellen White's writings are vulnerable to misinterpretation. She reacted to many different situations through the years, and the historical context of the particular issue she was addressing must be taken into consideration.

4. Roy Graham, *Ellen G. White: Co-Founder of the Seventh-day Adventist Church* (New York: Peter Lang, 1985), 144.

5. Because Ellen White responded to many different theological extremes, these contexts cannot be ignored, as so many followers and critics do. For instance, critics often exploit her statements that Christians should never say, "I am saved," but fail to see the antinomian contexts in which these statements were made. Any compilation of her statements must reflect the immediate literary context of each individual statement before any major theme can be established.

6. Because of modern technology, such as the *Ellen G. White Writings Comprehensive Research Edition* CD-ROM (Silver Spring, Md.: Ellen G. White Estate), thematic research in Ellen White's writings is more efficient, effective, and accessible. If we fail to read the statements in their literary context, we lose the benefits of the CD-ROM.

7. See, for example, David Neff, "Ellen White's Alleged Literary and Theological Indebtedness to Calvin Stowe" (unpublished paper, Andrews University, 1979, Center for Adventist Research). Neff provides evidence that Ellen White used Stowe's words but reformulated them to fit her own idea of inspiration, which differed from Stowe's.

8. Ellen G. White, *Selected Messages* (Washington, D.C.: Review and Herald®, 1980), 3:56.

9. Ibid., 71.

10. Gerhard Pfandl, "Ellen White and Hermeneutics," in *Understanding Scripture: An Adventist Approach,* George W. Reid, ed. (Silver Spring, Md.: Biblical Research Institute, General Conference of Seventh-day Adventists, 2006), 324.

11. I have chosen not to engage the charges on the shut-door teaching and Ellen White in this book. This concise discussion only touches on an issue that would take many pages to cover thoroughly. The following studies provide the evidence for the claims made in the next two paragraphs: Merlin D. Burt, "The Historical Background, Interconnected Development, and Integration of the Doctrines of the Sanctuary, the Sabbath, and Ellen G. White's Role in Sabbatarian Adventism from 1844 to 1849" (PhD dissertation, Andrews University, Berrien Springs, Mich., 2002); Burt, "Shut Door," in *The Ellen G. White Encyclopedia,* Denis Fortin and Jerry Moon, eds. (Hagerstown, Md.: Review and Herald®, 2011); P. Gerard Damsteegt, *Foundations of the Seventh-day Adventist Message and Mission* (Grand Rapids, Mich.: Eerdmans, 1977; reprint: Berrien Springs, Mich.: Andrews University Press, 1995), 104–124; Herbert E. Douglass, *Messenger of the Lord: The Prophetic Ministry of Ellen G. White* (Nampa, Idaho: Pacific Press®, 1998), 500–512, 549–569; Francis D. Nichol, *Ellen G. White and Her Critics: An Answer to the Major Charges That Critics Have Brought Against Mrs. Ellen G. White* (Washington, D.C.: Review and Herald®, 1951), 161–252; and Robert W. Olson, "The Shut Door Documents: Statements

Relating to the 'Shut Door,' the Door of Mercy, and the Salvation of Souls by Ellen G. White and Other Early Adventists Arranged in a Chronological Setting From 1844 to 1851," April 11, 1982, Ellen G. White Estate, Silver Spring, Md. For online sources, see Jud Lake, "Answers to the Shut Door Charges," http://ellenwhiteanswers.org/answers/shutdoor.

12. See Merlin D. Burt, "The 'Shut Door' and Ellen White's Visions," in *The Unpublished Letters of Ellen G. White, 1845–1859*, vol. 1, forthcoming, Ellen G. White Estate.

13. E. G. White, "Letter From Sister Harmon," *Day-Star*, Jan. 24, 1846, 31; reprinted in George Knight, *1844 and the Rise of Sabbatarian Adventism* (Hagerstown, Md.: Review and Herald®, 1994), 146.

14. E. G. White, *The Great Controversy* (Mountain View, Calif.: Pacific Press®, 1911), 429–431.

15. For examples of the critics' shut-door charges over the years, see B. F. Snook and Wm. H. Brinkerhoff, *The Visions of E. G. White, Not of God* (Cedar Rapids, Iowa: Cedar Valley Times, 1866), 3–5; H. E. Carver, *Mrs. E. G. White's Claims to Divine Inspiration Examined* (Marion, Iowa: Published at the "Hope of Israel" Office), 1870, 42–62; Miles Grant, *The True Sabbath: Which Day Shall We Keep? An Examination of Mrs. Ellen White's Visions* (Boston: Advent Christian Publication Society, 1874), 88–96; A. C. Long, *Comparison of the Early Writings of Mrs. White With Later Publications* (Marion, Iowa: Advent and Sabbath Advocate, 1883), 3–5; D. M. Canright, *Seventh-day Adventism Renounced After an Experience of Twenty-Eight Years: By a Prominent Minister and Writer of That Faith* (Kalamazoo, Mich.: Kalamazoo Publishing, 1888), 45–47; Canright, *Life of Mrs. E. G. White, Seventh-day Adventist Prophet: Her False Claims Refuted*, reprint of 1919 version, (Salt Lake City: Sterling Press, 1998) 59–81; E. S. Ballenger, *Facts About Seventh-day Adventists* (Riverside, Calif.: E. S. Ballenger, circa, 1949), 10–29; and more recently, Dale Ratzlaff, *The Cultic Doctrine of Seventh-day Adventists* (Glendale, Az.: Life Assurance Ministries, 1996), 117–152. See note 11 for responses to these charges.

16. E. G. White, *Selected Messages*, 1:37.

17. Ibid., 416.

18. Ibid., 16.

19. George Knight, *Reading Ellen White: How to Understand and Apply Her Writings* (Hagerstown, Md.: Review and Herald®, 1997), 111. For examples of other minor difficulties in Scripture, see Roger Coon, "Infallibility, Inerrancy, and the Prophets: Does a True Prophet Ever Make a Mistake?" at http://ellenwhiteanswers.org/dyn/media/pdf/Coon-infall-inerr.pdf.

20. Alberto R. Timm, "How Reliable Is the Bible?" *College and University Dialogue*, 13/3, 12–14, 2001; accessible online: http://dialogue.adventist.org/articles/13_3_timm_e.htm. See also Peter M. van Bemmelen, "Revelation and Inspiration," in *Handbook of Seventh-day Adventist Theology*, Raoul Dederen, ed. (Silver Spring, Md.: Review and Herald® and the General Conference of Seventh-day Adventists, 2000), 43–45, on the truthfulness and clarity of Scripture in spite of these difficulties.

21. Knight, 110.

22. For examples of these minor mistakes and others in Ellen White's writings, see Roger Coon, "Infallibility, Inerrancy, and the Prophets," at http://ellenwhiteanswers.org/dyn/media/pdf/Coon-infall-inerr.pdf.

23. Pfandl, "Ellen White and Hermeneutics," 325.

24. "The 1911 Edition of 'The Great Controversy': An Explanation of the Involvements of the 1911 Revision," page 4. See also "The Great Controversy—1911 Edition," appendix A, in *Selected Messages*, 3:433, 444.

25. Ibid., page 1.

26. Pfandl, 325. See also "W. C. White Statement Made to W. W. Eastman, November 4,

1912," appendix B, in *Selected Messages*, 3:445–450.

27. For responses to the plagiarism charge, see the links at Jud Lake, "Answers to the Plagiarism Charge," at http://ellenwhiteanswers.org/answers/plagarism.

28. W. C. White in E. G. White, *Selected Messages* (Washington, D.C.: Review and Herald®, 1980), 3:460.

29. See Maddox's *Responsible Grace*, 16.

30. Herbert Douglass, *Messenger of the Lord: The Prophetic Ministry of Ellen G. White* (Nampa, Idaho: Pacific Press®, 1998), 256–266.

31. For two excellent presentations on the great controversy in Scripture, see Frank B. Holbrook, "The Great Controversy," in *Handbook of Seventh-day Adventist Theology*, Raoul Dederen, ed. (Silver Spring, Md.: Review and Herald®, and the General Conference of Seventh-day Adventists, 2000), 969–1009; and Norman Gulley, *Systematic Theology*, vol. 1, *Prolegomena* (Berrien Springs, Mich.: Andrews University Press, 2003), 387–453, who gives a thorough discussion on the "Biblical Cosmic Controversy Worldview," in Scripture and in the writings of other Christians through the centuries.

32. For the story of this vision, see Arthur L. White, *Ellen G. White: The Early Years 1827–1862* (Hagerstown, Md.: Review and Herald®, 1985), 1:366–375. For Ellen White's personal, detailed account, see E. G. White, *Spiritual Gifts: My Christian Experience, Views and Labors: In Connection With the Rise and Progress of the "Third Angel's Message,"* vol. 2, (Battle Creek, Mich.: James White, 1860), 262–272.

33. E. G. White, *Spiritual Gifts: The Great Controversy Between Christ and His Angels and Satan and His Angels*, vol. 1 (Battle Creek, Mich.: James White, 1858).

34. E. G. White, *The Spirit of Prophecy: The Great Controversy Between Christ and His Angels and Satan and His Angels*, vol. 1 (Battle Creek, Mich.: Steam Press, 1870); E. G. White, *The Spirit of Prophecy: The Great Controversy Between Christ and Satan. Life, Teachings and Miracles of Our Lord Jesus Christ*, vol. 2 (Battle Creek, Mich.: Steam Press, 1877); E. G. White, *The Spirit of Prophecy: The Great Controversy Between Christ and Satan. The Death, Resurrection and Ascension of Our Lord Jesus Christ*, vol. 3 (Battle Creek, Mich.: Steam Press, 1878); and E. G. White, *Spirit of Prophecy: The Great Controversy Between Christ and Satan From the Destruction of Jerusalem to the End of the Controversy*, vol. 4 (Battle Creek, Mich.: Steam Press, 1884). A second and enlarged edition of volume 4 was published in 1888. For the full story of publishing the great-controversy theme from 1858 to 1911, see Arthur White, "The Story of *The Great Controversy*," *Review and Herald*, August 1, 1963, 2–4; and Arthur White, "The Story of *The Great Controversy*, Part 2," August 8, 1963, 6, 7.

35. E. G. White, *Patriarchs and Prophets* (Mountain View, Calif.: Pacific Press®, 1890; 1958); E. G. White, *Prophets and Kings* (Mountain View, Calif.: Pacific Press®, 1917; 1943); E. G. White, *The Desire of Ages* (Mountain View, Calif.: Pacific Press®, 1898; 1940); E. G. White, *The Acts of the Apostles* (Mountain View, Calif.: Pacific Press®, 1911); E. G. White, *The Great Controversy* (Mountain View, Calif.: Pacific Press®, 1911; 1950).

36. E. G. White, Letter 281, 1905; *Colporteur Ministry* (Mountain View, Calif.: Pacific Press®, 1953), 127.

37. Joseph Battistone, *The Great Controversy Theme in E. G. White Writings* (Berrien Springs, Mich.: Andrews University, 1978), 110. For further analysis of the great-controversy theme in Ellen White's writings, see Douglass, *Messenger of the Lord*, 256–277; and Douglass, *God At Risk: The Cost of Freedom in the Great Controversy* (Roseville, Calif.: Amazing Facts, Inc., 2004).

38. E. G. White, *Patriarchs and Prophets*, 33.

39. E. G. White, *The Great Controversy*, 678.

40. Battistone, 110.

41. This was first stressed by George Knight in his *Meeting Ellen White: A Fresh Look at Her Life, Writings, and Major Themes* (Hagerstown, Md.: Review and Herald®, 1996), 94, 95.

42. John Wood, " 'We Must All Appear': The Investigative Judgment Theme in the Writings of Ellen G. White," in *The Sanctuary and the Atonement: Biblical, Historical, and Theological Studies,* Arnold V. Wallenkampf and W. Richard Lesher, eds. (Washington, D.C.: General Conference of Seventh-day Adventists, 1981), 639.

43. Ibid., 641.

44. Wood, "The Mighty Opposites: The Atonement of Christ in the Writings of Ellen G. White, Part 1," in ibid., 694.

45. E. G. White, *Gospel Workers* (Washington, D.C.: Review and Herald®, 1948), 315.

46. E. G. White, "Missionary Work," *Review and Herald,* September 29, 1891, 593.

47. E. G. White, "Circulation of *Great Controversy*," in *The Ellen G. White 1888 Materials,* facsimile reproductions (Washington, D.C.: Ellen G. White Estate, 1987), 2:806.

48. E. G. White, *Education* (Mountain View, Calif.: Pacific Press®, 1952), 125, 126.

49. Ibid., 190.

50. Roger W. Coon, "There Simply Is No Case: Interview With Attorney Vincent L. Ramik," 6. Ramik said he first heard this analogy from Warren Johns.

(Chapter 12)
The Big Picture, Part 2: Vindicating Ellen White's Message

1. Even if the critics were to have assembled a thousand pages of controversial sayings written by Ellen White (which is profoundly generous), that amounts to only 1 percent of the approximately one hundred thousand pages of her entire literary corpus. And, in fact, the actual number of pages of sayings that the critics challenge is far less than one hundred—0.1 percent of her writings! Do the math! (I'm not including in this calculation the pages of literary borrowing Ellen White did, only individual statements compiled from the anti-Ellen White Web sites. When one adds in all the literary borrowing material, the total does exceed the amount of the controversial sayings. But it still amounts to a small percentage of her entire literary corpus. See http://ellenwhiteanswers.org/gen_dyn.php?file=media/pdf/Coonplagiarism.pdf.

2. Martin Carey, "Are Other Worlds Watching Us?" *Proclamation!* (January–February 2008), 12.

3. Rodney Nelson, "The Great Controversy Theme and The Gospel," *Proclamation!* (May–June 2003), 13.

4. Colleen Tinker, "New, Improved! Investigative Judgment," *Proclamation!* (March–April 2005), 9.

5. Ibid.

6. Richard Davidson, "Cosmic Metanarrative for the Coming Millennium," *Journal of the Adventist Theological Society*, 11/1–2 (2000): 103, 104. For more discussion on this cosmic moral conflict in Scripture, see Sook-Young Kim, "The Trajectory of the 'Warrior Messiah' Motif in Scripture and Intertestamental Writings" (PhD dissertation, Andrews University, 2008), and Sigve K. Tonstad, *Saving God's Reputation: The Theological Function of "Pistis Iesou" in the Cosmic Narratives of Revelation,* Library of New Testament Studies, vol. 337 (New York: T&T Clark International, 2006).

7. Ibid., note 4.

8. Gregory A. Boyd, *God at War: The Bible and Spiritual Conflict* (Downers Grove, Ill.: InterVarsity Press, 1997); and Boyd, *Satan and the Problem of Evil: Constructing a Trinitarian Warfare Theodicy* (Downers Grove, Ill.: InterVarsity Press, 2001).

9. Tremper Longman III and Daniel G. Reid, *God Is a Warrior* (Grand Rapids, Mich.: Zondervan, 1995).

10. Frank B. Holbrook, "The Great Controversy," in *Handbook of Seventh-day Adventist Theology*, Raoul Dederen, ed. (Silver Spring, Md.: Review and Herald® and the General Conference of Seventh-day Adventists, 2000), 989.

11. Joseph Battistone, *The Great Controversy Theme in E. G. White Writings* (Berrien Springs, Mich.: Andrews University, 1978), 3, 4.

12. It is popular among antagonists of Ellen White to argue that she was wrong in stating that Adam wasn't present during Eve's conversation with the serpent in *Patriarchs and Prophets* (Mountain View, Calif.: Pacific Press®, 1958), 53, 54. Genesis 3:6, they argue, states, "She took of its fruit and ate. She also gave to her husband *with her,* and he ate" (NKJV; emphasis added). Much could be said on this charge, but Richard Davidson provides a concise response: "The Hebrew clause in 3:6 'she also gave some to her husband, who was *with her* ['*immāh*]' does not imply that Adam was right by her side at the tree; note the clarification for this preposition in Adam's reply to God (3:12)—'The woman whom you gave to be with me ['*immādî*]'—showing that it refers to the partnership and not their proximity of location at any one given time. This interpretation seems to be implied in the last half of 3:12: 'She gave me fruit from the tree, and I ate.' If Adam had been present and listened to the whole conversation between Eve and the serpent, it seems he would have implicated the serpent as well as the woman in his defense. Similarly, the woman's testimony in 3:13 ('The serpent tricked me') would also seem to have applied to Adam as well (he also would have been deceived) if he had been personally present at the tree next to Eve" (Richard M. Davidson, *Flame*

of Yahweh: Sexuality in the Old Testament [Peabody, Mass.: Hendrickson Publishers, 2007], 66, note 29.)

13. See the excellent study on Genesis 3:15 by Afolarin Olutunde Ojewole, "The Seed in Genesis 3:15: An Exegetical and Intertextual Study" (PhD dissertation, Andrews University, 2002), 388–392. See also O. Palmer Robertson, *The Christ of the Covenants* (Phillipsburg, N.J.: Presbyterian and Reformed Publishing Co., 1980), 93–103, who comes to similar conclusions on this momentous passage.

14. George Knight, *The Cross of Christ: God's Work for Us* (Hagerstown, Md.: Review and Herald®, 2008), 116.

15. E. G. White, *The Desire of Ages* (Mountain View, Calif.: Pacific Press®, 1898; 1940), 19, 20.

16. Ibid., 24, 25.

17. Ibid., 25, 26.

18. Ibid., 26.

19. E. G. White, "Without Excuse," *Review and Herald,* September 24, 1901, 615; E. G. White, "A Crucified and Risen Saviour," *Signs of the Times,* August 16, 1899, 6.

20. E. G. White, *Fundamentals of Christian Education* (Nashville, Tenn.: Southern Publishing Association, 1923), 370.

21. Knight, 10.

22. Ángel M. Rodríguez, *Spanning the Abyss: How the Atonement Brings God and Humanity Together* (Hagerstown, Md.: Review and Herald®, 2008), 129.

23. See ibid., for a biblical discussion of these different phases of the atonement.

24. E. G. White, *Gospel Workers* (Washington, D.C.: Review and Herald®, 1948), 315.

25. E. G. White, *The Desire of Ages,* 764.

26. For a helpful discussion of these theories, see Millard J. Erickson, *Christian Theology,* 2nd ed. (Grand Rapids, Mich.: Baker, 1998), 798–817. For concise definitions from which I have borrowed, see Erickson, *Concise Dictionary of Christian Theology* (Grand Rapids, Mich.: Baker, 1986).

27. For a careful evangelical discussion on the penal-substitution theory, see Erickson, *Christian Theology,* 818–840; also see David Duffie, "Some Contemporary Evangelical Views of the Atonement," in *The Sanctuary and the Atonement: Biblical, Historical, and Theological Studies,* Arnold V. Wallenkampf and W. Richard Lesher, eds. (Washington, D.C.: General Conference of Seventh-day Adventists, 1981), 500–515. For a contemporary Seventh-day Adventist discussion on the atonement of Christ in Scripture, history, and Ellen White, see Raoul Dederen, "Christ: His Person and Work," in *Handbook of Seventh-day Adventist Theology,* Raoul Dederen, ed. (Silver Spring, Md.: Review and Herald® and the General Conference of Seventh-day Adventists, 2000), 160–204.

28. Regarding the ransom theory, Ellen White never wrote that Satan's claim on human beings was valid and that he should be paid a ransom. She freely used the expression "ransom," but she understood it more in the sense of the penal-satisfaction concept. See Woodrow Whidden, "The Soteriology of Ellen G. White: The Persistent Path to Perfection, 1836–1902" (PhD dissertation, Drew University, 1989), 121, 122, for discussion.

29. E. G. White, *The Desire of Ages,* 753, 755, 756; emphasis added.

30. For a more detailed discussion on Ellen White and the theories of the atonement, see Whidden, "The Soteriology of Ellen G. White," 117–126. See also his *Ellen White on Salvation* (Hagerstown, Md.: Review and Herald®, 1995), 49–54.

31. For an important Seventh-day Adventist discussion on the doctrine of salvation in Scripture, history, and Ellen White, see Ivan T. Blazen, "Salvation," in *Handbook of Seventh-day Adventist Theology,* 271–313; note the helpful bibliography, 313.

32. The most thorough study to date on the influence of Wesleyan thought on Ellen White's soteriological (salvation) writings is Whidden, "The Soteriology of Ellen G. White."

33. See Jacob Arminius, *The Works of James Arminius,* James Nichols and William Nichols, ed., trans., 3 vols. (Grand Rapids, Mich.: Baker, 1996). For an excellent study that sets forth classical Arminian the-

ology and addresses misunderstandings of it, see Roger E. Olson, *Arminian Theology: Myths and Realities* (Downers Grove, Ill.: InterVarsity Press Academic, 2006). For other contemporary studies advocating Arminianism, see Clark H. Pinnock, ed., *Grace Unlimited* (Minneapolis, Minn.: Bethany House Publishers, 1975); and Pinnock, ed., *The Grace of God, The Will of Man* (Grand Rapids, Mich.: Zondervan Academie Books, 1989); and Jerry L. Walls and Joseph R. Donngell, *Why I Am Not a Calvinist* (Downers Grove, Ill.: InterVarsity Press, 2004). For biblical studies critiquing the Calvinistic doctrine of perseverance, see I. Howard Marshall, *Kept by the Power of God: A Study of Perseverance and Falling Away* (Minneapolis, Minn.: Bethany House Publishers, 1969); Robert Shank, *Life in the Son: A Study of the Doctrine of Perseverance*, 2nd ed. (Springfield, Mo.: Westcott Publishers, 1961); and Shank, *Elect in the Son: A Study of the Doctrine of Election* (Minneapolis, Minn.: Bethany House Publishers, 1970).

34. For the story of the debate between Calvinism and Arminianism over the centuries, see Alan P. F. Sell, *The Great Debate: Calvinism, Arminianism, and Salvation* (Grand Rapids, Mich.: Baker, 1983).

35. See John Wesley, *The Works of John Wesley*, Thomas Jackson, ed., 14 vols. (Grand Rapids, Mich.: Baker, 1991). See also the projected 35-volume set still in progress at the time of this writing: *The Bicentennial Edition of the Works of John Wesley*, W. Reginald Ward and Richard P. Heitzenrater, eds. (Nashville, Tenn.: Abingdon Press, 1976–). I will be referencing the Jackson edition. For an excellent study of Wesley and the movement he spawned, see Richard P. Heitzenrater, *Wesley and the People Called Methodists* (Nashville, Tenn.: Abingdon Press, 1994).

36. On Wesley, see, for example, Thomas C. Oden, *John Wesley's Scriptural Christianity: A Plain Exposition of His Teaching on Christian Doctrine* (Grand Rapids, Mich.: Zondervan, 1994); on Arminius, see Carl Bangs, *Arminius: A Study in the Dutch Reformation* (Grand Rapids, Mich.: Zondervan, 1985). For a concise historical study affirming both Arminius's and Wesley's evangelical Christianity and showing how Wesley's moved beyond Arminius's, see Mildred Bangs Wynkoop, *Foundations of Wesleyan-Arminian Theology* (Kansas City, Mo.: Beacon Hill Press, 1967). The scriptural focus of both Arminius and Wesley can be confirmed by studying their respective works and noting the profuse references to Scripture.

37. See Wesley's classical essay "The Question, 'What is an Arminian?' Answered by a Lover of Free Grace," in *Works* (Jackson), 10:358–361. For helpful studies on Wesley's theology, see Randy L. Maddox, *Responsible Grace: John Wesley's Practical Theology* (Nashville, Tenn.: Kingswood Books, 1994); Thomas C. Oden, *John Wesley's Scriptural Christianity*; Kenneth J. Collins, *The Scripture Way of Salvation: The Heart of John Wesley's Theology* (Nashville, Tenn.: Abingdon Press, 1997); and Collins, *The Theology of John Wesley: Holy Love and the Shape of Grace* (Nashville, Tenn.: Abingdon Press, 2007).

38. See the significant series "John Wesley Christian Perfection Library," by Mark K. Olsen, *John Wesley's "A Plain Account of Christian Perfection." The Annotated Version* (Fenwick, Mich.: Alethea In Heart, 2005); Olsen, *John Wesley's Theology of Christian Perfection: Developments in Doctrine and Theological System* (Fenwick, Mich.: Truth In Heart, 2007); and Olsen, *John Wesley Reader on Christian Perfection* (Fenwick, Mich.: Truth In Heart, 2008).

39. See Wesley's essay "Serious Thoughts Upon the Perseverance of the Saints," in *Works* (Jackson), 10:284–298; and his sermon "Privilege of Those That Are Born of God," in ibid., 5:227–233. See also J. Steven Harper, "Wesleyan Arminianism," in J. Matthew Pinson, ed., *Four Views on Eternal Security* (Grand Rapids, Mich.: Zondervan, 2002), 209–255; and Gareth Lee Cockerill, "A Wesleyan Arminian View," in Herbert W. Bateman IV, ed., *Four Views on the Warning Passages in Hebrews* (Grand Rapids, Mich.: Kregel, 2007), 257–292.

40. Wesley, "Serious Thoughts Upon the Perseverance of the Saints," 298.

41. For discussion, see Whidden, "The Soteriology of Ellen G. White," 18–48.

42. Ibid., 47, 48, note 2; and George Knight, *Sin and Salvation: God's Work for and in Us* (Hagerstown, Md.: Review and Herald®, 2008), 153.

43. Ibid.

44. Teresa and Arthur Beem, *It's Okay NOT to Be a Seventh-day Adventist* (North Charleston, S.C.: BookSurge Publishing, 2008), 93.

45. E. G. White, "The Truth as It Is in Jesus," *Review and Herald,* June 17, 1890; in *Selected Messages* (Hagerstown, Md., Review and Herald®, 1986), 1:314.

46. See the following studies on Ellen White's "never say, 'I am saved' " statements and the assurance of salvation: Herbert Douglass, *Should We Ever Say, "I Am Saved"? What It Means to Be Assured of Salvation* (Nampa, Idaho: Pacific Press®, 2003); Philip W. Dunham, *Sure Salvation: You Can Know You Have Eternal Life* (Nampa, Idaho: Pacific Press®, 2007). See also the exceptionally helpful article on Ellen White and assurance by Jerry Moon, "Assurance of Salvation," in *The Ellen G. White Encyclopedia*, Denis Fortin and Jerry Moon, eds. (Hagerstown, Md.: Review and Herald®, 2011).

47. E. G. White, *Life Sketches of Ellen G. White* (Mountain View, Calif.: Pacific Press®, 1915), 39; emphasis added. While obviously written years later, this statement describes the culmination of Ellen Harmon's conversion experience in 1843, which is covered in detail in Merlin Burt, "Ellen G. Harmon's Three-Step Conversion Between 1836 and 1843 and the Harmon Family Methodist Experience," unpublished research paper, Andrews University Seventh-day Adventist Theological Seminary, 1998. For a concise discussion of Ellen White's conversion, see Jud Lake, "Reading Ellen White Through the Lens of Joy," *Adventist World,* September 2009, 38, 39.

48. E. G. White, *A Sketch of the Christian Experience and Views of Ellen G. White* (Saratoga Springs, N.Y.: James White, 1851), 61; reprinted in E. G. White, *Early Writings* (Washington, D.C.: Review and Herald®, 1945), 73; emphasis added.

49. E. G. White, *Spiritual Gifts: Facts of Faith, In Connection With the History of Holy Men of Old,* vol. 3, (Battle Creek, Mich.: Steam Press, 1864), 52; emphasis added.

50. E. G. White, "Practical Remarks," *Review and Herald,* March 29, 1870, 113, 115; emphasis added. Although this article was published in 1870, it was a report of remarks Mrs. White made at a tent meeting in June 1869 (ibid., 113, footnote).

51. E. G. White, "Camp Meeting at Eagle Lake," *Review and Herald,* May 4, 1876, 139; emphasis added. While Ellen White is reporting what her husband said, it is clear from the context of the article that she approves of what he said, and thus that her view coincided with his words.

52. E. G. White, *The Spirit of Prophecy: The Great Controversy Between Christ and Satan. The Death, Resurrection and Ascension of Our Lord Jesus Christ,* vol. 3 (Battle Creek, Mich.: Steam Press, 1878), 261, 262; emphasis added.

53. E. G. White, *Selected Messages,* 1:354. From a morning talk to the ministers assembled at the General Conference, Battle Creek, Michigan, November 1883.

54. E. G. White, Ms. 36, 1890, in *Manuscript Releases* (Silver Spring, Md.: E. G. White Estate, 1990), 3:420–421; also in E. G. White, "Danger of False Ideas on Justification by Faith," *The Ellen G. White 1888 Materials,* vol. 2 (Washington, D.C.: Ellen G. White Estate, Silver Spring, Md.: 1987), 812; emphasis added.

55. E. G. White, Ms. 36, 1891: Sabbath morning sermon, Healdsburg, California, Camp Meeting, September 19, 1891, in *Ellen G. White: Sermons and Talks* (Silver Spring, Md.: Ellen G. White Estate, 1990), 202, 203; emphasis added.

56. E. G. White, *Manuscript Releases,* 10:175; letter 35, 1894.

57. E. G. White, *The Desire of Ages,* 356; emphasis added.

58. E. G. White, *Christ's Object Lessons* (Nampa, Idaho: Pacific Press®, 1941), 317; emphasis added.

59. Ibid., 420; emphasis added.

60. E. G. White, *General Conference Bulletin,* April 10, 1901, 183; emphasis added.

61. E. G. White, *Selected Messages,* 2:255; letter 45, 1905; emphasis added. For other lists of Ellen White statements on this theme, see Dunham's *Sure Salvation,* 149–154; and Clifford Goldstein, *Graffiti in the Holy of Holies: An Impassioned Response to Recent Attacks on the Sanctuary and Ellen White* (Nampa, Idaho: Pacific Press®, 2003), 167–171.

62. E. G. White, *Life Sketches,* 449. This sentence comes from Paul as he expressed his assurance of salvation in the face of death (2 Timothy 1:12).

63. See Moon, "Assurance of Salvation."

64. E. G. White, *The Great Controversy,* 482.

65. Ibid.

66. Ibid., 483.

67. Ibid., 484.

68. Goldstein, 171.

69. E. G. White, *The Great Controversy,* 490.

70. John Wesley, "The Great Assize," in *Works* (Jackson), 5:175–178.

71. Many critics label another statement in *The Great Controversy* as legalistic perfectionism: "Those who are living upon the earth when the intercession of Christ shall cease in the sanctuary above are to stand in the sight of a holy God without a mediator. Their robes must be spotless, their characters must be purified from sin by the blood of sprinkling. Through the grace of God and their own diligent effort they must be conquerors in the battle with evil. While the investigative judgment is going forward in heaven, while the sins of penitent believers are being removed from the sanctuary, there is to be a special work of purification, of putting away of sin, among God's people upon earth" (425). Full explanation of this passage would take up more space than our purpose in this chapter allows. Woodrow Whidden has provided an excellent discussion of this statement in its larger context in his "The Soteriology of Ellen G. White," 357–371; and Whidden, *Ellen White on Salvation,* 132–139.

72. Samuele Bacchiocchi, *The Advent Hope for Human Hopelessness* (Berrien Springs, Mich.: Biblical Perspectives, 1986), 298, 299.

73. E. G. White, *Steps to Christ* (Mountain View, Calif.: Pacific Press®, 1956).

74. For the Wesleyan-Arminian themes, see, for example, ibid., 43, 61, 62, 63, 69, 72. For the character of God, see 9–15, 43, 44.

75. Ibid., 72; emphasis in the original.

76. Tim Poirier, "Exhibits Regarding the Work of Ellen White's Literary Assistants," Ellen G. White Estate, Self Document, 21–25. For the story of *Steps to Christ,* see Poirier, "A Century of Steps," *Adventist Review,* May 14, 1992, 14, 15; and "The Story of 'Steps to Christ,'" Elmshaven Leaflets, vol. 2, no. 3, Ellen G. White Estate, Document File 297, 1–4. Because the Christ-centered message in the book is so clear and legalism cannot be read into it, some critics argue against Ellen White's authorship. But this argument has serious problems (see Jud Lake, "Ellen White Authored Steps to Christ," accessible at http://ellenwhiteanswers.org/dyn/media/pdf/EGWauthored-Steps-to-Christ.pdf.). The critics who do take issue with the contents of the book read foreign ideas into it. See, for example, Beem, *It's Okay NOT to Be a Seventh-day Adventist,* 97, 98. The authors of this book fail to listen to specific statements in light of the overall message of the book and its Wesleyan-Arminian biblical background.

77. George Knight, *Meeting Ellen White: A Fresh Look at Her Life, Writings, and Major Themes* (Hagerstown, Md.: Review and Herald®, 1996), 109.

78. Ibid., 109–127.

79. E. G. White, *Steps to Christ,* 70, 71.

(Chapter 13)
An Evangelical at Heart

1. For helpful overviews of contemporary evangelicalism, see Alister McGrath, "Evangelicalism," *The Blackwell Encyclopedia of Modern Christian Thought,* Alister McGrath, ed. (Oxford: Basil Blackwell, 1993), 183, 184; D. M. Bebbington, "Evangelicalism: Britain," ibid., 184–187; and Millard J. Erickson, "Evangelicalism: USA," ibid., 187–192. Also see R. V. Pierard and W. A. Elwell, "Evangelicalism," *Evangelical Dictionary of Theology* 2nd ed., Walter A. Elwell, ed. (Grand Rapids, Mich.: Baker, 2001), 405–410; David L. Smith, "Evangelicalism," *A Handbook of Contemporary Theology,* (Wheaton, Ill.: Victor Books, 1992), 58–71; and Donald G. Bloesch, "Evangelicalism," *A New Handbook of Christian Theology,* Donald W. Musser and Joseph L. Price, eds. (Nashville, Tenn.: Abingdon Press, 1992), 168–173. For an especially helpful historical overview, see Bruce L. Shelly, "Evangelicalism," *Dictionary of Christianity in America,* Daniel G. Reid, Robert D. Linder, Bruce L. Shelly, and Harry S. Stout, eds. (Downers Grove, Ill.: InterVarsity, 1990), 413–416.

2. David W. Bebbington, *The Dominance of Evangelicalism: The Age of Spurgeon and Moody,* A History of Evangelicalism: People, Movements, and Ideas in the English-Speaking World, vol. 3 (Downers Grove, Ill.: InterVarsity Press, 2005), 22.

3. Ibid., 23–40. It is important to note, however, that although evangelicals of the nineteenth century were united in these core areas, like the evangelicals of today, they were far from a monolith of faith and practice. They fought with each other over how to interpret the Scriptures, over the definition of Christian doctrines, over social issues, and over every imaginable kind of personality conflict. For further discussion, see Mark A. Noll, *America's God: From Jonathan Edwards to Abraham Lincoln* (New York: Oxford University Press, 2002),170, 175–179.

4. Bebbington, 83–85.

5. Historian Paul K. Conkin views Ellen White and Adventism as an "apocalyptic" version of Christianity in his book *American Originals: Homemade Varieties of Christianity* (Chapel Hill, N.C.: The University of North Carolina Press, 1997), 110–145.

6. This includes not only nineteenth-century evangelicalism but its counterpart today. On the theological continuity of evangelicalism over the last century, see Shelly's article; also the two forthcoming volumes in the series, "A History of Evangelicalism: People, Movements, and Ideas in the English-Speaking World," should be helpful: Geoff Treloar, *The Disruption of Evangelicalism: The Age of Mott, Machen and McPherson,* vol. 4; and Brian Stanley, *The Global Diffusion of Evangelicalism: The Age of Graham and Stott,* vol. 5, to be published by InterVarsity Press.

7. See Geoffrey E. Garne, "Are the Testimonies Legalistic?" *Australasian Record,* December 4, 1982, 6, 7, who provides evidence for the "centrality of the cross and of Jesus as our only Savior throughout the *Testimonies,*" 6.

8. E. G. White, *Testimonies* (Nampa, Idaho: Pacific Press®, 1948), 2:89–93; emphasis added.

9. Garne, 6, 7.

10. Richard Baxter, "A Christian Directory," in *The Practical Works of Richard Baxter* (London: George Virtue, 1846; reprint, Ligonier, Penn.: Soli Deo Gloria Publications, 1990), 1:1–904.

11. *American Biographical History of Eminent and Self-Made Men of the State of Michigan, Third Congressional District, 1878* (Cincinnati, Ohio: Western Biographical Company, 1874, 1878), 108.

12. E. G. White, *Spiritual Gifts: My Christian Experience, Views and Labors: In Connection With the Rise and Progress of the "Third Angel's Message,"* vol. 2 (Battle Creek, Mich.: James White, 1860), 301.

Pages 301–304 contain numerous testimonies signed by individuals who witnessed the events described by Mrs. White.

13. Jasper B. Canright to S. E. Wight, February 24, 1931.

14. For documented evidence on the real Ellen White of history, see the following studies: Arthur L. White's six-volume biography, *Ellen G. White*, vols. 1–6 (cited repeatedly throughout this book); Herbert Douglass, "The Real Ellen White," in *Messenger of the Lord: The Prophetic Ministry of Ellen G. White* (Nampa, Idaho: Pacific Press®, 1998), 44–131, and George Knight, *Walking With Ellen White: Her Everyday Life as a Wife, Mother, and Friend* (Hagerstown, Md.: Review and Herald®, 1999), all of which interact with primary sources and provide evidence for these character virtues in Ellen White.

15. See, for example, http://www.adventistarchives.org/DocArchives.asp and http://whiteestate.org/.

16. For examples of these cardinal doctrines as expressed in historic church creeds, see http://www.reformed.org/documents; concerning the doctrine of the Second Coming, see LeRoy E. Froom, *Prophetic Faith of Our Fathers*, 5 vols. (Washington, D.C.: Review and Herald®, 1950.

17. See, for example, her early testimonies in E. G. White, *Testimonies*, vols. 1, 2.

18. E. G. White, *Selected Messages* (Washington, D.C.: Review and Herald®, 1958), 1:16.

19. This conviction culminated in my doctoral dissertation, Jud Lake, "An Evaluation of Haddon Robinson's Homiletical Method: An Evangelical Perspective" (ThD dissertation, University of South Africa, 2003). See also Lake, "Preaching," in *The Ellen G. White Encyclopedia*, Denis Fortin and Jerry Moon, eds. (Hagerstown, Md.: Review and Herald®, 2011).

20. I agree with Jerry Moon's assessment that Ellen White's later statements on the Trinity do not contradict her earlier statements on it. He writes: "Her later statements are increasingly precise and explicit, whereas her earlier statements were more ambiguous. Some of the early statements are capable of being read from either a Trinitarian or non-Trinitarian perspective. But I have not found any statement from her pen that criticizes a biblical view of the Trinity" (Woodrow Whidden, Jerry Moon, and John W. Reeve, *The Trinity: Understanding God's Love, His Plan of Salvation, and Christian Relationships* [Hagerstown, Md.: Review and Herald®, 2002], 206).

21. E. G. White, *Evangelism* (Washington, D.C.: Review and Herald®, 1946), 614–617.

22. Ibid., 614, 615; emphasis added.

23. For a helpful compilation of Ellen White statements on the Godhead and Christ's place in it, see http://www.adventistbiblicalresearch.org/documents/Christ.htm.

24. Eric Claude Webster, *Crosscurrents in Adventist Christology* (Berrien Springs, Mich.: Andrews University Press, 1992), 74–109; and John Wood, "The Mighty Opposites: The Atonement of Christ in the Writings of Ellen G. White," parts I and II in *The Sanctuary and the Atonement: Biblical, Historical, and Theological Studies,* Arnold V. Wallenkampf and W. Richard Lesher, eds. (Washington, D.C.: General Conference of Seventh-day Adventists, 1981), 694–730.

25. E. G. White, *The Great Controversy* (Mountain View, Calif.: Pacific Press®, 1911; 1950), 644.

26. E. G. White, *Gospel Workers* (Washington, D.C.: Review and Herald®, 1948), 159, 160.

27. W. R. Lesher, "Ellen White's Concept of Sanctification" (PhD dissertation, New York University, 1970), 272, 273.

28. See the following studies: Herbert Douglass, *Messenger of the Lord*, "Appendix P: The Ellipse of Salvation Truth," 573–575; Hans LaRondelle, *Christ Our Salvation: What God Does for Us and in Us* (Sarasota, Fla.: First Impressions, 1998); and George Knight, *Sin and Salvation: God's Work for and in Us* (Hagerstown, Md.: Review and Herald®, 2008).

29. Gunnar Pedersen, "The Soteriology of Ellen G. White Compared with the Lutheran Formula of Concord: A Study of the Adventist Doctrine of the Final Judgment of the Saints and Their Justification Before God" (ThD dissertation, Andrews University, 1995), 197.

30. Ibid., 189.

31. Ibid., 197, 198.

32. Ibid., 199.

33. Hans K. LaRondelle, "The Seventh-day Adventist View of the Relationship of Justification-Sanctification-the Final Judgment," appendix D, in Woodrow W. Whidden, *E. J. Waggoner: From the Physician of Good News to Agent of Division* (Hagerstown, Md.: Review and Herald®, 2008), 395.

34. See the forthcoming volume by Woodrow W. Whidden on judgment and assurance in the Library of Adventist Theology Series.

35. E. G. White, *Life Sketches of Ellen G. White* (Mountain View, Calif.: Pacific Press®, 1915), 110, 111.

36. Whidden, et al., 196, 197.

37. Ibid., 198.

38. E. G. White, Manuscript 10, 1890. See George Knight, *A Search for Identity: The Development of Seventh-day Adventist Beliefs* (Hagerstown, Md.: Review and Herald®, 2000), 90–127, for an insightful discussion on what is Christian in Adventism and Ellen White's role in this issue.

39. Richard W. Schwarz and Floyd Greenleaf, *Light Bearers: A History of the Seventh-day Adventist Church* (Nampa, Idaho: Pacific Press®, 2000), 615, 616.

40. E. G. White, *Selected Messages*, 2:32, 33.

41. For further details on this movement and the impact of Ellen White's carefully prepared statement, see Arthur White, *Ellen G. White: The Early Elmshaven Years, 1900–1905*, 100–108.

42. John Harvey Kellogg, *The Living Temple* (Battle Creek, Mich.: Good Health Publishing Co., 1903), 28, 88.

43. E. G. White, *Selected Messages*, 1:200; for Ellen White's main statements on this issue, see ibid., 193–208; and *Testimonies*, 8:255–328.

44. Arthur White, 306. For detailed coverage of this story and the important role of Ellen White's counsels, see Arthur White, 280–306; see also Richard W. Schwarz, *John Harvey Kellogg: Pioneering Health Reformer* (Hagerstown, Md.: Review and Herald®, 2006); and Gilbert W. Valentine, *W. W. Prescott: Forgotten Giant of Adventism's Second Generation* (Hagerstown, Md.: Review and Herald®, 2005), 167–191.

45. Ellen White to W. C. White's first wife, Mary, who was dying of tuberculosis (Letter 2, Dec. 29, 1889).

(Chapter 14)
The Best Defense Is a Good Offense

1. See http://www.formeradventist.com for examples of such testimonies.

2. George Knight, *If I Were the Devil, Seeing Through the Enemy's Smoke Screen: Contemporary Challenges Facing Adventism* (Hagerstown, Md.: Review and Herald®, 2007), 20, 24.

3. E. G. White, "Fanaticism and Side Issues," Ms. 82, 1894, in *Manuscript Releases* (Silver Spring, Md.: E. G. White Estate, 1990), 3:25, 26; also in E. G. White, *Testimonies to Ministers and Gospel Workers* (Mountain View, Calif.: Pacific Press®, 1962), 227, 228.

4. James White, "To a Brother at Monroe, Wis.," *Review and Herald,* March 17, 1868, 220.

5. E. G. White, *Testimonies for the Church* (Mountain View, Calif.: Pacific Press®, 1948), 1:166; emphasis added.

6. E. G. White, "Be of One Mind," *Review and Herald,* May 29, 1888, 337.

7. George Knight, *Reading Ellen White: How to Understand and Apply Her Writings* (Hagerstown, Md.: Review and Herald®, 1997), 36.

8. Two excellent sources on how to read and study the Bible are Gordon D. Fee and Douglass Stuart, *How to Read the Bible for All Its Worth,* 3rd ed. (Grand Rapids, Mich.: Zondervan, 2003); and its companion, Stuart, *How to Read the Bible Book by Book: A Guided Tour* (Grand Rapids, Mich.: Zondervan, 2002). Plans on how to read the Bible through in a year abound on the Internet.

9. See Knight, *Meeting Ellen White: A Fresh Look at Her Life, Writings, and Major Themes* (Hagerstown, Md.: Review and Herald®, 1996), 91–106, for an excellent discussion of the different groupings of Ellen White's writings.

10. Knight gives excellent counsel on reading Ellen White widely in the chapter "Read With a Plan," in *Reading Ellen White,* 36–40.

11. Cited in ibid., 40; emphasis in the original. For the original context, see Frederick E. J. Harder, "Read It Like It Is," in Herbert Douglass, ed., *What Ellen White Has Meant to Me* (Washington, D.C.: Review and Herald®, 1973), 117. Harder's counsel also applies to the *Ellen G. White Writings Comprehensive Research Edition* CD-ROM (Silver Spring, Md.: Ellen G. White Estate). Its potential is maximized when statements are read in their context rather than in isolated sentences and paragraphs.

12. Dale Ratzlaff, *Truth Led Me Out* (Glendale, Ariz.: LAM Publications, 2008), 110; emphasis in the original. For the dramatic contrast between Ellen White's stance toward the Bible and Joseph Smith's stance toward the Bible, see George Knight, "Joseph Smith, Ellen White, and the Great Gulf," *Adventist Review Special Edition: Meet Ellen White for Yourself,* n.d., 35.

13. Robert W. Olson, *One Hundred and One Questions on the Sanctuary and on Ellen White* (Washington, D.C.: Ellen G. White Estate, 1981), 41.

14. Knight, *Reading Ellen White,* 36–123.

15. George Knight, *Meeting Ellen White: A Fresh Look at Her Life, Writings, and Major Themes*; Knight, *Reading Ellen White: How to Understand and Apply Her Writings*; Knight, *Walking With Ellen White: Her Everyday Life as a Wife, Mother, and Friend* (Hagerstown, Md.: Review and Herald®, 1999); and Knight, *Ellen White's World: A Fascinating Look at the Times in Which She Lived* (Hagerstown, Md.: Review and Herald®, 1998).

16. Arthur L. White, *Ellen G. White,* vol. 1, *The Early Years, 1827–1862* (Washington, D.C.: Review and Herald®, 1985); Arthur White, *Ellen G. White,* vol. 2, *The Progressive Years, 1862–1876* (Washington, D.C.: Review and Herald®, 1986); Arthur White, *Ellen G. White,* vol. 3, *The Lonely Years, 1876–1891* (Washington, D.C.: Review and Herald®, 1984); Arthur White, *Ellen G. White,* vol. 4, *The Australian Years, 1891–1900* (Washington,

D.C.: Review and Herald®, 1983); Arthur White, *Ellen G. White,* vol. 5, *The Early Elmshaven Years, 1900–1905* (Washington, D.C.: Review and Herald®, 1981); Arthur White, *Ellen G. White,* vol. 6, *The Later Elmshaven Years, 1905–1915* (Washington, D.C.: Review and Herald®, 1982).

17. Arthur White, *Ellen White: Woman of Vision* (Hagerstown, Md.: Review and Herald®, 1982, 2000).

18. Herbert Douglass, *Messenger of the Lord: The Prophetic Ministry of Ellen G. White* (Nampa, Idaho: Pacific Press®, 1998); see also Gerhard Pfandl, *The Gift of Prophecy: The Role of Ellen White in God's Remnant Church* (Nampa, Idaho: Pacific Press®, 2008).

19. *Ellen G. White Writings Comprehensive Research Edition* CD-ROM (Silver Spring, Md.: Ellen G. White Estate). The White Estate periodically updates the CD-ROM.

20. Denis Fortin and Jerry Moon, eds. *The Ellen G. White Encyclopedia* (Hagerstown, Md.: Review and Herald®, 2011).

21. Start with the official Ellen G. White Estate Web site, where you will find apologetic resources as well as basic information about Ellen White: http:whiteestate.org/. For other apologetic resources, see appendix D.

22. E. G. White, *Testimonies,* 5:708.

23. E. G. White, *Testimonies,* 4:583, 584.

24. By "argument" I do not mean a shouting match but a series of carefully crafted premises that lead to a valid conclusion.

25. James W. Sire, *Why Good Arguments Often Fail: Making A More Persuasive Case for Christ* (Downers Grove, Ill.: InterVarsity Press, 2006), 74.

26. See for example, Verle Streifling, "Logical Fallacies in Biblical Interpretation," *Proclamation!* March–April 2001, 9–12.

27. Irving M. Copi and Carl Cohen, *Introduction to Logic,* 8th ed. (New York: Macmillan Publishing Company, 1990), 92.

28. See ibid., 91–127; and Anthony Weston, *A Rulebook for Arguments,* 3rd ed. (Indianapolis, Ind.: Hackett Publishing Comany, 2000), 71–78.

29. Besides the two books mentioned in the previous notes, the following three books are useful guides in critical thinking and detecting fallacies: Norman L. Geisler and Ronald M. Brooks, *Come Let Us Reason: An Introduction to Logical Thinking* (Grand Rapids, Mich.: Baker, 1990); S. Morris Engel, *With Good Reason: An Introduction to Informal Fallacies,* 6th ed. (Boston: Bedford/St. Martin's, 2000); and Henry A. Virkler, *A Christian's Guide to Critical Thinking* (Eugene, Ore.: Wipf & Stock Publishers, 2006).

30. This fallacy is sometimes called "concealed evidence."

31. In his book *The Case of D. M. Canright* (Grand Rapids, Mich.: Baker Book House, 1964), 13, Norman Douty called Adventists to task for what he called their "assault on Canright."

32. In what I say here about what constitutes a good argument, I am drawing from Sire, 73.

33. E. G. White, *The Ministry of Healing* (Mountain View, Calf.: Pacific Press®, 1909), 470.

34. During the summer of 2009, for example, Dale Ratzlaff and his team traveled to six different cities across America on a "Tour of Encouragement" (see *Proclamation!* May–June 2009, 23). At the various evangelical churches, he claimed that Seventh-day Adventism and Ellen White teach unbiblical, heretical doctrines.

35. Geisler and Brooks, 16.

(Conclusion)

1. For the life story of Seventh-day Adventist evangelist Kenneth Cox, see his autobiography *Called to Serve* (Nampa, Idaho: Pacific Press®, 2010).

2. Francis D. Nichol, *Why I Believe in Mrs. E. G. White* (Washington, D.C.: Review and Herald®, 1964), 127, 128.

More Truths From a Messenger and Friend of God!

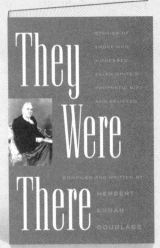

They Were There by Herbert Edgar Douglass:
Twenty-four fascinating stories of personal encounters with Ellen White are reported in this book—a preacher with two wives, a woman evangelist with a dark secret, a man whose presence made it impossible for Ellen White to speak, are just a few. Each individual was directly affected by Ellen White and her visions, and Mrs. White, ever the soul winner, urged each one to a closer walk with the Lord. 0-8163-2117-5

"Where the Word is Life"

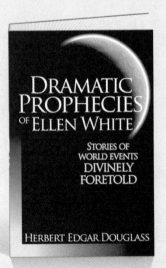

101 Questions About Ellen White and Her Writings:
If you could ask Ellen White one question, what would it be? Chances are it's answered in *101 Questions About Ellen White and Her Writings*. This book answers the most frequently asked and often most controversial inquiries that the White Estate receives on a daily basis about Ellen White, her writings, and her beliefs. Many of the myths that have developed over the years are exposed and readers will be introduced to the real truth about this inspirational author. 0-8163-2378-X

Dramatic Prophecies of Ellen White by Herbert Edgar Douglass:
Whether writing about war, segregation, spiritualism, healthful living, or the great controversy, God's messenger boldly spoke unpopular truths to those who needed to hear them. Today we need to listen once again. This book will rekindle your faith in the Spirit of Prophecy and inspire you to look carefully at those predictions yet to be fulfilled. 0-8163-2192-2

Three ways to order:

1. **Local** — Adventist Book Center®
2. **Call** — 1-800-765-6955
3. **Shop** — AdventistBookCenter.com